GÄRTEN Marokkos
Moroccan GARDENS
JARDINS du Maroc

© 2002 Feierabend Verlag OHG
Mommsenstraße 43, D-10629 Berlin

Design: Roman Bold & Black, Cologne
Drawings: H. A. Bohlmann
English Translation: Sheila Hardie for LocTeam, S.L., Barcelona
Traduction française: Claire Debard pour LocTeam, S.L., Barcelone
Lithography: divis, Cologne
Printing and Binding: Eurolitho, Milan
Printed in Italy

ISBN 3-936761-11-6
30 02 010 1

GÄRTEN Marokkos
Moroccan GARDENS
JARDINS du Maroc

Charlotte Seeling · Corinne Korda

Feierabend Verlag

Contents
Inhalt
Sommaire

Introduction
Einleitung
Introduction

Happiness is being in a garden at your own home. People have been convinced of this since they were driven out of Paradise. Since then, they have been on an endless search for a substitute for this lost Eden. The first earthly reflection of Paradise we know of is the Garden of the Hesperides. The delicious citrus fruits grew there, the so called "golden apples", which were already much sought-after by the Greek gods. Hercules, son of the almighty Zeus, was given the task of picking this celestial fruit. This was not easy. Because the only thing that was known about the Garden of the Hesperides was that it lay "at the end of the world" and was guarded by a dragon with a hundred heads.

According to the ancient Greeks, the world ended in North Africa, on the southern shores of the Mediterranean. For at that time Europe and Africa were still joined together. The demigod Hercules then ripped the land masses apart in order to force his way out of the Mediterranean and through to the Atlantic Ocean. The two legendary Pillars of Hercules remained: the Rock of Gibraltar on the northern bank of the strait and Djebel Musa on the Moroccan coast.

When he had done this, Hercules could begin the eleventh of the twelve labours he had been sentenced to perform after killing his own sons in a fit of madness: to seize the golden apples. They were protected in their garden by the Hesperides, the daughters of the mighty Atlas, who had to carry the vault of the sky on his shoulders. Hercules resorted to cunning in order to reach his goal: he talked the naive Atlas into getting his daughters to steal the divine fruit for him.

For Hercules this robbery had a happy end within the context of his twelve adventures. He was greeted in Olympus as the greatest hero in Greek mythology. According to legend, guileless Atlas on the other hand lies fossilised on his back – as a mountain range in Morocco. For the Berbers in that region he lives on today and they take care not to wake up the giant when they go walking in the Atlas Mountains.

It is quite clear that the first garden on Earth must have been in Morocco. Even those who do not believe there is much truth in myths can have no choice but to acknowledge that this North African kingdom was the birthplace of garden culture. Nowhere else is the idea of a garden so present, whether it is merely symbolised by a single plant or a fountain with hardly a little trickle of water. It is never a question of imitating nature, as is often the case in European gardens. On the contrary, in Islam, only that which has been created by human hand promises pleasure. Everything else is just desert...

All gardens start life as a hostile sea of sand. Without the desert the desire for an earthly paradise would never have been kindled – just as there would never have been a Garden of Eden in the hereafter if there had been no misery on Earth. Only a space protected by walls and ramparts could defy the threats of drought and barrenness. And so the oasis was created, the prototype for all gardens.

Whoever speaks of Moroccan gardens thinks of the *riyad*, the inner courtyard garden, which offers protection from the outside world. For a people born in the desert, which, with its barren enormity and wide horizons makes people appear small and abandoned, the intimate greenery of an enclosed space must seem like paradise. And to the familiar quotation "the Italians build their gardens, the English plant them and the French design them", we may add: "the Moroccans live in them".

In no other country does the garden have such an existential meaning as in Morocco. The writer Salah Stétié wrote: "In every person's soul there is a dimension that belongs to the garden – but especially in our souls. For us, the sons of the sand, the disinherited of water and the plant kingdom, every garden on the other side of a fata morgana is the Promised Land..."

Das Glück ist in einem Garten zu Hause. Davon sind die Menschen überzeugt, seit sie aus dem Paradies vertrieben wurden. Seither sind sie auf der ewigen Suche nach einem Ersatz für das verlorene Eden. Das erste irdische Abbild, von dem wir wissen, war der Garten der Hesperiden. Dort wuchsen die kostbaren Zitrusfrüchte, die „goldenen Äpfel", die schon von den griechischen Göttern begehrt wurden. Dem Kraftprotz Herkules, Sohn des allmächtigen Zeus, fiel die Aufgabe zu, diese himmlischen Früchte zu holen. Leicht war das nicht. Denn über den Garten der Hesperiden wusste man nur, dass er „am Ende der Welt" lag und von einem hundertköpfigen Drachen bewacht wurde.

Nach dem Verständnis der alten Griechen hörte die Welt in Nordafrika auf, an den südlichen Gestaden des Mittelmeeres. Denn damals waren Europa und Afrika noch miteinander verbunden. Erst Halbgott Herkules zerriss die Landmassen, um einen Weg aus dem Mittelmeer in den Atlantischen Ozean zu bahnen. Übrig blieb das legendäre Säulenpaar des Herkules: der Felsen von Gibraltar am Nordufer der Meeresstraße und das Felsmassiv des Djebel Musa an der marokkanischen Küste.

Als er das geschafft hatte, konnte Herkules sich an die elfte der zwölf Sühnetaten machen, die ihm auferlegt worden waren, nachdem er in einem Anfall von Wahnsinn seine Söhne getötet hatte: die goldenen Äpfel erobern. Gehütet wurden sie in ihrem Garten von den Hesperiden, Töchtern des Riesen Atlas, der auf seinen Schultern das Gewölbe des Himmels tragen musste. Herkules kam mit List an sein Ziel: Er überredete den naiven Atlas, seinen Töchtern die göttlichen Früchte abzuknöpfen.

Für Herkules nahm der Raub im Rahmen seiner zwölf Abenteuer ein gutes Ende. Er wurde als bedeutendster Held der griechischen Sage in den Olymp aufgenommen. Der tumbe Atlas hingegen liegt laut Legende versteinert auf seinem Rücken – als Gebirgskette in Marokko. Für die Berber dort ist er noch heute lebendig, sie hüten sich, den Riesen aufzuwecken, wenn sie im Atlasgebirge wandern.

Ganz eindeutig – der erste Garten der Erde muss in Marokko gelegen haben. Selbst wer nicht an einen gewissen Wahrheitsgehalt der Mythen glaubt, kann kaum umhin, das nordafrikanische Königreich als Ursprungsland der Gartenkultur anzuerkennen. Nirgendwo sonst ist die Idee des Gartens so allgegenwärtig, und sei sie nur durch eine einzelne Pflanze oder einen sparsam sprudelnden Brunnen symbolisiert. Dabei geht es nie darum, die Natur nachzuahmen, wie es in europäischen Gärten oft der Fall ist. Im Gegenteil, nur was von Menschenhand geschaffen wurde, verspricht im Islam Genuss. Alles andere ist Wüste ...

Am Anfang aller Gärten steht das feindliche Sandmeer. Ohne Wüste wäre wahrscheinlich nie der Wunsch nach einem irdischen Paradies wach geworden – wie es ohne Elend auf Erden keinen Garten Eden im Jenseits geben müsste. Nur ein durch Mauern und Wälle geschützter Raum konnte der Bedrohung durch Dürre und Kargheit trotzen. So entstand die Oase, das Urbild aller Gärten.

Wer vom marokkanischen Garten spricht, denkt an den *Riad,* den bepflanzten Innenhof, der Schutz vor der Außenwelt bietet. Für ein Volk, dessen Wiege in der Wüste steht, die mit ihrer kahlen Größe und ihrem weiten Horizont den Menschen klein und verlassen wirken lässt, muss das intime Grün eines umfriedeten Ortes das Paradies sein. Und dem geflügelten Wort „Die Italiener konstruieren ihren Garten, die Engländer pflanzen ihn an, die Franzosen designen ihn" kann man anfügen: „Die Marokkaner leben in ihm."

In keinem anderen Land hat der Garten eine so existentielle Bedeutung wie in Marokko. Der Schriftsteller Salah Stétié schrieb: „In der Seele eines jeden Menschen gibt es eine Dimension, die dem Garten gehört – aber ganz besonders in der unseren. Für uns, die Söhne des Sandes, die Enterbten des Wassers und des Pflanzenreichs, ist jeder Garten jenseits einer Fata Morgana das gelobte Land ..."

Le bonheur se trouve dans un jardin. Les hommes en sont convaincus depuis qu'ils ont été chassés du Paradis. Ils n'ont cessé depuis de chercher à remplacer l'Éden perdu. La première représentation terrestre connue est le Jardin des Hespérides. De précieux agrumes y poussaient, les « pommes d'or », déjà convoitées par les dieux grecs. C'est au beau parleur et fort Hercule, fils du tout-puissant Zeus, que reviendra la tâche de s'emparer de ces fruits célestes. Ce qui n'était pas chose aisée, car, du Jardin des Hespérides, on savait seulement qu'il se trouvait « au bout du monde » et était gardé par un dragon à cent têtes.

Selon la conception des anciens Grecs, le monde prenait fin en Afrique du Nord, sur les rivages sud de la Méditerranée. Car l'Europe et l'Afrique étaient alors encore reliées l'une à l'autre, et il faudra l'arrivée du demi-dieu Hercule pour rompre les masses de terre et ouvrir une voie à la Méditerranée dans l'océan Atlantique. Il reste de cet exploit le célèbre couple des colonnes d'Hercule : le rocher de Gibraltar, sur la rive septentrionale de la voie maritime, et le massif montagneux du Djebel Moussa sur la côte marocaine.

Après avoir réussi cela, Hercule put s'attaquer au onzième des douze travaux expiatoires qui lui avaient été imposés pour avoir tué ses fils dans un accès de folie : s'emparer des pommes d'or, surveillées dans leur jardin par les Hespérides, filles du géant Atlas, lui-même chargé de porter sur ses épaules la voûte du ciel. Hercule parviendra à son objectif par ruse : il convaincra le naïf Atlas de soutirer lui-même les fruits divins à ses filles.

Pour Hercule, le larcin aura un résultat positif : il sera accepté à l'Olympe comme héros le plus significatif des mythes grecs. Le pauvre Atlas, en revanche, aurait été, selon la légende, pétrifié sur le dos, formant une chaîne de montagnes au Maroc. Pour les Berbères, le géant y vit encore et ils prennent garde à ne pas le réveiller lorsqu'ils parcourent l'Atlas.

Aucun doute donc, le premier jardin sur Terre devait être situé au Maroc. Même sans croire à une part de vérité contenue dans les mythes, il est quasi impossible de ne pas reconnaître dans le royaume nord-africain le pays d'origine de la culture du jardin. Nulle part ailleurs, l'idée du jardin n'est aussi omniprésente, même simplement symbolisée par une seule plante ou une fontaine au faible clapotis. Il ne s'agit cependant jamais d'imiter la nature, comme c'est souvent le cas dans les jardins européens. Au contraire, seul ce qui a été créé par l'homme peut être une promesse de plaisir pour l'islam, et tout le reste ne peut être que désert ...

Avant tous les jardins, il y avait une mer de sable hostile. Sans le désert, le désir d'un Paradis terrestre n'aurait probablement jamais existé, de même que sans malheurs sur Terre, aucun jardin d'Éden n'aurait de raison d'être dans l'au-delà. Seul un espace protégé par des murs et des remblais pouvait contrer la menace de sécheresse et de pauvreté. L'oasis était née, modèle de tous les jardins.

Lorsqu'on évoque les jardins marocains, c'est au *riad* qu'on pense, cette cour intérieure plantée qui protège du monde extérieur. En effet, pour un peuple qui a son berceau dans le désert, dont la grandeur dépouillée et le vaste horizon donnent à l'homme un sentiment de petitesse et d'abandon, le vert et l'intimité d'un endroit clos devaient forcément représenter le Paradis. On pourrait même ajouter une partie à la sentence : « les Italiens dessinent leurs jardins, les Anglais les plantent, les Français les composent », à savoir, « les Marocains y vivent ».

Dans aucun autre pays du monde, le jardin n'a une telle signification existentielle qu'au Maroc. Comme l'écrit l'écrivain Salah Stétié : « Dans l'âme de tout homme se trouve une dimension qui relève du jardin, mais plus particulièrement dans la nôtre. Pour nous, les fils du sable, les déshérités de l'eau et du règne végétal, chaque jardin, plus qu'un mirage, est la Terre promise ... ».

In the Beginning there was the Desert
Am Anfang war die Wüste
Au début était le désert

A magnificent gate leading into the nowhere: somewhere between Ouarzazate and Zagora, some 250 kilometres southeast of Marrakech you can find this Arab arch in the rock desert of the pre-Sahara.

Grandioses Tor ins Nirgendwo: Zwischen Ouarzazate und Zagora, etwa 250 Kilometer südöstlich von Marrakesch, erhebt sich mitten in der Geröllwüste der Prä-sahara dieser arabische Bogen.

Porte grandiose vers le néant : En plein milieu du désert caillouteux du pré-Sahara, entre Ouarzazate et Zagora, à environ 250 km au sud-est de Marrakech, s'élève cet arche mauresque.

Without deserts gardens would not exist. What reason would people have to work the earth by the sweat of their brow if it turned green and covered itself in flowers without any human intervention – as once was the case in Paradise. However, the desert is infertile, inhospitable, a terrible place that forces people to design a counter-world. But the Tuaregs, the "blue sons" of the Sahara, see things diffrently: "God has created a world full of water on which people can live, and a land without water on which people can be thirsty, and a desert: a land with and without water on which people can find their soul…"

It is all very well for the nomads to talk: for as long as anyone can remember these Berber tribes, whose men wear indigo clothes, have driven through the western Sahara with their herds of camels, and God has always shown the devout Muslims the way. But civilisation has forced the Tuaregs to settle in the Moroccan cities and they are increasingly losing their knowledge of the desert and, with that, their belief in themselves and in God.

It can be no coincidence that the three large monotheistic religions – Judaism, Christianity and Islam – originated in the desert. Believers always considered it to be a place for reflection. Indeed, the prophet banished all life from the desert in order to have a peaceful place for himself – this was "Allah's garden", the "waterless sea".

In reality, there is a huge reservoir of water beneath the Sahara. It consists of stored up rainwater, which fell five to ten thousand years ago. And water millions of years old still emerges from the primitive rocks. It is a natural resource as valuable and limited as oil and therefore has to be rationed out equally carefully. In some regions, one only has to drill down half a metre and in others up to 1.5 kilometres to reach this precious liquid. Now, approximately every 100,000 years there is a brief wet period, which brings new water from the oceans with the monsoon.

Ohne Wüste gäbe es keinen Garten. Welchen Grund hätte der Mensch, im Schweiße seines Angesichts die Erde zu bearbeiten, wenn sie ganz von allein grünte und blühte – wie es einst im Paradies der Fall war? Die Wüste aber ist unfruchtbar, unwirtlich, ein schrecklicher Ort, der den Menschen zwingt, eine Gegenwelt zu entwerfen. Die Tuareg allerdings, die „blauen Söhne" der Sahara, sehen das anders: „Gott hat ein Land voll Wasser geschaffen, auf dass die Menschen leben können, und ein Land ohne Wasser, auf dass die Menschen Durst haben, und eine Wüste: ein Land mit und ohne Wasser, auf dass die Menschen ihre Seele finden…"

Die Nomaden haben leicht reden: Seit Menschengedenken ziehen diese Berberstämme, deren Männer indigoblau gefärbte Kleider tragen, mit ihren Kamelherden durch die westliche Sahara, und immer hat Gott den gläubigen Mohammedanern den Weg gewiesen. Aber die Zivilisation zwingt die Tuareg, in den Städten Marokkos sesshaft zu werden, und zunehmend verlieren sie ihr Wissen um die Wüste und damit ihren Glauben an sich selbst und an Gott.

Es kann kein Zufall sein, dass die drei großen monotheistischen Religionen Judentum, Christentum und Islam ihren Ursprung in der Wüste haben. Sie galt Gläubigen immer als Ort der Besinnung. Ja, der Prophet selbst verbannte alles Leben aus der Wüste, um einen Platz der Ruhe für sich zu haben – das war „der Garten Allahs", das „Meer ohne Wasser".

In Wahrheit existiert ein riesiges Reservoir an Wasser unter der Sahara. Es besteht aus gespeichertem Regen, der vor zehn- bis fünftausend Jahren gefallen ist. Und es gibt Millionen Jahre altes Wasser, das noch aus dem Urgestein kommt. Es ist so kostbar und begrenzt wie Öl und muss deshalb ebenso sorgfältig eingeteilt werden. In manchen Gebieten braucht man nur einen halben Meter zu bohren, in anderen bis zu eineinhalb Kilometer, um an das kostbare Nass zu kommen. Nur alle 100.000 Jahre etwa bricht eine kurze Feuchtzeit an, die mit dem

Sans désert, il n'y aurait pas de jardin. En effet, quelle raison aurait l'homme de cultiver la terre à la sueur de son front si elle verdoyait et fleurissait d'elle-même, comme autrefois au Paradis ? Le désert est inculte et inhospitalier, c'est un lieu d'épouvante qui contraint l'homme à concevoir un monde contraire. Les Touaregs, les « fils bleus » du Sahara, voient cependant les choses autrement : « Dieu a créé un pays avec beaucoup d'eau dans lequel les hommes peuvent vivre, un pays sans eau dans lequel les hommes connaissent la soif et un désert : un pays avec et sans eau dans lequel les hommes retrouvent leur âme … ».

Les nomades peuvent en parler à leur aise : de mémoire d'homme, on a toujours vu ces tribus berbères, dont les hommes portent des vêtements teintés de bleu indigo, parcourir le Sahara occidental avec leurs troupeaux de chameaux, et Dieu a toujours indiqué le chemin à ces musulmans croyants. Aujourd'hui cependant, la civilisation force les Touaregs à devenir sédentaires et à s'établir dans les villes marocaines, de sorte qu'ils perdent progressivement leur connaissance du désert, et avec elle leur croyance en eux-mêmes et en Dieu.

Ce n'est certainement pas un hasard si les trois grandes religions monothéistes, le judaïsme, le christianisme et l'islam, sont nées dans le désert. Pour les croyants, il a toujours été tenu pour un lieu où revenir à la raison, et même le Prophète en bannira toute vie, afin de pouvoir disposer d'un endroit calme, le « jardin d'Allah », la « Mer sans eau ».

En réalité, il existe sous le Sahara un immense réservoir d'eau où sont emmagasinées les eaux des pluies tombées il y a cinq à dix mille ans. Sans compter l'eau vieille de millions d'années qui sort encore des roches primitives. Elle est aussi précieuse et rare que le pétrole, et doit donc être aussi soigneusement répartie. Dans certaines régions, il suffit de creuser à un demi-mètre de profondeur pour atteindre le précieux liquide, dans d'autres jusqu'à un kilomètre et demi. Tous les 100 000 ans environ, et seulement, une courte période

Over the last ten years, climate researchers have registered a clear increase in precipitation. The reason for this is the greenhouse effect, which warms the earth, thus causing more moisture to evaporate over the seas; it is then driven by strong monsoon winds and produces rain in the deserts. Thus, today large expanses of land are covered with herbaceous vegetation where, in the past, not a single blade of grass would grow.

However, the desert is expanding; wherever any green plants sprout up, people in search of pastureland for their herds of goats and camels immediately appear. The animals eat all the plants, including the roots – and consequently the desert returns. Therefore, there are no meteorological grounds for the increasing desertification of the earth as there were in the Old World. Nowadays, this is due to the increase in the number of people and their grazing animals, which immediately destroy any budding plants.

Strictly speaking, areas can only be called desert where there is practically no precipitation, where there is no plant cover and life scarcely exists. Even in the Sahara with its ca. 10 million square kilometres, at the most 10 per cent in the east can be classified as pure desert. The majority of the Sahara is semi-desert or steppe, as occurs in Morocco.

According to legend, Allah showed some understanding: in order to make amends for the "desert-mistake", he created the camel. It is even better suited than the horse for walking on the sand. Moreover, during storms it can close its nostrils and eyelids in order to keep out the fine grains of sand. This is the one-humped camel, the dromedary, considered a sacred animal in Morocco.

Here's to the desert traveller, who is a match for his animal in terms of resistance! He is advised to take some dates with him as an emergency supply – they are tasty, nourishing and they keep well. They too are a gift from Allah. When he was creating the world, so the story goes, he had two lumps of clay left over and decided to make something with them that could allow people to survive in the desert: the dromedary and the date palm.

Monsun von den Meeren neues Wasser bringt. In den letzten zehn Jahren registrieren Klimaforscher eine deutliche Zunahme von Niederschlägen. Grund ist der Treibhauseffekt, der die Erde erwärmt, dadurch verdunstet mehr Feuchtigkeit über den Meeren, die durch verstärkte Monsunwinde über den Wüsten abregnet. So kommt es, dass heute weite Gebiete, in denen früher kein einziger Grashalm wuchs, mit krautiger Vegetation bedeckt sind.

Dennoch wächst die Wüste. Weil überall da, wo Grün sprießt, sofort Menschen auf der Suche nach Weiden mit ihren Ziegen- und Kamelherden auftauchen. Die Tiere fressen alle Pflanzen mit der Wurzel – so entsteht wieder Wüstengebiet. Die zunehmende Verwüstung der Erde hat also keine meteorologischen Gründe, wie es in der alten Welt der Fall war, sondern liegt an der zunehmenden Zahl der Menschen und ihrer Weidetiere, die jedes aufkeimende Leben sofort vernichten.

Streng genommen kann man nur solche Landstriche als Wüste bezeichnen, in denen praktisch kein Niederschlag fällt, wo jede Pflanzendecke fehlt und kaum Leben existiert. Selbst in der Sahara mit ihren rund zehn Millionen Quadratkilometern können allenfalls zehn Prozent im Osten als reine Wüste gelten. Der größte Teil ist Halbwüste oder Steppenlandschaft, so auch in Marokko.

Laut Legende hatte Allah ein Einsehen: Um den „Fehler Wüste" wieder gut zu machen, erschuf er das Kamel. Besser noch als das Pferd ist es dazu geeignet, im Sand zu laufen. Außerdem kann es bei Sturm seine Nüstern ebenso schließen wie seine Augenlider, sodass die feinen Körner nicht eindringen können. Gemeint ist das Kamel mit einem Höcker, das Dromedar, das in Marokko als geheiligtes Tier gilt.

Wohl dem Wüstendurchquerer, der es an Widerstandsfähigkeit mit seinem Tier aufnehmen kann! Als Notration empfehlen sich ihm Dattelfrüchte – wohlschmeckend, nahrhaft und haltbar. Auch sie sind ein Geschenk Allahs. Als er die Welt erschaffen hatte, so geht die Geschichte, blieben ihm zwei Lehmkügelchen übrig, und er beschloss, daraus etwas zu formen, was den Menschen das Überleben in der Wüste möglich machen sollte: das Dromedar und die Dattelpalme.

d'humidité apporte au désert avec la mousson de l'eau des mers et océans. Au cours des dix dernières années cependant, les climatologues ont enregistré une nette augmentation des précipitations. La raison invoquée en est l'effet de serre qui réchauffe la Terre, ce qui entraîne une évaporation accrue au-dessus de la mer, la vapeur d'eau étant ensuite portée par des vents de mousson plus forts jusqu'au désert, où elle retombe sous forme de pluie. Il arrive donc que de larges étendues où ne poussait autrefois pas le moindre brin d'herbe soient aujourd'hui couvertes d'une végétation herbacée.

Et pourtant le désert grandit. En effet, partout où jaillit du vert, les hommes se mettent aussitôt à la recherche de pâturages avec leurs troupeaux de chèvres et de chameaux, les bêtes dévorent alors toutes les plantes jusqu'à la racine, créant ainsi de nouveaux territoires désertiques. La désertification croissante n'est donc en aucun cas due à des raisons d'ordre météorologiques, comme cela a été le cas dans les temps anciens, mais à l'accroissement de la population et de son bétail, qui détruit aussitôt toute vie à peine germée.

Au sens strict du terme, on ne peut qualifier de déserts que les régions où les précipitations sont quasiment nulles, où tout tapis végétal manque et où la vie est quasi inexistante. Même le Sahara et ses près de dix millions de kilomètres carrés ne comprend au mieux que dix pour cent, dans sa partie orientale, de véritable désert et se compose pour l'essentiel de semi-désert ou de steppes, comme au Maroc.

Selon la légende, Allah serait revenu à la raison et, pour corriger « l'erreur du désert », il aurait créé le chameau. Plus encore que le cheval, il convient à la marche dans le sable. Par ailleurs, en cas de tempête, il peut fermer ses naseaux comme ses paupières, de sorte que les fins grains de sable ne peuvent y pénétrer. On parle ici du chameau à une bosse, donc du dromadaire, animal sacré au Maroc.

Bienheureux le voyageur du désert qui peut rivaliser d'endurance avec son compagnon à quatre pattes ! Comme ration alimentaire de base, les dattes sont à recommander, savoureuses, nourrissantes et résistantes. Par ailleurs, elles sont, elles aussi, un cadeau d'Allah : lorsqu'il a eu fini de créer le monde, dit la légende, il lui est resté deux boulettes d'argile et il décida d'en faire quelque chose qui permettrait à l'homme de survivre dans le désert, le dromadaire et le palmier dattier.

The Oasis
Die Oase
L'Oasis

Every oasis is a garden. It is not, as many believe, a mere whim of nature. The oasis must always be surrounded by desert and always has as its starting point a palm tree. Some oases might have originated from date stones someone carelessly spat out onto the sand; there is a reason for the Arab proverb that says: "Big things sometimes grow from little things –, just like the date palm from the stone". But even if the seed happens to land near a watering place and has the chance to germinate, it must be given lots of care and attention if it is to grow into a palm tree.

If human hands do not intervene to protect it, sand storms and the scorching heat will soon kill the delicate little plant. With a simple protective wall, on the other hand, an island of life can be created. An irrigated trough is sufficient to create a microclimate, which will not only allow the palm tree to flourish, but also allow other plants to germinate – and so we have an oasis.

At first, an oasis was nothing more than a couple of palm trees and a watering place, occasionally used as a resting spot by nomads. This was until the first tribes settled in the vicinity of the water and started to make demands on the oasis. Women would visit the spring all day long in order to fill their containers with water. Future marriages and intrigues were hatched here, children played, parties were held. Social life had its roots here. In the oases we find the idea of an Eden that can be traced back to the very distant past, to the time when the land was first cultivated and people adopted a sedentary way of life, which structured space and countered chaos with order.

Oases became spots where caravans would stop and get supplies on their way through the desert. They were places to exchange goods

Jede Oase ist ein Garten. Sie ist nicht, wie viele glauben, eine Laune der Natur. Immer muss sie der Wüste abgerungen werden, und am Anfang steht stets die Palme. Mag sein, dass die ein oder andere Oase aus einem achtlos ausgespuckten Kern entstanden ist, nicht umsonst sagt ein arabisches Sprichwort: „Manchmal entfaltet sich etwas ganz Großes aus etwas ganz Kleinem – wie die Dattelpalme aus einem Kern." Aber selbst wenn die Saat zufällig nahe einer Wasserstelle landet und die Chance hat zu keimen, muss sie gehegt und gepflegt werden, um zu einer Palme heranwachsen zu können.

Wenn nicht Menschenhände schützend eingreifen, werden Sandstürme und sengende Hitze dem zarten Pflänzchen schnell den Garaus machen. Mit einem einfachen Schutzwall dagegen kann man eine Insel des Lebens schaffen. Es genügt eine Mulde, die bewässert wird, schon entsteht ein Mikroklima, in dem nicht nur die Palme gut gedeiht, sondern das auch andere Pflanzen keimen lässt – schon ist eine Oase entstanden.

Zunächst waren Oasen nicht mehr als ein paar Palmen und eine Wasserstelle, dann und wann von Nomaden zur Rast genutzt. Bis sich die ersten Stämme in der Nähe des Wassers niederließen und die Oase für sich in Anspruch nahmen. Frauen kamen den Tag über an die Quelle, um Wasser in Behälter zu füllen. Hier entspannen sich zukünftige Ehen ebenso wie Intrigen, hier spielten Kinder, hier feierte man Feste. Hier entstanden die Wurzeln gesellschaftlichen Lebens. In Oasen findet man die Idee eines Eden, die man bis in die früheste Vergangenheit zurück verfolgen kann, in die Zeit der ersten Bodenbestellung und sesshafter Lebensweise, die dem Raum eine Geometrie gaben und dem Chaos eine Ordnung entgegen setzten.

Toutes les oasis sont des jardins. Et non, comme le croient beaucoup, un caprice de la nature. Elles doivent continuellement être arrachées au désert et toutes commencent par un palmier. Il se peut que l'une ou l'autre soit née d'un noyau de datte négligemment craché, un proverbe arabe dit bien que « le très grand naît parfois du très petit, comme le palmier dattier à partir de son noyau ». Mais même si la graine atterrit à proximité d'un point d'eau et a la chance de germer, elle doit encore être soignée et entretenue pour pouvoir devenir un palmier. En effet, sans l'intervention protectrice de l'homme, les tempêtes de sable et la chaleur torride auront vite fait de donner le coup de grâce à la fragile petite pousse. En revanche, un simple mur de protection suffit à former un îlot de vie, et un bassin approvisionné en eau crée ensuite un microclimat qui ne profite pas seulement au palmier, mais fait aussi germer d'autres plantes : une oasis est née.

Les premières oasis ne comportaient guère plus que quelques palmiers et un point d'eau où les nomades faisaient relâche de temps à autre. Jusqu'à ce que les premières tribus s'installent à proximité de l'eau et s'attribuent la propriété de l'oasis. On a alors commencé à voir les femmes se rendre à la source pendant la journée pour y remplir des récipients d'eau, c'est là que se sont décidés de futurs mariages et que se sont dénouées de nombreuses intrigues, là que jouent les enfants, là que sont célébrées les fêtes. Là, enfin, que toute vie sociale a pris racine. Dans une oasis se retrouve l'idée d'un Éden, que l'on peut faire remonter jusqu'au passé le plus ancien, à l'époque des premières cultures et des débuts de la vie sédentaire, qui ont assigné une géométrie à l'espace et opposé un ordre au chaos.

Where there is water, there is life. And where there is one palm tree, there will soon be an oasis.

Wo Wasser ist, entsteht Leben. Und wo erst eine Palme wächst, da entwickelt sich bald eine Oase.

Là où se trouve l'eau, la vie se développe. Et là où un palmier réussit à pousser, bientôt une oasis apparaît.

Palm tree groves used to line the banks of the river Drâa along a thousand kilometres; a green belt in the desert. Today, Morocco's longest river is slowly silting up.

Wie ein grüner Gürtel zogen sich einst die Palmenhaine am Ufer des Drâa tausend Kilometer lang durch die Wüste. Heute versandet Marokkos längster Fluss zunehmend.

Autrefois, telle une ceinture de verdure, des palmeraies s'étendaient sur mille kilomètres le long du Drâa. Aujourd'hui, le plus long fleuve du Maroc s'enlise peu à peu.

from far off lands and also a place to settle. Since they are situated in a hostile environment, from time immemorial it was the technically produced flooding that ensured their continued existence and protected them from being covered in sand and ceasing to exist.

To maintain these islands of fertility, settlers thought of a way of exploiting the crucially essential subterranean water. The most highly-developed method was to dig out long, underground channels, called *foggara*, in the Sahara. These tunnel irrigation systems tap the ground water layers and also carry the condensation that forms every night on the sand. These man-made underground watercourses have been partly driven over thousands of kilometres and create miracles with moisture and vegetation in areas of arable land.

Taking care of the gardens is a never-ending task, because of the constant presence of wind and sand. That's why artificial barriers are built

Oasen wurden Halte- und Versorgungspunkte für Karawanen auf ihrem Zug durch die Wüste. Sie waren Tauschorte für Waren aus fernen Ländern und sie sind Siedlungsorte. Da sie sich in einer feindlichen Umgebung befinden, war es von jeher die Technik gesteuerter Überschwemmung, die ihnen die Weiterexistenz sicherte und sie vor dem Ende durch Versanden schützte.

Um die Inseln der Fruchtbarkeit zu erhalten, haben sich ihre Siedler einiges einfallen lassen, denn es galt, das unterirdische Wasser zu nutzen. Die ausgereifteste Methode besteht im Ausheben langer unterirdischer Gänge, die im Sahara-Gebiet als *foggara* bezeichnet werden. Diese Stollen-Brunnen-Systeme zapfen die Grundwasserschichten an und nehmen auch das sich über Nacht im Sand bildende Kondenswasser auf. Diese künstlichen Wasseradern werden teils über Tausende von Kilometern vorgetrieben und sorgen in den Anbauflächen für Wunder an Feuchtigkeit und Vegetation.

Les oasis étaient des lieux de halte et d'approvisionnement pour les caravanes qui traversaient le désert. Elles étaient des points d'échange pour les marchandises des pays lointains et elles sont des zones d'habitat. Situées au milieu d'un environnement hostile, c'est depuis toujours la technique de l'inondation contrôlée qui a assuré leur survie et les a protégées de la disparition par ensablement. Pour préserver ces îlots fertiles, leurs habitants ont dû faire preuve d'imagination. Il s'agissait alors d'exploiter l'eau souterraine. La méthode la plus élaborée consiste à creuser de longs passages souterrains, connus dans les régions sahariennes sous le nom de *foggara*. Ces systèmes de galeries et de puits captent l'eau des nappes phréatiques et absorbent l'eau de condensation qui se forme pendant la nuit sur le sable. Ces voies d'eau artificielles sont dans certains cas étendues à des milliers de kilomètres et assurent le miracle de l'humidité et de la végétation dans les zones cultivées.

An oasis-village with the typical clay buildings, near Ouarzazate. It is surrounded by fertile fields, olive- and palm tree groves.

Ein typisches Oasen-Dorf mit Lehmbauten in der Nähe von Ouarzazate. Umgeben ist es von fruchtbaren Feldern, Oliven- und Palmenhainen.

Près de Ouarzazate, un village d'oasis typique avec ses constructions en pisé. Il est entouré de champs fertiles, d'oliveraies et de palmeraies.

and put in place with the idea of keeping the sand still, thus encouraging the creation of dune chains. Fences made from interwoven palm fronds shape the landscape and the fabric of the cultivated plots of land is structured by channels and clay brick walls, which surround houses and estates.

Today, clay bricks are the still the most commonly used construction material in the oases and at the same time the oldest wall building system, as shown in the city walls that surround the historic *médinas* in Morocco. Without these bricks made of earth and water and baked in the sun, there would be no walls – and therefore no gardens in this desert climate.

Also, without the shade provided by the palm trees, none of the other plants here could survive: apricot, orange, fig and pomegranate trees, under which in turn beans, carrots, lettuce, turnips, tomatoes, cabbages, fennel, coriander, mint and parsley grow. Typical oasis plants include henna, which does not flourish in our latitudes, and marigolds.

Die Instandhaltung der Gärten hört niemals auf, denn Wind und Sand lassen sich nicht fernhalten. So baut man künstliche Barrieren, platziert sie mit Überlegung, sodass der Sand sich ablagert und die Entstehung von Dünenketten begünstigt. Zäune aus ineinander verflochtenen Palmenblättern modellieren die Landschaft, und das Gewebe der landwirtschaftlich genutzten Parzellen erhält eine Struktur durch Kanäle und Mauern aus Lehmziegeln, die Häuser und Besitz umschließen. Lehmziegel sind das heute noch gebräuchlichste Baumaterial in der Oase und gleichzeitig das älteste System des Mauerbaus, wie die Stadtwälle um die historischen *médinas* von Marokko bezeugen. Ohne die aus Erde und Wasser geformten und von der Sonne gebrannten Ziegel gäbe es keine Mauern – und keine Gärten im Wüstenklima.

Ohne den Schatten, den die Palme von oben spendet, könnten alle anderen Pflanzen hier nicht überleben: Aprikosen-, Orangen-, Feigen- und Granatapfelbäume, unter denen wiederum Bohnen, Karotten, Salat, Rüben, Tomaten, Kohl, Fenchel, Koriander, Minze und Petersilie wachsen. Typische Oasengewächse sind Henna, das in unseren Breiten nicht gedeiht, und *Calendula,* die Ringelblume.

L'entretien du jardin qu'est l'oasis ne cesse jamais, car ni le vent, ni le sable, ne se laissent tenir à l'écart. On construit ainsi des barrières artificielles, qu'on dispose à des endroits calculés pour que le sable s'y accumule et favorise la formation de chaînes de dunes. Les clôtures de palmes tressées modèlent le paysage et le tissu des parcelles exploitées par l'agriculture est structuré par les canaux et les murs en briques d'argile qui entourent maisons et propriétés. Aujourd'hui encore, les briques d'argile sont le matériau le plus usité dans les oasis, ainsi que le plus ancien système de construction de murs, comme l'attestent les remparts qui entourent les médinas historiques du Maroc. Sans ces briques faites de terre et d'eau et brûlées par le soleil, il n'y aurait pas de murs, et pas de jardins sous le climat du désert.

Et sans l'ombre que les palmiers dispensent d'en haut, aucune des autres plantes ne pourrait survivre ici : abricotiers, orangers, figuiers et grenadiers, qui à leur tour abritent haricots, carottes, salades, navets, tomates, choux, fenouil, coriandre, menthe et persil. Parmi les plantes les plus typiques des oasis figurent le henné, qui ne pousse pas sous nos latitudes, et le *calendula,* ou souci.

Hospitality in the Desert
Gastlichkeit in der Wüste
L'Hospitalité dans le désert

The unwritten law of the desert guarantees unlimited hospitality to all travellers, including one's most deadly enemies. As long as he is under your roof or in your tent, you are not allowed to harm your guest; on the contrary, you must share even your last supplies of food and drink with him. This strict code of honour arose because hospitality in the desert was a question of survival. In Morocco, this archaic need has resulted in a highly developed tradition, which is not just restricted to private houses.

Even in the most inhospitable regions, inns and hotels are of an exceptionally high standard. And the modern traveller, who arrives in Agadir and drives out into the desert in the dark of night, reaching Taroudant in roughly one hour, is just as happy to drink tea in the Palais Salam as travellers of old when they reached a life-saving oasis.

Moreover, the five-hour journey over the 2,120 m high Tizi n'Test pass in the direction of Marrakech, which goes past a palm tree bearing a sign announcing the "snow line", makes one receptive to the hospitality offered in even the smallest Berber villages such as Ouled Berhil.

One should never be put off by outside appearances. The most exclusive accommodation is often hidden behind high walls and nondescript doors. Since an outward display of luxury is forbidden in such a barren milieu, all the more extravagance is offered inside.

Das ungeschriebene Gesetz der Wüste garantiert jedem Wanderer uneingeschränkte Gastfreundschaft. Das gilt sogar für den Todfeind. So lange er sich unter seinem (Zelt-)Dach befindet, darf der Gastgeber ihm nichts antun, im Gegenteil, er muss auch die letzten Vorräte noch mit ihm teilen. Entstanden ist dieser strikte Ehrenkodex, weil Gastlichkeit in der Wüste eine Frage des Überlebens war. Aus dieser archaischen Notwendigkeit ist in Marokko eine hoch entwickelte Tradition entstanden, die nicht nur in Privathäusern gepflegt wird. Selbst in der unwirtlichsten Gegend halten Gasthäuser und Hotels einen ungewöhnlich hohen Standard. Der moderne Reisende, der in Agadir landete, in finsterer Nacht Richtung Wüste fährt und nach etwa einer Stunde Taroudant erreicht, ist über den Tee im Palais Salam bestimmt ebenso erfreut wie der frühe Wanderer, der eine rettende Oase erreichte. Auch die fünf Stunden dauernde Fahrt über den 2.120 m hohen Pass Tizi n'Test Richtung Marrakesch, vorbei an einer Palme, deren Schild die „Schneegrenze" ankündigt, macht jeden empfänglich für Gastfreundschaft – und die wird noch im kleinsten Berberdorf wie Ouled Berhil geboten.

Dabei darf man sich vom Äußeren nie abschrecken lassen. Die exklusivsten Herbergen verbergen sich oft hinter hohen Mauern und unscheinbaren Toren. Luxus nach außen zu demonstrieren, verbietet sich in einem so kargen Umfeld – innen wird dafür umso mehr geboten.

Une loi non-écrite du désert garantit à chaque voyageur une hospitalité sans limites. Même à son ennemi mortel, nul ne peut attenter quoi que ce soit tant qu'il se trouve sous son propre toit (de tente). Au contraire, l'hôte est tenu de partager avec lui, même ses dernières provisions. Si un code d'honneur aussi strict a pu s'imposer ainsi, c'est parce que dans le désert, l'hospitalité était une question de survie. Cette nécessité aujourd'hui révolue a donné naissance à une tradition très vivante au Maroc, que les hôtes privés ne sont pas seuls à entretenir. Ainsi, même dans les endroits les moins accueillants, les hôtels et auberges offrent un niveau d'hospitalité inhabituellement haut ; et le touriste moderne qui, après avoir atterri à Agadir, a pris en pleine nuit la direction du désert et atteint Taroudant au bout d'une heure, se réjouit sans aucun doute autant du thé au Palais Salam que le voyageur d'autrefois à l'arrivée dans une oasis salvatrice.

Les cinq heures de route vers Marrakech par le col Tizi n'Test, à 2 120 m d'altitude et où un panneau indicateur près d'un palmier annonce la « limite des neiges », prédisposent, elles aussi, chacun à l'hospitalité, offerte à tous jusque dans le plus petit village berbère, comme Ouled Berhil. À condition cependant de ne pas se laisser décourager par l'aspect extérieur des lieux. Les gîtes les plus agréables se dissimulent souvent derrière de hauts murs et des portes austères, chacun s'interdisant de faire étalage du moindre luxe dans un environnement aussi pauvre.

The scene that greets one's eyes upon arriving at the *Palais Salam* at night is as unreal as the backdrop for an oriental period film: two black guards, one dressed in blood red and the other in snow white, keep watch over the mighty entrance to this famous hotel, which nestles in the historical 16th century city walls. According to ancient tradition, guests are greeted in the foyer by a tea maker proffering boiling hot, sugary mint tea – the only drink capable of even reviving exhausted desert travellers.

Once refreshed, at a later hour, travellers make their way to the garden, where their senses will be further indulged. In quite a classical manner, four flowerbeds spread out to the right of the main axes, which are covered in black and white tiles. At the point where they meet, water gently splashes about from a blue and white fountain. This is how the Islamic *riyad* should be: rigorously structured, so one can find one's way around immediately, and filled with cool air, soft sounds and exquisite scents which diffuse bewitchingly especially at night. Two hundred-year-old fig trees grow here as well as a large number of banana, orange and hibiscus trees and the flame-coloured Indian Shot *(canna indica)*. The first impression promises more enjoyment the following day.

At half past five, a concert of an amazing variety of different bird songs announces the awakening of nature. Only the turtle doves are merciful and sleep for another hour, and all lovers follow suit.

The *Palais Salam* is situated in grounds measuring over a hectare and was built at the beginning of the 19th century for a pasha before being turned into a hotel in 1930. It is above all a paradise for birds; their presence fills the air with constant movement and a profusion of sounds. They chirp, sing joyfully or scold shrilly, take long baths in the typical water channels that run through all Arab gardens and are particularly fond of nesting in the weathered city walls, which protectively encircle these grounds. The multitude of

Unwirklich wie die Kulisse für einen orientalischen Kostümfilm wirkt die Szenerie bei der nächtlichen Ankunft im *Palais Salam:* Zwei schwarze Wächter, einer blutrot, der andere schneeweiß gekleidet, hüten den mächtigen Eingang des berühmten Hotels, das eingebettet in die historischen Stadtmauern aus dem 16. Jahrhundert liegt. Nach alter Tradition werden die Gäste in der Halle von einem Teekoch mit glühend heißem, zuckersüßem Minztee begrüßt – das einzige Getränk, das selbst erschöpfte Wüstenwanderer wieder belebt.

Erfrischt begibt sich der Reisende noch zu später Stunde in den Garten, wo seine Sinne weiter verwöhnt werden. Ganz klassisch entfalten sich vier Beete rechts und links der schwarz-weiß gekachelten Hauptachsen, an deren Kreuzpunkt eine blau-weiße Fontäne plätschert. So soll er sein, der islamische *Riad:* streng gegliedert, aufdass man sich sofort zurecht findet, und erfüllt mit kühler Luft, sanften Geräuschen und erlesenen Düften, die sich besonders in der Nacht betörend verbreiten. Zwei hundertjährige Feigen wachsen hier, viele Bananen, Orangen, Hibiskus und feuerfarbenes Blumenrohr *(Canna)*. Der erste Eindruck verheißt größere Gartenfreuden für den nächsten Tag.

Um fünf Uhr dreißig kündigt ein Konzert der unterschiedlichsten Vogelstimmen das Erwachen der Natur an. Nur die Turteltauben sind gnädig und schlafen eine Stunde länger, und alle Verliebten tun's ihnen gleich. Der gut einen Hektar große Grund des *Palais Salam*, das Anfang des 19. Jahrhunderts für einen Pascha erbaut und 1930 zum Hotel umgewandelt wurde, ist in erster Linie ein Paradies für Vögel, ihre Gegenwart erfüllt die Luft mit steter Bewegung und vielfältigen Klängen. Sie zirpen, flöten, jubilieren oder zetern, baden ausgiebig in den typischen Wasserkanälen, die jeden arabischen Garten durchziehen, und nisten mit Vorliebe in der verwitterten Stadtmauer, die das Gelände schützend umgibt. Die Erinnerung an das *Palais Salam* ist für immer von der Vielzahl der Vögel

Le décor d'une arrivée nocturne au Palais Salam semble aussi peu réel que les coulisses d'un film oriental en costumes : deux gardiens noirs, l'un vêtu de rouge sang, l'autre de blanc pur, surveillent l'entrée massive du célèbre hôtel, enchâssé dans les remparts historiques de la ville, qui datent du 16ᵉ siècle. Selon une tradition ancienne, les hôtes sont accueillis dans le hall par un tisanier avec un thé à la menthe bouillant et sucré, la seule boisson capable de ranimer même les voyageurs du désert les plus épuisés.

Rafraîchi, le voyageur peut encore se rendre à une heure avancée dans les jardins pour de nouveaux plaisirs des sens. Dans un style des plus classiques, quatre parterres s'étalent à gauche et à droite des axes principaux carrelés de noir et de blanc, à l'intersection desquels clapote une fontaine bleue et blanche. C'est ainsi que doit être le *riad* islamique : strictement cloisonné pour que le visiteur s'y retrouve aussitôt et empli d'air frais, de doux bruits et de parfums choisis qui diffusent leur magie avec encore plus de force pendant la nuit. Ici, on trouvera deux figuiers bicentenaires, ainsi que de nombreux bananiers, orangers, hibiscus et balisiers *(Canna)* couleur de feu : la première impression du jardin promet un plaisir accru pour le lendemain.

À cinq heures trente, un concert des voix d'oiseau les plus diverses annonce l'éveil de la nature. Seules les tourterelles ont la grâce de dormir une heure de plus, imitées par tous les amoureux. Le terrain d'au moins un hectare du Palais Salam, construit au début du 19ᵉ siècle pour un pacha et transformé en hôtel en 1930, est avant tout un paradis pour les oiseaux, dont la présence emplit l'air d'un mouvement constant et des sons les plus divers. Ils pépient, chantent, exultent ou criaillent, se baignent abondamment dans les canaux qui traversent chaque jardin arabe digne de ce nom et nichent de préférence dans le rempart rongé par le temps qui enclot et protège le terrain. Pour tous, les souvenirs du Palais Salam

One-hundred-year-old palm trees tower over the city wall of Taroudant and offer the Palais Salam shade.

Hundertjährige Palmen überragen die Stadtmauer von Taroudant. Sie gewähren auch dem Palais Salam Schutz.

Des palmiers centenaires surplombent le mur d'enceinte de Taroudant. Ce mur protège également le Palais Salam.

Palais Salam

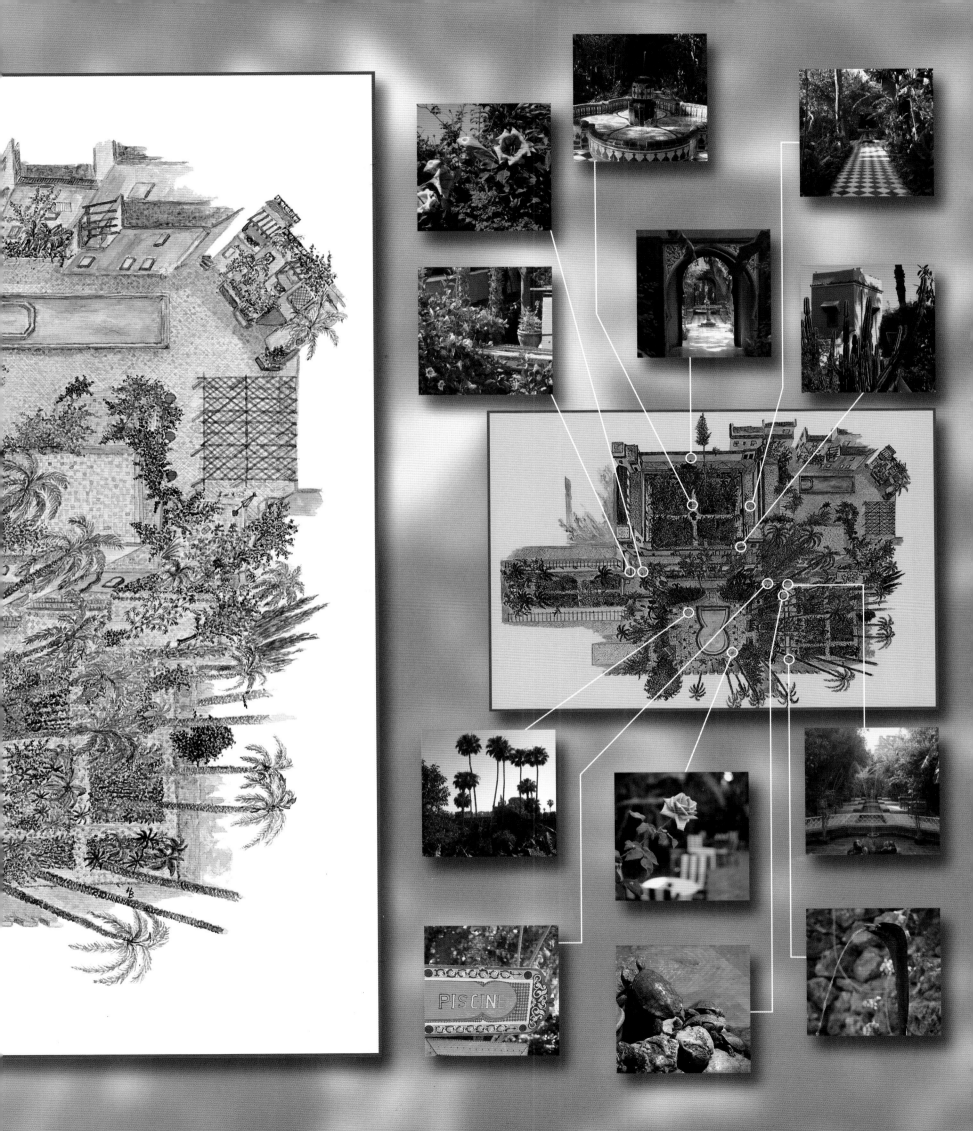

birds at the *Palais Salam* is engraved on one's mind forever. In addition, the grounds, which are cared for by the head gardener and his ten assistants, offer an astonishingly luxuriant flora.

The hundred-year-old palm trees, which rise around the pool and grow far beyond the battlements of the city walls are outstanding. Invitingly shaped like an Arab gateway, the large swimming pool is sheltered on all sides by lush plants. Nevertheless, some people prefer the small pool, which is situated a floor higher up and belongs to the newer hotel complex that was added in 1970. Perhaps they are seduced by the impressive cup of gold vine *(solandra maxima)*, whose giant blossoms appear to be made of wax; it flourishes so magnificently up here that

geprägt. Dabei bietet die Anlage, die von einem Chefgärtner und seinen zehn Mitarbeitern gepflegt wird, eine staunenswert üppige Flora.

Herausragend die hundertjährigen Palmen, die sich rund um den Pool erheben und weit über die Zinnen der Stadtmauer hinaus wachsen. Das große Schwimmbecken ist einladend wie ein arabisches Tor geformt und nach allen Seiten durch dichte Pflanzungen abgeschirmt. Gleichwohl ziehen manche den kleineren Pool vor, der ein Stockwerk höher liegt und zu dem neueren Hotelkomplex gehört, der ab 1970 hinzugefügt wurde. Vielleicht fühlen sie sich verführt von dem beeindruckenden Goldkelch *(Solandra maxima)*, dessen riesige Blüten wirken, als wären sie aus Wachs, und der hier oben so unglaublich gedeiht, dass er nicht

restent à jamais marqués par ses oiseaux. L'endroit offre par ailleurs, grâce aux soins d'un jardinier-chef et de ses dix aides, une végétation étonnamment luxuriante.

Sous la domination des palmiers centenaires qui se dressent tout autour du bassin et dépassent largement les créneaux du rempart, la grande piscine, bordée de tous côtés par un écran végétal épais, présente la forme engageante d'une porte arabe. Certains préféreront cependant le petit bassin, situé un étage plus haut et qui appartient au nouveau complexe hôtelier ajouté au début des années 1970, peut-être séduits par l'impressionnante solandra *(Solandra maxima)* dont les énormes fleurs donnent l'impression d'être en cire et qui se développe si incroyablement à cette hauteur qu'elle ne se

The tower is the favourite resting place for turtle doves, while the pool is the main attraction for the turtles.

Der Turm ist bevorzugter Platz der Turteltauben – während das Wasserbecken Anziehungspunkt der Schildkröten ist.

La tourelle est le coin preféré des tourterelles – tandis que le bassin reste le centre d'attraction des tortues.

it has not only grown over the roof but also climbed up the city wall. The view from above should not be missed either: over the restaurant, hidden under a heavy load of bougainvillea flowers, you can see the rear part of the old garden, which contains wonderful roses and a remarkable collection of giant cacti.

nur das Dach überwuchert, sondern auch noch die Stadtmauer erklimmt. Der Blick von oben hinunter ist auch nicht zu verachten: Über das Restaurant hinweg, das sich unter der Blütenlast der Bougainvillea verbirgt, sieht man auf den rückwärtigen Teil des alten Gartens, der wunderbare Rosen und eine beachtliche Samm-

contente pas d'envahir le toit, mais fait aussi l'ascension du rempart. La vue vers le bas n'est pas non plus à négliger : au-delà du restaurant, croulant sous la charge fleurie des bougainvillées, on aperçoit la partie arrière de l'ancien jardin, qui abrite des roses somptueuses et une collection appréciable de cactus géants.

This is the famous fountain of the Palais Salam's traditional *riyad*. The fountain is the centre of the garden, which is divided into four parts.

Der berühmte Brunnen im traditionellen *Riad* des Palais Salam. Er bildet den Mittelpunkt des viergeteilten Gartens.

La célèbre fontaine du traditionnel *riad* du Palais Salam. Elle constitue le centre du jardin découpé en quatre parties.

Directly in front of the breakfast terrace lies the tiled channel, which flows into an octagonal basin. But only those sitting down below can watch the turtles in the pool – and the birds that love to bathe in this channel and are guaranteed to peck the crumbs off the guests' tables afterwards...

lung riesiger Kakteen beherbergt. Direkt vor der Frühstücksterrasse liegt der gekachelte Kanal, der in ein achteckiges Becken mündet. Aber nur wer unten sitzt, kann die Schildkröten im Wasserbecken beobachten – und die Vögel, die gerne in diesem Kanal baden und hinterher die Krümel vom Tisch der Gäste picken...

Juste devant la terrasse du petit déjeuner, le canal pavé débouche dans un bassin octogonal, il faut cependant être assis en bas pour pouvoir y observer les tortues et les oiseaux, dont le canal est le lieu de baignade favori, d'où ils ne manquent pas de venir picorer les miettes des tables après le départ des hôtes...

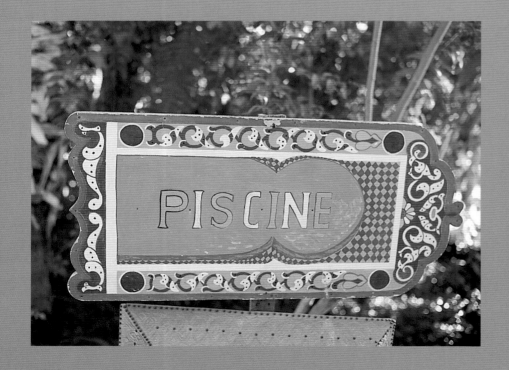

PISCINE

The traditional fountain, the impressive cup of the *solandra maxima* or the hand-painted signpost are only a few of the Palais Salam's charming details. In a Morrocan garden, roses are indispensable, but turtles come as a surprise. An iron cobra supplies the channel with water.

Einige der Details, die den Charme des Palais Salam ausmachen, vom klassischen Brunnen über die imposanten Blüten der *Solandra maxima* bis zum handbemalten Wegweiser. Schildkröten sind eine Überraschung, Rosen ein Muss im marokkanischen Garten. Die eiserne Kobra speist den Kanal mit Wasser.

Quelques uns des détails qui font le charme du Palais Salam, de la fontaine classique aux fleurs imposantes de la *Solandra maxima* au poteau indicateur peint main ... Si les roses sont le nec plus ultra dans un jardin marocain, les tortues, elles, restent une surprise. Le cobra en fer alimente un cours d'eau.

La Gazelle d'Or

In order to reach the "Golden Gazelle", which is one of Morocco's finest hotels, visitors must travel for two kilometres along the dusty country road from Taroudant. At the end of the drive, a black guard in white uniform stands in front of a half-open door – in this world this is a symbol meaning that you are welcome, but also that the private sphere of the guests is to be protected. After a quick inspection, the second half of the door is opened.

The guests immediately find themselves in a garden. It is small and, with its pool, seems typically Islamic. The entrance to the hotel almost disappears beneath a luxuriant, rampant bougainvillea plant. From the lobby on the left-hand side a long corridor leads to the bar with a large terrace. From this spot, there is a view over the garden itself, which is full of surprises.

A long water channel forms the "backbone" and leads from a small basin to an Olympic-sized pool. At the starting point there are palm trees, and roses and cacti grow in the middle. Two alleys, whose splendour can scarcely be surpassed, flank the watercourse: in front of the tender green backdrop of sturdy banana trees the red or white leaves of countless poinsettias *(euphorbia pulcherimma)* spread out. Here these plants, often better know as Christmas stars, can grow to be as tall as a man. In the red and white palette one can also include the impressive collection of large-blossomed *hippeastrum*, whose red and white striped flowers attract our attention. The owner, Madame Bennis, has new

Um die „Goldene Gazelle" zu erreichen, die als das feinste Landhotel Marokkos gilt, muss der Besucher von Taroudant aus zwei Kilometer staubige Landstraße hinter sich bringen. Am Ende der Auffahrt wartet ein schwarzer Wächter in weißer Kleidung vor einem halb geöffneten Tor – in dieser Welt der Symbole ein Zeichen dafür, dass man willkommen ist, gleichzeitig aber die Privatsphäre der illustren Gäste geschützt werden soll. Nach kurzer Kontrolle wird auch der zweite Flügel geöffnet.

Sofort befindet man sich in einem Garten. Er ist klein und mutet mit seinem Wasserbecken typisch islamisch an. Der Eingang des Hotels verschwindet fast unter einer üppig wuchernden Bougainvillea. Von der Lobby führt linker Hand ein langer Gang zur Bar mit der großen Terrasse. Von hier hat man Blick auf den eigentlichen Garten, der voller Überraschungen steckt.

Das „Rückgrat" bildet ein langer Wasserkanal, der von einem kleinen Bassin zu einem Pool mit olympischen Maßen führt. Am Ausgangspunkt wachsen Palmen, Rosen und mittendrin Kakteen. Den Wasserlauf flankieren zwei Alleen, die an Pracht kaum zu überbieten sind: Vor dem zartgrünen Hintergrund kräftiger Bananenstauden entfalten sich die roten oder weißen Hochblätter unzähliger Poinsettien *(Euphorbia pulcherimma)*, die bei uns besser bekannt sind als Weihnachtssterne – hier entwickeln sie sich zu mannshohen Sträuchern. In der Rot-Weiß-Palette bleibt auch die beeindruckende Sammlung großblütiger

Pour atteindre « La Gazelle d'Or », considéré comme l'hôtel de campagne le plus raffiné du Maroc, le visiteur doit d'abord parcourir deux kilomètres d'une route de terre poussiéreuse depuis Taroudant. À la fin de l'ascension, un gardien noir vêtu de blanc l'attend devant un portail à moitié ouvert, dans ce monde de symboles, un signe de bienvenue, mais aussi que la vie privée de l'illustre hôte doit être protégée. Après un contrôle rapide, le deuxième vantail est ouvert à son tour. Aussitôt, on se trouve au cœur d'un jardin, de dimensions modestes et de pur style islamique avec son bassin. L'entrée de l'hôtel disparaît presque sous un bougainvillier des plus foisonnants. Dans le vestibule, un long couloir à gauche mène au bar et à sa vaste terrasse, d'où l'on peut admirer la vue sur le véritable jardin, et les nombreuses surprises qu'il recèle.

Sa « colonne vertébrale » est constituée d'un long canal reliant un petit bassin à une piscine de dimensions olympiques. Le point de départ est planté de palmiers et de rosiers entourant des cactus. La voie d'eau est flanquée de deux allées à la splendeur inégalable : sur le fond vert tendre de vigoureux bananiers s'épanouissent les bractées rouges ou blanches d'innombrables poinsettias *(Euphorbia pulcherimma)*, plus connus dans nos pays sous le nom d'Étoile de Noël et qui forment ici des arbustes à hauteur d'homme. Toujours dans les teintes rouge et blanc, on admire également l'impressionnante collection de *hippeastrum* à grandes fleurs, et notamment les

hippeastrum bulbs sent in specially from Holland each year.

The large central lawn around which the guest pavilions are grouped is clearly inspired by British style. Horses and a flock of sheep are allowed to graze here. Opposite lies the golf course.

On principle, no insecticides are used in the "Gazelle d'Or", simply because the produce has as final destination: the plates of the discerning guests. The hotel is famous for its cuisine, in which herbs play a major role. In the kitchen garden you can find vervain, wild basil, sage, oregano, camomile, rosemary, thyme, lemon balm, peppermint, mugwort and dill, that "exotic" northern herb. They are not just used to season the meals; they are also tied into little aromatic bouquets and used to decorate the tables in the pool-restaurant.

At lunchtime a buffet is set out there, with a view of the large orange grove, whose fruits are naturally also used. Other fruit and vegetables grown here include apricots, peaches, figs, olives, mandarin oranges, grapefruits, Seville oranges, pomegranates and lemons. In addition,

Hippeastrum, wobei die rot-weiß-gestreiften Exemplare die größte Aufmerksamkeit auf sich ziehen. Madame Bennis, die Besitzerin, lässt jedes Jahr neue *Hippeastrum*-Knollen eigens aus Holland kommen.

Vom englischen Gartenstil inspiriert ist die große zentrale Rasenfläche, um die herum die Gästepavillons gruppiert sind. Pferde und eine Schafherde dürfen hier grasen. Gegenüber liegt der Golfplatz.

Auf Inzektizide wird in der „Gazelle d'Or" grundsätzlich verzichtet, schon allein deswegen, weil die Erträge den verwöhnten Gästen vorgesetzt werden. Das Hotel ist berühmt für seine Küche, in der Kräuter eine Hauptrolle spielen. Im Potager wachsen Verveine (Eisenkraut), wildes Basilikum, Salbei, Oregano, Kamille, Rosmarin, Thymian, Zitronenmelisse, Pfefferminze, Beifuß und das „exotische" nordische Kraut Dill. Sie würzen nicht nur die Gerichte, sondern werden auch zu aromatischen Sträußchen gebunden, die im Pool-Restaurant die Tische schmücken. Dort wird unter Olivenbäumen mittags ein Buffet aufgebaut, mit Blick auf den großen Orangenhain, dessen Früchte natür-

étonnants exemplaires rayés de rouge et de blanc. Madame Bennis, la propriétaire de l'hôtel, fait venir chaque année de nouveaux bulbes de *hippeastrum* de Hollande.

La grande pelouse centrale autour de laquelle sont groupés les pavillons destinés aux hôtes, elle, rappelle plutôt le style anglais. Des chevaux et un troupeau de mouton y paissent tranquillement, tandis qu'en face se trouve le terrain de golf.

À la « Gazelle d'Or », on a renoncé par principe à tout insecticide, ne serait-ce que parce que les produits du jardin sont servis aux hôtes choyés de l'hôtel. L'établissement est en effet célèbre pour sa cuisine, où les herbes jouent un rôle majeur : dans le potager poussent verveine, basilic sauvage, sauge, origan, camomille, romarin, thym, mélisse citronnée, menthe et estragon, sans oublier l'herbe nordique et « exotique » qu'est ici l'aneth. Outre leur fonction culinaire, ils sont aussi utilisés pour les petits bouquets aromatiques qui décorent les tables du restaurant au bord de la piscine. Un buffet sous les oliviers y est servi le midi, avec vue sur l'orangeraie, dont les fruits sont également utilisés. De même, abricots, pêches,

Aloes blossom in the "Mexican garden", while the entrance of the marquee, the *tente caïdale*, is covered by white bougainvillea flowers. Thanks to the horses and sheep there is no need to mow the lawn in front of the guest pavilions. The photo is framed by a poinsettia, also known as Christmas star.

Im „mexikanischen Garten" blüht die Aloe, während der Eingang zum Festzelt, der *tente caïdale*, von weißer Bougainvillea beschützt wird. Pferde und Schafe betätigen sich als Rasenmäher vor den Gästebungalows. Im Vordergrund eine ausgewachsene *Poinsettie* (Weihnachtsstern).

L'aloès fleurit au « jardin mexicain », tandis que l'entrée de la tente caïdale est abritée par des bougainvilliers blancs. Chevaux et moutons remplacent la tondeuse devant les bungalows des clients. Au premier plan, un poinsettia adulte.

The garden "Gazelle d'Or" offers the most beautiful flowers such as (clockwise form top left): amaryllis, Indian shot, iceberg-roses and *clivia*.

Blütenstars aus dem Garten der „Gazelle d'Or", im Uhrzeigersinn von links oben: Amaryllis, Canna, Iceberg-Rose, Clivie.

Parmi les fleurs qui tiennent la vedette à la Gazelle d'Or : amaryllis, canna, rosier « iceberg », clivia (dans le sens des aiguilles d'une montre, en partant d'en haut à gauche).

They grow useful plants such as avocados, papayas, bananas, sunflowers and alfalfa for the horses.

Madame Bennis is however prouder of her formal garden elements than of the luxuriant diversity, which in some places is reminiscent of the tropics: at certain times of the years the alleys are flanked with red and white blossoms and at others they display a host of blue flowers (e.g. *agapanthus*). And she is proud of her pure white rose garden, where only the "Iceberg" variety grows. Lots of thought has also gone into planting the gardens around the guest bungalows: here jasmine and Solanum vine climb up the walls and nicotiana and lilies bloom – at night the guests are allowed to get carried away with their bewitching scent.

The path to the swimming pool is lined by the red and white striped *hippeastrum* "carnival" (an amaryllis); the bulbs are imported from the Netherlands.

Der Weg zum Swimmingpool ist gesäumt von rot-weiß gestreiften *Hippeastrum* „Carnival" (Amaryllis), deren Knollen aus Holland kommen.

Le chemin qui mène à la piscine est bordé d'*hippeastrum* « carnival » (amaryllis), dont les bulbes viennent de Hollande.

lich Verwertung finden. Aus eigener Anzucht kommen außerdem Aprikosen, Pfirsiche, Feigen, Oliven, Mandarinen, Pampelmusen, Bitterorangen, Granatäpfel und Zitronen. Andere Nutzpflanzen sind Avocados, Papayas, Bananen, Sonnenblumen und Saatluzerne für die Pferde.

Stolzer jedoch als auf die üppige Vielfalt, die in manchen Teilen an die

figues, olives, mandarines, pamplemousses, bigarades, grenades et citrons sont cultivés sur place, ainsi que d'autres plantes utiles comme les avocats, les papayes, les bananes, les tournesols et la luzerne pour les chevaux. Plus cependant que l'extraordinaire variété dont certains éléments ne sont pas sans rappeler les

Tropen erinnert, ist Madame Bennis auf ihre streng durchkomponierten Gartenteile: Auf die Alleen, die zu einer bestimmten Jahreszeit nur in Rot und Weiß blühen, sich in einer anderen Saison dagegen durchgehend mit blauen Blüten (zum Beispiel *Agapanthus*) präsentieren. Und auf ihren rein weißen Rosengarten, in dem nur die Sorte „Ice-

tropiques, ce qui fait la fierté de Madame Bennis, ce sont la composition et l'ordonnance strictes des différentes parties du jardin : les allées qui fleurissent en rouge et blanc à certaines saisons pour ne se présenter qu'en bleu à d'autres (notamment grâce aux fleurs d'*agapanthus*). Sans oublier sa roseraie d'un blanc de

berg" wächst. Wohl durchdacht ist auch die Anpflanzung bei den Gästebungalows: Hier klettern Jasmin und Solanum, blühen Nicotiana und Lilien – erlaubt ist nur, was die Gäste nachts mit betörendem Duft umfängt.

neige, dont l'unique occupante est la variété « Iceberg ». Les plantations aux abords des bungalows ne sont pas élaborées avec moins de soin : le jasmin et le *solanum* y grimpent, tandis qu'y fleurissent le nicotiana et les lis ; les seules plantes autorisées sont celles dont les parfums grisants charment les hôtes pendant la nuit.

Riad Hida

The signpost to *Riad Hida* is large and striking. Nevertheless, western travellers tend not to follow it, as they find it too unlikely that this primitive gravel path that crosses straight through an impoverished market selling vegetables and plastic bowls could lead to a palace hotel with luxurious gardens. But yet this is indeed the case.

Moments after stepping through the gateway in the high enclosure wall you are greeted with the scent of freshness. This is not just because on the left hand side there is a pool inviting you to cool off. It is also the atmosphere of abundance and hospitality, which is all the more overwhelming because the surrounding area is almost life-threateningly barren. There is a real oasis feel about the *Riad Hida*. Fuchsia coloured bougainvilleas are draped over all the walls, light blue bindweeds climb upwards entwining themselves around the palm trees. Roses bloom with marguerites, pelargoniums and busy lizzies, all trying to outdo one another – even most of the cacti are in flower. It is no wonder that a rich Dane bought this palace (built by Pasha Hida in the 19th century) for this reason alone, because he had fallen in love with the garden. For 30 years now he has been sharing his passion with the hotel and restaurant guests.

Behind the reception and the bar a few steps lead down to the large rectangular fruit garden, where bananas and citrus fruits grow in abundance. You will never find larger grapefruit anywhere! In

Der Wegweiser zum *Riad Hida* ist groß und auffallend. Dennoch folgt der westliche Reisende ihm nicht – zu unwahrscheinlich findet er die Möglichkeit, über diesen primitiven Schotterweg, quer durch einen ärmlichen Markt für Gemüse und Plastikschüsseln, zu einem Hotel-Palast mit luxuriösen Gärten zu gelangen. Und doch ist es so.

Kaum tritt man durch das Tor in der hohen Umfriedungsmauer, riecht es nach Erfrischung und Labsal. Das liegt nicht nur daran, dass linker Hand sofort ein Pool zur Abkühlung einlädt. Es ist diese Atmosphäre von Überfluss und Gastlichkeit, die umso überwältigender wirkt, da die Umgebung geradezu lebensbedrohlich karg ist. Im *Riad Hida* stellt sich echtes Oasen-Gefühl ein. Fuchsiafarbene Bougainvilleen ergießen sich über alle Mauern, hellblaue Winden ranken an Palmen empor, Rosen blühen mit Margeriten, Pelargonien und Fleißigen Lieschen um die Wette, und selbst die Kakteen tragen zum großen Teil Blüten. Kein Wunder, dass ein reicher Däne diesen Palast, der im 19. Jahrhundert für Pascha Hida erbaut wurde, nur deswegen kaufte, weil er sich in den Garten verliebt hatte. Seit 30 Jahren teilt er seine Passion mit Hotel- und Restaurantgästen.

Hinter Rezeption und Bar führen einige Stufen hinunter in das große Rechteck des Obstgartens, in dem vor allem Bananen und Zitrusfrüchte willig wachsen. Größere Pampelmusen wird man nirgendwo finden! Im Mikro-Klima des groß-

Le panneau indiquant la direction du *Riad Hida* est grand et très visible. Et pourtant, le voyageur occidental ne le suit généralement pas, trouvant trop invraisemblable la simple possibilité que ce chemin caillouteux traversant un pauvre marché aux légumes et ustensiles plastiques puisse conduire à un palace et à ses somptueux jardins. Il en est pourtant ainsi.

À peine franchie la porte dans le haut mur d'enceinte, on sent la fraîcheur et l'apaisement. La piscine, à gauche, qui invite de suite à se rafraîchir n'en est pas seule responsable, mais bien une atmosphère d'opulence et d'hospitalité, qui se manifeste avec d'autant plus de force que les environs sont si misérables. Au *Riad Hida* s'impose la sensation authentique d'être dans une oasis. Des bougainvilliers fuchsia s'épandent sur tous les murs, des volubilis bleu clair grimpent le long des palmiers, les roses rivalisent en floraison avec les marguerites, les pélargoniums et les impatientes, et même les cactus sont presque tous fleuris. Rien d'étonnant donc, si un riche Danois n'a acheté ce palais, construit au 19e siècle pour le pacha Hida, que parce qu'il était tombé amoureux de son jardin. Depuis 30 ans, il partage sa passion avec les hôtes de l'hôtel et du restaurant.

Derrière la réception et le bar, quelques marches descendent jusqu'au grand verger rectangulaire, où bananes et agrumes se partagent la vedette : vous ne trouverez nulle part d'aussi gros pamplemousses ! Sous le microclimat du carré géné-

---

An impressive bougainvillea greets the guests of the *Riad Hida* enthusiastically once they arrive at the hotel after their dusty trip.

Von Bougainvillea überschwänglich begrüßt fühlt sich der Gast im „Riad Hida", nachdem er die staubige Anfahrt überstanden hat.

Les bougainvilliers semblent offrir un accueil enthousiaste au visiteur qui a réussi à surmonter l'arrivée poussiéreuse.

A little pavilion crowns the water channel. Protected by cypresses, pelargonia and marguerites are in flower.

Ein kleiner Pavillon krönt den Wasserkanal. Unter der Schirmherrschaft von Zypressen wachsen Pelargonien und Margeriten.

Un petit pavillon couronne le chemin d'eau. Sous le haut patronage des cyprès, s'épanouissent pélargoniums et marguerites.

the microclimate of this liberally watered square, the giant shining yellow fruit grow into genuine showpieces – only the numerous peacocks rival them with their vain cartwheels.

Whoever thought that Ouled Berhil was a godforsaken Berber village, finds clear proof here that the Creation is at home everywhere; even if the laboriously worked soil under such luxuriant heavily-laden plants is as naked and karstic as the desert, from which this garden was wrested.

zügig bewässerten Gevierts entwickeln sich die leuchtend gelben Riesenfrüchte zu wahren Schauobjekten – nur die zahlreichen Pfauen machen ihnen mit eitlem Radschlagen Konkurrenz.

Wer dachte, Ouled Berhil sei ein gottverlassenes Berberdorf, der findet hier augenfälligen Beweis dafür, dass die Schöpfung überall zu Hause ist. Auch wenn der mühsam bearbeitete Boden unter den so reich tragenden Pflanzen nackt und karstig ist wie die Wüste, der dieser Garten abgerungen wurde.

reusement irrigué, les fruits géants d'un jaune éclatant se développent jusqu'à devenir de véritables pièces de musée. Seuls les nombreux paons leur font concurrence, à grand renfort de roues vaniteuses.

Tous ceux qui ont pu penser qu'Ouled Berhil n'était qu'un village berbère désolé trouvent ici la preuve indiscutable que la créativité n'a pas de frontières. Même lorsque le sol péniblement cultivé sous la végétation luxuriante est aussi nu et aride que le désert auquel a été arraché ce jardin.

A pleasant seating is designed around the octagonal fountain. In the background the entrance to the restaurant (above) is visible. Peacocks love to walk up and down the restaurant entrance.

Um den achteckigen Brunnen mit Fontäne gruppiert sich eine Sitzecke. Dahinter liegt der Eingang zum Speisesaal (Foto rechts), vor dem die Pfauen gern auf und ab spazieren.

Autour de la fontaine octogonale, les fauteuils invitent au repos. Juste derrière, l'entrée de la salle à manger (photo de droite), devant laquelle les paons aiment se pavaner.

Marrakech – Morocco's Biggest Oasis

Marrakesch – Marokkos größte Oase

Marrakech – La Plus grande oasis du Maroc

Legend has it that a nomad was forced by heavy rains to pitch his tent for a long time in the desert. He found the spot – with a view of the crystalline peaks of the snow-capped Atlas – so beautiful it seemed unreal, like a fata morgana, and he stayed for another week and then another... During this time he ate a large number of dates and unthinkingly spat the stones onto the desert sand. There they germinated and took root thus creating Morocco's largest oasis with over 150,000 palm trees: Marrakech. Historians tell a different tale of the founding of Morocco's fourth biggest city: in the month of May 1070, a caravan of warlike Almoravids chose the immense plain at the foot of the High Atlas as the centre of their new kingdom, despite the fact that nothing grew there except bird's foot trefoil, jujube and thorn apple. The nomads, used to living off the milk and meat from their sheep and goats, settled down there, cultivated the plains until they were green and covered with flowers and created the most beautiful city in Morocco. This red city, which is praised in many songs, often referred to as a "rose amongst palm trees", together with its 12-kilometre long and 6 to 9 metre high fortified walls, was created using trampled clay, which upon drying immediately takes on a highly sought-after pink patina and proves indestructible in this climate. From the very start, this incomparable place cast its spell over people, it was not given the name marrakouch for nothing - in the language of the city's founders this means something like "come here quickly".

Those who follow this call never regret it. Marrakech has been honoured by being given the name Bahja, 'the happy one', a reflection of this city's "joie de vivre".

Es geht die Legende, dass ein Nomade durch heftige Regenfälle gezwungen war, sein Zelt für längere Zeit in der Wüste aufzuschlagen. Der Platz – mit Blick auf die kristallenen Gipfel des schneebedeckten Atlas – erschien ihm unwirklich schön wie eine Fata Morgana, und er verlängerte seinen Aufenthalt um eine Woche und eine weitere ... In dieser Zeit aß er viele, viele Dattelpalmen und spuckte die Kerne achtlos in den Wüstensand. Dort keimten sie und schlugen Wurzeln, und so entstand Marokkos größte Oase mit mehr als 150.000 Palmen: Marrakesch. Die Geschichtsschreiber erzählen die Gründung der viertgrößten Stadt Marokkos anders: Es war im Monat Mai des Jahres 1070, dass die Karawane der kriegerischen Almoraviden die immense Ebene am Fuße des Hohen Atlas zum Mittelpunkt ihres neuen Reiches erwählte, obwohl dort nichts wuchs außer Hornklee, Judendorn und Teufelsapfel. Die Nomaden, gewöhnt sich von Milch und Fleisch ihrer Schafe und Ziegen zu ernähren, wurden hier sesshaft, brachten die Ebene zum Grünen und Blühen und stampften die schönste Stadt Marokkos aus dem Boden – was wörtlich zu nehmen ist, denn die viel besungene rote Stadt, diese „Rose inmitten von Palmen", ist einschließlich ihrer 12 Kilometer langen und sechs bis neun Meter hohen Befestigungsmauern aus gestampftem Lehm entstanden, der beim Trocknen sofort die begehrte rosarote Patina annimmt und sich in diesem Klima als unverwüstlich erweist. Der unvergleichliche Ort zog von Anfang an die Menschen in seinen Bann, nicht ohne Grund leitet sich sein Name ab von marrakouch, was in der Sprache seiner Gründer soviel wie „komm schnell hierher" bedeutet.
Wer dem Aufruf folgt, bereut es nicht. Marrakesch trägt den Ehrennamen Bahja, Stadt der Lebensfreude.

Selon la légende, un nomade aurait été contraint par les pluies torrentielles de monter sa tente pour un séjour prolongé dans le désert. L'endroit – et la vue sur les sommets cristallins de l'Atlas neigeux – lui parut d'une beauté incroyable, telle une illusion, et il prolongea son séjour d'une semaine, puis d'une autre... Pendant ce temps, il mangea beaucoup, beaucoup de dattes, dont il cracha négligemment les noyaux dans le sable du désert. Ces derniers germèrent et prirent racine, et c'est ainsi que fut créée la plus grande oasis du Maroc avec plus de 150 000 palmiers : Marrakech.
Les historiens racontent autrement la fondation de la quatrième ville du Maroc : au mois de mai de l'année 1070, la caravane des guerriers Almoravides choisit l'immense plaine au pied du Haut-Atlas pour en faire le centre de son nouvel empire, alors que rien n'y pousse que du trèfle cornu, de l'épine-du-Christ et de l'herbe au diable. Les nomades, habitués à se nourrir du lait et de la viande de leurs moutons et chèvres, s'y établissent, font fleurir et verdir la plaine et surtout font sortir du sol la plus belle ville du Maroc, littéralement sortir du sol, car la ville rouge tant chantée, cette « rose au milieu des palmiers », est tout entière, y compris ses remparts fortifiés longs de 12 kilomètres et hauts de six à neuf mètres, construite en argile foulée, qui s'avère inusable sous ce climat et qui, en séchant, prend la patine rouge-rosé si recherchée. Dès le début, cet endroit incomparable entre tous a pris les hommes sous son charme, ce n'est d'ailleurs pas sans raison que son nom vient de marrakouch, ce qui, dans la langue de ses fondateurs, signifie à peu près « viens vite ! ».
Aucun de ceux qui suivent son appel ne le regrette et Marrakech s'honore également du nom de Bahja, cité de la joie de vivre.

The Palmeraie Gardens
Die Gärten der Palmerie
Les Jardins de la Palmeraie

I t is almost a miracle that the Palmeraie was able to grow in this landscape as the only palm grove of its kind north of the mountain range of the High Atlas. Legend tells us, that the stones of the dates eaten and thrown away by nomads traveling through the desert, were the reason for it. These billions of seeds from all over the Sahara all came together at this particular place to germinate, and thus the Palmeraie offers a wide variety of the most beautiful dates. No-one really knows how it originated; all that is known for sure is that countless eagerhands must have taken part in the work, but certainly also several clever minds.

For without the underground irrigation system, with its ditches and channels, which carry the meltwater from the High Atlas to the far-off wadis, this perfect oasis could never have been created. Additionally, a network of natural springs also runs under the fertile clay soil of the Palmeraie.

Today, the *khettara* have only a historical value, since the water supply has long been guaranteed by nearby reservoirs. Many people feared that this new system would disrupt the ecological balance and bring about the demise of the palm grove. Paradise was already showing its dark side: the first documented measurement of the Palmeraie gave a surface area of roughly 15,000 ha, covered in several hundred thousand palm trees. At the end of the 1950s, only 12,000 ha were recorded and at the beginning of the 1980s it had dropped to 6,000 – thus, in 70 years 60% of this area, which has been protected by law since 1929, had disappeared.

C'est presque un miracle que la palmeraie ait pu se développer, seule de ce type, au nord de la chaîne montagneuse du Haut-Atlas. La légende dit que des millions de noyaux de dattes, consommées par des nomades lors de leur traversée du désert et provenant de tous les coins du Sahara, se seraient retrouvés à cet endroit pour germer. Ainsi serait née la palmeraie aux belles et multiples espèces de dattiers. Nul ne sait véritablement comment elle a été créée, on sait seulement que d'innombrables petites mains diligentes ont dû participer à l'ouvrage. Et quelques cerveaux aussi. Car sans le système d'irrigation souterrain, ses fossés et canaux amenant l'eau de la fonte des neiges depuis de lointains wadis du Haut-Atlas, jamais cet idéal d'oasis n'aurait vu le jour, et cela malgré les puits naturels se trouvant en son sol argileux fertile.

Aujourd'hui, les *khettara* n'ont plus de valeur qu'historique et l'approvisionnement en eau est depuis longtemps assuré par des lacs de retenue voisins. Nombreux sont cependant ceux qui craignent que l'équilibre écologique n'en soit troublé et le déclin de la palmeraie précipité. En effet, le paradis a déjà commencé à dévoiler sa face cachée : si le premier relevé attesté donnait une estimation de surface de 15 000 hectares plantés de quelques centaines de milliers de palmiers, à la fin des années 1950, seuls 12 000 hectares étaient encore enregistrés et 6 000 au début des années 80. En 70 ans, ce sont donc 60 pour cent d'une surface classée site naturel protégé depuis 1929 qui ont été perdus. La principale raison en est la tendance croissante des gens aisés à s'assurer la propriété de vastes terrains à l'extérieur des villes trop étroites. Un mouvement qui garantit, certes, l'existence future de la ceinture verte que forme la palmeraie, mais morcelée en jardins

The large estates of the Palmeraie are a welcome area to experiment ideas – for both architects and garden designers. Nearby dams secure the necessary water supply.

Willkommenes Experimentierfeld für Architekten und Gartengestalter sind die großen Grundstücke der Palmerie. Die Wasserversorgung ist durch nahe gelegene Stauseen gesichert.

Les grandes propriétés de la Palmeraie offrent un terrain d'expérimentation de choix aux architectes et paysagistes. Des lacs artificiels à proximité garantissent le ravitaillement en eau.

Es grenzt an ein Wunder, dass sich die Palmerie als einzige ihrer Art nördlich der Kette des Hohen Atlas entwickeln konnte. Der Legende nach trug sich folgendes zu: Millionen von Dattelkernen, verzehrt von Nomaden, die durch die Wüste zogen, wären aus allen Ecken der Sahara an diesem Platz zusammen gekommen, um hier zu keimen, und so entstand die Palmerie mit den schönsten und vielfältigsten Dattelarten. Niemand weiß, wie sie wirklich entstanden ist, sicher ist nur, dass unzählige fleißige Hände daran beteiligt gewesen sein müssen. Und einige kluge Köpfe. Denn ohne das unterirdische Bewässerungssystem mit seinen Gräben und Kanälen, die das Schmelzwasser des Hohen Atlas aus fernen Wadis heran führten, wäre niemals dieses Idealbild einer Oase entstanden, obwohl sich zusätzlich ein Netz natürlicher Brunnen unter dem fruchtbaren Lehmboden der Palmerie entlang zieht.

Heute haben die *khettara* nur noch historischen Wert, längst ist die Wasserversorgung durch nahe Stauseen gesichert. Viele befürchten, dass genau dadurch das ökologische Gleichgewicht gestört und der Untergang der Palmerie herauf beschworen wird. Schon zeigt das Paradies seine Schattenseiten: Die erste beurkundete Vermessung ergab eine Oberfläche von geschätzten 15.000 Hektar, bewachsen mit einigen hunderttausend Palmen. Ende der 1950er Jahre wurden nur noch 12.000 Hektar registriert und Anfang der 80er Jahre 6.000 – in 70 Jahren gingen also 60 Prozent der seit 1929 unter Naturschutz stehenden Fläche verloren. Grund dafür ist der zunehmende Drang der Wohlhabenden, sich große Grundstücke außerhalb der engen Stadt zu sichern. Dadurch ist zwar garantiert, dass die Palmerie ein grüner Gürtel bleiben wird, aber zerstückelt in exklusive

The reason for this being the increasing pressure from well-to-do people wanting to secure a large plot of land on the outskirts of the cramped city. In this way it is guaranteed that the Palmeraie will continue to be a green belt, but broken up into exclusive private gardens with palatial villas behind high walls, whilst all around windswept isolated palm trees stand on the waste land. At least, it was not permitted to cut down any of the palm trees or to damage the area surrounding them. At any rate, the late King Hassan II saw to it that 11,000 ha land would be reforested so that all parts of the Palmeraie could be joined up.

Some ecologists may be concerned about the development of the area, but the town planners are convinced that the project is carried out with responsibility and care. The strict order that every plot can only be sold at a minimum of one hectar of land, ensures that the area of the Palmeraie is not going to be overdeveloped into tiny pieces of land. Nevertheless, for architects, this is a paradise. Where else could they build on such a large scale?

It does not really come as a surprise, that Marrakech is considered the stronghold of a new, modern, typically Moroccan style of architecture, having its roots dating back to the "golden age", in the times of the Almoravid and Almohad rulers of the 11th and 12th centuries. The same materials, which have been in use for centuries, are still employed today: the reddish clay soil of the *Haouz,* a region which is the artrium of the real desert, the Sahara. One of the material's characteristic is the famous warm and beautiful shade, that it gives to the buildings. At dusk, Marrakech is bathed in red light and the "red city" has been celebrated in many songs. The material also allows a variety of forms and designs, ranging from cupolas and arches to battlements and the decorated façades. The Palmeraie gardens follow the style of the houses, which are clearly modern but also quite unequivocally Morrocan style.

Privatgärten mit palastartigen Villen hinter hohen Mauern, während drumherum windzerzauste Palmen vereinzelt auf Brachland stehen. Immerhin darf bei Bauvorhaben in der Palmerie keine einzige Palme gefällt oder in ihrem Lebensraum gestört werden. König Hassan II. veranlasste, dass 11.000 Hektar Land wieder aufgeforstet und der Palmerie angeschlossen wurden.

Manche Ökologen mögen die Erschließung des Geländes mit Sorge betrachten, doch die Städteplaner sind überzeugt, dass hier verantwortungsbewusst gehandelt wird. Allein die Vorschrift, dass kein Grundstück unter einem Hektar verkauft werden darf, sorge dafür, dass die Palmerie nicht zersiedelt werden könne. Für Architekten jedenfalls ist sie ein Paradies – wo sonst können sie so großzügig bauen?

So kommt es, dass Marrakesch als Hochburg einer neuen typisch marokkanischen Architektur gilt, die ihre Wurzeln im „goldenen Zeitalter" der Almoraviden- und Almohaden-Herrscher (11.–12. Jahrhundert) hat. Gebaut wird mit dem selben Material wie damals: mit dem rötlichen Lehmboden der Haouz-Gegend, die sozusagen der Vorhof zur wirklichen Wüste, der Sahara, ist. Das Material garantiert die schöne warme Tönung, die Marrakesch im Abendlicht zur viel besungenen „roten Stadt" macht. Ebenso ermöglicht diese moderne Architektur vielfältige Formen, sie reichen von Kuppeln über Bögen bis zu Zinnen und Verzierungen der Fassade. Die Gärten der Palmerie folgen dem Vorbild der Häuser, die eindeutig modern – aber auch eindeutig marokkanisch sind.

privés fermés aux villas dignes de palais enfermées derrière de hauts murs, alors que tout autour, des palmiers ébouriffés par le vent se dressent solitaires dans des champs en friche. Toutefois, aucun palmier ne doit être abattu ou dérangé dans son espace vital lors de travaux dans la palmeraie. Le roi Hassan II décida également le reboisement de 11 000 hectares qui furent rattachés à la palmeraie.

Si quelques écologues considèrent la mise en valeur du terrain d'un œil critique, les urbanistes croient agir en toute conscience. Seule l'ordonnance concernant l'interdiction de la vente de terrains de moins d'un hectare veille à ce que la palmeraie ne soit pas dégradée par de nouvelles constructions. En tout cas, elle représente un véritable paradis pour les architectes – où pourraient-ils construire sinon aussi généreusement ? C'est ainsi que Marrakech devient la citadelle d'une nouvelle architecture typiquement marocaine, qui a trouvé ses racines dans « l'âge d'or » des souverains des Almoravides et des Almohades (11e–12e siècles). On construit dans le même matériau qu'autrefois : la terre argileuse rougeâtre de la région de Haouz, avant-cour pour ainsi dire du vrai désert du Sahara. Ce matériau garantit une belle teinte chaude qui fait de Marrakech, baignée dans la lumière du soir, une « ville rouge ». Cette terre argileuse permet également de réaliser diverses formes : les dômes au-dessus des arceaux, les créneaux et les enjolivures des façades. Les jardins de la palmeraie suivent l'exemple des maisons qui sont résolument modernes – mais aussi incontestablement marocaines.

Dar Asseraf

The first impression of this place is that this is the Mediterranean because of the soft terracotta archway, covered in dark green vegetation, which climbs up in shallow steps. This appears somewhat mysterious and leads one to expect an abundantly planted "homely" garden. Instead, you find yourself at the end of the shady archways in another sparsely decorated atrium, which would be well suited as the entrance to a Japanese Zen cloister: austerely structured stone floors with a precisely positioned water tank in the centre and bamboo bushes in the corner.

When you step out again the atmosphere changes. Waving grass and rustling banana trees create the impression that this is a very natural garden. Moreover, the extremely decorative crown-of-thorns (euphorbia milii) which grows here spreads naturally in this climate. Its yellow flowers are small and unspectacular, but are surrounded by red leaves and well protected by sharp thorns.

The entry to the house is covered by a tent-like porch, which disappears beneath honeysuckle and bougainvillea. Here, a white stone fountain provides fresh air. Both the latter and the carved house door remind us we are in Morocco. The owners of the property, who are locals, have deliberately avoided the customary colourful folklore, although they have chosen a quite traditional method of construction.

They had their house designed by Elie Mouyal, who is famous for his new interpretation of old mud-and-clay architecture. Despite its typical carved wood balcony, even the bathhouse appears as masculine and modern as the whole estate. The pool, spanned by a wooden bridge,

Der erste Eindruck ist mediterran. Das liegt an dem Bogengang in sanftem Terrakotta, berankt von sattem Grün, der in flachen Stufen hinan führt. Ein wenig geheimnisvoll wirkt er und lässt einen reich bepflanzten, „wohnlichen" Garten erwarten. Stattdessen findet man sich am Ende der schattigen Arkaden in einem kargen Vorhof wieder, der auch als Eingang zu einem japanischen Zen-Kloster taugen würde: streng gegliederter Steinfußboden, in der Mitte eine exakt platzierte Wasserschale und Bambusbüsche in den Ecken.

Der Schritt hinaus bringt wieder einen Stimmungswechsel. Wehende Gräser und raschelnde Bananenstauden lassen den Eindruck eines naturnahen Gartens entstehen. Auch die überaus dekorative Christusdorn-Wolfsmilch (Euphorbia milii), die hier wächst, breitet sich in diesem Klima natürlich aus. Ihre gelben Blüten sind klein und unscheinbar, aber von leuchtend roten Hochblättern umgeben – und von scharfen Dornen beschützt.

Der Eingang zum Haus trägt einen zeltartigen Vorbau, der unter Lonicera und Bougainvillea verschwindet. Hier sorgt ein weißer Steinbrunnen für frische Luft. Er und die geschnitzte Haustür verweisen darauf, dass man sich in Marokko befindet. Die übliche farbige Folklore haben die einheimischen Besitzer bewusst vermieden, obwohl sie eine ganz traditionelle Bauweise gewählt haben.

Sie ließen ihr Haus von Elie Mouyal entwerfen, der für seine Neu-Interpretation der alten Lehmarchitektur berühmt ist. Selbst das Badehaus wirkt, trotz typischem geschnitztem Holzbalkon, so modern und männlich wie das ganze An-

La première impression est méditerranéenne. Cela tient au chemin en arcades, d'un doux ton de terre cuite, sur lesquelles grimpe le vert foncé, qui mène vers le haut en marches plates. L'effet produit est quelque peu mystérieux et fait attendre un jardin « confortable » richement planté. Au lieu de cela, la voûte ombragée débouche de nouveau sur une pauvre avant-cour, entrée supposée d'un cloître zen japonais : sol rigoureusement découpé de dalles pavées avec au milieu une vasque parfaitement positionnée et dans les coins des bosquets de bambou.

Il suffit d'un pas de plus pour changer de nouveau d'atmosphère. Les herbes flottant au vent et les bananiers froufroutants donnent cette fois l'impression d'un jardin très naturel. L'euphorbe épines du Christ (Euphorbia milii), particulièrement décoratif, se propage lui aussi naturellement sous ce climat : ses fleurs jaunes sont, certes, petites et très simples, mais entourées de bractées protectrices d'un rouge lumineux et d'épines acérées.

L'entrée de la maison est surmontée d'un avant-corps en forme de tente qui disparaît sous les lonicera et les bougainvillées. Une vasque de pierre blanche y assure la fraîcheur de l'air ; avec la porte sculptée, il rappelle que nous sommes au Maroc. Pour le reste, les propriétaires marocains ont délibérément évité le folklore coloré habituel, bien qu'ils aient opté pour une construction des plus traditionnelles. La maison a été conçue par Elie Mouyal, célèbre pour sa ré-interprétation de l'architecture ancienne en torchis, et même le pavillon de bains, malgré son balcon typique de bois sculpté, présente le caractère moderne et masculin du reste de la propriété. La piscine,

The olive trees, lined along the overgrown wall, were standing here already at a time when there were no private gardens in the Palmeraie. Fairly new is the grove of orange trees behind the rosemary bush to the left.

Die Olivenbäume vor der überwucherten Mauer wuchsen hier schon, als es noch keine Privatgärten in der Palmerie gab. Neu ist die Anpflanzung eines Orangenhains hinter der Rosmarinhecke links.

Les oliviers devant le mur recouvert de verdure existaient bien avant qu'il n'y ait des jardins privés dans la Palmeraie. En revanche, l'orangeraie à gauche derrière la haie de romarin est toute nouvelle.

lies right at the end of the vast grounds in a separate garden-room in which exclusively red pelargoniums and white oleander bloom.

The extensive lawn takes up most of the garden, the widest variety of fruit trees grow on the left-hand side and on the right olive trees, and every year annuals in bloom are newly planted.

wesen. Der Pool, den eine hölzerne Brücke überspannt, liegt ganz am Ende des riesigen Geländes in einem eigenen Gartenraum, in dem ausschließlich rote Pelargonien und weißer Oleander blühen.

Den größten Teil des Gartens nimmt die ausgedehnte Rasenfläche ein, auf der linker Hand die verschiedensten Obstbäume und rechts Olivenbäume wachsen, die jedes Jahr aufs Neue mit blühenden Einjährigen unterpflanzt werden.

enjambée par un pont de bois, est située tout à l'extrémité de l'immense terrain, dans son propre jardin clos où fleurissent exclusivement des pélargoniums rouges et des lauriers-roses blancs.

L'essentiel du jardin est occupé par la vaste pelouse, garnie du côté gauche des arbres fruitiers les plus divers, et du côté droit d'oliviers, plantés chaque année de nouveau sous couverture avec d'autres âgés d'un an et en fleurs.

To offer a view has always been an important element of Morrocan garden design as we can see here. The pavilion that covers the end of the basin is also an interpretation of another classical element.

Durchblicke spielen seit jeher eine große Rolle in Marokkos Gärten, so auch hier. Der Pavillon, der über dem Pool thront, ist ebenfalls die Interpretation eines klassischen Elements.

Comme ici, les vues jouent un rôle prépondérant dans les jardins marocains. Le pavillon qui trône au-dessus de la piscine est également l'interprétation d'un élément classique.

...ach orange tree has its individual irrigation ditch. Strong thorns defend
...he striking flowers of the *euphorbia*. The agave is able to preserve its upright
...rowth during long periods of dryness.

...edes Orangenbäumchen steht in seiner eigenen Bewässerungsmulde.
...Mit wehrhaften Stacheln verteidigt die *Euphorbie* ihre auffallenden Blüten.
...ie Agave erhält ihren aufrechten Wuchs auch über längere Trockenperioden.

...haque oranger est entouré d'un creux qui facilite son irrigation.
...*euphorbe* protège ses fleurs somptueuses grâce à ses épines guerrières.
...agave conserve son port altier même après une longue période de sécheresse.

Once an olive grove flourished on this spot, and many of the former trees, including the palm trees, which served as a protective barrier, still stand today. But the most striking of all are the countless small orange trees whose fruit ripen at an accessible height. The impressive avenue of orange trees begins behind the rose-bed lined entry area on the left of which the guesthouse is situated. The dainty trees with their spherical crowns run up to the main house in a sweeping semi-circle.

In all its simplicity the preliminary portal of the entrance to the house appears as grandiose as a modern triumphal arch. The signature of the renowned grassroots architect, Elie Mouyal, is once again easy to recognise. Even the garden, most of which lies in front of the house, appears modern, although it dates back to traditional models. It could be described as a "Moroccan style near-natural garden", which is incidentally much older than the famous English version. Its roots reach back to the 12th century, when the Almohad rulers laid out the *Agdal* in the then capital Marrakech and thus created a new style of garden. For the first time, views over the surrounding landscape were included in the design. Care was taken to ensure that, in spite of the monumental buildings such as the enormous water reservoir, "plants prevailed over stone". The Schubnel Garden follows this model.

The view from the house looks out through two trunks of an ancient olive tree towards the classical cruciform water channel. The "olive tree twins" have a stone border, which looks like the plinth surrounding a monument – and this seems quite appropriate. As a rule, all root areas are at least provided with

Einst gedieh an diesem Platz ein Olivenhain, und viele der früheren Bäume, einschließlich der Palmen, die als Schutzwall dienten, stehen heute noch. Aber am meisten prägen sich die zahllosen Orangenbäumchen ein, deren Früchte in handlicher Höhe reifen. Die beeindruckende Orangenallee beginnt hinter dem mit Rosenbeeten gesäumten Eingangsbereich, in dem linker Hand das Gästehaus liegt. In schwungvollem Halbrund ziehen sich die zierlichen Bäume mit den kugeligen Kronen bis zum Haupthaus hin. Man geht auf Natursteinplatten, die in Rasen gebettet sind.

Das vorgelagerte Portal des Hauseingangs wirkt bei aller Schlichtheit grandios wie ein neuzeitlicher Triumphbogen. Die Handschrift des renommierten Grassroots-Architekten Elie Mouyal ist unschwer wieder zu erkennen. Auch der Garten, der zum größten Teil vor dem Haus liegt, mutet modern an, obwohl er auf traditionelle Vorbilder zurückgeht. Man könnte ihn als „naturnahen Garten marokkanischer Art" bezeichnen, der übrigens viel älter ist als die berühmte englische Version. Seine Wurzeln reichen ins 12. Jahrhundert, als die Almohaden-Herrscher in der damaligen Hauptstadt Marrakesch den *Agdal* anlegten und damit einen neuen Gartenstil kreierten. Zum ersten Mal wurden Ausblicke auf die umgebende Landschaft in die Gestaltung mit einbezogen. Und es wurde darauf geachtet, dass trotz monumentaler Bauten wie dem riesigen Wasserreservoir „die Pflanze über den Stein siegt". Der Schubnel-Garten folgt diesem Vorbild.

Der Blick vom Haus wird durch die zwei Stämme eines uralten Olivenbaumes hindurch auf den klassischen Wasserkanal in Kreuzform gelenkt. Der „Olivenzwilling" bekam

Une oliveraie s'étendait autrefois à cet endroit et bon nombre des anciens arbres, dont les palmiers qui formaient alors un mur protecteur, sont encore debout aujourd'hui. Mais le plus marquant reste les innombrables petits orangers, dont les fruits mûrissent à hauteur d'homme : l'imposante allée des oranges commence après l'entrée, bordée de massifs de roses et à la gauche de laquelle se dresse l'hôtellerie. Dans un demi-cercle parfait, les gracieux arbres aux cimes sphériques se succèdent jusqu'au bâtiment principal. On marche sur des dalles de pierre enchâssées dans l'herbe.

Le portail avant de l'entrée fait l'effet, dans toute sa sobriété, d'un arc de triomphe des temps modernes : on reconnaît sans peine la signature du célèbre architecte Elie Mouyal. Le jardin lui aussi, dont la majeure partie précède la maison, donne une impression de modernité, bien qu'il se réclame de modèles traditionnels. On pourrait le qualifier de « jardin naturel de style marocain », par ailleurs beaucoup plus ancien que les célèbres versions anglaises. Ses origines remontent au 12e siècle, lorsque les souverains Almohades plantèrent l'*Agdal* dans leur capitale d'alors, Marrakech, créant ainsi un nouveau style. Pour la première fois, on a intégré au jardin des vues sur le paysage environnant et on a veillé à ce que, malgré la présence de constructions monumentales, comme l'énorme réservoir d'eau, « la plante l'emporte sur la pierre ». Le jardin Schubnel suit ce modèle.

Depuis la maison, le regard est dirigé, entre les deux troncs d'un olivier séculaire, vers le canal classique en forme de croix. « L'olivier jumeau » a été doté d'une ceinture de pierre rappelant le socle d'un monument et,

Carefully pruned orange trees line this avenue, which leads in smooth curves to the main house.

Sorgfältig beschnittene Orangenbäum säumen die sanft geschwungene Allee die auf das Haupthaus zuführt.

Les orangers soigneusement taillés bordent l'allée doucement incurvée qu mène à la maison principale.

Villa Schubnel

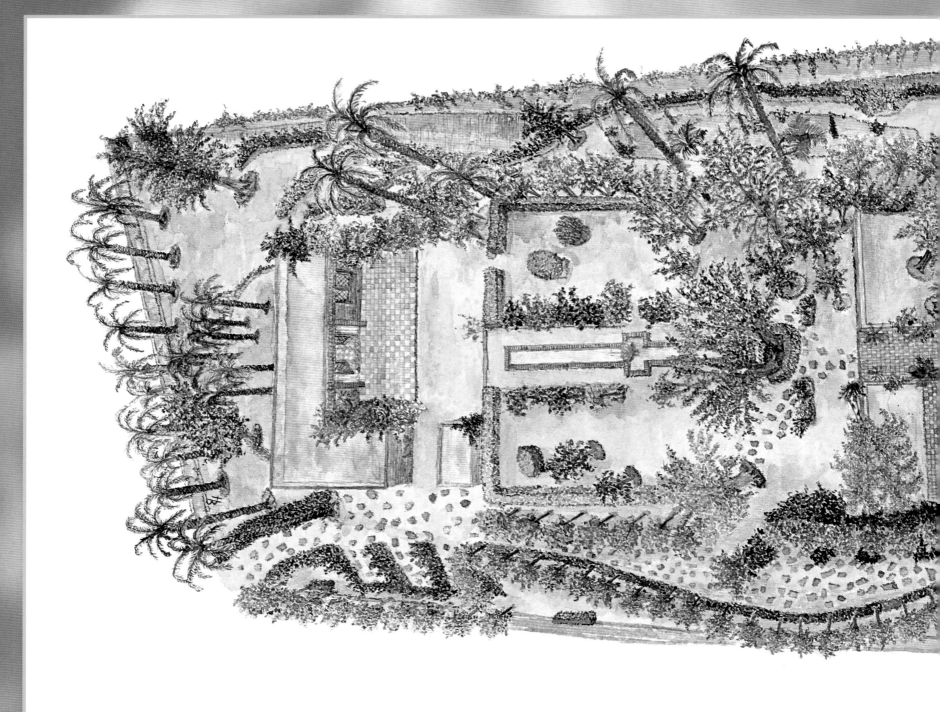

The swimming pool was especially designed, while the main entrance with its modern *porticus* door reminds the spectator of a historical palace.

Der Swimmingpool wurde von einem Designer entworfen. Der Hauseingang erinnert mit seinem modernen Porticus an historische Paläste.

La piscine est l'œuvre d'un créateur. L'entrée de la maison avec son portique fait penser aux palais historiques.

mulched areas, most even have a border and often enough proper flowerbeds can be found under the trees. In Morocco, palm trees in particular, for many people the quintessence of exotic beauty, are often laden with additional decoration. In this garden too there are palm trees, with sumptuous flowering bougainvilleas climbing up their trunks.

Gilda and André Schubnel, who divide their time between Paris and Marrakech, love roses. The finest specimens grow by the channel, where the air is refreshing thanks

eine steinerne Einfassung, die wie der Sockel eines Denkmals wirkt – was durchaus angemessen scheint. Grundsätzlich wurden alle Wurzelbereiche mindestens mit Baumscheiben versehen, meistens sogar mit einer Einfassung, und oft genug finden sich richtige Blumenbeete unter den Bäumen. Insbesondere die Palmen, für viele Inbegriff exotischer Schönheit, erhalten in Marokko oft zusätzlich Schmuck. Auch in diesem Garten finden sich Palmen, an deren Stämmen reich blühende Bougainvilleen emporranken.

par conséquent, tout à fait appropriée. En règle générale d'ailleurs, les zones racinaires de tous les arbres comportent des rondelles et le plus souvent également des rebords. C'est pourquoi il n'est pas rare que de véritables parterres de fleurs s'y forment, les palmiers notamment, pour beaucoup l'incarnation de la beauté exotique, qui se voient souvent offrir des ornements supplémentaires au Maroc, ont ici les troncs recouverts de bougainvillées richement fleuries.

Gilda et André Schubnel, qui partagent leur vie entre Paris et Marra-

The traditional Islamic garden contains the axes of co-ordinates, which is here reflected by the water channel. The ancient twin-olive tree (right) is an eye-catcher and at the same time a lookout.

An das Achsenkreuz des klassischen islamischen Gartens erinnert der Wasserkanal. Der uralte Oliven-Zwilling (rechts) ist Blickfang – und bietet Durchblick.

Le petit canal avec son axe en forme de croix rappelle le jardin islamique classique. « L'olivier-jumeau » séculaire capte le regard – tout en offrant une vue encadrée.

Pink bougainvillea twines itself around the trunk of a palm tree. White bougainvillea is a splendid background for the *solanum* (right).

Rosa Bougainvillea berankt den Stamm einer Palme. Vor weißer Bougainvillea kommt *Solanum* gut zur Geltung (großes Foto).

Des bougainvilliers roses grimpent le long d'un palmier. Le *solanum* est mis en valeur par les bougainvilliers blancs (grande photo).

to the constantly bubbling fountain. The whole garden is watered generously; a fact that can be inferred from the large number of discretely placed sprinklers.

The art of irrigation had already been mastered by the 10th century in Marrakech. Proof of this are the countless *khettara* (irrigation channels), which run through the whole palm grove. Anyone who has these *khettara,* which are classified as historic monuments, on their plot of land is responsible for their upkeep. Most are used as plant containers, and this is what Gilda and André Schubnel have done with theirs.

The newest element in the Schubnel garden is the designer pool behind the house, which blends in perfectly thanks to its undulating shape. Behind it there is another kitchen garden and a fruit tree plantation.

Gilda und André Schubnel, die ihre Zeit zwischen Paris und Marrakesch teilen, lieben Rosen. Die edelsten Exemplare stehen am Kanal, wo die Luft dank stetig sprudelnder Fontäne erfrischend ist. Der gesamte Garten wird großzügig bewässert, das verraten viele diskret platzierte Wasserhähne.

Die Kunst des Bewässerns beherrschte man in Marrakesch schon im 10. Jahrhundert. Davon zeugen zahlreiche *khettara* (Bewässerungskanäle), die sich durch die gesamte Palmerie ziehen. Wer auf seinem Grundstück denkmalgeschützte *khettara* vorfindet, ist verpflichtet, sie zu erhalten. Meistens werden sie als Pflanzbecken genutzt, so auch von Gilda und André Schubnel.

Das neueste Element in ihrem Garten ist der Designer-Pool hinter dem Haus, der sich dank seiner gewellten Form perfekt einfügt. Dahinter liegen noch ein Nutzgarten und eine Obstplantage.

kech, sont tous deux amoureux des roses. Les exemplaires les plus rares se dressent au bord du canal, où l'air est rafraîchi par des fontaines jaillissant en permanence. L'ensemble du jardin est, du reste, généreusement irrigué, comme le trahissent de nombreux robinets placés à des endroits discrets.

L'art de l'irrigation a été maîtrisé à Marrakech dès le 10e siècle. De nombreux *khettara* (canaux d'irrigation) en témoignent, qui parcourent toute la palmeraie. Les propriétaires trouvant sur leur terrain l'un de ces *khettara* classés monuments historiques sont tenus de le conserver, et l'utilisent généralement comme bac à plantes, ce qui est aussi le cas de Gilda et André Schubnel.

L'élément le plus moderne de leur jardin est la piscine de designer située derrière la maison et qui, grâce à sa forme ondulée, s'intègre parfaitement à l'ensemble. Par-derrière se trouvent encore un jardin potager et une plantation d'arbres fruitiers.

Dar Rachad

It has only taken two years for a piece of neglected desert with date palms to be transformed into this garden. One can see that it is still fairly new, but the structure promises that a luxuriant paradise will soon be growing here, in a true traditional style. This is important to Aziz Rachad, a Moroccan by birth who grew up in Switzerland where he studied veterinary medicine and still works today. When creating his estate in the Palmeraie, he bases the design on old models.

It begins with the drive, which, following Moroccan traditions, is bordered with rose beds. They indicate an open house, because in this country the rose is the symbol of hospitality, which in turn is considered to be the greatest virtue. From time immemorial, visitors have been served purifying rose water, distilled from wild roses, which grow at a height of 1,500 metres in the High Atlas and are harvested at the beginning of May. In Dr. Rachad's garden, everything is done to ensure that the flowers constantly renew themselves the whole summer long. How would you otherwise be able to greet guests if you do not have a constant supply of fresh rose leaves floating in the fountains and water basins?

The Rachad estate is geared towards the visitors. There is a guesthouse and a *hammam*, which display the best Moroccan craftwork, from *tadlekt* (polished plaster wall) to *zellij* (ceramic mosaic tiles). The meeting place at the pool is a *Caïd*'s tent, similar to the ones formerly

Nur gut zwei Jahre hat es gedauert, bis aus einem Stück vernachlässigter Wüste mit Dattelpalmen dieser Garten wurde. Noch merkt man ihm an, dass er jung ist, aber die Struktur verspricht, dass hier bald ein üppiges Paradies wächst, ganz im traditionellen Stil. Das ist wichtig für Aziz Rachad, Marokkaner von Geburt, aber aufgewachsen in der Schweiz, wo er Veterinärmedizin studiert hat und nach wie vor tätig ist. Bei der Gestaltung seines Anwesens in der Palmerie orientiert er sich ganz an alten Vorbildern.

Das beginnt bei der Auffahrt, die nach Landessitte mit Rosenbeeten eingefasst wurde. Sie signalisieren ein offenes Haus, denn die Rose gilt in Marokko als Symbol für Gastlichkeit, und die wiederum zählt als größte Tugend. Besuchern wird seit altersher reinigendes Rosenwasser kredenzt, das aus wilden Rosen destilliert wird, die im Hohen Atlas in einer Höhe von 1.500 Metern wachsen und Anfang Mai geerntet werden. In Dr. Rachads Garten wird alles getan, damit die Blüten sich den ganzen Sommer über immer wieder erneuern. Denn wie sollte man Gäste empfangen, wenn nicht stets frische Rosenblätter zur Verfügung stehen, die in Brunnen und Wasserschalen schwimmen?

Das Rachad-Anwesen ist ganz auf Besucher ausgerichtet. Für sie gibt es ein Gästehaus und einen *hammam*, die bestes marokkanisches Kunsthandwerk demonstrieren, von *tadlekt* (polierter Wandverputz) bis *sillij* (Keramikmosaik).

Il n'aura pas fallu plus de deux ans pour qu'à partir d'un morceau de désert à l'abandon planté de palmiers dattiers, un jardin voie le jour. On remarque bien encore qu'il est jeune, mais son arrangement est la promesse d'un futur paradis luxuriant, de style parfaitement traditionnel. Car c'est important pour Aziz Rachad, Marocain de naissance, mais qui a grandi en Suisse, où il a étudié la médecine vétérinaire et exerce encore aujourd'hui : pour la réalisation de sa propriété de la palmeraie, il s'inspire exclusivement de modèles anciens.

On le voit dès la montée, sertie de massifs de roses selon l'usage local. Ils indiquent une demeure accueillante, car au Maroc, la rose est le symbole de l'hospitalité, elle-même considérée comme la première des vertus. Depuis toujours, on présente au visiteur une eau de rose purifiante, distillée à partir de roses sauvages qui poussent dans le Haut-Atlas à 1 500 mètres d'altitude et sont récoltées début mai. Dans le jardin du Dr Rachad cependant, tout est fait pour que les fleurs se renouvellent pendant tout l'été. Comment sinon pourrait-on recevoir des hôtes, sans disposer en permanence de pétales de roses fraîches flottant sur l'eau des fontaines et des vasques ?

La propriété Rachad est toute entière tournée vers les visiteurs. Ils y bénéficient d'une hôtellerie et d'un *hammam* ornés du plus bel artisanat d'art marocain, du *tadlekt* (crépi de mur poli) au *zellij* (mosaïque de céramique) ; le lieu de réunion au bord de la piscine est une tente de caïd telle

The bronze sculpture, as high as a man, is the work of a Tunisian artist, who is a friend of the landlord. Garden parties always end up in the *tente caïdale*.

Die mannshohe Bronzeskulptur am Pool ist das Werk eines tunesischen Künstlers, der als Freund des Hauses oft zu Gast ist. Gartenfeste nehmen stets in der *tente caïdale* ihren Ausgang.

L'imposante sculpture de bronze au bord de la piscine est l'œuvre d'un artiste tunisien. Les garden-parties se terminent sous la tente caïdale.

erected by tribal leaders for their assemblies.

Amongst the customary palm trees, olive trees, succulents and cacti, the avenue of lantana *(lantana camara)* seems out of place. Considered by many to be a weed, its indestructibility proves a big advantage here, as it guarantees flowers all year long even under the blazing sun. The evergreen climber *solanum crispum* on the other hand only opens out its scented purple-blue blossoms on the shaded side of the house.

Sammelplatz am Pool ist ein *Caïd-*Zelt, wie es Stammesfürsten früher für Versammlungen aufstellten.

Zwischen den üblichen Palmen, Oliven, Sukkulenten und Kakteen fällt die Allee aus Wandelröschen *(Lantana camara)* aus dem Rahmen. Von vielen als Unkraut betrachtet, erweist sich ihre Unverwüstlichkeit hier als Vorteil, weil sie auch in praller Sonne ganzjährig Blüte garantiert. Dagegen entfaltet der immergrüne Kletterer *Solanum crispum* seine duftenden blauvioletten Blüten nur auf der Schattenseite des Hauses.

que les chefs de tribus du désert en faisaient autrefois dresser pour le rassemblements.

Entre les inévitables palmiers les oliviers, les plantes succulente et les cactus, l'allée de lantanier *(Lantana camara)* sort de l'ordinaire Souvent considéré comme une mau vaise herbe, sa résistance s'avère ic des plus avantageuses car elle est la promesse de fleurs toute l'année e plein soleil, tandis que la vivace grim pante *Solanum crispum* ne déploie ses corolles bleu-violet et odorante que du côté ombragé de la maison

This rather new garden is dominated by beds of roses. Every day the roses' flowers are used to decorate the water ponds. Roses tolerate various pink *verbena* as well as lantana. A rather unusual mix is the combination of roses and wild grass. A corner of the garden is reserved for desert plants such as *opuntia* and aloe.

In dem noch jungen Garten dominieren die Rosenbeete. Mit ihren Blütenblättern werden alle Wasserbecken täglich frisch dekoriert. Rosen vertragen sich auch gut mit Verbenen in verschiedenen Rosa-tönen und mit Lantana. Am ungewöhnlichsten ist die Kombination mit wilden Gräsern. Ein Teil des Gartens ist reserviert für typische Wüstenpflanzen wie Opuntien und Aloen.

Les parterres de roses dominent dans ce jardin encore jeune. Les pétales servent à orner bassins et fontaines. Les roses s'harmoni-sent également avec les verveines dans des dégradés de rose et les *lantana*. Associées aux hautes herbes, elles jouent la surprise. Une partie du jardin est réservée aux plantes du désert comme l'aloès et l'*opuntia*.

In front of the marquee, the *tente caïdale*, an "Andalusian garden" has been created.

Vor dem großen Festzelt, der *tente caïdale*, wurde ein „andalusischer Garten" angelegt.

Devant la tente caïdale s'étend un « jardin andalou ».

Six graceful Asil Arabs were the crucial factor in Walter Gunz's decision to buy this five-hectare plot of land. He wanted to spare his thoroughbred horses, which were reared in Egypt and used to the desert climate, the move to Munich. So he purchased the land in the palm grove, even though he already owned a house with *riyad* in the old part of Marrakech. Amongst the existing 386 palm trees he created a mini-village for friends and employees, for horses and his dog, Felix, who, true to his name, when half-starved was lucky enough to collapse right in front of the car belonging to Walter Gunz of all people. And in this way he entered this earthly paradise.

Indeed, according to the guests, Walter Gunz has created nothing less than that here. The university-educated religious scholar strove for a place of beauty and understanding, where members of the three large monotheistic religions could meet one another and exchange ideas. Hundreds of lorry loads of humus and plants were required to create this earthly paradise. It became an Arab garden – as befits the surroundings – only a few of the paths do not follow the strict geometric pattern, quite simply because horses have difficulty galloping around right angles. For their sake, there are plenty of gentle curves and thus some corners of the garden appear rather English whilst others look joyously Italian. What Walter Gunz really likes is to link up different cultures. This is why he employed two landscape designers, one from Arabia and the other from Europe. The entrance gate entwined with honeysuckle and lantana and the two-part pond at the end of the plot are proof of a happy association.

Only in front of the large *Caïd's* tent is the garden maintained in a

Sechs zierliche Asil-Araber gaben den Ausschlag für den Kauf dieses fünf Hektar großen Grundstücks. Walter Gunz wollte seinen edlen Pferden, die in Ägypten gezüchtet wurden und Wüstenklima gewöhnt sind, nicht den Umzug nach München zumuten, und so erstand er das Gelände in der Palmerie, obwohl er bereits ein Haus mit *Riad* in der Altstadt von Marrakesch besitzt. Zwischen den vorhandenen 386 Palmen entstand ein Mini-Dorf für Freunde und Angestellte, für Pferde und den Hund Felix, der das Glück hatte – nomen est omen –, mitten auf der Straße ausgerechnet vor Walter Gunz' Auto halb verhungert zusammen zu brechen. So kam er ins Paradies.

Nichts Geringeres nämlich hat Walter Gunz nach Meinung aller Gäste hier erschaffen. Der studierte Religionswissenschaftler strebte einen Ort der Schönheit und der Verständigung an, wo Angehörige der drei großen monotheistischen Religionen zum Austausch zusammen treffen. Hunderte von Lastwagen-Ladungen mit Humus und Pflanzen waren nötig, um das irdische Paradies entstehen zu lassen. Es wurde ein arabischer Garten, wie er hierher gehört – nur manche Wege folgen nicht dem streng geometrischen Muster, ganz einfach, weil Pferde schwerlich um rechte Winkel galoppieren. Ihretwegen gibt es viele sanfte Schwünge, und deswegen mutet der Garten in manchen Ecken ein wenig englisch an und in anderen wiederum heiter italienisch. Was Walter Gunz freut, geht es ihm doch um das Verbindende zwischen den Kulturen. So hat er zwei Landschaftsgestalter beschäftigt, einen aus Arabien, einen aus Europa. Vom mit Lonicera und Lantana berankten Eingangstor bis zum zweigeteilten Teich am Ende des Grundstücks zeugt die Gestaltung von einer glücklichen Verbindung.

Dar Gunz

Ce sont six graciles pur-sang arabes qui ont fait pencher la balance en faveur de l'achat de cette propriété de cinq hectares : Walter Gunz n'a pas voulu exiger de ses nobles montures, élevées en Égypte et habituées au climat du désert, qu'elles déménagent à Munich, et a donc fait l'acquisition d'un terrain dans la palmeraie, bien qu'il possède déjà une maison avec *riad* dans la vieille ville de Marrakech. Entre les 386 palmiers a vu le jour un mini-village pour les amis et les em-

ployés, ainsi que pour les chevaux et le chien Félix qui eut la chance – prédestination du nom – de s'effondrer à moitié affamé au milieu de la rue, précisément devant la voiture de Walter Gunz. Ce qui lui a valu d'entrer au paradis de son vivant.

Car ce n'est rien de moins que le paradis que, de l'avis de tous ses hôtes, Walter Gunz a créé ici. Spécialiste de l'histoire des religions, il aspirait à un lieu de beauté et d'harmonie, où les fidèles des trois grandes religions monothéistes viendraient

échanger. Plusieurs centaines de camions d'humus et de plantes ont été nécessaires pour réaliser le paradis terrestre. Le résultat est un jardin arabe, comme il se doit ici, à la différence près que bon nombre de chemins ne suivent pas un motif strictement géométrique, tout simplement parce que les chevaux galopent difficilement à angle droit. Pour eux, on trouve donc beaucoup de douces envolées, qui font paraître le jardin à certains endroits quelque peu anglais, et à d'autres en revanche joyeu-

sement italien, ce qui ne peut que réjouir Walter Gunz, lui qui s'intéresse à tout ce qui relie les différentes cultures entre elles. Pour la même raison, il a engagé deux architectes paysagistes, un Arabe et un Européen, et, depuis le portail d'entrée bordé de lonicera et de lantaniers jusqu'à l'étang divisé en deux à l'extrémité du terrain, la composition témoigne d'une association réussie.

Le seul endroit où le jardin conserve un style andalou classique, c'est devant la grande tente de caïd. Là, les

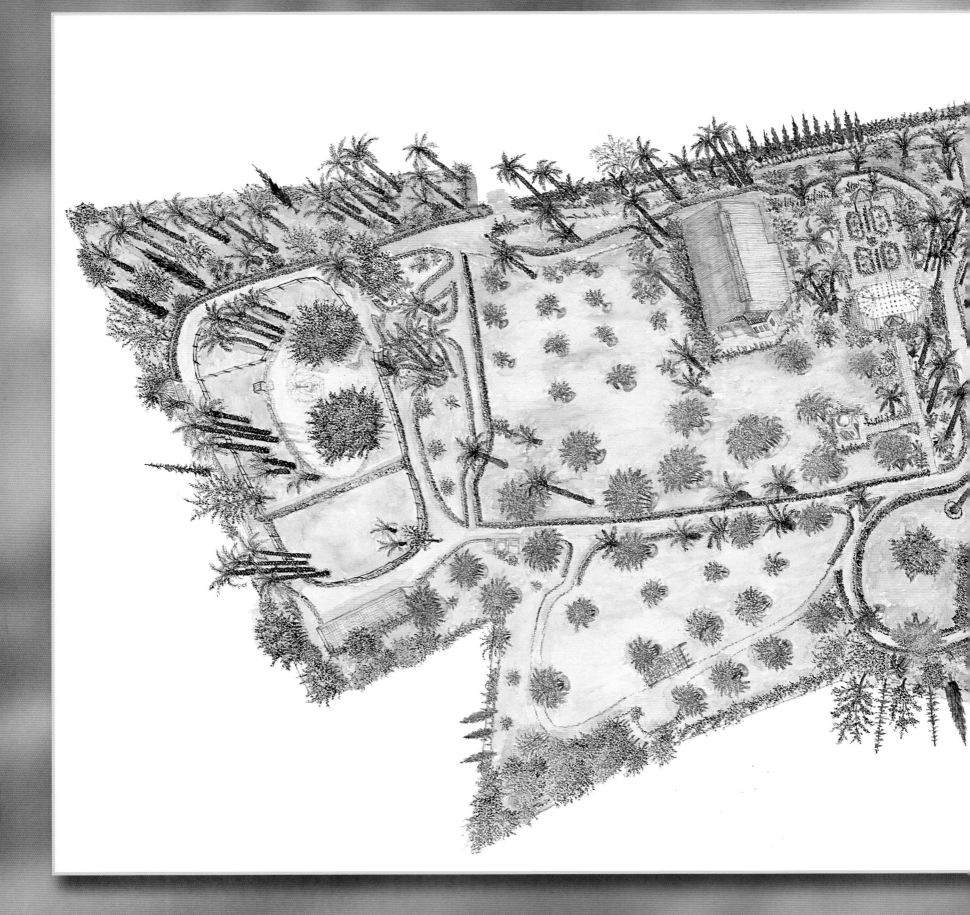

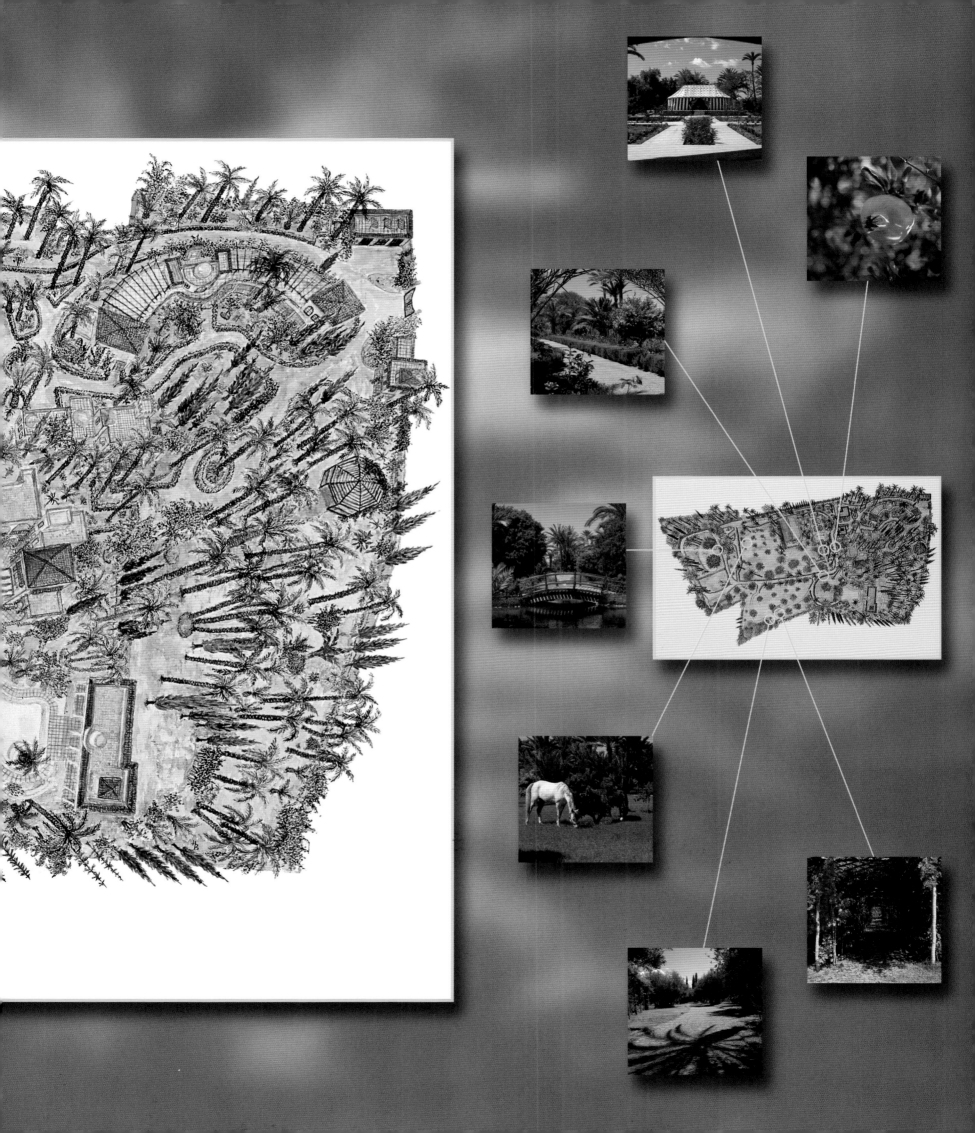

classical Andalusian style. Mainly roses grow in its rectangular flowerbeds, but there are also many other plants such as vines, jasmine, pomegranate and citrus trees, which, according to the Koran, belong to paradise. The Moroccan custom of decorating the trunks of date palms with climbing bougainvillea was also adopted. The reason for this is that, since palm leaves quickly become ugly and thus have to be chopped off, the trunk becomes increasingly bare.

All the buildings, including the stables, have been built using adobe.

This method of construction, formerly common in the Maghreb, ensures a constant, pleasantly cool temperature and humidity level in the house. Nevertheless, they had to give way to modern materials. So, Walter Gunz took the trouble to obtain clay bricks made according to the old design – he had to order the machines to produce them from a museum. But it has been worth it; inside the 40-cm thick walls, both people and animals feel as if they are in the Garden of Paradise and would love to copy Felix and stay in this happy place forever.

Nur vor dem großen *Caïd*-Zelt ist der Garten ganz im klassischen andalusischen Stil gehalten. In seinen rechteckigen Beeten wachsen Rosen, aber auch viele andere Pflanzen, die laut Koran ins Paradies gehören, wie Wein, Jasmin, Granatapfel und Zitrusfrüchte. Übernommen wurde auch die marokkanische Sitte, die Stämme der Dattelpalmen mit rankender Bougainvillea zu schmücken. Da Palmblätter schnell hässlich und deswegen abgeschlagen werden, wird der Stamm immer kahler.

Alle Bauten, einschließlich der Ställe, sind aus ungebrannten Lehm-

steinen errichtet. Diese Bauweise, die früher im Maghreb üblich war, sorgt für gleichbleibendes, angenehm kühles Raumklima. Dennoch musste sie modernem Material weichen, und so hatte Walter Gunz Mühe, Lehmsteine nach altem Muster zu bekommen – er musste sich die Maschinen für die Herstellung aus einem Museum kommen lassen. Es hat sich gelohnt, Mensch und Tier fühlen sich im Innern der 40 cm dicken Mauern genau so wohl wie im paradiesischen Garten und würden es Hund Felix am liebsten nachtun und für immer an diesem glücklichen Ort bleiben.

The palm trees generously offer shade (left). The wooden pergola is covered with lush wine tendrils (right). All flower beds are framed by pruned rosemary (below).

Der Schatten beweist, wie großzügig eine Palme ihren Schatten spendet (links). Die hölzerne Pergola trägt schwer am üppig rankenden Wein (rechts). Alle Beete sind mit beschnittenem Rosmarin eingefasst (unten).

L'ombre du palmier dit toute la générosité de cet arbre. La pergola croule sous la vigne opulente (à droite). Tous les chemins sont bordés de romarins taillés (en bas).

massifs rectangulaires sont plantés essentiellement de roses, mais aussi de nombreuses autres plantes qui, selon le Coran, poussent au paradis : vigne, jasmin, grenades et agrumes. On a également repris l'habitude marocaine de décorer le tronc des palmiers dattiers de bougainvilliers grimpants, ce qui s'explique par le fait que, comme les palmes perdent rapidement leur beauté et doivent être coupées, le tronc des palmiers ne cesse de se dénuder avec le temps.

Tous les bâtiments, y compris les écuries, sont construits en briques d'argile crue, une méthode autrefois usuelle au Maghreb et qui garantit une température ambiante régulière et agréablement fraîche. Aujourd'hui, elle a cependant cédé la place à des matériaux plus modernes et Walter Gunz a eu bien du mal à trouver des briques d'argile correspondant au modèle ancien. Les machines pour leur fabrication ont finalement été empruntées à un musée. Cela en valait la peine cependant, car, à l'intérieur des murs de 40 cm d'épaisseur, hommes et animaux se sentent exactement aussi bien qu'au paradis et tous seraient prêts à rester pour toujours dans ce lieu bienheureux.

To spare his Arab horses a move to Munich, Germany, the owner had bought this property. Now, the horses share the pasture peacefully with the donkeys (top left). The pomegranate is always spectacular, in every phase of ripeness (bottom left). A wooden bridge spans the big pond (right).

Für seine Araberpferde hat der Besitzer das Grundstück angeschafft – sie teilen die Weide friedlich mit Eseln. Granatäpfel sind in allen Stadien der Reife schön. Eine hölzerne Brücke überspannt den großen Teich.

C'est pour ses purs-sangs arabes que le propriétaire a acheté ce domaine – ceux-ci partagent l'herbe paisiblement avec les ânes. Les grenades sont belles à chaque étape de leur croissance. Un pont en bois surplombe le grand étang.

Palmeraie Golf Palace

If you ask which is the most beautiful garden in Marrakech, many people will reply, the *Palmeraie Golf Palace*. Europeans may be surprised at this, but anyone who knows that immaculate green is the most beautiful thing in the world for a Moroccan will grasp the real significance of this garden. Green is the sacred colour of the Koran and should not be stepped on, which is why this colour never appears in rug patterns. A lawn, on the other hand, is a miracle in this desert land and the one in the *Golf Palace* is indeed incredibly dense and well-kept. Not a single weed dare spoil the appearance of the green on the golf course – assistants see to this by removing each and every stalk and stem that has not begun life as a grass seed.

Equally significant are the seven lakes, which the internationally renowned golf architect Robert Trent Jones incorporated into the 18-hole golf course in order to enhance the appeal of the game and the landscape. Water is the most important element in any Islamic garden and certainly here the springs, fountains and pool put the spotlight on this precious liquid. The bunkers, created using sand from the Atlantic coast, create the impression of white beaches in the middle of the oasis.

However, the most fascinating thing of all for foreign visitors is the view of the High Atlas, whose lofty peaks are capped with snow until the late spring. This view was very consciously included in the planning, since the rules of Moroccan garden art require panoramic

Fragt man nach dem schönsten Garten Marakeschs, verweisen viele auf das *Palmeraie Golf Palace*. Das mag den Europäer verwundern, aber wer weiß, dass ein makelloses Grün das Schönste ist, was ein Marokkaner sich vorstellen kann, dem erschließt sich die Bedeutung dieser Anlage. Grün ist die heilige Farbe des Koran, sie darf nicht mit Füßen getreten werden, deswegen kommt sie in keinem Teppichmuster vor. Ein Rasen dagegen ist in diesem Wüstenland wie ein Wunder, und der vom *Golf Palace* ist in der Tat unglaublich dicht und gepflegt. Kein einziges Unkraut darf das Grün des Courses verunzieren – dafür sorgen Hilfskräfte, die per Hand jeden Halm entfernen, der nicht aus Grassaat entstanden ist.

Ebenso bedeutend sind die sieben Seen, die der international renommierte Planer Robert Trent Jones so in den 18-Loch-Golfkurs eingebettet hat, dass sie den Reiz des Spieles ebenso erhöhen wie den der Landschaft. Wasser ist das wichtigste Element in jedem islamischen Garten, und hier setzen Brunnen, Fontänen und ein Becken mit einem großen Wasserspiel das kostbare Nass in Szene. Sandhindernisse, für die das Material von der Atlantikküste geholt wurde, erwecken den Eindruck weißer Strände mitten in der Oase.

Am faszinierendsten für fremde Besucher jedoch ist der Ausblick auf den Hohen Atlas, dessen Gipfel bis spät ins Frühjahr hinein mit Schnee bedeckt sind. Diese Sicht ist sehr bewusst in die Planung mit einbezogen worden, denn die Regeln

Reed is growing around the big lakes, which are one of the main attractions of the golf course. The property is of such a size, that the visitor can even encounter little islands planted with palm trees.

Schilf wächst an den Rändern des großen Teiches, der zu den Attraktionen des Golfplatzes zählt. Er ist so groß, dass sogar Palmen bewachsene Inseln Platz darin finden.

Des roseaux bordent le grand étang, qui fait partie des attractions du terrain de golf. Celui-ci est si grand qu'il abrite même des îlots couverts de palmiers.

Si l'on demande quel est le plus beau jardin de Marrakech, nombreux sont ceux qui citeront le *Palmeraie Golf Palace*. La plupart des Européens en seront sans doute étonnés, mais ceux qui savent qu'un vert sans tache est le plus beau qu'un Marocain puisse s'imaginer comprendront pleinement la signification de ce parc. Le vert, en effet, est la couleur sacrée du Coran, qu'il est interdit de fouler aux pieds et qui, pour cette raison, n'apparaît jamais dans les motifs de tapis. Une pelouse en revanche, dans ce pays désertique, fait l'effet d'un véritable miracle, et celle du *Golf Palace* est incroyablement épaisse et soignée. Aucune mauvaise herbe ne vient déparer le vert parfait du parcours. Une main d'œuvre attentionnée y veille, qui coupe à la main le moindre brin non issu de semence d'herbe.

Tout aussi remarquables, les sept lacs ont été intégrés au parcours de 18 trous par l'architecte de golf à la renommée internationale Robert Trent Jones d'une manière telle qu'ils rehaussent autant l'attrait du jeu que celui du paysage. L'eau est l'élément principal de tout jardin islamique et ici, fontaines, points d'eau et le bassin agrémenté d'un grand jet d'eau mettent en scène à merveille le précieux liquide. La présence d'obstacles sablonneux, dont la matière première a été apportée de la côte atlantique, donne l'impression de plages blanches au cœur de l'oasis.

Le plus fascinant pour les visiteurs étrangers reste cependant la vue sur le Haut-Atlas, dont les sommets demeurent couverts de neige jusqu'à la fin du printemps. Le panorama a été délibérément intégré à

Waterworks are the symbol of luxury. Hotel and golf course offer various waterworks, ranging from the classical marble fountain to the "water ballet", which consist of spraying water jets.

Wasserspiele sind der Inbegriff des Luxus, und davon bieten Hotel und Golfclub unzählige, vom klassischen Marmorbrunnen bis zum „Wasserballett", das aus schäumenden Fontänen besteht.

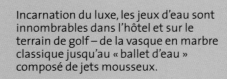

Incarnation du luxe, les jeux d'eau sont innombrables dans l'hôtel et sur le terrain de golf – de la vasque en marbre classique jusqu'au « ballet d'eau » composé de jets mousseux.

viewpoints looking out over the surrounding land.

In this respect, the *Palmeraie Golf Palace* is actually quite excellent as a garden. The view is spectacular. Especially for golf players it is a rewarding destination, both for a day's outing and for a longer stay in the adjoining hotel. They will meet enthusiastic players, since golf is Morocco's number one sport and was introduced at the beginning of the last century even before football. King Hassan II, who died in 1999, was the country's biggest golf supporter and patron.

der marokkanischen Gartenkunst verlangen es, Perspektiven auf die Umgebung zu öffnen.

In diesem Sinne ist das *Palmeraie Golf Palace* in der Tat ein äußerst gelungener Garten. Und für den Golfspieler ist es ein lohnendes Ziel, sowohl für einen Tagesausflug als auch für einen längeren Aufenthalt im angeschlossenen Hotel. Er wird auf begeisterte Spieler treffen, denn Golf ist in Marokko Nationalsport Nr. 1, wurde zu Beginn des letzten Jahrhunderts sogar noch vor Fußball eingeführt. Größter Anhänger und Förderer war der im Jahr 1999 verstorbene König Hassan II.

la conception du terrain pour respecter les règles de l'art des jardins marocain, qui exigent que soient ouvertes des perspectives sur les alentours.

Dans ce sens, le *Palmeraie Golf Palace* est un jardin particulièrement réussi. Et une destination profitable pour tout joueur de golf, que ce soit pour une journée ou pour un séjour plus long à l'hôtel tout proche. Il y rencontrera d'autres joueurs passionnés car le golf est au Maroc le sport national n°1, introduit, avant même le football, dès le début du siècle dernier et dont le roi Hassan II, disparu en 1999, était l'un des adeptes et défenseurs les plus actifs.

This spacious ground combines architecture and nature in perfect harmony. Even the ducks are aware of the immaculate green lawn and the fact that each single weed is picked by hand.

Architektur und Natur gehen in der großzügigen Anlage eine perfekte Harmonie ein. Selbst die Enten wissen das makellose Grün zu schätzen, aus dem jedes Unkraut per Hand entfernt wird.

Architecture et nature sont en parfaite harmonie dans cette propriété généreuse. Même les canards apprécient le gazon immaculé, dont on retire les mauvaises herbes à la main, une par une.

Tikida Garden

Before night falls in the *Palmeraie* the setting sun bathes everything in a romantic red light. That's when Marrakech's palm grove appears as a veritable Garden of Eden. In reality, here the desert only disappears in places continually cultivated and tended by man. Well looked after, the gardens do indeed flourish more magnificently here than anywhere else. Since only invited guests are allowed to enter private property – and Arab society is very closed – guests in search of peace go to the *Tikida Garden* Hotel, situated ten kilometres outside the town on the road to Fez. This is a house especially loved by French families, who dine alfresco here in the evenings, gently caressed by the scents of jasmine and *Solanum* vine.

The garden is kept very tidy. At the hotel entrance, whose arches are overgrown with red bougainvillea, neat lawns are bordered by bushes in bloom, such as oleander and flowerbeds of marguerites. If you cross the lobby, you will come to the *riyad*, bordered to the right and left by long buildings with guestrooms. At weekends, the courtyard turns into a bazaar where hand-crafted Moroccan goods such as babouche slippers and djellabahs are sold – and people can have their hands painted with henna.

Symmetrically placed and paved paths lead to the rooms and divide the garden into flowerbeds of equal size, planted with pomegranate and citrus trees. Spanning over the wide central axis there is a pergola covered in a thick roof of white bougainvillea, which is the dominant plant in the inner courtyard: it climbs up arches, pillars and protruding sections of the walls. Even the *hammam* is cloaked in the sumptuous white blooms.

At midday, a buffet lunch is served at the pool situated right at the end of the garden. And in the evening, you can sit there on a raised terrace and watch the sun set...

Bevor es Nacht wird in der Palmerie, taucht die untergehende Sonne alles in ein romantisierendes rotes Licht. Dann sieht es tatsächlich so aus, als sei Marrakeschs Palmenhain ein einziger Garten Eden. In Wahrheit ist er nur da keine Wüste, wo er ständig von Menschenhand gepflegt wird. Dann allerdings gedeihen die Gärten prächtiger als anderswo. Da zu Privatbesitz nur Geladene Zutritt haben – und die arabische Gesellschaft ist eine sehr geschlossene! –, gehen Ruhe suchende Gäste gern ins Hotel *Tikida Garden*, das zehn Kilometer außerhalb der Stadt an der Straße nach Fès liegt. Es ist ein Haus, das besonders bei französischen Familien beliebt ist, die hier am Abend im Freien dinieren, umschmeichelt von Jasmin- und *Solanum*-Düften.

Saubere Rasenflächen, eingefasst von blühenden Büschen wie Oleander und Blumenbeeten mit Margeriten liegen vor dem Hotel-Eingang, dessen Arkaden von roter Bougainvillea überwuchert werden. Wenn man die Lobby durchquert hat, kommt man in den *Riad*, der rechts und links von langgestreckten Gebäuden mit Gästezimmern begrenzt ist. Der Hof wird an Wochenenden zum Bazar, in dem die Gäste marokkanisches Kunsthandwerk, Babouchen und Djellabahs kaufen – oder sich die Hände mit Henna bemalen lassen können.

Symmetrisch angelegte, gepflasterte Wege führen zu den Zimmern und teilen den Garten in gleich große Beete, die mit Granatäpfeln und Zitrusfrüchten bepflanzt sind. Die breite Mittelachse wird überspannt von einer Pergola, die ein dichtes Dach aus weißer Bougainvillea trägt – die übrigens die dominierende Pflanze im ganzen Innenhof ist; sie rankt an Arkaden, Pfeilern und Mauervorsprüngen. Auch der *hammam* hüllt sich in das reich blühende weiße Kleid.

Juste avant la tombée de la nuit dans la palmeraie, le soleil couchant plonge tout le décor dans une lumière rouge des plus romantiques. On a vraiment l'impression alors que la palmeraie de Marrakech n'est plus qu'un seul jardin d'Éden. En vérité, les seuls endroits où le désert a disparu sont ceux que l'homme a en main et là, il faut le reconnaître, les jardins croissent et embellissent mieux qu'ailleurs. Comme seuls les invités ont accès aux propriétés privées – et que la société arabe est des plus fermées ! – les hôtes à la recherche de calme optent volontiers pour l'hôtel *Tikida Garden,* à dix kilomètres en dehors de la ville, sur la route de Fès. L'endroit est particulièrement apprécié des familles françaises, qui viennent y dîner dehors le soir, flattées par sa splendeur et les effluves du jasmin et du *solanum.*

Devant l'entrée de l'hôtel, dont les arcades sont envahies de bougainvilliers rouges, s'étendent des pelouses bien entretenues encadrées de bosquets fleuris de lauriers-roses ou de massifs de marguerites. Après avoir traversé le vestibule, on parvient au *riad,* délimité à gauche et à droite par les longs bâtiments qui abritent les chambres. La cour est transformée en bazar les week-ends et l'on peut y acheter des objets artisanaux marocains, des babouches et des djellabas, ou s'y faire peindre les mains au henné.

Des chemins pavés disposés symétriquement mènent aux chambres et partagent le jardin en parterres de dimensions égales plantés de grenades et d'agrumes. Le large axe central est recouvert d'une pergola qui supporte une épaisse couverture de bougainvilliers blancs, une plante par ailleurs dominante dans l'ensemble de la cour intérieure, où elle grimpe le long des arcades, des piliers et des avancées du mur. Même le *hammam* se voile de cette parure blanche si richement fleurie.

One of the characteristics of the hotel complex is the pergolas that cover the paths. Female gardeners in typical green habit tend to them.

Die Hotelanlage ist geprägt von überwachsenen Laubengängen. Gepflegt wird sie von Gärtnerinnen in typischer grüner Tracht.

Typiques de l'hôtel, les arcades recouvertes de verdure. Le jardin est entretenu par des jardinières portant l'uniforme vert.

The Palm Tree   Die Palme   Le Palmier

The palm tree is the most generous tree of all: it gives shade to everyone except itself. That's what the Arabs say, and they treat their tree with love and respect. For them, the palm tree is a symbol of life. From far off, the waving tops of the palm trees are a sign to desert travellers that water and food are nearby. In many countries, and particularly those of the Maghreb, oases and palm groves are one and the same thing, so omnipresent is the date palm. Biblical pictures too have always been linked to palm trees. Nonetheless, the palm tree is older than the Bible, even older than human memory itself.

Thanks to this tree, mankind has a wide variety of products. The family of the *palmae* is the cornucopia for many different people in the tropical and subtropical regions of the world and ensuring their existence. In these regions up to 3,400 species of palm trees with up to 236 types are growing. Generally, most people associate the palm tree with the African continent and the Mediterranean region, but in fact, there are more palm categories in Asia and America than in Africa. Only 50 types of palm trees are counted in Africa.

The most beloved species is the date palm, also called *phoenix dactylifera*. From time immemorial, it has been associated with the heavenly fire, the sun. As the Arabs say, "the King of the oases dips his feet into the water and stretches his head up into the heavenly fire". Just like the legendary phoenix, who burns to death and then rises up again from its ashes, the *phoenix* date palm also renews itself continually: all year round it produces new leaves when the old ones die, thus promising immortality and perpetual prosperity. The date palm grows up to 30 metres in height and can live

Die Palme ist der großzügigste aller Bäume: jedem spendet sie Schatten, nur nicht sich selbst. So sagen die Araber und begegnen ihrem Baum mit Liebe und Respekt. Für sie ist die Palme ein Symbol des Lebens. Schon von weitem signalisieren wehende Palmenwipfel dem Wüstenwanderer, dass er sich Wasser und Nahrung nähert. In vielen Ländern, und besonders in denen des Maghreb, sind Oasen und Palmenhaine ein und dasselbe, so omnipräsent ist dort die Dattelpalme. Auch biblische Bilder waren stets mit Palmen verbunden. Gleichwohl ist die Palme älter als die Bibel, älter als unsere Erinnerung.

Die Menschheit hat gerade dieser Baumart eine reiche Palette von Produkten zu verdanken. Die Familie der *palmae* ist ein wahres Füllhorn für die Existenz zahlreicher Bevölkerungsgruppen in tropischen und subtropischen Gebieten der Erde. In diesen Zonen gedeihen an die 3400 Palmenarten in 236 Gattungen. Obwohl wir die Palme gern mit dem afrikanischen Kontinent und dem Mittelmeerraum in Verbindung bringen, gibt es mehr Gattungen in Asien und Amerika als in Afrika, wo gerade fünfzig Sorten vorkommen.

Die am häufisten besungene ist die Dattelpalme, *Phoenix dactylifera*. Sie wurde seit jeher dem himmlischen Feuer, der Sonne, zugeordnet. Bei den Arabern heißt es: „Der König der Oasen taucht seine Füße ins Wasser und reckt sein Haupt in das Feuer des Himmels." Wie der sagenhafte Vogel Phoenix, der sich selbst verbrennt und aus der Asche neu ersteht, so erneuert sich auch die Phoenix-Palme ununterbrochen: Das ganze Jahr über bringt sie neue Blätter hervor, während alte absterben. So verheißt sie Unsterblichkeit und dauernden Wohlstand. Die Dattelplame wird bis 30 Meter hoch und bis zu

Le palmier est le plus généreux de tous les arbres : il dispense son ombre à tous, sauf à lui-même. Ainsi du moins en parlent les Arabes, qui ne l'abordent qu'avec amour et respect, car pour eux, le palmier est un symbole de vie et ses cimes flottant au vent annoncent de loin au voyageur du désert la présence d'eau et de nourriture. Dans de nombreux pays, et plus particulièrement ceux du Maghreb, oasis et palmeraies ne font qu'un, tant le palmier dattier y est omniprésent. Les images bibliques ont elles aussi été de tout temps associées aux palmiers. Pourtant, le palmier est plus vieux que la Bible, plus vieux que tous nos souvenirs.

L'humanité doit beaucoup à cet arbre offrant une palette de produits considérable. En effet, la famille des palmacées est une véritable corne d'abondance pour de nombreuses catégories de la population des régions tropicales et subtropicales. Il y pousse 3 400 espèces de palmiers de 236 genres. Même si on associe volontiers le palmier au continent africain ou au bassin méditerranéen, force est de constater qu'il existe plus de genres en Asie et en Amérique qu'en Afrique, où seuls cinquante espèces y règnent.

Le plus célébré est le palmier dattier, *Phoenix dactylifera*. Depuis toujours, il est associé au feu du ciel, le soleil, et pour les Arabes, il s'agit du « roi de l'oasis trempant les pieds dans l'eau et dressant la tête dans le feu céleste ». De même que le phénix, l'oiseau de légende qui s'immole lui-même et renaît de ses cendres, le palmier-phoenix se renouvelle continuellement et produit toute l'année de nouvelles palmes tandis que d'autres meurent, promesse d'immortalité et de prospérité éternelle. Le palmier dattier peut atteindre 30 mètres de haut et vivre jusqu'à 300 ans. Aucune tempête ou presque ne peut le briser ou le plier, encore moins le déraciner car, contrairement

for up to 300 years, almost never being bent or uprooted by storms. Unlike our European forest trees, whose trunks grow from the inside to the outside with the hardest wood being in the centre, palm trees grow in the opposite direction and form a cylindrical tubular trunk, hard on the outside but soft on the inside. This explains why the palm tree dances in the wind but hardly ever bends or breaks.

The palm tree's beautiful pose and its abundant yields have inspired Arab poets, who have compared the tree with the beauty of young women: "her long black hair adorned her back like a fruit-laden palm branch", wrote Imru'l-Qays in the 6th century. But the palm tree is not only a subject of poetry. Thanks to its long, slender trunk and its crown of palm leaves, the palm tree stands for more than just being a pretty plant. The tree offers many practical advantages: palm leaves cover the roofs of houses or protect dunes, they are also used for woven mats and cushions; cages, tables and chairs are designed out of palm stems; ropes are woven out of its fibres. Last but least, the hollow trunk serves as a pipe or gutter.

Every year in Morocco, 82,000 tonnes of dates are harvested. From September on, the blows of machetes can be heard in the palm groves and orange-coloured dates can be seen falling onto outspread tarpaulins. Dates are harvested shortly before the ripening. When they are ripe, they acquire a shining brown colour. There is a wide range of different types, long or round, brown or caramel-coloured, hard or soft. They grow mainly in the Ziz Valley in southwest Morocco. Some varieties spoil easily and are only consumed locally. Others are more resistant and so can be exported.

In Morocco, the date is a basic foodstuff like milk. Both, milk and date, are served at family reunions such us births, weddings and funerals. An honoured guest or a pilgrim who has come back from Mecca, must be welcomed with dates and milk. In the southern regions dates are tossed over newly-married couples to ensure that peace and prosperity will accompany their marriage.

300 Jahre alt, und sie wird so gut wie nie vom Sturm geknickt oder gar entwurzelt. Anders als unsere Waldbäume, deren Stämme von innen nach außen wachsen und daher das härteste Holz im Kern haben, wachsen Palmen entgegengesetzt und bilden einen zylindrischen Röhrenstamm, der außen fest, innen aber weich ist. So kommt es, dass die Palme sich zwar im Winde bewegt, sich aber kaum krümmt oder beugt.

Die aufrechte Haltung der Palme und der Reichtum ihrer Ernte haben arabische Dichter inspiriert, die sie mit der Schönheit junger Mädchen verglichen: „Ihr langes schwarzes Haar schmückte ihren Rücken gleich einem fruchtbeladenen Palmenzweig", schrieb Imru'l-Qays im 6. Jahrhundert. Die Palme ist jedoch nicht nur ein schöner Baum, mit seinem langen Stamm und seiner aus mehr oder minder langen Palmwedeln bestehenden Krone. Sie ist vor allem einer der nütztlichsten überhaupt: Palmblätter bedecken Dächer und schützen Dünen, werden zu Matten und Steckkissen geflochten; aus den Blattstielen konstruiert man Käfige, Tische und Stühle; aus ihren Fasern werden starke Seile gedreht. Der ausgehöhlte Stamm findet als Regenrinne oder als Rohr Verwendung.

In Marokko werden jährlich 82.000 Tonnen Datteln geerntet. Ab September hört man in den Palmenhainen die Schläge der Machete und sieht orangefarbene Dattel-Trauben auf ausgebreitete Planen fallen. Datteln werden kurz vor der Reife geerntet. Wenn sie reif sind, färben sie sich glänzend braun. Es gibt eine Unzahl verschiedener Sorten, lang oder rund, braun oder karamelfarben, hart oder weich. Sie wachsen vor allem im Ziz-Tal im Südosten von Marokko. Einige Sorten verderben leicht und werden nur regional konsumiert. Andere überstehen mehrere Monate und sind somit exportfähig.

In Marokko ist die Dattel ein Grundnahrungsmittel wie Milch. Beides reicht man bei Geburt, Hochzeit und Beerdigung. Ein hoher Gast oder ein Pilger, der aus Mekka zurückkehrt, wird mit Milch und Datteln empfangen. In den südlichen Regionen regnet es Datteln über jedes jungverheiratete Paar, auf dass Frieden und Wohlstand die Ehe begleiten mögen.

aux arbres de nos forêts, dont les troncs croissent de l'intérieur vers l'extérieur et dont le bois le plus dur se trouve donc au centre, les palmiers se développent en sens inverse et forment un tronc cylindrique en forme de tube, dur à l'extérieur mais tendre à l'intérieur. Ainsi, le palmier s'agite, certes, dans le vent, mais ne s'incline ni ne ploie quasiment jamais.

Le maintien du palmier et l'abondance de la récolte ont inspiré les poètes arabes, qui ont comparé sa beauté à celle de jeunes filles, comme par exemple Imru'l-Qays qui écrira au 6e siècle : « Ses longs cheveux noirs ornaient son dos, telle une branche de palmier chargée de fruits ».

Le palmier n'est pas uniquement un bel arbre au stipe allongé et au toupet de feuilles pennées plus ou moins longues. Il est avant tout un des arbres les plus utiles : ses feuilles couvrent les toits et protègent les dunes, sont tressées en tapis et en mattes ; les branches servent à construire des cages, des tables et des chaises ; et des cordes sont réalisées avec ses fibres. Le tronc, une fois creusé, est utilisé comme gouttière ou tuyau.

Au Maroc, on récolte chaque année 82 000 tonnes de dattes. Dès septembre, dans les palmeraies, on entend résonner les coups de machettes qui font tomber les régimes orange de dattes sur des bâches tendues sur le sol. Les dattes sont récoltées juste avant maturité et prennent en mûrissant une teinte brune et luisante. Il en existe une multitude de variétés différentes, longues ou rondes, brunes ou couleur caramel, dures ou tendres. On les trouve essentiellement dans la vallée du Ziz, au sud-est du Maroc. Certaines sortes sont fragiles et donc réservées à la consommation régionale, tandis que d'autres sont plus résistantes et peuvent être exportées.

Au Maroc, la datte est un aliment de base au même titre que le lait. Tous deux sont offerts lors des naissances, des mariages et des funérailles, et un hôte de marque ou un pèlerin de retour de la Mecque doivent également être reçus avec du lait et des dattes. Dans les régions méridionales du pays, on fait pleuvoir des dattes sur les couples de jeunes mariés, afin que leur union s'accompagne de paix et de prospérité.

The Green City
Die grüne Stadt
La Cité verte

A green belt surrounding the fortified clay castle was something typical of oases. The dwellings were built in a raised position so that water could be supplied to the lower-lying gardens through a complex system of underground channels. This principle was taken up in many Arab towns, to the amazement of early travellers, who were mad about the "garden cities". Today, the outskirts of Moroccan cities, like those in other countries, are deafeningly noisy. Marrakech is no exception. However, some of the green belt still remains here, not just thanks to the palm grove. As in days of old, around the city there are extensive estates, which serve for fruit

and vegetable growing. Initially, they might have been communal gardens, where each family cultivated its own plot. Today, most of the kitchen gardens are also in private hands and are sometimes known as *buhayra*, namely if they have a water tank or at least channels to ensure a sufficient water supply. The term *bustân* is used to describe the fruit gardens in general, but this Persian word originally meant "the place of fragrances" and was associated with pleasure gardens. In the meantime, fruit and vegetables as well as oriental herbs grow alongside one another in the *bustân*, and thus please the senses whilst at the same time serving as food.

Typisch für Oasen war der grüne Gürtel, der die festungsartigen Lehmburgen umgab. Die Behausungen lagen erhöht, sodass durch ein kompliziertes System an unterirdischen Kanälen den tiefer liegenden Gärten Wasser zugeführt werden konnte. Dieses Prinzip wurde für viele arabische Städte übernommen, zum Erstaunen früher Reisender, die von den „Gartenstädten" schwärmten. Heute haben die Städte in Marokko, genau wie überall, eine von ohrenbetäubendem Lärm geplagte Peripherie. So auch Marrakesch. Dennoch hat sich hier etwas von dem grünen Gürtel erhalten, nicht nur dank der Palmerie. Wie zu Urzeiten gibt es um die Stadt herum ausgedehnte Ländereien, die dem Obst- und Gemüseanbau dienen. In den Anfangszeiten mögen das Gemeinschaftsgärten gewesen sein, in denen jede Familie ihre eigene Parzelle bestellte. Heute liegen auch die Nutzgärten meist in privater Hand und werden entweder als *buhayra* bezeichnet, nämlich dann wenn sie ein Wasserbecken enthalten oder mindestens Kanäle zur ausreichenden Versorgung. Der Ausdruck *bustân* wird allgemein für Obstgärten angewendet, aber der persische Ursprung des Wortes bedeutet „Ort des Geruchs" und galt eher den Lustgärten – mittlerweile wachsen im bustân alle Früchte, Gemüse und Kräuter des Orients gemeinsam, sodass er die Sinne erfreut und der Ernährung dient.

The "green belt" surrounding the city accommodates all sorts of gardens: commercial plantations (below) as well as "potagers" containing both flowers and vegetables and modern interpretations of the *hortus conclusus*.

Im „grünen Gürtel" der Stadt finden sich alle Arten von Gärten: kommerzielle Plantagen (unten) ebenso wie „potagers" mit Blumen und Gemüse oder moderne Interpretationen des *hortus conclusus*.

Dans la « ceinture verte » qui entoure la ville, se trouvent toutes sortes de jardins : plantations destinées au commerce (en bas), potagers fleuris ou interprétations modernes du *hortus conclusus* (jardin clos).

La ceinture verte qui entourait les palais de torchis fortifiés est un élément caractéristique de toute oasis. Les habitations y étaient surélevées et un système complexe de canaux souterrains permettait d'amener l'eau aux jardins en contrebas. Le principe a été repris dans de nombreuses villes arabes, suscitant l'étonnement des premiers voyageurs qui s'enthousiasmeront pour ces « villes-jardins ». Aujourd'hui les villes marocaines, comme toutes les villes du monde, sont entourées d'une périphérie résonnant en permanence d'un bruit assourdissant. Marrakech ne fait pas exception à la règle. Néanmoins, toute trace de la ceinture verte n'y a pas encore disparu. Outre la palmeraie, les alentours de la ville demeurent entourés, comme aux premiers temps, de vastes terrains voués à la culture des fruits et légumes, sans doute d'anciens jardins collectifs où chaque famille cultivait sa propre parcelle. Aujourd'hui encore, les jardins de rapport sont le plus souvent privés et sont désignés, soit de *buhayra* lorsqu'ils comportent un bassin, ou au moins quelques canaux garantissant un approvisionnement suffisant en eau, soit par le terme *bustân*, employé pour les vergers ou jardins fruitiers en général, bien que l'origine persane du mot signifie « lieu des parfums » et qualifie plutôt les jardins d'agrément. Aujourd'hui, les *bustân* rassemblent tous les fruits, légumes et herbes de l'Orient et servent autant les plaisirs des sens que la nécessité de l'alimentation.

Bustân Ruspoli

Hospitality is his business – gardens his passion. Prince Fabrizio Ruspoli combines the two in the most beautiful way when he drives guests out in a minibus from his fine small city hotel *La Maison Arabe* to his vegetable garden north of the city. This long, narrow piece of land is a typical *bustân*, which combines all the elements of an ornamental flower garden with those of a kitchen garden, just like a French *potager* – which is no coincidence, since this Italian Prince grew up in both France and Morocco. Beautiful flowers such as roses and jasmine flourish among the usual vegetables such as leeks and cabbages. As in every *bustân* there are tiled channels, decorative wells, citrus fruits and naturally fields of fresh mint, which is indispensable for the Moroccan national drink, *thé à la menthe*. This tea is served to the guests at the side of the pool, as they mostly come out here to swim. Prince Ruspoli offers this service because his exclusive hotel is situated in the historical *médina* where there is no room for a pool as all patios have been used since time immemorial by the restaurant trade. *La Maison Arabe* gained its legendary reputation primarily for being a gourmet restaurant; those who have dined here include Winston Churchill, crowned heads, cult writer Paul Bowles and pretty well all prominent visitors to Marrakech. A few more hotel rooms were added in 1997, and house guests staying there are able to visit Prince Ruspoli's private garden at any time.

Visitors often stay late into the night. For nowhere else can you find

Gastlichkeit ist sein Gewerbe – das Gärtnern seine Leidenschaft. Beides kann Prinz Fabrizio Ruspoli aufs Schönste verbinden, wenn er Gäste aus seinem feinen kleinen Stadthotel *La Maison Arabe* mit einem Shuttlebus hinausfährt in seinen Gemüsegarten nördlich der Stadt. Dieses lange, schmale Stück Land ist ein typischer *bustân*, der alle Elemente des Ziergartens mit denen des Nutzgartens vereint, ähnlich einem französischen *potager* – was kein Zufall ist, denn in diesen beiden Ländern ist der italienische Prinz aufgewachsen. Edle Blumen wie Rosen und Jasmin gedeihen zwischen gewöhnlichem Gemüse wie Lauch und Kohl. Wie in jedem *bustân* findet man gekachelte Kanäle und dekorative Brunnen, Zitrusfrüchte und natürlich Felder mit frischer Minze, die für das marokkanische Nationalgetränk *Thé à la menthe* unabdingbar ist.

Den Tee bekommen die Gäste am Pool serviert, denn meistens lassen sie sich zum Schwimmen hierher fahren. Diesen Service bietet Prinz Ruspoli an, weil sein exklusives Hotel in der historischen *médina* liegt, wo kein Platz für einen Pool ist, weil alle Patios seit jeher für den Restaurantbetrieb genutzt werden. *La Maison Arabe* hat seinen legendären Ruf zunächst als Gourmet-Adresse gewonnen, von Winston Churchill über gekrönte Häupter bis zu Kultschriftsteller Paul Bowles dürfte so ziemlich jeder prominente Marrakesch-Besucher hier gespeist haben. Einige wenige Hotelzimmer kamen erst 1997 hinzu, und für diese Hausgäste steht Prinz Ruspolis Privatgarten jederzeit offen.

Nicht selten bleiben Besucher bis spät in die Nacht. Denn nirgendwo

L'hospitalité est sa profession, le jardinage sa passion. Le prince Fabrizio Ruspoli parvient à réunir les deux de la plus belle façon qui soit lorsqu'il conduit en minibus les hôtes de son petit hôtel de ville raffiné, *La Maison Arabe,* dans son jardin potager situé au nord de la ville. Le terrain, long et étroit, est un *bustân* typique, qui réunit tous les éléments du jardin d'agrément à ceux du jardin de rapport à la manière d'un potager français, rien d'étonnant puisque le prince italien a grandi dans ces deux pays. Ici, des fleurs de choix comme les roses ou le jasmin prospèrent parmi des légumes courants comme les poireaux ou le chou. Et comme dans chaque *bustân,* on trouve des canaux pavés et des fontaines ornementales, des agrumes et, bien sûr, des carrés de menthe fraîche, indispensable pour préparer la boisson nationale marocaine, le *Thé à la menthe.*

Le thé est servi aux hôtes au bord de la piscine, car c'est le plus souvent pour venir nager qu'ils se font conduire jusqu'ici. Le prince Ruspoli propose ce service, car son hôtel distingué est situé dans la *médina* historique, où la place n'est pas suffisante pour une piscine et où tous les patios sont depuis toujours réservés aux restaurants. *La Maison Arabe* doit sa réputation légendaire tout d'abord à sa cuisine, car c'est une adresse pour les gourmets où, de Winston Churchill aux têtes couronnées ou à l'écrivain-culte Paul Bowles, chaque visiteur de marque à Marrakech se doit d'avoir dîné. Les quelques chambres d'hôtel n'ont été ajoutées qu'en 1997 et pour ses invités, les jardins privés du prince

Generally, the use of right angles dominates the walkways of a garden. Here, we find the exception of paths winding their ways trough the green.

Wo sonst der rechte Winkel vorherrscht schlängelt sich hier ausnahmsweise ein gewundener Pfad durch die Gartenanlage.

Là où normalement domine le droit chemin, ici l'exception confirme la règle : un chemin ondulé traverse le jardin.

a traditional *Caïd's* tent – used nowadays in the larger gardens as reception areas – quite as invitingly furnished as here. Decorated with red velvet, embroidered wall hangings and luxurious silk cushions, bathed in a mysterious light by hundreds of lanterns and with an intense aroma of "sun-ripened" roses in the air, many fabulous parties take place here – Arabian nights right out of a fairy-tale. Many of the ingredients for the banquet come straight from the garden onto the table. The Prince also supplies his restaurant in the city with vegetables and herbs he has grown himself. He has "green fingers", something that he discovered after taking over this house as a private residence. The far-sighted architect Duhon built it in 1960 "out in the wilds" at a time when no-one wanted to live outside the city. Today, these plots of land are highly sought after, but only a few know how to revive the

sonst ist das tradionelle *Caïd*-Zelt, das heute in jedem größeren Garten als „Empfangsraum" zu finden ist, so einladend ausgestattet worden wie hier. Ausgeschlagen mit rotem Samt, mit bestickten Wandbehängen und kostbaren Seidenkissen, von Hunderten von Laternen in geheimnisvolles Licht getaucht und intensiv nach „sonnengereiften" Rosen duftend, finden hier viel gerühmte Feste statt – arabische Nächte wie im Märchen.

Für die Festgelage kommen viele der Zutaten aus dem Garten frisch auf den Tisch. Auch sein Restaurant in der Stadt versorgt der Prinz mit Gemüse und Kräutern eigener Zucht. Er hat einen „grünen Daumen", das erwies sich, nachdem er dieses Haus als privaten Wohnsitz übernommen hatte. Es wurde 1960 vom weitsichtigen Architekten Duhon „auf freier Wildbahn" erbaut – zu einem Zeitpunkt, als noch niemand außerhalb der Stadt wohnen wollte. Heute sind diese Grundstücke begehrt, aber nur

Ruspoli sont naturellement toujours ouverts.

Il n'est pas rare que les visiteurs y restent jusque tard dans la nuit, car nulle part ailleurs, la tente de caïd traditionnelle, qui tient aujourd'hui lieu de « salle de réception » dans tous les grands jardins, n'est aussi accueillante. Tendue de velours rouge, garnie de tentures brodées et de précieux coussins de soie, inondée d'une lumière mystérieuse par des centaines de lanternes et embaumée de l'arôme intense de roses « mûries au soleil », de nombreuses fêtes d'exception y ont lieu, des nuits arabes comme dans les contes.

Pour les banquets, bon nombre des ingrédients sont apportés encore frais du jardin à la table. Le prince fournit aussi son restaurant en ville avec des légumes et des herbes qu'il cultive lui-même. Il a en effet les « doigts verts » et s'en est aperçu lorsqu'il a repris la maison pour en

A luxury version of a tent is the so-called *tente caïdale:* the interior is lined with purple velvet and the air is filled with the scent of roses. Serving as a contrast and surrounded by a wall is 'the inner courtyard, which encloses a narrow watercourse flanked by slender palm trees.

Ein Luxuszelt ist diese *tente caïdale*, die mit rotem Samt ausgeschlagen und mit Rosenduft erfüllt ist. Streng dagegen der ummauerte Innenhof mit dem schmalen Wasserlauf, der von schlanken Palmen flankiert wird.

Cette tente caïdale est une véritable tente de luxe, tapissée à l'intérieur de velours cramoisi et imprégnée d'un envoûtant parfum de rose. Plus sobre, la cour entourée de murs, et son mince filet d'eau flanqué de palmiers élancés.

tradition of the kitchen garden as well as Ruspoli.

He installed an irrigation system made from intersecting *seguias* (narrow ditches) with troughs around each fruit tree. Each pear or citrus tree can be watered whenever required. All the other plants also benefit from the resulting damp microclimate, especially the countless climbers, which grow up the high red walls made from tabia, the red mud of the plains. Particularly spectacular are the white bougainvillea blossoms.

All the pathways are classically bordered with clipped box or rosemary hedges. Only the main axes are paved with large natural stone slabs: smaller paths are covered in an artistic pattern made out of coloured pebbles, which is just as decorative as the traditional Moroccan tiled mosaics. Red and black pebbles also frame the main irrigation channel.

wenige verstehen es so wie Ruspoli, die Tradition des Nutzgartens wieder aufleben zu lassen. Er installierte ein Bewässerungssystem aus sich kreuzenden *seguias* (schmalen Gräben) mit Mulden rund um jeden Obstbaum. Bei Bedarf kann jeder Pfirsich, jede Birne oder Zitrusfrucht gewässert werden. Von dem dadurch entstehenden feuchten Mikroklima profitieren auch alle anderen Pflanzen, vor allem die zahlreichen Kletterer, die an den hohen Mauern im lokalen Rotton emporranken. Besonders spektakulär blüht eine weiße Bougainvillea.

Alle Wege sind mit beschnittenen Buchsbaum- oder Rosmarinhecken eingefasst. Nur die Hauptachsen sind mit großen Natursteinplatten belegt; kleinere Wege bekamen ein kunstvolles Muster aus farbigen Kieselsteinen, das so dekorativ wirkt wie das landesübliche Fliesenmosaik.

Whether red cabbage, roses or mint – all plants equally grow in this garden. Additionally, onions and beans are cultivated.

Ob Rotkohl, Rosen oder Minze – alles wächst in diesem Garten gleichberechtigt nebeneinander. Auch Zwiebeln und Bohnen werden angebaut.

Choux rouge, roses, menthe – dans ce jardin, tout trouve sa place. On y cultive aussi oignons et haricots.

faire sa résidence personnelle. Cette dernière a été construite en 1960 « à l'état sauvage » par l'architecte visionnaire Duhon, à une époque où personne ne voulait encore vivre en dehors de la ville. Aujourd'hui, ces terrains sont recherchés, mais seuls bien peu savent comme Ruspoli faire revivre la tradition du jardin de rapport. Le système d'irrigation qu'il a installé se compose de *seguias* (tranchées étroites) croisés et de

creux autour de chaque arbre fruitier, permettant d'arroser au besoin chaque pêcher, chaque poirier ou chaque agrumier séparément, tandis que le microclimat humide qui en résulte bénéficie à l'ensemble des autres végétaux, notamment aux nombreuses plantes grimpantes qui couvrent les hauts murs au ton rouge traditionnel. Les fleurs d'un bougainvillier blanc sont particulièrement spectaculaires.

Tous les chemins ont été entourés à la manière classique de haies taillées de buis ou de romarin et seuls les axes principaux sont pavés de grosses pierres. Les chemins plus petits ont été dotés d'un ingénieux motif de graviers colorés, tout aussi décoratif que les mosaïques pavées en usage dans la région. Le canal principal est lui aussi bordé de graviers rouges et noirs.

Roseraie Habiba

The jeep drive takes you out through an olive grove, where each of the trees is at least 200 years old – and, according to Dr. Berrada, might even be ten times that age.

The university-educated doctor, who comes from a family of physicians and is also married to one, is considered to be an olive specialist. He runs an *olea europea* tree school and, naturally, produces his own olive oil. The doctor gave up medicine for his plantations, which, in addition to olive trees, also include apricots, pomegranates, apples, pears, tomatoes and melons. The kitchen garden that he and his brothers cultivate in Marrakech's green belt covers one thousand hectares.

His greatest success has been with rose growing, which he began in 1994. Indeed, some 70,000 long-stemmed roses are ordered on a single day, St. Valentine's day on 14th February, to be given as signs of affection. The rest of the year scarcely any orders come from Europe, where old English or robust garden roses are now more fashionable.

These tall beauties are not easy to grow. In April/May strong winds blow through the fertile plain and can decapitate all the buds. For this reason, all the rose plantations (with 60,000 bushes per hectare) look alike and do not fit the romantic idea of a scented Moroccan rose field. The queen of flowers is grown under plastic tunnels, using either "the canary system" with long wooden

Die Fahrt mit dem Jeep führt durch einen Hain mit Olivenbäumen, von denen jeder einzelne mindestens 200 Jahre alt ist – und laut Dr. Berrada noch zehnmal so alt werden kann. Der studierte Mediziner, der aus einer Arztfamilie kommt und mit einer Ärztin verheiratet ist, gilt als Olivenspezialist. Er hat eine Baumschule für *Olea europaea*, und natürlich stellt er sein eigenes Olivenöl her. Für seine Plantagen, auf denen außer Oliven auch Aprikosen, Granatäpfel, Äpfel, Birnen, Tomaten und Melonen wachsen, hat er die Heilkunst aufgegeben. Eintausend Hektar umfasst das Nutzland im Grüngürtel von Marrakesch, das er und seine vier Brüder bewirtschaften.

Den größten Erfolg hat er mit seiner 1994 begonnenen Rosenzucht – allerdings nur an einem einzigen Tag: 70.000 langstielige rote Rosen werden bei der *Roseraie Habiba* für den Valentinstag am 14. Februar geordert, um als Zeichen der Zuneigung verschenkt zu werden. Die übrige Zeit des Jahres kommen kaum Aufträge aus Europa, wo alte englische oder robuste Gartenrosen jetzt mehr in Mode sind.

Die hochgewachsenen Schönheiten sind nicht leicht zu ziehen. Im April/Mai wehen starke Winde durch die fruchtbare Ebene, die alle Knospen köpfen können. Deshalb ähnelt die Rosenplantage, wo 60.000 Sträucher pro Hektar angepflanzt sind, nicht im mindesten der romantischen Vorstellung von einem duften-

Le trajet en Jeep passe par un bois d'oliviers où chaque arbre est vieux d'au moins 200 ans et, selon le Dr Berrada, peut encore vivre dix fois aussi longtemps. Ce médecin érudit, issu d'une famille de médecins et marié avec une médecin, passe pour être un spécialiste de l'olivier. Il exploite une pépinière d'*Olea europaea*, et, bien sûr, produit sa propre huile d'olive. Il a abandonné la médecine pour ses plantations, où l'on trouve, outre des oliviers, des abricotiers, des grenadiers, des pommiers, des poiriers, des tomates et des melons. La surface totale, qu'il cultive avec ses quatre frères, comprend un millier d'hectares dans la ceinture verte de Marrakech.

Son plus grand succès lui vient de la culture des roses, commencée en 1994, mais seulement un jour par an : 70 000 roses rouges à longue tige sont commandées à la *Roseraie Habiba* le 14 février, pour être offertes en signe d'affection à la Saint-Valentin. Le reste de l'année, les commandes d'Europe sont rares, car on y préfère les anciennes roses anglaises ou les roses de jardin plus résistantes.

Les beautés sur leurs longues tiges nécessitent des soins particuliers. En avril/mai, de forts vents soufflent sur la plaine fertile et peuvent étêter d'un coup tous les boutons. Dans ces conditions, on comprendra que la plantation de roses et ses 60 000 plants par hectare ne présente pas le moins du monde l'apparence romantique d'un champ de roses parfumées. La reine

As soon as the roses start to grow, they are covered by a plastic roof which is fixed to wooden stilts to protect the roses from the wind and the burning sun.

Sobald die Rosen heranwachsen, kommen Plastikplanen über die Holzpfähle, um sie vor Winden und sengender Sonne zu schützen.

Dès que les roses commencent à pousser, les poteaux en bois sont recouverts de bâches plastiques qui les protégent du vent et de la brûlure du soleil.

The *Roseraie Habiba* does not only survive on roses, but also cultivates pomegranates (left) and melons (above) in great quantities.

Die „Roseraie Habiba" lebt nicht von Rosen allein; Granatäpfel (links) und Melonen (oben) werden in Mengen angebaut.

Il n'y a pas que les roses qui font vivre la « roseraie Habiba » ; on y cultive également grenades et melons en quantité.

stilts, or resting them on metal posts. Storms pull at the tarpaulins so strongly that they have to be completely replaced every two years.

Cultivating watermelons and honeydew melons, on the other hand, is straightforward. The visitors' enthusiasm for the large glossy fruit makes the keen farmer so happy that he immediately gives several melons away as gifts.

den marokkanischen Rosenfeld. Die Königin der Blumen wird unter Plastiktunneln angebaut, die entweder „nach System Kanarienvogel" auf langen Holzstelzen oder auf Metallpfosten ruhen. Die Stürme zerren so stark, dass die Planen alle zwei Jahre komplett erneuert werden müssen.

Unproblematisch dagegen ist die Anzucht der Wasser- und Honigmelonen. Die Begeisterung der Besucher über die großen glänzenden Früchte freut den Landwirt aus Leidenschaft so sehr, dass er gleich mehrere Melonen zum Geschenk macht.

des fleurs est cultivée sous des tunnels de plastique qui reposent, soit, « système volière », sur de longues perches de bois, soit sur des poteaux métalliques. Les tempêtes exercent une telle force que les bâches doivent être complètement renouvelées tous les deux ans.

La culture des pastèques et des melons, elle, pose bien moins de problèmes, et l'enthousiasme des visiteurs envers les gros fruits luisants réjouit tellement l'agriculteur par passion qu'il leur en offre souvent aussitôt plusieurs exemplaires.

The big day of the long-stemmed,
red rose is Valentine's Day.

Ihren großen Auftritt erleben die
unter Planen herangezogenen lang-
stieligen roten Rosen am Valentinstag.

Grandies sous bâche, les roses
élancées vivent leur heure de gloire
à la Saint Valentin.

The Monumental Garden
Der monumentale Garten
Le Jardin monumental

In all countries the history of garden design has always been written by the ruling classes. It is not determined by a need for survival but rather it is limited to aesthetics and the expansion of power. In the Arab-Islamic world, there are three varieties of monumental gardens.

1. *Palace gardens:* garden courtyards that belong to a palace surrounded by courtly buildings, in which the grandiose architecture is the main focus and the garden simply a decorative addition.

2. *Garden palace:* the pleasure garden situated outside the residence and far away from the city in the form of a walled park. Here, the buildings, such as the only occasionally inhabited summer palaces, play a secondary role. In most cases there are just pavilions and often the ruler and the court would camp in festive tents.

3. *The rauda* also started out as an irrigated pleasure garden, but found its true role only after the death of its creator, when it became his last resting-place. Then the *rauda*, literally translated as "blessed peace", became a place of reverence and contemplation.

Die Geschichte der Gartenkunst wurde zu allen Zeiten und in allen Ländern von den Herrschenden geschrieben. Sie ist nicht bestimmt von der Notwendigkeit des Überlebens, sondern einzig und allein der Ästhetik und der Machtentfaltung verpflichtet. Im arabisch-islamischen Raum bildeten sich dabei drei Spielarten des monumentalen Gartens heraus.

1. *Palastgarten:* Der zum Palast gehörende, von höfischen Bauten umrahmte Gartenhof, bei dem die grandiose Architektur im Mittelpunkt steht und der Garten schmückende Ergänzung ist.

2. *Gartenpalast:* Der Lustgarten außerhalb der Residenz und abseits der Stadt als ummauerter Park. Hier spielen Bauten, wie zeitweilig bewohnte Sommerpaläste, eine untergeordnete Rolle. Meist gibt es nur Pavillons, und oft campierten Herrscher und Hofstaat auch in festlichen Zelten.

3. *Der Rauda* nimmt seinen Anfang ebenfalls als bewässerter Lustgarten, findet seine wahre Bestimmung aber erst nach dem Ableben seines Erbauers als dessen letzte Ruhestätte. Dann wird der *Rauda,* wörtlich übersetzt „selige Ruhe", zu einer Stätte der Verehrung und einem Ort der Kontemplation.

The garden courtyard of the Palais Royal (far left) is designed for representation, whereas the fruit plantations lining the big water basin of the Agdal (above) and the Menara (left) are fruit and pleasure gardens, open for all.

Der Repräsentation verpflichtet ist der Gartenhof im Palais Royal (links). Dagegen sind die Obstplantagen bei den großen Wasserbecken des Agdal (oben) und der Menara (links) als Nutz- und Lustgärten für alle da.

La cour arborée du Palais Royal est entretenue à des fins de représentation (à gauche). Les vergers qui entourent les grands bassins de l'Agdal et de la Menara, en revanche, sont simplement conçus pour l'agrément de tous.

De tous temps et dans tous les pays, l'histoire des jardins a été écrite par les souverains. Elle n'est en aucun cas déterminée par le besoin de survie, mais uniquement par l'esthétique et l'étalage du pouvoir. Dans la zone arabo-islamique, trois sortes de jardins monumentaux se sont ainsi développées.

1. *Jardin de palais :* appartenant au palais et entouré des bâtiments de la cour, il s'organise autour de l'architecture grandiose dont le jardin est un complément décoratif.

2. *Palais-jardin :* jardin d'agrément sous la forme d'un parc entouré de murs situé à l'extérieur de la résidence du souverain et à l'écart de la ville. Les bâtiments, comme par exemple des palais d'été habités seulement provisoirement, n'y jouent qu'un rôle secondaire. On n'y trouve généralement que des pavillons car bien souvent, les souverains et leur suite se contentaient eux aussi de tentes d'apparat où camper.

3. *Le rauda* commence généralement sa carrière aussi comme jardin d'agrément irrigué et ne prend sa signification réelle qu'après le décès de son créateur, dont il devient la dernière demeure. Le rauda, littéralement « repos bienheureux », devient alors un lieu de vénération et de contemplation.

Palais Royal

It is thanks to King Hassan II that the Royal Palace has today regained its former splendour. Although the seat of the government moved to Rabat in 1956, the former ruler, who died in 1999, saw to it that the palace in the ancient royal city of Marrakech was lavishly restored. 3000 craftsmen were employed to carry out the restoration, with which the King – who was also know as *El Bani* (a person who loves building) – was able to instigate the renaissance of traditional craftwork that he had intended.

The access road to the former *Kasbah Royale*, built in the 12th century outside the *médina*, is closely guarded. However, the new King Mohammed VI has announced that all palaces will be made accessible to the public. Apart from the *Palais Royal*, scarcely anything else remains of the magnificent historical grounds that once contained baths, fountains and gardens, the largest indoor bazaar in the world, an open-air oratorio, racecourses, a park, cemeteries and the most progressive hospital of its day.

The strict symmetry of the garden courtyard enclosed with arches is emphasised by the geometrically laid out tiles, the axially positioned fountain and the perfect line of orange trees. Here, as in all courtly grounds, everything serves the allegorical glorification of power. Nevertheless, the palace owners and their guests could never do without sumptuous greenery: the view looks out over the enormous plantations of the nearby *Agdal*.

Es ist König Hassan II. zu verdanken, dass der Königspalast heute wieder im alten Glanz erstrahlt. Obwohl der Regierungssitz seit 1956 in Rabat ist, hat der im Jahr 1999 verstorbene Herrscher dafür gesorgt, dass der Palast in der alten Königsstadt Marrakesch aufwändig restauriert wurde. 3000 Kunsthandwerker waren mit der Wiederherstellung beschäftigt, womit dem König, den man auch *El Bani* (den Baulustigen) nannte, die beabsichtigte Renaissance des traditionellen Handwerks gelang.

Die Zufahrt zur ehemaligen *Kasbah royale*, die im 12. Jahrhundert außerhalb der *Médina* erbaut wurde, wird streng bewacht. Aber der neue König Mohammed VI. hat angekündigt, alle Paläste der Öffentlichkeit zugänglich zu machen. Außer dem *Palais royal* ist kaum noch etwas erhalten von der prunkvollen historischen Anlage, die einst Bäder, Brunnen und Gärten, den größten überdachten Bazar der Welt, ein Oratorium im Freien, Pferderennbahn, Park, Friedhöfe und das fortschrittlichste Krankenhaus seiner Zeit beherbergte.

Die strenge Symmetrie des mit Arkaden eingefriedeten Gartenhofes wird von den geometrisch verlegten Fliesen, den axial aufgestellten Brunnen und den in Reih und Glied stehenden Orangenbäumen betont. All dieses dient, wie in jeder höfischen Anlage, der allegorischen Verherrlichung der Macht. Auf reiches Grün mussten die Bewohner des Palastes dennoch nie verzichten: Man blickt weit über die riesigen Plantagen des nahe gelegenen *Agdal*.

Si le Palais royal rayonne de nouveau de son éclat passé, c'est au roi Hassan II qu'on le doit. En effet, bien que le siège du gouvernement soit situé à Rabat depuis 1956, le souverain disparu en 1999 a veillé à ce que le palais de l'ancienne ville royale de Marrakech soit restauré à grands frais. Trois mille artisans d'art ont participé aux travaux grâce auxquels le roi, également appelé *El Bani* (le bâtisseur), est parvenu comme il le souhaitait à faire renaître l'artisanat traditionnel du Maroc.

L'accès de l'ancienne *Kasbah royale*, construite au 12e siècle en dehors de la *médina*, est très surveillé. Cependant, le nouveau roi Mohammed VI a annoncé qu'il ouvrirait au public tous les palais. À Marrakech, outre le *Palais royal*, il ne reste quasiment rien du somptueux domaine historique qui abritait jadis bains, fontaines et jardins, ainsi que le plus grand bazar couvert du monde, un oratoire en plein air, un hippodrome, un parc, des cimetières et l'hôpital le plus moderne de son époque.

La stricte symétrie de la cour du jardin, entourée d'arcades, est encore renforcée par les dalles à motifs géométriques, les fontaines disposées sur le même axe et les orangers en rangs. Tout ici, comme c'est le cas dans chaque bâtiment de cour, sert à la glorification allégorique du pouvoir. Les habitants du palais n'ont pour autant jamais eu à renoncer aux vastes étendues de verdure : la vue s'étend loin sur les immenses plantations de l'*Agdal* tout proche.

The royal palace's courtyard, enclosed with arches, presents itself in perfect symmetry. Marble fountains underline the central axis.

In schöner Symmetrie präsentiert sich der Arkadenhof des Königspalastes. Die Mittelachse ist durch eine Reihe marmorner Brunnen betont.

La cour aux arcades du palais Royal arbore une belle symétrie. L'axe du milieu est mis en valeur par une série de vasques en marbre.

Agdal

If there is one garden that should be seen as a model for the gardens in Marrakech, then it is the *Agdal*. The name comes from the Berber language and means "meadow on the banks of a *wadi* enclosed with a stone wall". In the *Agdal* there are extensive, walled plantations, which are located in the outer districts of the Palace, similar to those in Rabat and Meknes. The special characteristic of the 440-hectare enclosed *Agdal* in Marrakech is the fact that it is divided into several sections linked one with another. First there is the orange grove, which is situated next to the large pool, in order to profit from the precious water. Then there is the olive plantation, which takes up much more space. Yet farther away there are grape vines. In this way you can wander from one garden to the next, from the pome-

Wenn es eine Anlage mit Modellcharakter für die Gärten von Marrakesch gibt, dann ist es der *Agdal*. Die Bezeichnung kommt aus der Berbersprache und bedeutet „Wiese an den Ufern eines *Wadi*, eingefriedet mit einer Steinmauer". Beim *Agdal* handelt sich um großflächige ummauerte Kulturen in den äußeren Palastbezirken, wie man sie auch in Rabat und Meknès findet. Die Besonderheit des 440 Hektar umfassenden *Agdal* in Marrakesch ist seine Unterteilung in mehrere Abschnitte, die miteinander verbunden sind. Zuerst kommt der Orangenhain, er findet sich ganz nah am großen Bassin, um vom kostbaren Wasser zu profitieren. Dann folgt die Olivenplantage, die sehr viel mehr Raum einnimmt. Noch weiter entfernt wächst der Wein. So wandert man von einem Garten zum

S'il est un jardin qui tient lieu de modèle à tous ceux de Marrakech, c'est l'*Agdal*. Son nom vient du berbère et signifie « Prairie au bord d'un *oued* entourée d'un mur de pierres ». Dans le cas de l'*Agdal*, il s'agit de vastes surfaces cultivées murées, appartenant aux enceintes extérieures des palais, comme on en trouve aussi à Rabat et Meknès. La particularité des 440 hectares de l'*Agdal* de Marrakech est sa division en plusieurs parties reliées les unes aux autres. Tout d'abord l'orangeraie, à proximité immédiate du grand bassin, pour profiter de la présence de l'eau si précieuse ; elle est suivie de la plantation d'oliviers, qui occupe un espace beaucoup plus vaste. Encore un peu plus loin, c'est la vigne qui pousse, et l'on passe ainsi d'un jardin à un autre, des grenadiers aux figuiers, puis aux noyers, aux amandiers et aux palmiers.

The large pool of Dâr al-Hana feeds water to the gigantic olive plantations. Of the southern pavilion, only ruins have remained.

Riesige Olivenhaine werden gespeist vom Wasser des großen Beckens Dâr al-Hanâ. Vom Süd-Pavillon stehen nur noch Ruinen.

Les gigantesques oliveraies sont ravitaillées en eau par le grand bassin Dâr al-Hana. Du pavillon sud ne subsistent plus que des ruines.

granates to the figs, then pass alongside the walnut trees, or the almond and palm trees.

Many Moroccans spend their weekends in the *Agdal*, and have picnics under the shade of the trees or feed the carps in both the large pools. This garden was originally called *Buhayra*, or "small sea", a term that may well have referred to the rolling expanse of the garden as well as the lakes. Nowadays the term *buhayra* is used to refer to a well-irrigated vegetable garden, and the royal park is known as the *Agdal*. Laid out between 1156 and 1157, like the Menara Gardens, it is one of the oldest examples of Arab-Islamic garden art, several hundred years older than the famous gardens of the Alhambra in Spain and the Taj Mahal in India.

nächsten, von Granatäpfeln zu Feigen, zu Nussbäumen, Mandeln und Palmen.

Viele Marokkaner verbringen ihr Wochenende im *Agdal*, machen Picknick unter den schattigen Bäumen oder füttern die Karpfen in den beiden großen Wasserbecken. Ursprünglich hieß die Anlage *Buhayra*, was „kleines Meer" bedeutet und sich sowohl auf die Wassermengen als auch auf die wogende Weite des gesamten Gartens bezogen haben mag. Heute bezeichnet man mit dem Wort *Buhayra* gut bewässerte Gemüsegärten, während der königliche Park als *Agdal* gilt. Entstanden zwischen 1156 und 1157, genau wie die Gärten der Menara, ist er eines der ältesten Beispiele arabisch-islamischer Gartenkunst, einige Jahrhunderte älter als die berühmten Anlagen der Alhambra in Spanien und des Taj Mahal in Indien.

Les Marocains sont nombreux à venir passer le week-end à l'*Agdal*, pour pique-niquer à l'ombre des arbres ou nourrir les carpes des deux grands bassins. L'endroit s'appelait à l'origine *Buhayra*, ce qui signifie « petite mer », un nom pouvant désigner aussi bien l'importante quantité d'eau que l'étendue ondoyante du jardin dans son ensemble. Aujourd'hui, le mot *Buhayra* est employé pour des jardins potagers bien irrigués et le parc royal est appelé *Agdal*. Créé entre 1156 et 1157, comme les jardins de la Menara, l'*Agdal* de Marrakech est l'un des plus anciens exemples de l'art des jardins arabo-islamique, plus vieux de quelques siècles que les célèbres parcs de l'Alhambra en Espagne ou du Taj Mahal en Inde.

Menara

According to legend, the Menara Gardens bear witness to Sultan Moulay Ismail's unrequited love for the daughter of the Sun King Louis XIV. In actual fact, the Sultan received a painting of the royal family from the French monarch, with whom he corresponded. He fell head over heels in love with the beauty of Princess Conti, who was portrayed in the painting, and sent a negotiator to ask for her hand in marriage. But, alas – a marriage between the "white rose" and the "black sultan" did not take place. As a result of this, the rejected sultan entered the pleasure gardens of Menara one last time to plant two cypress trees – as a symbol of his unrequited love.

Whether it is true or not, the story fits the atmosphere of the Menara Gardens very well; they are more elegiac, but also more elegant than the far larger *Agdal* Gardens. Both were laid out by the Almohads in the 12th century, but their present structure was set up during the restoration in the 19th century. Standing in the centre of the relatively small (1200 x 800 m) gardens with its olive groves and fruit plantations is the 200 x 150 m pool, supplied with water from the High Atlas, which passes through a series of underground canals. On clear spring days, the snow-capped peaks of the Atlas Mountains and the outline of the small pavilion (one of Marrakech's landmarks) are reflected on its smooth surface.

Laut Legende legen die Gärten der Menara Zeugnis ab von der unglücklichen Liebe des Sultans Moulay Ismail zur Tochter des Sonnenkönigs Louis XIV. In der Tat bekam der Sultan von dem französischen Regenten, mit dem er korrespondierte, ein Gemälde der königlichen Familie geschenkt. Er verliebte sich Hals über Kopf in die Schönheit der abgebildeten Prinzessin Conti und schickte einen Unterhändler, der um ihre Hand anhielt. Aber ach – eine Hochzeit zwischen der „weißen Rose" und dem „schwarzen Sultan" kam nicht zustande. Daraufhin ging der Abgewiesene ein letztes Mal in die Lustgärten der Menara, um zwei Zypressen zu pflanzen – als Symbol seiner unerfüllten Liebe.

Ob wahr oder nicht, die Geschichte passt zur Stimmung der Menara, die elegischer, aber auch eleganter ist als im viel größeren Park *Agdal*. Angelegt wurden beide im 12. Jahrhundert von den Almohaden, aber ihre jetzige Form erhielten sie bei der Restaurierung im 19. Jahrhundert. Mittelpunkt der relativ kleinen (1200 x 800 m) Anlage mit Olivenhainen und Obstplantagen ist das 200 x 150 m große Becken, das durch unterirdische Kanäle mit Wasser aus dem Hohen Atlas gespeist wird. An klaren Frühlingstagen spiegeln sich auf seiner glatten Oberfläche die schneebedeckten Gipfel des Atlas und die Umrisse des kleinen Lustschlosses, das eines der Wahrzeichen von Marrakesch ist.

Selon la légende, les jardins de la Menara témoignent de l'amour malheureux du sultan Moulay Ismail pour la fille du Roi-Soleil, Louis XIV. En fait, le sultan avait reçu du régent français, avec lequel il entretenait une correspondance, un tableau représentant la famille royale et s'était follement épris de la beauté de la Princesse de Conti. Il enverra un parlementaire demander sa main mais, hélas, le projet d'union entre la « rose blanche » et le « sultan noir » n'aboutira pas. Là-dessus, l'amoureux éconduit se rendit une dernière fois dans ses jardins d'agrément de la Menara pour y planter deux cyprès, symboles de son amour malheureux.

Vraie ou non, l'histoire convient à l'atmosphère de la Menara, plus élégiaque, mais aussi plus distinguée que celle du parc de l'*Agdal*, de dimensions très supérieures. Tous deux ont été créés au 12e siècle par les Almohades, mais ont reçu leur forme actuelle au 19e siècle, sous la Restauration. Le centre du domaine relativement modeste (1200 x 800 m) planté de bosquets d'oliviers et d'arbres fruitiers est occupé par le grand bassin de 200 x 150 m, alimenté en eau depuis le Haut-Atlas par des canaux souterrains.

Aux clairs jours de printemps, sa surface lisse reflète les sommets enneigés de l'Atlas et les contours du petit château de plaisance, devenu l'un des emblèmes de Marrakech.

The finely built Menara pavilion has become the landmark of Marrakech. In pure light, the former summer residence is reflected in the large water basin, once the place of happy boat tours.

Der zierliche Pavillon der Menara hat sich zum Wahrzeichen von Marrakesch entwickelt. Bei klarem Licht spiegelt sich das ehemalige Lustschlösschen in dem großen Wasserbecken, das einst für vergnügliche Bootsfahrten genutzt wurde.

Le délicat pavillon de la Ménara est devenu au fil du temps l'emblême de Marrakech. Par temps clair, l'ancien châtelet de plaisance se mire dans le grand bassin d'eau, qui autrefois servait aux parties de bateau.

Street-traders, offering ice-cream and beverages, are awaiting the visitors, who are allowed to walk the Menara fruit plantations only at a certain time.

Auf die Spaziergänger, die nur zu bestimmten Zeiten Zutritt zu den Obstplantagen der Menara haben, warten fliegende Händler, die Eis und Getränke verkaufen.

Les promeneurs, qui n'ont accès aux vergers de la Ménara qu'à heure fixe, sont attendus par des marchands ambulants, proposant glaces et boissons fraîches.

Heavenly Gardens
Von himmlischen Gärten
Des jardins célestes

The garden is the believer's idea of paradise, which in fact can only be a *hortus conclusus,* an enclosed space sheltered from the hostile outside world. That's because for desert dwellers nature is a terrible place where hunger, thirst and heatstroke are constant threats. Accordingly, for them a garden has nothing to do with nature – it is a human creation. In ideal circumstances, this earthly paradise looks like a heavenly garden, which is described quite precisely in the Koran: four rivers flowing with water, wine, milk and honey, divide the kingdom of the true servant of Allah, in which heavy shadows "spread over them protectively, and fruit ... hang low..." *(76th Surah, 13–15).*

The Arab-Islamic garden is committed to geometry and architecture. The four-part pattern was probably developed in Persia and brought to the Mediterranean at the time of the conquests. The oldest examples from the 8th century were dug up in Syria and Spain. The oldest garden laid out in axial lines in Morocco belongs to Koutoubia (built between 1106 and 1142). The Almohad mosque whose minaret rises 77 metres above the ground is one of Marrakech's most famous landmarks.

Private gardens follow the same heavily symbolic patterns: the four rivers are represented by axial channels in the middle of which there is a pond or a fountain, which in rich houses may be covered by a pavilion. The four beds are planted with flowers, evergreen shrubs and trees and also fruit trees. To make them easier to water, the beds are often set deeper than the paths – the fruit is therefore within easy reach. "The boundaries of the prop-

Das Paradies ist in der Vorstellung der Gläubigen ein Garten. Und dieser kann nur ein *hortus conclusus* sein, ein eingefriedeter Ort, der abgeschirmt ist gegen die feindliche Außenwelt. Denn die Natur ist für Wüstenbewohner ein schrecklicher Ort, in dem Hunger, Durst und Hitzschlag drohen. Entsprechend hat ein Garten für sie nichts mit Natur zu tun – er ist Menschenwerk. Im Idealfall sieht das irdische Paradies aus wie der himmlische Garten, der im Koran ziemlich genau beschrieben wird: Vier Ströme, die Wasser, Wein, Milch und Honig führen, teilen das Reich der aufrichtigen Diener Allahs, in dem dichte Schatten „sich behütend über ihnen ausbreiten, und Früchte ... tief herabhängen..." *(76. Sure, 13–15)*

Der arabisch-islamische Garten ist der Geometrie verpflichtet und der Architektur. Das viergeteilte Schema wurde wahrscheinlich in Persien entwickelt und mit den Eroberungszügen in den Mittelmeerraum getragen. Die ältesten Beispiele aus dem 8. Jahrhundert wurden in Syrien und Spanien ausgegraben. Der älteste auf einem Achsenkreuz angelegte Garten Marokkos gehört zur Koutoubia (zwischen 1106 und 1142 erbaut). Die Almohaden-Moschee mit ihrem 77 Meter hohen Minarett gilt als das Wahrzeichen von Marrakesch.

Die privaten Gärten folgen den gleichen symbolträchtigen Mustern: Die vier Ströme werden durch Kanäle in Form eines Achsenkreuzes versinnbildlicht, in deren Mitte sich ein Teich oder ein Brunnen befindet, der in reichen Häusern von einem Pavillon überdacht sein kann. Die vier Beete sind bepflanzt mit Blumen, immergrünen Sträuchern und Bäumen und Fruchtgehölzen. Aus

Private gardens may follow the traditions of the Islamic art of gardening (left) or may be designed freely (below). Every fruit plantation like the one near the Menara (right) needs a huge water basin.

Private Gärten können den Regeln islamischer Gartenkunst folgen (links) oder ganz frei gestaltet werden (unten). Zu Obstplantagen wie bei der Menara (rechts) gehört ein großes Wasserbassin.

Les jardins privés peuvent suivre les règles de l'art du jardin islamique (à gauche) ou être façonnés de manière tout á fait libre (en bas). Les vergers comme ceux de la Ménara (à droite) se doivent d'être accompagnés d'un grand bassin.

Dans la représentation des croyants, le Paradis est un jardin. Il ne peut être qu'un *hortus conclusus,* un lieu clos et abrité du monde extérieur hostile. Car, pour les habitants du désert, la nature est un lieu d'épouvante où les menacent la faim, la soif et l'insolation. Par conséquent, un jardin n'a pour eux rien à voir avec la nature, mais est œuvre des hommes. Idéalement, le paradis terrestre ressemble au jardin céleste décrit avec précision dans le Coran : quatre fleuves où coulent l'eau, le vin, le lait et le miel partagent l'empire des serviteurs fidèles d'Allah, où des ombres épaisses « se déploient au-dessus d'eux pour les protéger, et où les fruits... pendent bas aux arbres... » *(76ᵉ sourate, 13–15).*

Le jardin arabo-islamique est tenu à une certaine géométrie et architecture. Le plan divisé en quatre parties a probablement été inventé en Perse et amené jusqu'en Méditerranée avec les guerres de conquête. Les exemples les plus anciens remontent au 8ᵉ siècle et ont été exhumés en Syrie et en Espagne. Le plus vieux jardin du Maroc à être aménagé selon deux axes en croix est celui de la Koutoubia (construite entre 1106 et 1142) : la mosquée des Almohades, avec son minaret de 77 mètres, passe pour être l'emblème de Marrakech.

Les jardins privés suivent le même modèle hautement symbolique : les quatre fleuves sont incarnés par des canaux formant deux axes en croix et se rejoignant au centre dans un étang ou une fontaine, éventuellement surmontés d'un pavillon dans les riches demeures. Les quatre parterres sont plantés de fleurs, d'arbustes à feuilles persistantes, d'arbres et de bosquets fruitiers. Pour des raisons d'irrigation, ils sont souvent en contrebas par rapport aux chemins, plaçant les fruits directement à portée de main.

erty are created by grape vines", wrote Ibn Luyun in a 14th century agricultural treatise, "and along the paths that cross it, grape vines are grown on the arboured paths".

Today it is more common to find jasmine growing on the archways or pergolas, but otherwise the garden of paradise's design remains scarcely unaltered. It can be found as the *riyad,* the inner courtyard in all dwellings within the *médina,* the medieval centre of Moroccan cities. Small houses surround with their four walls a single inner courtyard, which serves as a *patio* and a *riyad* simultaneously. In spacious houses, however, a distinction is made between the privately used *patio,* which forms the heart of a residential estate and the *riyad,* which also has social functions.

In Arabic, the garden was originally called *rawda.* In Andalusia, however, where Moorish garden culture blossomed most fully only the plural, *riyad* was used and this expression is still used today. In Marrakech the term *riyad* is used not only to describe the garden in the inner courtyard, but every house that has this type of garden courtyard. Nowadays, the term *rawda* on the other hand is only used to refer to a cemetery garden.

Like the *riyad,* the *arsa* was designed as a pleasure garden, but without decorative buildings and used for growing fruit and vegetables.

The *gulistân* was originally intended as a garden exclusively planted with roses. Today, all fragrant gardens with fountains are given this name.

Bustân is the name given to any cultivated garden, large plantation or orchard. The *bustân* is the garden of taste and aromas.

If a kitchen garden is situated outside the town walls and is watered, it is called a *buhayra* or *sâniya.*

Agdal is a Berber word, which refers to large plantations of olive and orange trees.

« La propriété est délimitée par des vignes », écrit Ibn Luyun au 14ᵉ siècle dans un traité d'agriculture, « et le long des chemins qui la traversent, on fait grimper des vignes sur des charmilles ».

Aujourd'hui, c'est plus souvent du jasmin qui couvre arches ou pergolas, mais sinon, le schéma du jardin de Paradis n'a guère changé. On le trouve sous forme de *riad*, de cour intérieure, dans toutes les demeures des médina et les centres médiévaux des villes marocaines. Les petites maisons enclosent de leurs quatre ailes une seule cour intérieure, qui doit alors tenir lieu à la fois de patio et de *riad*. Dans les habitations plus vastes, on distingue le patio, à usage strictement privé et qui forme le cœur de toute demeure, et le *riad*, qui a aussi un rôle de représentation.

Autrefois, jardin se disait en arabe *rawda*, mais en Andalousie, où l'art des jardins maure a été poussé à son extrême, on n'utilisait que le pluriel du mot, *riad*, resté jusqu'à aujourd'hui. À Marrakech, on appelle *riad*, outre le jardin d'une cour intérieure, toute maison qui dispose d'un tel jardin. Le terme *rawda*, en revanche, n'est plus utilisé qu'exclusivement pour les jardins des cimetières.

L'*arsa* est conçu exactement comme le *riad* pour tenir lieu de jardin d'agrément, mais sans bâtiments ornementaux. Il est aussi utilisé pour la culture de fruits et de légumes.

Le *gulistân* était à l'origine uniquement un jardin de roses. Aujourd'hui, on désigne ainsi tout jardin parfumé possédant des fontaines.

On appelle *bustân* les jardins cultivés, ainsi que toute grande plantation ou verger. Le *bustân* est le jardin du goût et des arômes.

Dès qu'un jardin de rapport est situé hors des murs de la cité et est irrigué, il porte le nom de *buhayra* ou *sâniya*.

Agdal est un mot berbère qui fait référence aux grandes plantations d'oliviers et d'orangers.

Bewässerungsgründen liegen die Beete oft tiefer als die Wege – so sind die Früchte zum Greifen nahe. „Begrenzt wird der Besitz von Reben", schreibt Ibn Luyun in einem landwirtschaftlichen Traktat aus dem 14. Jahrhundert, „und entlang den Wegen, die ihn durchqueren, zieht man Reben an Laubengängen."

Heute ist es häufiger Jasmin, der an Bögen oder Pergolen wächst, ansonsten hat sich das Schema des Paradiesgartens kaum verändert. Er findet sich als *Riad*, als Innenhof, in allen Wohnstätten der *médina*, der mittelalterlichen Zentren marokkanischer Städte. Kleine Häuser umschließen mit ihren vier Flügeln nur einen Innenhof, der gleichzeitig als *Patio* und *Riad* dienen muss. In weitläufigen Behausungen jedoch unterscheidet man zwischen dem nur privat genutzten *Patio*, der das Herz einer Wohnanlage bildet, und dem *Riad*, der auch der Repräsentation dient.

Ursprünglich hieß der Garten im Arabischen *rawda*, in Andalusien aber, wo die maurische Gartenkunst zu höchster Blüte getrieben wurde, benutzte man nur den Plural *Riad* – dieser Ausdruck ist bis heute geblieben. In Marrakesch bezeichnet man nicht nur den Garten im Innenhof, sondern jedes Haus, das über einen solchen verfügt, als *Riad*. Die Bezeichnung *rawda* dagegen verwendet man ausschließlich noch für den Garten-Friedhof.

Genau wie der *Riad* als Lustgarten konzipiert, aber ohne Schmuckbauten und auch für den Anbau von Obst und Gemüse genutzt, ist der *arsa*.

Als reiner Rosengarten war ursprünglich der *gulistân* gedacht. Heute bezeichnet man jeden duftenden Garten mit Brunnen so.

Bustân nennt man den bestellten Garten, jede größere Anpflanzung, jeden Obstgarten. Der *bustân* ist der Garten des Geschmacks und der Aromen.

Sobald ein Nutzgarten außerhalb der Stadtmauern liegt und bewässert wird, heißt er *buhayra* oder *sâniya*.

Agdal ist ein Wort aus der Berbersprache, das sich auf große Anpflanzungen von Oliven und Orangen bezieht.

Henna – Fortune on Earth

On the *Jemaa El Fna* in Marrakech, the square that for foreigners – and perhaps locals too – constitutes the fulfilment of their oriental dream, everyone can make fate smile upon them. All you need for this can be found here and in the adjoining *souk*: amulets such as the protective hand of Fatima, objects to ward off the "Evil Eye", textiles with cabbalistic patterns, which avert disaster, and jewellery that promises eternal life. But above all there is henna. Like pedlars, the veiled henna artists follow their potential clientele carrying folding stands. Especially for the female tourists they have made the effort to supply pattern books – as if everyone understood the symbolism of the signs. For most tourists, henna patterns look like exotic lace gloves, for the knowledgeable visitors they are full of symbols that ward off evil spirits and bring good fortune.

Henna tattoos are far more than just a type of make-up. Of course, the deep orange patterns on the hands and feet are meant to please a man's eye and kindle his desire, and that is why all brides are decorated with them. But extravagant henna patterns of varying degrees of complexity are also painted on a woman's skin on the birth of a child or when she is ill. The magical signs will invoke good fortune and exorcise the evil spirits that can enter through all the orifices of the body. Women in particular are in

Henna – Glück auf Erden

Auf dem *Jemaa El Fna* in Marrakesch, jenem Platz, der für Fremde – und vielleicht auch für Einheimische – die Erfüllung des Traums vom Orient ist, kann jeder das Schicksal gnädig stimmen. Alles was er dazu braucht, findet er hier und im angrenzenden *souk:* Amulette wie die schützende Hand der Fatima, Objekte, die den „bösen Blick" abwehren, Textilien mit kabbalistischen Mustern, die Unheil abwenden, und Schmuck, der ewiges Leben verspricht. Vor allem aber Henna. Wie fliegende Händler folgen verschleierte Henna-Künstlerinnen mit klappbaren Ständen der potentiellen Kundschaft. Extra für Touristinnen haben sie sich Musterbücher angeschafft – als könnten jene die Symbolik der Zeichen verstehen. Für sie sieht Henna aus wie ein exotischer Spitzenhandschuh, für Eingeweihte sind alle Symbole darin enthalten, die Böses bannen und Glück herbeischwören.

Tätowierungen aus Henna sind weit mehr als eine Art Make-up. Sicher, das tief orangefarbene Muster auf Händen und Füßen soll das Auge des Mannes erfreuen und seine Lust entfachen, deswegen wird jede Braut damit geschmückt. Aber auch zur Geburt eines Kindes oder bei Krankheit bekommen Frauen mehr oder weniger aufwändige Henna-Muster auf die Haut gemalt. Mit den magischen Zeichen wird das Glück beschworen, und böse Geister, die durch alle Körperöffnungen eindringen

Le Henné – bonheur terrestre

Sur la *Jemaa El Fna* de Marrakech, cette place où pour les étrangers – et peut-être aussi pour les gens du pays – tous les rêves d'Orient se réalisent, chacun peut se faire accorder la clémence du destin. Tout ce dont il a besoin pour cela se trouve ici et dans le *souk* voisin : des amulettes représentant par exemple la main protectrice de Fatima, des objets qui écartent le « mauvais œil », des tissus aux motifs cabalistiques qui détournent les catastrophes ou des bijoux qui garantissent la vie éternelle. Mais surtout du henné. Comme des marchands ambulants, les dessinatrices-artistes voilées suivent toute clientèle éventuelle avec leurs stands pliants. Elles se sont procuré spécialement pour les touristes des livres de motifs, comme si ces dernières pouvaient comprendre la symbolique des différents signes. Pour elles, le henné ne semble rien d'autre qu'un gant de dentelle exotique, tandis que pour les initiés, il contient tous les symboles qui écartent le mal et attirent le bonheur.

Les tatouages au henné sont bien plus qu'une sorte de maquillage. Certes, les dessins d'un orange profond ont pour objet de réjouir le cœur de l'homme et d'attiser son désir, et ornent pour cela les pieds et les mains de chaque épousée, mais des motifs plus ou moins élaborés sont aussi peints sur la peau des femmes pour la naissance d'un enfant ou en cas de maladie. Les signes magiques sont autant de promesses de bonheur et conjurent les mauvais esprits

danger, and the artistic henna paintings were developed for them over generations. Since time immemorial men have coloured their beard with henna, as Mohammed once did: "This pleases the angels," the prophet said.

Henna *(lawsonia inermis)* is a relatively inconspicuous small bush with small leaves and fine white, pleasantly scented flowers. It only grows in genuine desert oases like Ouarzazate. The dried green leaves are sold from large baskets in the market. The powder obtained from the crushed leaves is lime green and sold either loose, piled up in high pyramids, or packed in colourful boxes. It is mixed to a paste with water, and sometimes also with tea to which lemon juice has been added and then used to colour the hair, nails and skin orange to brick red. They say that the greener the powder, the stronger the effect.

Painting the whole of the body with henna takes around three hours. In the past, henna artists used a small pointed stick, today the paste is applied using a syringe, with which they quickly and deftly draw a network of extremely fine lines on the skin. Patterns differ from one tribe to another; in the north of Morocco they merge artistically into one another, in the south they are geometrical, simple and bucolic. The patterns always contain symbols of fertility and marital peace.

Apart from that, henna artists can add anything they find beautiful and elegant. Each *hannaya* (henna artist) invents her own details, after all they are artists and put all their skill and love into this ephemeral body work. Only then does the henna painting bring the invoked *barraka,* the fortune we all need in order to cope with the inevitable *mektoub* (destiny).

können, werden abgewehrt. Vor allem Frauen sind gefährdet, und für sie wurden die kunstvollen Henna-Bemalungen über Generationen hinweg entwickelt. Männer haben sich seit jeher, wie einst Mohammed, den Bart mit Henna gefärbt: „Das erfreut die Engel", sagte der Prophet.

Henna *(Lawsonia inermis)* ist ein relativ unscheinbarer kleiner Strauch mit kleinen Blättern und feinen weißen Blüten, die angenehm duften. Er wächst nur in reinen Wüsten-Oasen wie Ouarzazate. Die getrockneten grünen Blätter werden in großen Körben auf dem Markt angeboten. Das Puder, das aus den zerstoßenen Blättern gewonnen wird, ist limettengrün und wird entweder lose in hohen Pyramiden oder abgepackt in bunten Schachteln zum Verkauf angeboten. Es wird mit Wasser, manchmal auch mit Tee, dem Zitronensaft beigesetzt wird, zu einer Paste gerührt, die Haare, Nägel und Haut orange bis backsteinrot färbt. Je grüner der Puder, umso stärker ist der Effekt, heißt es.

Drei Stunden etwa dauert eine volle Bemalung. Früher nahmen die Henna-Künstlerinnen dafür ein zugespitztes Stöckchen, heute tragen sie die Paste mit einer Spritze auf, zeichnen damit schnell und geschickt ein Netzwerk feinster Linien auf die Haut. Die Muster sind von Stamm zu Stamm verschieden, im Norden Marokkos sind sie eher kunstvoll ineinander verlaufend, im Süden sind sie geometrisch, einfach und ländlich. Immer gehören Symbole für Fruchtbarkeit und ehelichen Frieden dazu. Ansonsten kann die Henna-Malerin alles hinzufügen, was sie schön und elegant findet. Jede *hannaya* denkt sich eigene Details aus, schließlich ist sie Künstlerin und legt ihr ganzes Können und ihre ganze Liebe in die vergängliche Körperarbeit. Nur dann nämlich bringt die Henna-Bemalung das beschworene *barraka,* das Glück, das wir alle brauchen, um mit dem unausweichlichen *mektoub* (Bestimmung) fertig zu werden.

susceptibles de pénétrer dans le corps par tous ses orifices. Les femmes y sont le plus exposées et c'est pour elles que les peintures au henné si artistiques ont été élaborées pendant des générations. Les hommes, eux, se colorent depuis toujours, comme autrefois Mahomet, la barbe au henné : « qui réjouit les anges », aurait dit le Prophète.

Le henné *(Lawsonia inermis)* est un arbuste relativement insignifiant aux petites feuilles et dont les fleurs blanches et délicates répandent un parfum agréable. Il ne pousse que dans les vraies oasis du désert, comme Ouarzazate. Les feuilles vertes séchées sont vendues dans de grands paniers sur les marchés. La poudre obtenue à partir des feuilles broyées est d'une couleur vert citronné et peut être achetée en vrac sous forme de hautes pyramides ou emballée dans des paquets colorés. Elle est mélangée à de l'eau, ou parfois à du thé additionné de jus de citron, pour former une pâte qui colore cheveux, ongles et peau d'une teinte orange à rouge brique. Plus la poudre est verte, plus l'effet sera fort, dit-on.

Autrefois, les artistes du henné utilisaient pour cela une petite baguette affûtée. Aujourd'hui, elles emplissent de pâte une seringue qui leur sert à tracer avec rapidité et brio un réseau de lignes très fines sur la peau. Les motifs sont différents selon les tribus ; dans le nord du Maroc, ils ont tendance à se fondre artistiquement les uns dans les autres ; dans le sud, ils sont géométriques, simples et villageois. Les symboles de la fécondité et de la paix domestique en font toujours partie, mais sinon, la dessinatrice est libre d'ajouter les motifs qui lui paraissent élégants et beaux. Chaque *hannaya* imagine ses propres détails, comme de véritables artistes qu'elles sont, qui mettent tout leur savoir et leur amour au service d'un travail éphémère sur le corps. En effet, ce n'est qu'à cette condition que la peinture au henné apportera la *barraka* invoquée, la chance dont nous avons tous besoin pour venir à bout de l'inéluctable *mektoub* (destin).

The Hortus Conclusus

Der Hortus conclusus

L'Hortus conclusus

It is hot. 40° Celsius on a summer's day. In the narrow streets and alley-ways of the *médina* the heat is building up. It is sticky and the often praised fragrances become so intense that they start to smell bad. The sky is now just a far-off hazy streak. Nearby, on the other hand, you can hear the cries of beggars imploring with their well-worn phrases as they follow the foreigners. When a nondescript wooden gate opens at the end of a cul-de-sac, it is like a release: order replaces chaos, fresh air replaces dust, peace replaces noise – the silence is broken only by chirping birds and the relaxing sound of a gently splashing fountain.

Anyone who has ever experienced this can understand why the *hortus conclusus* is like a reflection of Paradise on Earth. It is however only in Marrakech that this has quite simply become a synonym for living per se. In fact, the walled garden constitutes a component of a large house, containing several courtyards and patios. The largest of these rooms, which are open to the sky, was originally called a *riyad* mostly consisting of a long narrow rectangle, divided up precisely into four flowerbeds arranged around a central fountain. Today, all homes with inner courtyard gardens are called *riyads* – proof of garden's status in this city.

Es ist heiß. 40 Grad an einem Sommertag. In den engen Gassen der *médina* staut sich die Hitze. Stickig ist es hier, und die oft besungenen Düfte verdichten sich zu Gerüchen, zu Gestank. Der Himmel ist nur ein ferner diesiger Streifen. Nah dagegen sind die beschwörenden Formeln der Bettler, die den Fremden verfolgen. Wenn sich am Ende einer Sackgasse ein unscheinbares Holztor öffnet, ist es wie eine Erlösung: Ordnung statt Chaos, Frische statt Staub, Ruhe statt Lärm – belebt nur von Vogelgezwitscher und dem leisen Plätschern eines Brunnens.

Wer das einmal erlebt hat, versteht, warum der *Hortus conclusus* als Abbild des Paradieses auf Erden gilt. Aber nur in Marrakesch ist er zum Synonym des Wohnens schlechthin geworden. Eigentlich ist der von Mauern umschlossene Garten Bestandteil eines größeren Wohnhauses, das mehrere Höfe und Patios umschließt. *Riad* wurde ursprünglich der größte dieser zum Himmel hin offenen Räume genannt, meist ein längliches Rechteck, das ganz präzise in vier Beete aufgeteilt war, die sich um einen Brunnen im Mittelpunkt gruppierten. Heute bezeichnet man in Marrakesch jeden Wohnsitz als *Riad,* dessen Innenhof bepflanzt ist – Beweis für den Stellenwert des Gartens in dieser Stadt.

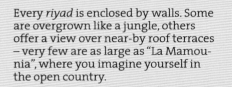

Every *riyad* is enclosed by walls. Some are overgrown like a jungle, others offer a view over near-by roof terraces – very few are as large as "La Mamounia", where you imagine yourself in the open country.

Jeder *Riad* ist ringsum von Mauern eingeschlossen. Manchmal ist er dschungelartig bewachsen, ein andermal gibt er Ausblicke auf benachbarte Dachterrassen frei – selten ist er so groß, dass man sich in freiem Gelände wähnt wie bei „La Mamounia".

Chaque *riad* est entouré de murs. Quelquefois, il abrite une végétation luxuriante, d'autres fois il permet de voir les terrasses voisines. Il arrive aussi – rarement – qu'il soit si grand qu'on se croit en terrain libre, comme à la « Mamounia ».

Il fait très chaud. Quarante degrés l'été. La chaleur s'accumule dans les ruelles étroites de la *médina.* L'atmosphère y est étouffante et les parfums si souvent célébrés s'épaississent jusqu'à ne plus devenir que des odeurs, voire des puanteurs. Le ciel n'est qu'une bande brumeuse et lointaine. Toutes proches en revanche sont les litanies implorantes des mendiants, qui ne laissent aucun répit à l'étranger. Aussi, lorsque à l'extrémité d'une impasse, une porte de bois toute simple s'ouvre, c'est comme une délivrance : le chaos cède la place à l'ordre, la poussière à la fraîcheur et le bruit au calme, seulement animé par des gazouillis d'oiseaux et le doux clapotis d'une fontaine.

Il faut en avoir fait l'expérience pour comprendre ce qui fait de l'*hortus conclusus* un modèle du Paradis sur terre. Mais ce n'est qu'à Marrakech qu'il est aussi devenu un synonyme d'habitation. En effet, le jardin entouré de murs appartient généralement à une vaste demeure comprenant plusieurs cours et patios. La plus grande de ces pièces ouvertes sur le ciel était autrefois appelée *riad,* il s'agissait généralement d'un rectangle allongé, divisé très précisément en quatre parterres groupés autour d'une fontaine centrale. Aujourd'hui, à Marrakech, on appelle *riad* toutes les demeures dont la cour intérieure est plantée, une preuve de la place qu'occupent les jardins dans cette ville.

Riad Sozzani

At the beginning of the 1990s Franca Sozzani fell in love with Marrakech: "It is so different, so full of life...". This Italian woman was quite determined to buy a house there – precisely because Marrakech was not at all fashionable then. And that appealed to this fashion expert. With her practised eye, Franca, editor-in-chief of Italian *Vogue*, which is more avant-garde and artistic than its sister magazines, recognised the unspoilt beauty of this city. Especially *Jemaa el Fna* cast its spell over her, this "frayed" square on the edge of the *médina*, before it enters the alluring *souks*. Each evening it changes from an asphalted void into a stage with changing actors: storytellers, snake charmers, people selling roast meat, fortune-tellers, dancers and quacks all gather here in a chaotic jumble.

"It's a magical place", says Franca. She wanted her house to be just as authentic. She found it in the *médina*, the historical old town: a typical *dâr*, which was still in Moroccan hands and, to a large extent, had been kept in its original form. The biggest advantage of the house was that it had three inner courtyards. So, it was not so difficult to sacrifice one to install a swimming pool. The other two were laid out as classical gardens.

The first patio with its square pool is surrounded by arches, with bougainvillea climbing up the columns. In the passageways there are narrow kilims, which pick up the

Anfang der 90er Jahre verliebte Franca Sozzani sich in Marrakesch: „So anders, so voller Leben ..." Die Italienerin war fest entschlossen, sich hier ein Haus zu kaufen – gerade weil Marrakesch damals überhaupt nicht in Mode war. Das reizte die Mode-Expertin. Franca, Chefredakteurin der italienischen *Vogue*, die avantgardistischer und künstlerischer als ihre internationalen Schwester-Zeitschriften ist, erkannte mit geübtem Auge die unverdorbene Schönheit dieser Stadt. Vor allem der *Jemaa El Fna* hatte sie in ihren Bann gezogen, dieser „ausgefranste" Platz am Rande der *médina*, bevor es in die lockenden *souks* geht. Jeden Abend verwandelt er sich vom asphaltierten Nichts in eine Bühne wechselnder Schauspiele: Geschichtenerzähler, Schlangenbeschwörer, Garköche, Wahrsager, Tänzer und Quacksalber geben sich ein chaotisches Stelldichein.

„Ein magischer Platz", sagt Franca. Genauso authentisch wünschte sie sich ihr Haus. Sie fand es in der *médina*, der historischen Altstadt: ein typisches *dâr*, das noch in marokkanischen Händen und weitgehend in seiner ursprünglichen Form erhalten war. Der größte Vorzug des Hauses bestand darin, dass es über drei Innenhöfe verfügt. So fiel es nicht schwer, einen dieser Höfe für einen Swimmingpool zu opfern. Die beiden anderen wurden als klassische Gärten angelegt.

Der erste Patio mit dem quadratischen Pool ist von Arkaden umgeben,

For a few years only, this *riyad* shone as one complete work of art, designed by a contemporary artist.

Für ein paar Jahre nur glänzte dieser *Riad* als das Gesamtkunstwerk eines zeitgenössischen Künstlers.

Pendant quelques années seulement, ce *riad* a fait figure « d'œuvre globale » d'un artiste contemporain.

Au début des années 90, Franca Sozzani tombe amoureuse de Marrakech : « si différente, si pleine de vie … » L'Italienne est alors fermement décidée à s'y acheter une maison, entre autres raisons parce que Marrakech n'est alors pas du tout recherchée, ce qui attire cette spécialiste de la mode. Franca, rédactrice en chef du *Vogue* italien, plus à l'avant-garde et plus artistique que ses homonymes du monde entier, reconnaît de son regard exercé la beauté intacte de la ville. Elle tombe surtout sous le charme de la *Jemaa El Fna*, cette place « en lambeaux » en bordure de la *médina*, qui précède l'entrée des *souks* si attirants. Chaque soir, l'asphalte anonyme de la place se transforme en une tribune où se succèdent les spectacles : conteurs, charmeurs de serpents, gargotiers, diseurs de bonne aventure, danseurs et charlatans s'y donnent rendez-vous dans un indescriptible chaos.

« Un endroit magique » pour Franca, qui cherche une maison tout aussi authentique. Elle la trouvera dans la *médina*, la vieille ville historique : un *dâr* typique, resté pour l'essentiel entre les mains de Marocains et dans sa forme d'origine. Son avantage principal est qu'elle dispose de trois cours intérieures. Cela ne posera donc aucun problème d'en sacrifier une pour la piscine, les deux autres étant aménagées en jardins classiques.

Le premier patio où se trouve la piscine carrée est entouré d'arcades

The garden of this terracotta-coloured *riyad* spreads out over several courtyards and roofs. The typical high and slender clay pots can be found everywhere.

Über mehrere Höfe und Dächer verteilt sich der Garten des terrakottafarbenen *Riad*. Überall finden sich die charakteristischen hohen schmalen Tontöpfe.

Le jardin du *riad* couleur terre cuite s'étale sur plusieurs cours et toits. Partout, on trouve les hautes amphores caractéristiques.

faded red colour of the walls. The water in the turquoise pool appears to be in constant movement, thanks to the pattern on the bottom, which gives the impression of waves and whirlpools. Like amorphous shapes that appear to come from nature, these patterns are repeated on the archways and grilles. They are typical of the American artist Kris Ruhs, a friend of the family, who was given free rein and allowed to design the whole *riyad* as one complete work of art. The columns, decorated in the traditional way with bright mosaic tiles, were covered in a painted leaf pattern and the double doors provided with frames painted in abstract paisley patterns instead of mosaics.

Despite the presence of a large amount of the artist's decorative latticework, the two smaller patios are dominated by plants. The first courtyard is laid out like an Andalusian garden, with cruciform tiled

deren Säulen von Bougainvillea berankt werden. In den Durchgängen liegen schmale Kelims, die das verwaschene Rot der Wände wieder aufnehmen. Das Wasser des türkisen Pools scheint ständig in Bewegung, da ein Muster an seinem Grund Wellen und Strudel suggeriert. Ähnlich amorphe Formen, die aus der Natur zu kommen scheinen, wiederholen sich an Torbögen und Gittern. Sie sind typisch für den amerikanischen Künstler Kris Ruhs, einen Freund der Familie, der freie Hand bekam und den ganzen *Riad* zu einem Gesamtkunstwerk gestalten durfte. Die Säulen, die traditioneller Weise mit buntem Fliesenmosaik geschmückt sind, bekamen ein gemaltes Blattmuster, und die Flügeltüren wurden statt mit Mosaik mit gemalten Rahmen in abstrahiertem Paisleymuster versehen.

In den beiden kleineren Patios dominieren, trotz viel zierendem Gitterwerk des Künstlers, die Pflanzen. Der erste ist wie ein andalusischer

dont les colonnes sont envahies de bougainvillées. Dans les passages sont posés d'étroits kilims du même rouge délavé que les murs. L'eau de la piscine turquoise semble sans cesse en mouvement, car un motif au fond suggère vagues et tourbillons. Des formes amorphes similaires, qui semblent tirées de la nature, se répètent sur les arches des portes et les grilles. Elles sont une spécialité de l'artiste américain Kris Ruhs, un ami de la famille, qui a reçu carte blanche pour transformer le *riad* tout entier en une œuvre d'art. Les colonnes, traditionnellement ornées de carreaux de mosaïque colorés, ont été ici peintes d'un motif de feuillage et les portes à deux battants ont vu la mosaïque remplacée par un cadre peint d'un motif paisley abstrait.

Dans les deux patios plus petits, les plantes dominent malgré les nombreux grillages ornementaux de l'artiste. Le premier est aménagé en jardin andalou, avec des chemins

Classical fountain with sunken beds and black-and-white tiles. The decoration of the arches and columns is new.

Klassisch die Brunnenanlage mit versenkten Beeten und schwarz-weißen Fliesen – neu die Bemalungen an Bögen und Säulen.

Si la fontaine au carrelage noir et blanc entourée de parterres escamotés est classique, les ornements peints sur les arcades et les colonnes sont une innovation.

paths and a fountain in the centre. The four equal-sized flowerbeds have been planted with different species of palm trees, banana trees and agaves to provide shade for the roses. In the final courtyard there are three tiled fountains, linked by a water channel. They are surrounded by a circular flowerbed – a surprising shape, since right angles predominate in Islamic gardens.

This modern interpretation of the classical Moroccan *riyad* has inspired some new owners of old houses in Marrakech to follow a similar path. Franca on the other hand got fed up with the sight of the experiment after a few years. She had expert craftsmen come and restore her whole *riyad* in a historic style with faience mosaics, tadlekt and sumptuously decorated stucco.

Garten angelegt, mit kreuzförmigen gefliesten Wegen, in deren Mitte ein Brunnen steht. Die vier gleich großen Beete sind mit verschiedenen Palmenarten, Bananen, Agaven als Schattenspender für Rosen bepflanzt.

Im letzten Innenhof stehen drei gekachelte Brunnen, verbunden durch einen Wasserkanal. Umgeben sind sie von einem kreisrunden Beet – eine überraschende Form, im islamischen Garten herrscht der rechte Winkel vor.

Die moderne Interpretation des klassischen marokkanischen *Riad* hat einige neue Besitzer alter Häuser in Marrakesch inspiriert, einen ähnlichen Weg zu gehen. Franca dagegen hat sich nach einigen Jahren an dem Experiment übergesehen. Sie ließ geübte Kunsthandwerker kommen und ihren gesamten *Riad* im historischen Stil restaurieren, mit Fayence-Mosaiken, Tadelakt und reich verziertem Stuck.

pavés en croix et une fontaine au centre. Les quatre parterres de taille identique sont plantés de différentes espèces de palmiers, de bananiers et d'agaves qui dispensent de l'ombre aux rosiers.

Dans la dernière cour intérieure, trois fontaines carrelées sont reliées par un canal et entourées d'un massif circulaire, une forme plutôt surprenante pour un jardin islamique, où règne normalement l'angle droit.

Cette interprétation moderne du *riad* marocain classique a inspiré d'autres nouveaux propriétaires de vieilles demeures de Marrakech, qui ont à leur tour emprunté cette voie. Franca, elle, s'est lassée de son expérience après quelques années et a fait venir des artisans d'art expérimentés pour restaurer entièrement son *riad* en style historique, à grands renforts de mosaïques de faïence, de tadelakt et de stuc richement ornémenté.

The sun hitting on fan palms, banana trees and delicate lianas makes various patterns.

Fächerpalmen, Bananenhaine und zartes Lianengeranke brechen die Sonne in vielfältigen Mustern.

Palmiers éventails, bananiers et tendres lianes sont transformés en motifs variés par le soleil.

Riad Gunz

Actually, it was a trip to Japan that led Walter Gunz to buy a house in the *médina* of Marrakech. In the fully air-conditioned 34th floor of a Tokyo hotel he felt cut off from the pulsating city life: there were "no noises, no smells". Therefore, on his next trip, which took him to Morocco, Gunz was all the more receptive to the different sensory impressions: "the narrow streets, the smells, the traces of the Middle Ages…".

Walter Gunz wanted to know what was hidden behind these high walls and solid doors. But Arab houses are closed to foreigners. He was only allowed to enter an old, unoccupied building – which he was then forced to buy. Thus he became the owner of a *dâr* and soon an expert in Moroccan architecture.

He made sure that the palatial building with the unusually large *riyad* (over 1,000 square metres) was "arabised" again when it was renovated. The *zellij* had lost their traditional blue colour, so he had to have new mosaic tiles made. Nowadays the whole house is lit up with the elegant blue and white geometrical mosaics.

The swimming pool was converted again into a water tank with fountains, as befits an Islamic garden courtyard. Nine jets on either side spray out water, which clashes in the air and forms arches. The long, narrow basin is framed with red roses and lavender and box hedges. At one end, it widens out into a water-lily pond.

Ivy and grape vines climb all over the walls, and plumbago, *lantana*

This *riyad* was conceived in the Andalusian style. Lilies, lavender and roses grow alongside the water basin with several jets. In the background, alocasia leaves dominate.

Eigentlich ist eine Japanreise schuld daran, dass Walter Gunz ein Haus in der *médina* von Marrakesch kaufte. Im vollklimatisierten 34. Stock eines Hotels in Tokio fühlte er sich ausgeschlossen vom pulsierenden Leben: „Keine Geräusche, keine Gerüche." Das machte ihn bei seiner nächsten Reise, die nach Marokko führte, umso empfänglicher für alle Sinneseindrücke: „Die Gassen, die Düfte, die Spuren des Mittelalters …"

Walter Gunz wollte wissen, was sich hinter den hohen Mauern und massiven Toren verbarg, aber arabische Häuser bleiben Fremden verschlossen. Einlass wurde ihm nur in ein leerstehendes altes Gebäude gewährt – das man ihm dann zum Kauf aufdrängte. So wurde er zum Besitzer eines *Dâr* und bald darauf zum Kenner marokkanischer Architektur. Er sorgte dafür, dass der palastartige Bau mit dem ungewöhnlich großen *Riad* (mehr als tausend Quadratmeter) beim Restaurieren wieder „arabisiert" wurde. Das Blau der traditionellen *sillij* gab es nicht mehr, und so musste Gunz seine Mosaikfliesen neu brennen lassen. Jetzt erstrahlt das ganze Hofhaus in elegantem Blau-Weiß.

Aus dem Swimmingpool wurde wieder ein Wasserbecken mit Brunnen, wie es sich für einen islamischen Gartenhof gehört. Neun Düsen an jeder Seite sprühen Fontänen, die sich zu hohen Wasserbögen treffen. Umrahmt ist das lange schmale Becken von roten Rosen und Hecken aus Lavendel und Buchs. An einem Ende erweitert es sich zu einem Seerosenteich.

Nach andalusischem Muster wurde dieser *Riad* angelegt. Am Wasserkanal mit den vielen Fontänen wachsen Taglilien, Lavendel und Rosen. Das dominierende Blattwerk sind Alocasien.

C'est à la suite d'un voyage au Japon que Walter Gunz a acheté une maison dans la *médina* de Marrakech : enfermé au 34e étage d'un hôtel de Tokyo ultra-climatisé, il s'est senti exclus de toute animation et de toute vie, « sans le moindre bruit ni la moindre odeur », et a développé en conséquence chacun de ses sens au cours de son voyage suivant, qui le menait au Maroc : « les ruelles, les parfums, les traces du Moyen-âge … »

Walter Gunz a toujours voulu savoir ce qui se cache derrière les hauts murs et les portails massifs, mais les maisons arabes demeurent le plus souvent fermées aux étrangers. Il ne sera autorisé à pénétrer que dans un vieux bâtiment vide qu'on le pressera ensuite d'acheter. C'est ainsi qu'il deviendra propriétaire d'un *dâr* et peu après connaisseur de l'architecture marocaine. Il veillera à ce que le bâtiment digne d'un palais, avec son *riad* exceptionnellement grand (plus de mille mètres carrés), soit de nouveau « arabisé » pendant sa restauration. Comme le bleu des *zellij* traditionnels ne se trouvait plus, il a dû faire cuire spécialement ses carreaux de mosaïque, et aujourd'hui, toute la cour rayonne d'une élégante harmonie de bleu et de blanc.

La piscine a été de nouveau transformée en bassin avec fontaine, comme il se doit pour un jardin islamique. Neuf buses de chaque côté font jaillir des jets d'eau, qui parcourent de hauts arcs de cercles avant de se rencontrer. Le bassin long et étroit est encadré de roses rouges et de haies de lavande et de buis, et s'élargit à l'une de ses extré-

Ce *riad* a été conçu suivant le modèle andalou. Le long du canal aux multiples fontaines croissent hémérocalles, lavande et roses. Le feuillage dominant vient des alocasies.

and Indian shot *(canna indica)* bloom in the flowerbeds. Elephant ear, fan palms and rubber plants provide shade. The showpiece, however, is the rare African tulip tree *(spathodea campanulata)* with its large orangey-red flowers.

When Walter Gunz discovered a Star of David on the old grounds he knew he had made the right decision: he wanted to bring different religions together here and for them to be reconciled. It is quite appropriate that he can hear the call of the Muezzin loud and clear from this house: "It is nice to be reminded of God several times a day".

Die Wände ringsum sind mit Efeu und Wein berankt, in den Beeten blühen Plumbago, Lantana und *Canna*. Elefantenohr, Fächerpalme und Gummibaum spenden Schatten. Schaustück aber ist der seltene afrikanische Tulpenbaum *(Spathodea campanulata)* mit seinen großen orangeroten Blüten.

Als Walter Gunz im alten Geländer einen Judenstern entdeckte, wusste er, dass er die richtige Entscheidung getroffen hatte: An diesem Ort wollte er verschiedene Religionen zusammen führen und versöhnen. Dazu passt, dass er den Ruf des Muezzins laut und deutlich hört: „Es ist schön, mehrmals am Tag an Gott erinnert zu werden."

mités en un étang aux nénuphars. Sur les murs tout autour grimpent la vigne et le lierre, dans les parterres fleurissent plumbagos, lantanas et cannas, tandis qu'oreilles d'éléphant, palmiers éventails et caoutchoucs dispensent à tous de l'ombre. Mais le clou du spectacle reste le tulipier du Gabon *(Spathodea campanulata)*, arbre rare aux grandes fleurs rouge-orange.

Lorsque Walter Gunz a découvert une étoile de David dans la vieille balustrade, il a su qu'il avait pris la bonne décision : à cet endroit, il réunirait et réconcilierait différentes religions. Et la voix forte et claire du muezzin qui se fait entendre toute proche n'est qu'un signe de plus « c'est beau de se voir rappeler Dieu plusieurs fois par jour ».

The trimmed laurel tree draws nearly as much attention as the rare African tulip tree or the impressive leaf of the alocasia.

Das beschnittene Lorbeerbäumchen zieht fast genauso viel Aufmerksamkeit auf sich wie der seltene afrikanische Tulpenbaum oder das eindrucksvolle Blatt der Alocasie.

Le laurier taillé attire presqu'autant l'attention que le tulipier du Gabon peu commun ou l'impressionante feuille de l'alocasie.

Riad Enija

Ursula Haldimann and Björn Conerding sit in their closed *riyad* in the heart of the labyrinth of the medieval *médina* and claim that this is the most central place in the world.

The beach on the Atlantic coast at the small artist's town of Essaouira, where they own a weekend house is 150 kilometres away. It is only half that distance to the ski resorts in the High Atlas. The solitude of the desert is also within reach, and if they feel like seeing other exotic places the airport is close by. Well-travelled Björn knows why he has made Marrakech the centre of his life. For years he travelled all over the world in order to save cultural monuments for UNESCO. Then his trained eye fell on the dilapidated *Riad Enija* – if one thing seemed worth saving to him, then it was this formerly splendid residence, which used to belong to a large clan.

A *Caïd* built this house some 200 years ago and had it extended for his descendants bait by bait . The next owner, a rich silk merchant from Fez, added a few more precious objects to the sumptuous decoration and furnishings. After that the property became dilapidated. Today the *Riad Enija* has recovered the splendour it possessed 200 years ago.

With the furnishings, he avoided anything that might turn the *Riad Enija* into some kind of folklore museum. The occasional furniture was designed by André Dubreuil, the lamps by Carolyn Quartermaine, the lanterns by Med Hajlani and the fabrics by Brigitte Perkins, who also furnished the palace for the King. These are one of the best and most expensive furnishings that modern design has to offer. With their sensuous

Ursula Haldimann und Björn Conerdings sitzen in ihrem geschlossenen *Riad* mitten im Labyrinth der mittelalterlichen *médina* und behaupten: „Dies ist der zentralste Ort der Welt."

150 Kilometer sind es zum Strand an der atlantischen Küste im Künstlerstädtchen Essaouira, wo sie ein Wochenendhaus besitzen. Halb so weit nur ist der Weg zum Skilaufen im Hohen Atlas. Die Einsamkeit der Wüste liegt ebenfalls in erreichbarer Nähe, und einen Flughafen gibt es schließlich auch. Björn, der Vielreisende, weiß, warum er Marrakesch zum Mittelpunkt seines Lebens gemacht hat. Jahrelang war er in der ganzen Welt unterwegs, um für die UNESCO Kulturdenkmäler zu retten. Dann fiel sein geübtes Auge auf den herunter gekommene *Riad Enija* – wenn ihm etwas erhaltenswert schien, dann dieser ehemals prächtige Wohnsitz einer großen Sippe. Ein *Caïd* hatte ihn vor etwa 200 Jahren erbauen lassen. Der nächste Besitzer, ein reicher Seidenhändler aus Fès, fügte der prunkvollen Innenausstattung noch einige Kostbarkeiten hinzu. Danach aber verfiel der Palast nach und nach.

Heute erstrahlt *Riad Enija* wieder im selben Glanz wie vor 200 Jahren. Für die Restaurierung zog der darin erfahrene Björn nur die besten Kunsthandwerker Marokkos heran. Bei der Inneneinrichtung dagegen wurde alles vermieden, was *Riad Enija* zu einem Folklore-Museum machen könnte. Beistellmöbel von André Dubreuil, Lampen von Carolyn Quartermaine, Laternen von Med Hajlani und Stoffe von Brigitte Perkins, die auch den Palast für den jungen König ausstatten durfte, zählen zum Besten und Teuersten,

Ursula Haldimann et Björn Conerding se sont établis dans un *riad* clos au cœur du labyrinthe de la *médina* médiévale, en affirmant « qu'il s'agit de l'endroit le plus central du monde ».

Il faut rouler 150 kilomètres pour atteindre la plage sur la côte Atlantique de la petite ville d'artistes d'Essaouira, où ils possèdent une maison de vacances. La distance pour aller skier dans le Haut-Atlas est de moitié moins. La solitude du désert est également à proximité et de surcroît la ville possède un aéroport. Björn, grand voyageur, sait parfaitement pourquoi il a fait de Marrakech le centre de sa vie : pendant des années, il a parcouru le monde pour sauver au nom de l'UNESCO des monuments culturels et son œil exercé est tombé sur le *Riad Enija,* alors à la dérive. Si un bâtiment lui a jamais semblé digne d'être conservé, c'est bien cette résidence, autrefois somptueuse, d'une grande famille.

Un *caïd* l'avait fait construire il y a environ 200 ans. Le propriétaire suivant, un riche négociant en soie de Fès, ajoutera quelques objets précieux au somptueux mobilier intérieur, mais ensuite le palais tombera en ruine peu à peu.

Aujourd'hui, le *Riad Enija* rayonne de nouveau du même éclat qu'il y a deux siècles. Björn, doué pour la restauration, n'a embauché que les meilleurs artisans d'art marocains. Pour l'ameublement intérieur en revanche, on a évité tout ce qui pourrait transformer le *Riad Enija* en un musée populaire, au profit de tout ce que le design actuel offre de mieux et de plus cher : meubles bas d'André Dubreuil, lampes de Carolyn Quartermaine, lanternes de Med Hajlani et tissus de Brigitte Perkins,

It is a traditional custom to place freshly cut roses into the high basin. Here, this custom is celebrated every day. The classical tiles also border all four flowerbeds in this courtyard.

Der alte Brauch, jeden Tag frische Rosen in das erhöhte Brunnenbecken zu legen, wird hier jeden Tag aufs Neue zelebriert. Die klassischen Fliesen ziehen sich auch als Rand um die vier Beete des Hofes.

Ici, on célèbre tous les jours l'ancienne coutume de garnir les bassins de roses fraîches. Les carrelages classiques servent également à encadrer les quatre parterres de la cour.

The exceptionally beautiful faience mosaics *(zellij)* covering walls and columns and the chased plaster stucco above were restored to perfection.

Perfekt restauriert wurden die selten schönen Fayence-Mosaiken *(sillij)* an Wänden und Säulen und der kunstvoll ziselierte Stuck aus Gips darüber.

Les splendides faïences *(zellij)* des murs et des colonnes, ainsi que les stucs ciselés au dessus ont été parfaitement restaurés.

colours and shapes they fit perfectly in this historic setting.

Ursula, who used to spoil her guests as a confectioner in her café in Berne, Switzerland, takes care of the exclusive small hotel business. *Riad Enija* has two rooms and seven suites, all with access to the terrace. From breakfast to the evening *table d'hôte*, it all happens in the *riyad*, the inner courtyard. Its beauty lies in the architecture; as in all Islamic garden courtyards, the plants play a supporting role – providing shade. *Washingtonia* and *phoenix* palms grow here – the winters are too cold for other, more exotic species, since temperatures can drop to as low as minus three to four degrees Celsius. Too much sun on the other hand brings out the lice, which have caused many of the old orange trees to die. But what is important is that the Seville orange trees *(citrus aurantium)* are still there – bitter oranges have always been used to clean brass and silver. Moreover, the large round fruit still hangs in the trees when all other citrus fruits have been picked: "these are our only Christmas decorations", says Björn.

was modernes Design zu bieten hat.

Ursula, die früher als Zuckerbäckerin die Gäste in ihrem Café in Bern verwöhnt hat, kümmert sich um den exklusiven kleinen Hotelbetrieb, für den zwei Zimmer und sieben Suiten bereit gestellt wurden, alle mit Zugang zur Terrasse. Vom Frühstück bis zur abendlichen *table d'hôte* spielt sich alles im *Riad*, dem Innenhof, ab. Seine Schönheit liegt in der Baukunst, wie bei allen islamischen Gartenhöfen – die Pflanzen spielen eine (Schatten spendende) Nebenrolle. Es wachsen *Washingtonia* und *Phoenix*, für exotischere Palmenarten ist der Winter hier mit drei bis vier Grad unter Null zu kalt. Zuviel Sonne wiederum fördert Läuse, woran viele der alten Orangenbäume eingegangen sind. Hauptsache, die Pomeranzen *(Citrus aurantium)* sind noch da – Bitterorangen nämlich braucht man in Marokko seit altersher zum Putzen von Messing und Silber. Außerdem hängen die großen runden Früchte noch in den Bäumen, wenn alle anderen Zitrusfrüchte bereits abgeerntet sind: „Unser einziger Weihnachtsschmuck", sagt Björn.

qui a également équipé le palais du jeune roi.

Ursula, dont les talents de pâtissière ont autrefois fait les délices des clients de son café bernois, se consacre exclusivement au petit hôtel raffiné, composé de deux chambres et de sept suites, donnant toutes sur la terrasse. Du petit-déjeuner à la table d'hôte du soir, tout se passe dans le *riad*, la cour intérieure. Sa beauté vient de son architecture, la végétation ne jouant qu'un rôle (dispensateur d'ombre) secondaire. Ici poussent des *Washingtonia* et des *Phoenix*. L'hiver, avec trois à quatre degrés en dessous de zéro, est trop froid pour les espèces de palmiers plus exotiques. Trop de soleil, en revanche, attire des insectes nuisibles, auxquels ont succombé bon nombre des anciens orangers, mais l'essentiel, les bigarades *(Citrus aurantium)*, est resté. En effet, depuis toujours au Maroc, on utilise les oranges amères pour le nettoyage du laiton et de l'argent. De plus, les gros fruits ronds sont encore suspendus aux arbres lorsque tous les autres agrumes ont déjà été récoltés : ils sont « notre unique décoration de Noël », dit Björn.

La Mamounia

In the world there are only a handful of hotels that the connoisseurs praise. The legends woven about a house count more than luxury and service. In this respect, *La Mamounia* surpasses a *Ritz,* an *Oriental* or an *Adlon.* And this is the stuff that dreams are made of: the kind leader Sidi Mohammed – who was known as the "Benefactor of Marrakech", because he restored his ancestors' palaces, mausoleums and mosques as well as the old city walls before he went on to build his own palace – gave each of his four sons a large *arsa* (pleasure garden) when they got married. One of them became famous. It belonged to Mamoun, the youngest prince, who had a small, perfectly proportioned pavilion built, in which he spent happy hours with his wife, the legendary beauty, Lalla Fatma. Over 200 years have gone by since then, but the garden is still named after the prince, and the luxury hotel *La Mamounia,* on its 15-hectare grounds, which opened in 1929, was also named in his honour. The Prince's olive trees still form a line along the main avenue, which runs straight up to the pavilion where important politicians and high-ranking military officers, envoys and adventurers of all persuasions used to enjoy themselves. However, this pavilion has now closed forever: an important *Marabout* (saint) is apparently buried there, and no one would ever dare disturb his eternal peace.

Instead of this, there are now three villas tucked away in the garden, which are just as highly sought after by prominent guests as the Prince's pavilion was long ago. An underground corridor links them directly to the hotel kitchen, thus enabling the most unusual wishes to be fulfilled discreetly – including secret visits.

Weltweit gibt es nur wenige Hotels, die Kenner zum Schwärmen verleiten. Mehr noch als Luxus und Service zählen dabei die Legenden, die sich um ein Haus ranken. Was das angeht, übertrifft *La Mamounia* vielleicht sogar ein *Ritz, Oriental* oder *Adlon.* Und dies ist der Stoff, aus dem die Träume sind: Der gütige Herrscher Sidi Mohammed – man nannte ihn „Wohltäter von Marrakesch", weil er die Paläste seiner Vorgänger, ihre Mausoleen und Moscheen sowie die alte Stadtmauer restaurieren ließ, bevor er daran ging, seinen eigenen Palast zu errichten – schenkte jedem seiner vier Söhne zur Hochzeit einen großen *arsa* (Lustgarten). Einer davon hat Berühmtheit erlangt. Er gehörte Mamoun, dem jüngsten Prinzen, der einen kleinen Pavillon mit vollkommenen Proportionen erbauen ließ, in dem er glückliche Stunden mit seiner legendär schönen Frau Lalla Fatma verbrachte.

Mehr als 200 Jahre sind seither vergangen, der Garten trägt immer noch den Namen des Prinzen, und das 1929 auf dem 15 Hektar großen Grund eröffnete Luxushotel *La Mamounia* wurde ebenfalls nach ihm benannt. Noch immer säumen die Olivenbäume des Prinzen die Hauptallee, die direkt auf den Pavillon zuläuft, in dem sich einst hohe Politiker und Militärs, Gesandte und Abenteurer aller Couleur amüsierten. Heutzutage ist er geschlossen: ein hoher *Marabout* (Heiliger) soll dort begraben liegen, und niemand wagte es, seine ewige Ruhe zu stören.

Stattdessen gibt es versteckt im Garten drei Villen, die bei prominenten Gästen ebenso begehrt sind wie ehemals der Pavillon. Ein unterirdischer Gang verbindet sie direkt mit der Hotelküche, was eine diskrete Erfüllung der ausgefallensten Wünsche ermöglicht.

Seuls peu d'hôtels dans le monde séduisent les initiés jusqu'à la passion. Plus encore que le luxe et le service, ce sont alors les légendes créées autour d'une maison qui importent. Dans ce domaine, *La Mamounia* l'emporte sans doute, même sur un *Ritz,* un *Oriental* ou un *Adlon.* Et ces légendes sont de l'étoffe des rêves : le bon souverain Sidi Mohammed – appelé le « bienfaiteur de Marrakech » parce qu'il avait fait restaurer les palais de ses prédécesseurs, ainsi que leurs mausolées et mosquées, et l'ancien rempart de la cité avant de commencer la construction de son propre palais – avait offert à chacun de ses quatre fils pour son mariage un grand *arsa* (jardin d'agrément). L'un d'entre eux est devenu célèbre. Il appartenait à Mamoun, le plus jeune des princes, qui y fera construire un petit pavillon aux proportions parfaites, où il passera des heures de bonheur avec son épouse à la beauté légendaire, Lalla Fatma.

Plus de deux cent ans se sont écoulés, le jardin porte encore le nom du prince et le luxueux hôtel *La Mamounia,* qui occupe depuis 1929 les 15 hectares de la propriété, a également été baptisé d'après lui. Les oliviers du prince y bordent encore l'allée principale, qui mène directement au pavillon. Ce dernier, cependant, utilisé jadis comme lieu de plaisirs par des chefs politiques et militaires ou des ministres et aventuriers de tout poil, est aujourd'hui fermé pour toujours : un grand *marabout* (saint) y serait enterré et nul ne saurait se risquer à troubler son repos éternel.

En compensation, trois villas sont cachées dans le jardin, tout aussi recherchées des hôtes de marque qu'autrefois le pavillon du prince. Un passage souterrain les relie directement aux cuisines de l'hôtel, permettant la réalisation discrète des

A Moorish portal with view over an arched courtyard is an invitation to the world of "Arabian Nights".

Ein maurisches Tor mit Blick auf einen Arkadenhof lädt ein in eine Welt wie aus Tausendundeinenacht.

Véritable invite au pays des milles et unes nuits, le portail arabe ouvre sur une cour à arcades.

The traditional hotel even offers its own little golf course. In front of the club house is a small pond, shaded by tall papyrus trees.

If the gnarled olive trees could talk, they would have something to say about the famous guests such as Josephine Baker, who adopted a Moroccan child, or Marlene Dietrich and Gary Cooper who, with their film "Morocco", turned the country into a popular holiday destination, or about Alfred Hitchcock, in whose thriller "The man who knew too much" Marrakech and *La Mamounia* played leading roles, and also the couturier Pierre Balmain, who lavished white camellias, silk scarves,

Das Traditionshotel verfügt auch über einen eigenen kleinen Golfplatz. Vor dem Clubhaus liegt ein Teich, der von hohen Papyrus-Pflanzen beschattet wird.

Wenn die knorrigen Oliven reden könnten, sie wüssten einiges zu erzählen über Berühmtheiten wie Josephine Baker, die ein marokkanisches Kind adoptierte, über Marlene Dietrich und Gary Cooper, die mit ihrem Film „Marocco" das Land als Reiseziel in Mode brachten, über Alfred Hitchcock, in dessen Thriller „Der Mann, der zuviel wusste" Marrakesch und *La Mamounia* Hauptrollen spielten, bis zu dem Couturier Pierre Balmain, der die weiblichen Gäste seiner Modenschau mit wei-

L'hôtel de tradition dispose également d'un petit terrain de golf. Devant le *clubhouse* se trouve un étang, abrité par de hauts papyrus.

souhaits les plus inhabituels, dont les visites secrètes.

Si les oliviers noueux pouvaient parler, ils auraient bien des choses à raconter sur des célébrités comme Josephine Baker, qui adoptera un enfant marocain, Marlene Dietrich et Gary Cooper, qui mettront le pays à la mode avec leur film « Maroc », Alfred Hitchcock et son film policier « L'homme qui en savait trop », dont Marrakech et *La Mamounia* occupent les rôles principaux, jusqu'au couturier Pierre Balmain, qui inondait

141

perfumes and champagne on the female guests at his fashion shows ... But the high, bougainvillea-covered walls keep all the secrets of the *Arsat Al-Mamounia* pleasure garden. Yet the only thing that has been advertised for marketing purposes is the fact that Sir Winston Churchill often visited this place to pursue his great passion, painting nature. His sketch-es, an easel, brushes, a hat and a stick are kept in the suite named after him.

The garden is looked after by 40 gardeners who, twice a year, plant 60,000 new annuals, such as snapdragons, nicotiana, petunias and the like, which are cultivated in greenhouses. *La Mamounia* is one the only hotel in the world to offer this sort of luxury.

ßen Kamelien, Seidentüchern, Parfüms und Champagner geradezu überschüttete ... So aber bewahren die sechs Meter hohen und mit Bougainvillea dick gepolsterten Mauern alle Geheimnisse des eingefriedeten *Arsat Al Mamounia*. Nur dass der britische Premier Sir Winston Churchill hier mehrfach seiner großen Leidenschaft, dem Malen nach der Natur, nachging, wird bis heute werbewirksam vermarktet.

40 Gärtner pflegen die Anlage und pflanzen zweimal pro Jahr 60.000 frische Einjährige, wie Löwenmaul, Ziertabak, Petunien und ähnliches, die in eigenen Gewächshäusern gezogen werden. Ein Luxus, den außer *La Mamounia* wahrscheinlich kein Hotel der Welt bietet.

The alley of olive trees was planted over 200 years ago and leads to a pavilion that is now a mausoleum.

Die Oliven-Allee wurde vor über 200 Jahren angelegt, sie führt auf einen Pavillon zu, der als Mausoleum dient.

L'allée d'oliviers a été plantée il y a plus de 200 ans ; elle mène à un pavillon servant de mausolée.

littéralement les invitées à son défilé de camélias blancs, de mouchoirs de soie, de parfum et de champagne ... Mais les murs de six mètres de haut et rembourrés d'épais bougainvilliers gardent en réalité tous les secrets de l'*Arsat Al Mamounia*. Seule la grande passion du Premier ministre britannique Sir Winston Churchill pour la peinture naturaliste, à laquelle il

s'adonnera ici plusieurs fois, est encore évoquée à titre de publicité.

40 jardiniers prennent soin et y plantent deux fois par an 60 000 annuelles, gueules-de-loup, tabac d'ornement, pétunias ou autres, cultivées dans leurs propres serres. Un luxe que certainement bien peu d'hôtels dans le monde peuvent offrir à leur clientèle, à part *La Mamounia*.

Twice a year, about 60,000 annuals are planted, among them snap-dragon, ornamental tobacco and petunias.

Zweimal jährlich werden 60.000 frische Einjährige, wie Löwenmaul, Ziertabak und Petunien gepflanzt.

Deux fois par an, on plante 60 000 annuelles fraîches, comme l'antirrhine, les nicotiana et les pétunias.

The bougainvillea-covered wall that makes the 15 hectares into a *hortus conclusus* is six metres high.

Sechs Meter hoch ist die mit Bougainvillea bewachsene Mauer, die aus den 15 Hektar einen *hortus conclusus* macht.

Le mur couvert de bougainvilliers, qui transforme les 15 hectares en jardin clos, fait six mètres de haut.

A masterpiece made the French painter Jacques Majorelle (1886–1962) world famous. This is not one of his paintings, which were not held in high esteem. It is the garden he created on the edge of the Palmeraie in Marrakech, which attracts admirers from round the globe. And it is a single colour that makes it immortal: the harsh metallic cobalt blue, with which he imbued walls, steps, borders, benches, plant containers, pergolas and the façade of his studio – which has gone down in art history as "Majorelle blue".

Jacques Majorelle bought the grounds in 1924 and later increased the size of the gardens by purchasing more land. In the end, he owned almost four hectares. Although he was a great admirer of the Maghreb, he did not follow the style of Moorish (Islamic) gardens, but instead he modelled it on the exotic ones he had known in his youth on the French Côte d'Azur. Admittedly, he installed typical Moroccan-style marble pools and fountains covered in mosaics and a pavilion with a raised island set amidst water-lilies. In this way all around he created a tropical paradise. Over the course of 35 years, this passionate plant collector gathered no fewer than 1800 different types of cacti and 400 species of palm tree. The usual citrus and date trees were set aside in favour of figs trees, cypresses, arborvitaes, eucalyptuses, carob trees, agaves, aloes, giant euphorbias, cycads and tree ferns. Majorelle provided shade for the small goldfish pond with a metre-high bamboo grove. He even imported peacock butterflies, pink flamingos and small monkeys to create his *jardin exotique*.

But the real Caribbean feel began when, in 1937, Majorelle picked up his paint pot and brushes and 'painted' his garden in the true sense of the word – paths, bridges, railings, flowerbed borders… He chose "Anton blue", for most things, the colour of the overalls all workers wear in France. By doing this the painter took the bold step of intro-

146

Ein Meisterwerk machte den französischen Maler Jacques Majorelle (1886–1962) weltberühmt. Es ist nicht etwa eines seiner Gemälde, mit denen er wenig Anerkennung fand. Es ist der Garten, den er am Rande der Palmerie in Marrakesch schuf, der Bewunderer aus aller Welt anzieht. Und es ist eine einzige Farbe, die ihn unsterblich macht: Jenes metallisch harte Kobaltblau, mit dem er Mauern, Treppen, Einfassungen, Bänke, Pflanzgefäße, Pergola und die Fassade seines Ateliers tränkte – das in die Kunstgeschichte eingegangene „Majorelle-Blau".

Jacques Majorelle kaufte den Grund 1924 und erwarb in den folgenden Jahren immer wieder Land hinzu, bis er schließlich fast vier Hektar besaß. Obwohl ein großer Bewunderer des Maghreb, orientierte er sich nicht an maurisch-islamischen Gärten, sondern an exotischen, wie er sie in seiner Jugend an der Côte d'Azur kennen gelernt hatte. Zwar installierte er landestypische Wasserbecken und Brunnen aus Mosaik und Marmor und einen Pavillon auf erhöhter Insel inmitten von Seerosen, doch drum herum kreierte er ein tropisches Paradies. Nicht weniger als 1800 verschiedene Kakteensorten und 400 Palmenarten trug der leidenschaftliche Pflanzensammler im Laufe von 35 Jahren zusammen. Den üblichen Zitrus- und Dattelbäumen setzte er Feigen, Zypressen, Thujas, Eukalyptus, Johannisbrotbäume, Agaven, Aloë, riesige Euphorbien, Palmfarne und Baumfarne zur Seite. Ein kleines Goldfischbecken ließ er von einem meterhohen Bambushain beschatten. Ja, er importierte sogar einige Pfauenauge-Schmetterlinge, rosa Flamingos und kleine Affen für seinen *jardin exotique*.

Aber das richtige Karibik-Gefühl stellte sich erst ein, als Majorelle 1937 zu Pinsel und Farbtopf griff und seinen Garten im wahrsten Sinne des Wortes anmalte – Wege, Brücken, Geländer, Beetumrandungen … Für das meiste wählte er die Farbe des „Blauen Anton", jenes Overalls, den in Frankreich jeder Arbeiter trägt.

Un chef-d'œuvre a rendu célèbre dans le monde entier le peintre français Jacques Majorelle (1886–1962), non pas l'un de ses tableaux, qui ne lui ont valu que peu de reconnaissance, mais le jardin qu'il a créé à Marrakech en bordure de la palmeraie et qui attire les admirateurs des quatre coins du monde. Une couleur en particulier l'immortalise : ce bleu cobalt métallique et dur dont l'artiste a imprégné murs, escaliers, bordures, bancs, pots de fleurs, pergola et la façade de son atelier et qui est entré dans l'histoire de l'art sous le nom de « bleu Majorelle ».

Jacques Majorelle achète sa propriété en 1924 et ne cesse au cours des années suivantes d'acquérir des terrains supplémentaires, jusqu'à ce qu'il possède près de quatre hectares. Bien qu'il soit un grand admirateur du Maghreb, il ne s'inspire pas des jardins maures islamiques, mais des jardins exotiques qu'il avait appris à connaître pendant sa jeunesse sur la Côte d'Azur. Il installe bien un bassin et une fontaine typiques de mosaïque et de marbre, ainsi qu'un pavillon sur une île surélevée au milieu des nénuphars, mais c'est pour créer tout autour un paradis tropical. Collectionneur passionné de plantes, il ne rassemblera pas moins de 1800 espèces différentes de cactus et 400 sortes de palmiers pendant 35 ans. Les arbres à agrumes et les dattiers habituels sont accompagnés de figuiers, de cyprès, de thuyas, d'eucalyptus, de caroubiers, d'agaves, d'aloès, d'euphorbes géantes, de cycadacées et de fougères arborescentes, un petit bassin à poissons rouges est ombragé par une haie de bambous de plusieurs mètres et le peintre importera même des papillons-paons, des flamants roses et de petits singes pour son jardin.

L'impression des Caraïbes ne se met cependant véritablement en place qu'à partir de 1937, lorsque Majorelle se saisit de ses pinceaux et pots de peinture pour peindre son jardin, au sens littéral du terme : chemins, ponts, balustrades, bordures de parterres … Il optera dans la plupart des cas pour la couleur du

Majorelle

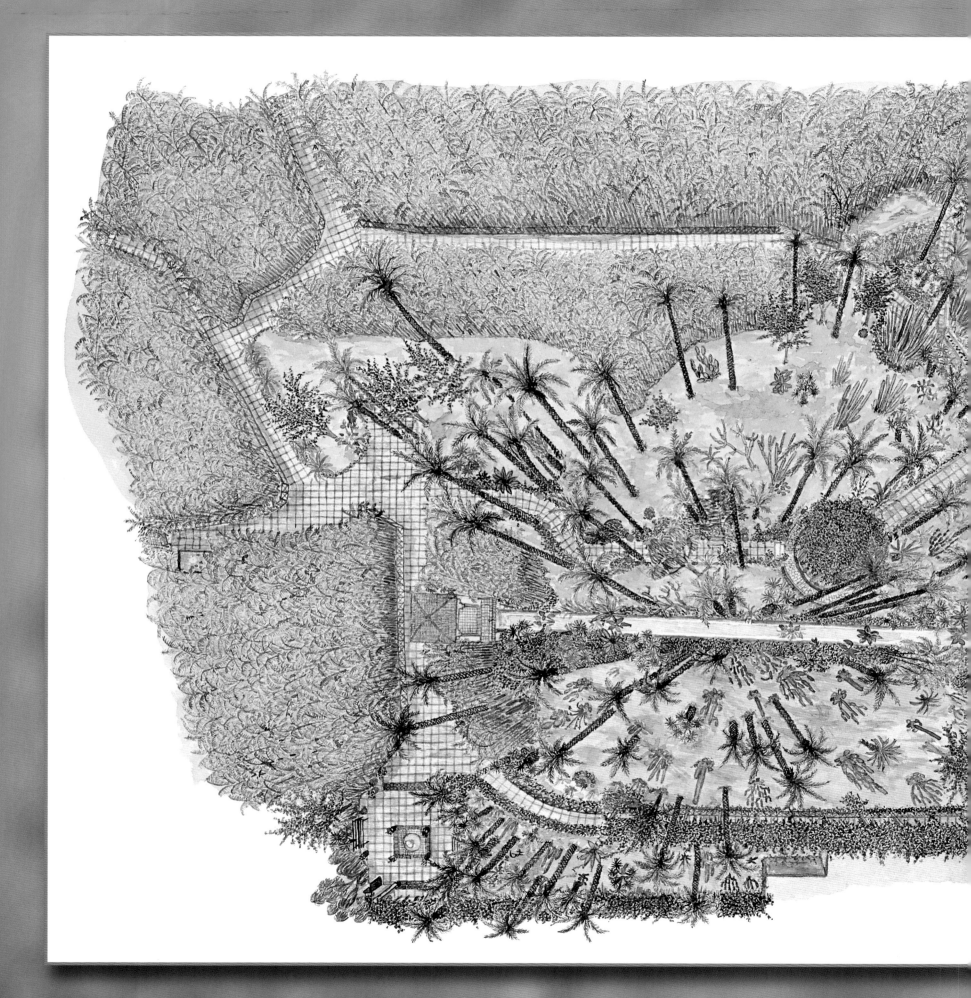

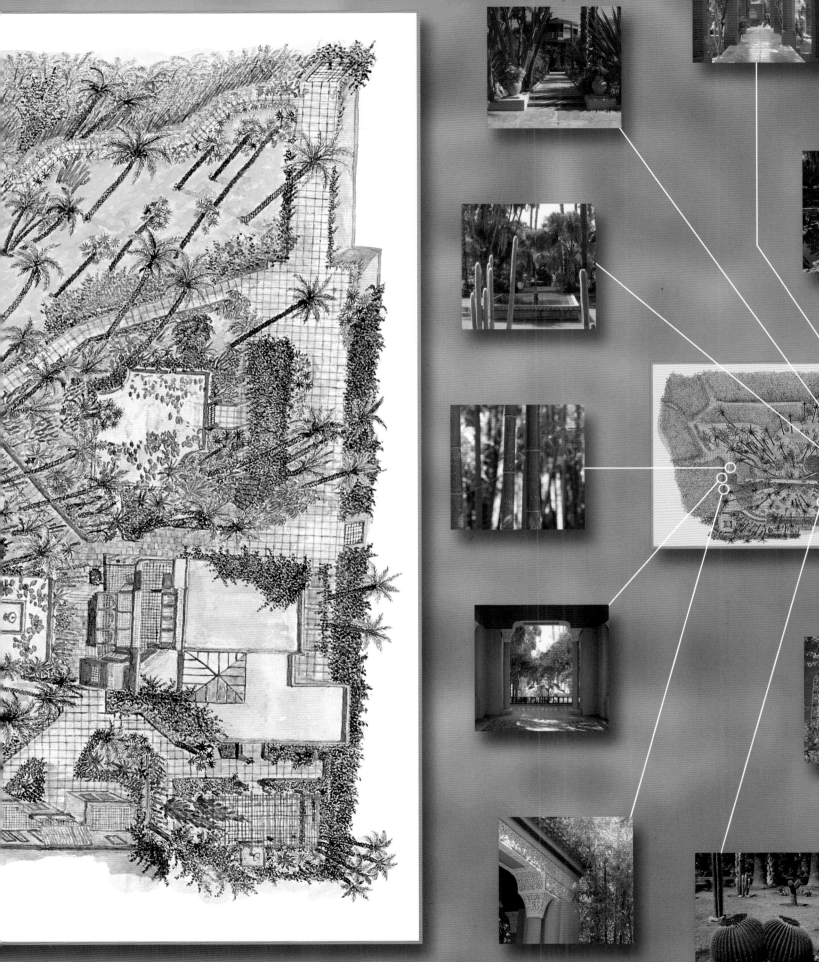

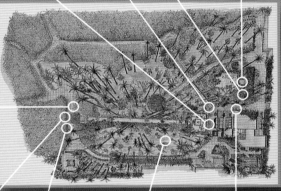

A stuccoed pavilion is raised above the water channel that flows into a basin in front of the studio. The eye wanders over alocasia leaves and bamboo stretching above them. The famous Majorelle-blue is showcased on the pergola between the studio and water-lily-pond.

Ein stuckverzierter Pavillon sitzt über dem Wasserkanal, der in einem Becken vor dem Atelier mündet. Eine Alocasie reckt ihre Blätter ins Blickfeld, überragt von Bambus. Das berühmte Majorelle-Blau kommt bei der Pergola zwischen Atelier und Seerosenteich am besten zur Geltung.

ducing a disturbing note that prevailed over all others. And yet, this gaudy colour actually does the densely planted garden good by showcasing it quite dramatically – Majorelle had now completed his masterpiece.

In a 1928 Marrakech guidebook tourists were already being recommended visits to the garden of the Villa *Bou Saf Saf* (poplar tree in Arabic). Majorelle had bought the plot of land because of these trees, as they were proof to him of the presence of water. The poplars had to be removed, in order for Majorelle's extravagant vision to take shape. He always welcomed interested visitors and was a generous host to his international friends. Towards the end of his life, however, Majorelle was

Damit wagte der Maler einen verstörenden Akzent, der sich gegen alles andere durchsetzt. Und doch, gerade diese grelle Farbe tut dem dicht bepflanzten Garten gut, setzt ihn dramatisch in Szene – Majorelles Meisterwerk war vollendet.

Schon in einem Marrakesch-Führer von 1928 war Touristen der Garten der Villa *Bou Saf Saf* (arabisch für Pappel) empfohlen worden. Wegen der Pappeln hatte Majorelle das Grundstück gekauft, waren sie doch Beweis für vorhandenes Wasser. Die Pappeln mussten weichen, dafür nahm Majorelles extravagante Vision Gestalt an. Interessierte Besucher waren ihm immer willkommen. Gegen Ende seines Lebens jedoch war er gezwungen, Eintrittsgeld zu verlangen – zuviel hatte der Garten

« bleu », du bleu de travail porté par tous les ouvriers. Le peintre parvient ainsi à une intensité troublante, qui s'impose contre tout le reste. Pourtant, cette couleur crue profite justement au jardin luxuriant et le met en scène de façon spectaculaire, le chef-d'œuvre de Majorelle est parfaitement achevé.

Dès 1928, un guide de Marrakech recommandait aux touristes le jardin de la villa *Bou Saf Saf* (peupliers en arabe). En effet, c'est à cause des peupliers que Majorelle avait acheté le terrain, voyant en eux des témoins de la présence d'eau. Ils devront céder la place lorsque la vision extravagante de Majorelle prendra forme. Les visiteurs intéressés étaient alors toujours les bienvenus. Vers la fin de sa vie cependant, il se verra contraint

Le canal menant à un bassin devant l'atelier est surplombé d'un pavillon garni de stucs. Une alocasie expose son feuillage, dépassée par les bambous. La pergola entre atelier et bassin aux nénuphars met superbement en valeur le célèbre « bleu majorelle ».

forced to charge an entry fee – the garden had cost too much and his painting had brought in too little. This man, who went to Morocco in 1917 to become a great painter, died a famous gardener.

The garden then fell into disrepair until the French couturier Yves Saint-Laurent and his partner Pierre Bergé took over the residence and restored it to its former glory. They divided off their own private house, the *Villa Oasis,* christened the remaining garden with the name of its creator and opened it to paying visitors. The former studio was turned into a small museum for Islamic art – and a few of Majorelle's paintings now receive the attention here they were denied during the artist's lifetime.

Basins with fountains mark the end of the narrow, long water channel. In front of it lies the cactus garden, behind, palm trees grow. *Cressula* leaves show up beautifully in front of the studio's decorative railings. Water-lilies and goldfish are the most-photographed objects in the Majorelle garden.

Becken mit Brunnen bilden den Endpunkt des langen schmalen Wasserlaufs. Davor liegt der Kakteengarten, dahinter erheben sich Palmen. Das Dickblatt *(Cressula)* behauptet sich vor dem dekorativen Gitterwerk am Atelier. Seerosen und Goldfische sind das meist fotografierte Motiv im Majorelle-Garten.

Le bassin à la fontaine forme la fin du mince cours d'eau. Devant, se trouve le jardin de cactus, derrière s'élèvent des palmiers. La cressule s'impose devant la grille ouvragée qui orne l'atelier. Nénuphars et poissons rouges sont le motif le plus photographié à Majorelle.

verschlungen und zuwenig die Malerei eingebracht. Der Mann, der 1917 nach Marokko gegangen war, um ein großer Maler zu werden, starb als berühmter Gärtner.

Der Garten verfiel zunächst, bis der französische Couturier Yves Saint-Laurent und sein Partner Pierre Bergé den Besitz übernahmen und auf das Schönste restaurierten. Ihr Privathaus, die *Villa Oasis,* trennten die beiden ab, den übrigen Garten benannten sie nach ihrem französischen Schöpfer und öffneten ihn für zahlende Besucher. Aus dem ehemaligen Atelier wurde ein kleines Museum für islamische Kunst – und auch einige Werke Majorelles finden jetzt hier die Beachtung, die ihnen zu Lebzeiten des Künstlers verwehrt war.

d'exiger un droit d'entrée, car le jardin avait trop englouti d'argent et la peinture n'en avait pas rapporté suffisamment. L'homme venu en 1917 au Maroc dans l'espoir de devenir un grand peintre mourra dans la peau d'un célèbre jardinier.

Le jardin commence alors à dépérir, jusqu'à ce que le grand couturier français Yves Saint-Laurent et son partenaire Pierre Bergé le rachètent et le restaurent de la plus belle façon. Ils construiront à part leur demeure privée, la *Villa Oasis,* donneront au reste du jardin le nom de son créateur et en ouvriront l'accès aux visiteurs payants. L'ancien atelier est devenu un petit musée d'art islamique et quelques œuvres de Majorelle y trouvent l'attention qui leur fut défendue du vivant de l'artiste.

The pavilion's stucco ornaments are a true work of art. *Echinocactus grusonii* sit in state in the cactus garden. Many visitors left their marks on the soft bark of the bamboo trunks.

Die Stuckarbeiten am Pavillon sind wahre Kunstwerke. Im Kakteen-Garten thronen Schwiegermuttersessel *(Echinocactus grusonii)*. Viele Besucher verewigen sich in den weichen Rinden der Bambusstämme.

Les stucs du pavillon sont de véritables œuvres d'art. Les échinocactus trônent dans le jardin de cactus. Beaucoup de visiteurs s'immortalisent dans l'écorce tendre des bambous.

Water means life

There is no life without water: water is required for a seed to begin to germinate in the nourishing Mother Earth. Human life begins in water too – in the amniotic fluid of the womb. If one goes back to the start of life itself, as mythology and later science have done, then the ocean is the place where life on Earth began over three billion years ago. The name of our planet Earth is a misnomer, since over 70% of its surface is covered in water...

Without water, there are neither any gardens: water is necessary to create an oasis in the desert. For a long time, people believed that oases were the result of the fortunate intervention of the Gods. A "water miracle" was often cited at the beginning of their descriptions. However, in general there was nothing celestial about the irrigation of oases or gardens, it was simply a question of hydraulic technology. Think of the Hanging Gardens of Babylon, one of the Seven Wonders of the Ancient World.

The Ancient Greeks ascribed their creation to the Assyrian Queen Seimiramis: a highly developed system of aqueducts led water from a river up to the highest point of the Hanging Gardens, where it was then directed through channels in order to water all the trees and plants. In Egypt, early engineers practised controlled flooding of the Nile. Dikes plus over and underground channels transported water to the population and onto the fields. Meanwhile, today's well-boring systems make life easier in hot parts of the world. However, the effects of damns are not all positive. The famous Aswan Dam has contributed to Egypt's water supply. But at the same time it also holds back the fertile Nile mud, which

Wasser bedeutet Leben

Ohne Wasser kein Leben: Wasser ist nötig, damit ein Samenkorn in der nährenden Mutter Erde zu keimen beginnt. Auch das Leben eines Menschen beginnt im Wasser – im Fruchtwasser der Gebärmutter. Geht man zu den Ursprüngen des Lebens zurück, wie es zuerst die Mythologie und später die Wissenschaft getan haben, dann ist der Ozean der Ort, an dem irdisches Leben vor mehr als drei Milliarden Jahren seinen Anfang genommen hat. Die Erde trägt ihren Namen eigentlich zu Unrecht, denn ihre Oberfläche ist zu 70 % mit Wasser bedeckt...

Ohne Wasser kein Garten: Wasser ist notwendig, um eine Oase in der Wüste entstehen zu lassen. Lange Zeit glaubte man an ein glückliches Eingreifen der Götter, wenn Oasen enstanden. Ein „Wasser-Wunder" wird häufig zu Beginn ihrer Beschreibung zitiert. Dabei war meist an der Bewässerung von Oasen und Gärten nichts Überirdisches, sondern Hydraulik-Technik. Man denke an die hängenden Gärten von Babylon, einem der sieben Weltwunder. Ihre Kreation schrieben die alten Griechen der Königin Semiramis zu: Ein hochentwickeltes System von Aquaedukten brachte Wasser aus einem Fluss bis auf die höchste Spitze der hängenden Gärten, von wo Kanäle es weiter zur Bewässerung aller Bäume und Pflanzen leiteten. In Ägypten praktizierten die frühen Ingenieure eine Art kontrollierte Überschwemmung des Nils. Deiche, über- und unterirdische Kanäle transportierten das Wasser zur Bevölkerung und auf die Felder. Die heutigen Systeme des Brunnenbohrens erleichtern in heissen Zonen inzwischen das Leben. Dafür haben Staudämme nicht nur positive Auswirkungen. Der berühmte Staudamm in Assuan hat zur Wasserversorgung von Ägypten beigetragen. Er hält aber

L'eau, symbole de vie

Sans eau, pas de vie : c'est l'eau qui fait commencer à germer une graine de semence dans la terre nourricière. La vie des hommes aussi commence dans l'eau, le liquide amniotique de l'utérus maternel. Et si l'on remonte aux origines de la vie, comme l'ont fait, d'abord la mythologie, puis la science, c'est dans l'océan que la vie sur Terre a commencé, il y a plus de trois milliards d'années, Terre par ailleurs injustement nommée, puisque 70 % de sa surface est recouverte d'eau...

Sans eau, pas de jardin : c'est l'eau qui fait surgir les oasis dans le désert. Pendant longtemps, on a cru à une intervention réussie des dieux et la description des oasis commence souvent par la mention d'un « miracle aquatique ». L'irrigation des oasis et des jardins n'a pourtant jamais rien eu à voir avec le surnaturel, mais bien plus avec la technique hydraulique. Il suffit de penser aux jardins suspendus de Babylone, l'une des sept merveilles du monde de l'Antiquité. Les anciens Grecs en attribuaient la création à la reine Sémiramis : un système d'aqueducs des plus élaborés amenait l'eau d'un fleuve jusqu'au sommet des jardins, d'où des canaux allaient ensuite irriguer les arbres et les plantes. En Égypte, les premiers ingénieurs parvenaient plus ou moins à contrôler la crue du Nil, tandis que des digues et des canaux en partie souterrains transportaient l'eau jusqu'à la population et dans les champs. Les systèmes actuels de creusement de puits, eux aussi, facilitent la vie dans les zones torrides. Les barrages n'ont cependant pas que des effets positifs : si le grand barrage d'Assouan a contribué à l'alimentation en eau de l'Égypte, il retient aussi les boues fertiles du Nil, qui ont servi pendant des millénaires d'engrais naturels pour les cultures.

had been used on the fields for thousands of years as a natural fertiliser.

In the *gulistân* (rose garden) the meaning of a water body as a mirror of eternity is highlighted. The pool in the centre of the garden is just like the gate to the Garden of Eden. The architects of the Alhambra in Granada played with the pool's mirror function: the magnificently adorned façades and arches of the palace are reflected in the garden ponds – and these mirror pictures are the reality that most Alhambra tourists take pictures of. The cisterns, simple water reservoirs in the kitchen garden or *bustân*, become mirrors in the pleasure garden's *gulistân* and the irrigation channels in the former become rivers of paradise in the latter. In the Dar Batha garden in Fez, restored in 1914 by the French landscape designer Forestier, every façade is reflected in a water display on the terraces, which were laid out on the cruciform garden. It is not just here that the primarily aesthetic quality of water is used, before it fulfils its purpose in the irrigation channels.

It was only later that fountains were constructed creatively. One could say the Christian fountain cracked the Muslim mirror. That way one takes a step back from the symbolic meaning of the element water and a step towards the direction of decoration. Whilst the spring gently murmurs, the bubbling of the fountain is a considerably clearer auditory experience. Sometimes it is deafening, as in the courtyard of the Generalife. Some architects even use fountains with the aim to drown out the noise from nearby streets.

More than anything else, the garden is a musical place: throughout history, poets have associated the murmur of water in the garden with women singing while they work and the ringing voices of children. In the *riyad*, religious or family celebrations, singing and dancing take place. And the gentle splashing of the fountain answers the cooing of the turtle doves that bathe there ...

auch den fruchtbaren Nilschlamm zurück, der Jahrtausende lang als natürlicher Dünger auf die Felder gelangte.

Im *gulistân* wird die Bedeutung einer Wasserfläche als Spiegel der Ewigkeit hervor gehoben. Das Bassin in der Gartenmitte ist gleichsam das Tor zum Garten Eden. Mit dieser Funktion des Spiegels von Wasserbecken haben die Architekten der Alhambra in Granada gespielt: Die wunderbar geschmückten Fassaden und Arkaden des Palastes spiegeln sich in den Wasserbecken der Gärten wider – und es sind diese Spiegelbilder der Wirklichkeit, die Alhambra-Touristen am meisten fotografieren. Die Zisterne, einfaches Wasser-Reservoir im Nutzgarten *bustân*, wird zum Spiegel im Lustgarten *gulistân*, und die Bewässerungskanäle im ersteren werden zu den Flüssen des Paradieses im letzteren. Im Garten von Dar Batha in Fès, 1914 von dem französischen Landschaftsarchitekten Forestier restauriert, spiegelt sich jede Fassade in einem Wasserspiegel auf den Terrassen, die über dem kreuzförmig angelegten Garten angelegt wurden. Nicht nur hier wird zunächst die ästhetische Qualität des Wasser genutzt, bevor es in Bewässerungskanälen seinen Zweck erfüllt.

Erst später entstanden Springbrunnen als Gestaltungsmittel. Man kann sagen, der Springbrunnen der Christen hat den Spiegel der Muselmanen zerstört. Damit ging man einen Schritt weg von der symbolischen Bedeutung des Elements Wasser und einen Schritt weiter in Richtung Dekoration. Während die Quelle leise murmelt, ist das Sprudeln von Springbrunnen ein wesentlich deutlicheres Hörerlebnis. Manchmal wird es betäubend, wie im Patio des Generalife. Manche Architekten setzen Brunnen heute sogar ein, um die Geräusche naheliegender Straßen zu übertönen...

Mehr als alles andere ist der Garten ein musikalischer Ort: Zu allen Zeiten haben die Dichter das Murmeln des Wassers im Garten mit dem Gesang der Frauen bei der Arbeit und den hellen Stimmen der Kinder assoziiert. Im *Riad* fanden und finden religiöse oder familiäre Feste, Gesang und Tanz statt. Und das sanfte Plätschern des Brunnens antwortet auf das Gurren der Turteltauben, die sich an ihm laben...

Dans le *gulistân*, on souligne l'importance d'une surface d'eau comme miroir de l'éternité. Le bassin au centre du jardin est également la porte du jardin d'Éden. Les architectes de l'Alhambra de Grenade ont joué avec cette fonction de miroir: les façades et arcades merveilleusement décorées du palais se réfléchissent dans les bassins du jardin, et ce sont ces reflets de la réalité que les touristes photographient le plus. Ainsi, la citerne, simple réservoir d'eau dans un jardin de rapport, un *bustân*, devient miroir dans un jardin d'agrément, un *gulistân*, et les canaux d'irrigation du premier se transforment dans le second en fleuves du paradis. Dans le jardin de Dar Batha, à Fès, restauré en 1914 par l'architecte-paysagiste français Forestier, chaque façade se reflète dans un miroir d'eau sur les terrasses aménagées au-dessus du jardin disposé en croix: ici aussi, on a tiré parti des qualités esthétiques de l'eau avant de la laisser remplir sa fonction dans les canaux d'irrigation.

Les jets d'eau ne sont apparus que plus tardivement dans l'aménagement des jardins. On peut même dire que le jet d'eau des chrétiens a détruit le miroir des musulmans. Avec lui, on s'éloigne d'un pas de la symbolique de l'élément liquide, tandis qu'on avance d'un pas vers la décoration, d'autant plus que, si la fontaine murmure doucement, le jaillissement d'un jet est sensiblement plus sonore. Il peut même être assourdissant, comme dans le patio du Generalife, et aujourd'hui, certains architectes choisissent même de disposer des fontaines pour couvrir les bruits des rues avoisinantes dans les jardins qu'ils réalisent...

Plus que tout, le jardin est un lieu musical: de tous temps, les poètes ont associé le murmure de l'eau dans les jardins au chant des femmes au travail et aux voix claires des enfants. Dans les *riad* avaient et ont toujours lieu des fêtes religieuses ou familiales, des chants et des danses. Et le doux clapotis de la fontaine répond alors aux roucoulades des tourterelles qui s'y rafraîchissent.

Fez – Historic Capital
Fès – Historische Hauptstadt
Fès – Capitale historique

"Balak, balak!" *Watch out! Watch out! No-one can escape this cry. The words "balak, balak", resound incessantly, ringing in your ears and driving people forward through the narrow alleyways of the* médina, *forcing them through the last eye of the needle. It is impossible to get out of the way. Nowhere are passageways narrower. Nowhere do more people push their way through a historic old town than in Fez. Only here can you find* zerzayas, *or human carriers, because the alleyways are too narrow even for a donkey.*

Fez is home to many refugees. When the city was founded at the beginning of the 9th century they came from Kairouan in Tunisia. After that there was the arrival of the Muslims from Andalusia and 500 years later the Jews forced to leave Spain. All of them brought with them their knowledge and skills, and so Fez became a flourishing capital of the arts, crafts and trade. It was already an intellectual and spiritual centre thanks to El Kairaouine, the 9th century university mosque. It is the oldest centre of Islamic faith and knowledge and indeed one of the oldest universities in the world.

Right up to the 20th century Fez was the largest and richest city in Morocco. Its decline began in 1911 with the French protectorate. Rabat was made the seat of government and Casablanca became the financial centre. Fez became poor, especially when new waves of refugees came rolling in: in the 1940s farmers arrived in the city in search of work and shelter, driven off the land by drought. The devastating earthquake of 1960 brought in homeless people from Agadir, who constructed a new part of the city above the marble Merinid Necropolis, the fourth district after the historic centre Fez El Bali (old Fez), the "white city" Fez El Jedid (new Fez) constructed by the Merinid sultans and the French Ville Nouvelle.

If things continue at this rate, the city will soon have one million inhabitants. Almost 400,000 people live in Fez El Bali alone, a district built for only 100,000. UNESCO wants to preserve this perfect testimony to the Islamic Middle Ages just as it is. In 1990, Fez El Bali declared the inestimable treasures that hide in its labyrinth of narrow streets a world cultural heritage. However, up to now it has not been possible to carry out any of the projects to rescue these treasures. There is simply no way through – "balak, balak!".

„Balak – Balak!" Vorsicht, Vorsicht! Diesem Ruf entkommt keiner. „Balak, Balak", ertönt ununterbrochen, setzt sich fest im Ohr, treibt die Menge voran durch die Enge der médina, zwingt sie auch noch durchs letzte Nadelöhr. Ausweichen unmöglich. Nirgendwo sind die Durchgänge schmaler, drängen sich mehr Menschen durch die historische Altstadt als in Fès. Nur hier gibt es Zerzayas, menschliche Lastenträger, weil die Gassen selbst für Esel zu eng sind.

Fès ist Heimat von Flüchtlingen. Bei Gründung der Stadt Anfang des 9. Jahrhunderts kamen sie aus dem tunesischen Kairouan, dann folgten Moslems aus Andalusien. 500 Jahre später waren es Juden, die Spanien verlassen mussten. Sie alle brachten ihr Wissen und Können mit, und so wurde Fès zur florierenden Hauptstadt von Kunst, Handwerk und Handel. Intellektueller und spiritueller Mittelpunkt war es ohnehin dank El Kairaouine, der Universitäts-Moschee aus dem 9. Jahrhundert. Sie ist das älteste Zentrum islamischen Glaubens und Wissens und die älteste Universität der Welt überhaupt.

Fès blieb bis ins 20. Jahrhundert hinein die größte und reichste Stadt Marokkos. Der Untergang begann 1911 mit dem Protektorat der Franzosen. Rabat wurde zum Regierungssitz ernannt, Casablanca entwickelte sich zum Wirtschaftszentrum. Fès verarmte, vor allem als neue Flüchtlingswellen anrollten: In den 40er Jahren kamen die Bauern, von der Dürre vertrieben suchten sie Zuflucht und Arbeit in der Stadt. Das verheerende Erdbeben von 1960 brachte Heimatlose aus Agadir, die oberhalb der marmornen Meriniden-Nekropole einen neuen Stadtteil anlegten – den vierten nach dem historischen Kern Fès El Bali, nach der „weißen Stadt" Fès El Jédid von den Meriniden-Sultanen und der Ville Nouvelle der Franzosen.

Wenn es so weiter geht, ist die Stadt bald eine Millionen-Metropole. Allein in Fès El Bali, das einst für 100.000 Einwohner erbaut wurde, leben jetzt bereits fast 400.000 Menschen. Die UNESCO will dieses perfekte Zeugnis des islamischen Mittelalters so erhalten, wie es ist. 1990 wurde Fès El Bali, das unermessliche Kostbarkeiten in seinem Gassen-Labyrinth birgt, zum Weltkulturerbe erklärt. Doch bis jetzt konnte noch keines der Projekte zu seiner Rettung durchgesetzt werden. Es ist einfach kein Durchkommen – „Balak, Balak!"

« Balak – Balak ! », « Attention, attention ! » Impossible de ne pas entendre cet appel. « Balak, Balak » retentit sans cesse de toutes parts, se loge dans l'oreille, chasse la foule dans l'étroitesse de la médina, la force encore jusqu'au dernier trou d'aiguille. Impossible d'y échapper. Nulle part les passages ne sont plus étroits et nulle part ne se pressent plus de gens dans la vieille ville historique qu'à Fès. On ne voit également qu'ici les zerzayas, les porteurs à pied, car les ruelles sont trop étroites même pour les ânes. Fès est une cité de réfugiés. À la fondation de la ville, au début du 9e siècle, les premiers sont venus de Kairouan, en Tunisie ; ils seront suivis de musulmans d'Andalousie, eux-mêmes suivis 500 ans plus tard de Juifs chassés d'Espagne. Tous ont apporté leur savoir et leur savoir-faire, de sorte que Fès est devenue la capitale florissante de l'art, de l'artisanat et du commerce. Elle était déjà un foyer intellectuel et spirituel grâce à El Kairaouine, la mosquée-université créée au 9e siècle et est aujourd'hui le plus ancien centre de la foi et de la science islamiques, ainsi que l'une des plus anciennes universités du monde.

Fès restera jusqu'au 20e siècle la plus grande et la plus riche ville du Maroc. Le déclin s'amorce en 1911 avec le protectorat français. Rabat est alors désignée comme siège du gouvernement et Casablanca devient un grand centre économique, tandis que Fès s'appauvrit, notamment avec l'arrivée de nouvelles vagues de réfugiés. Dans les années 40, les paysans chassés par la sécheresse viennent chercher refuge et travail à la ville, puis, en 1960, le tremblement de terre dévastateur amène les sans-abri d'Agadir, qui occuperont un nouveau quartier surplombant la nécropole marmoréenne des Mérinides, le quatrième après le cœur historique de la ville Fès El Bali, la « ville blanche » des sultans mérinides Fès El Jédid et la Ville Nouvelle des Français. Si sa croissance continue au même rythme, la ville sera bientôt une métropole d'un million d'habitants.

Rien qu'à Fès El Bali, construit à l'origine pour 100 000 habitants, vivent déjà près de 400 000 hommes et ce, alors que l'UNESCO voudrait conserver en l'état ce témoignage incomparable du Moyen-Âge islamique.

En 1990, Fès El Bali, qui abrite des trésors inimaginables dans son labyrinthe de ruelles, a été déclaré patrimoine mondial de l'humanité ; aucun des projets de sauvetage n'a cependant encore pu être réalisé. Il n'y a simplement pas moyen de passer, « Balak, Balak ! »

Traditional and Modern Gardens
Traditionelle und moderne Gärten
Jardins traditionnels et modernes

The "Andalusian garden", Palais Jamaï for example (left), can be divided into several room-like compartments. Modern gardens rather show themselves as "landscape". The eldest gardens like Bou Jloud are hidden behind historic town walls.

Ein „andalusischer Garten" wie im Palais Jamaï (links) kann in viele verschiedene Räume unterteilt werden. Moderne Gärten dagegen präsentieren sich eher als „Landschaft". Die ältesten Gärten wie Bou Jloud sind vor historischen Stadtmauern umgeben.

On peut découper un « jardin andalou », comme celui du Palais Jamaï (à gauche), en une multitude de pièces. Les jardins modernes, en revanche, se présentent plutôt comme un « paysage ». Les jardins les plus anciens, comme celui de Bou Jloud, sont entourés de murs d'enceinte historiques.

Fez is the largest preserved medieval city in the whole of Islamic world – except for its gardens. Most of them have fallen victim to poverty and lack of space. There was a time when each house, rich or poor, had an open inner courtyard with a round fountain in the middle, under the shade of a lemon tree. In the Maghreb, the existence of these basic elements is enough for a place to be classified as a garden. Bubbling water and cooling faience mosaics made of small green, blue, black and white chipped ceramic tiles turn any enclosed space into a reflection of paradise. Fez was once a proud, beautiful and rich city, famous for its inhabitants' palaces with their magnificently planted patios and courtyards. They were owned by all the "influential families" in whose hands lay the city's destiny; the city gates still bear their names today. The rise of these families was democratic, although not as a system with elections but rather one based on trust and experience. Each craft guild was led by an *Al Amin* (the trustworthy and faithful one). The offspring of the influential families had to go to Rabat and Casablanca in order to continue their businesses. Their palaces and gardens fell into disrepair. Houses formerly inhabited by one family were now divided up between ten or more, mostly farmers, who had fled to the city during the great drought. When the grand houses became unin-

habitable they moved on to one of the new districts of Fez. But there is hope. Firstly, foreigners and the influential families' heirs are gradually coming to the city and renovating the old palaces. The number of courtyards with a fountain bubbling in the centre under the shade of a lemon tree is increasing once again ... Nowhere are people prouder of the glorious past than in Fez, which has the largest surviving Islamic medieval city. Sometimes, however, this significant legacy can also be a burden. Since there is wide public interest all over the world in restoring the city's historic treasures, it is hard for modern architects and landscape designers to make a name for themselves. Nevertheless, a guild of young architects, who have deliberately broken free from all the old models, has gained acceptance in Fez. With their work they want to be an example for their era. Their clients are primarily young lawyers, doctors and the businessmen, people who settle in the district which the French named the *Ville Nouvelle*. They want houses that are modern but still remain "typical of Fez". The gardens of these houses are no longer based on the Andalusian model; instead they are inspired by garden designs from South Africa or Provence. Another trend is the exotic garden, reminiscent of a South American jungle. Only the avant-garde still concentrate on using single plant families such as the cacti.

Fès ist die größte erhaltene mittelalterliche Stadt des Islam – bis auf ihre Gärten. Die meisten von ihnen sind der Platznot und der Armut zum Opfer gefallen. Einst hatte jedes Haus, ob arm oder reich, einen offenen Innenhof mit einem runden Springbrunnen in der Mitte, beschattet von einem Zitronenbaum. Diese Grundausstattung genügt im Maghreb, um den Namen Garten zu verdienen. Sprudelndes Wasser und kühlende Fayence-Mosaike aus blauen, grünen, weißen und schwarzen Keramikstückchen machen jeden umfriedeten Raum zu einem Abbild des Paradieses.

Einst war Fès, die stolze, schöne und reiche Stadt, berühmt für die Paläste ihrer Bürger, die prächtige bepflanzte Patios und Höfe hatten. Sie gehörten jenen „großen Familien", von denen die Geschicke der Stadt bestimmt wurden; die Stadttore tragen heute noch ihre Namen. Der Aufstieg dieser Familien entsprach einem demokratischen System. Jede Handwerksgilde wurde von einem *Al Amin* (der Vertrauensvolle und Treue) geführt. Die Nachkommen dieser Familien mussten nach Rabat und Casablanca gehen, um ihre Geschäfte fortzuführen. Ihre Paläste und Gärten verfielen. Wo früher eine Familie residierte, teilen sich heute zehn oder mehr den Raum, meist Bauern, die vor der großen Dürre in die Stadt flohen. Wenn die herrschaftlichen Häuser unbewohnbar geworden sind, ziehen sie weiter in die neuen Viertel von Fès.

Aber es gibt Hoffnung. Zunächst kamen Fremde und nach und nach auch die Erben der großen Familien, um die alten Paläste instand zu setzen. Es mehren sich die Höfe, in deren Mitte wieder ein Springbrunnen unter einem Zitronenbäumchen plätschert ...

Nirgendwo ist man stolzer auf die große Vergangenheit als in Fès, das eine bestens erhaltene Altstadt aus dem islamischen Mittelalter besitzt. Doch das bedeutende Erbe kann auch eine Last sein. Da das Interesse der Weltöffentlichkeit sich darauf konzentriert, die historischen Schätze zu restaurieren, haben moderne Architekten und Landschaftsgestalter es schwer, sich einen Namen zu machen. Dennoch hat sich in Fès eine Gilde junger Architekten durchgesetzt, die sich bewusst von allen alten Vorbildern löst. Ihr Ziel ist es, eine neue Formensprache zu entwickeln. Ihre Klienten wünschen sich moderne Häuser, die dennoch „typisch Fès" sind. Die dazu gehörenden Gärten orientieren sich nicht mehr am andalusischen Modell, sondern nehmen bevorzugt Anregungen aus Südafrika oder der Provence auf. Ein anderer Trend sind exotische Gärten, die an einen südamerikanischen Dschungel erinnern. Nur die Avantgarde konzentriert sich auf eine einzige Pflanzen–Familie: Reine Kakteengärten sind hier sehr selten.

Fès est la plus importante ville médiévale du monde islamique qui soit encore conservée, à l'exception de ses jardins, dont la plupart ont été victimes du manque de place et de la pauvreté. Autrefois, chaque maison, riche ou pauvre, possédait une cour intérieure ouverte avec une fontaine ronde au milieu, ombragée par un citronnier. Il suffit en effet de ces quelques éléments pour mériter le nom de jardin au Maghreb : le clapotis de l'eau et la fraîcheur des mosaïques en petits morceaux de faïence bleus, verts, blancs et noirs y font de chaque espace clos une image du paradis.

Fès était autrefois une ville fière, belle et riche, célèbre pour ses palais aux patios et cours plantés d'une végétation luxuriante. Ils appartenaient aux « grandes familles » qui ont marqué le destin de la ville et dont les noms ornent encore les portes de la cité. L'ascension sociale de ces familles se faisait alors selon un système démocratique. Chaque gilde d'artisans était menée par un *Al Amin* (digne de confiance et fidèle). Leurs descendants ont malheureusement dû rejoindre Rabat et Casablanca, pour y poursuivre leurs affaires. Les palais et les jardins se sont délabrés et, là où autrefois vivait une seule famille, dix ou plus se partagent aujourd'hui l'espace, généralement des paysans ayant fui à la ville pour échapper à la grande sécheresse et qui, lorsque les demeures princières deviennent inhabitables, déménagent ailleurs dans les nouveaux quartiers de Fès. Il reste cependant de l'espoir. Les étrangers d'abord, puis peu à peu les héritiers des grandes familles, sont revenus afin de remettre en état les anciens palais. Aujourd'hui, les cours où une fontaine clapote au centre sous un petit citronnier se multiplient ...

Dans aucune autre ville les habitants ne sont plus fiers de leur passé glorieux qu'à Fès. Cependant, cet héritage médiéval remarquable peut parfois devenir aussi une charge. En effet, comme l'intérêt de l'opinion publique mondiale est concentré sur la restauration des trésors historiques, les architectes et paysagistes modernes ont beaucoup de mal à se faire un nom. Malgré tout, un groupe de jeunes architectes a su s'imposer à Fès en se détachant délibérément des modèles anciens. Leur objectif est de développer un nouveau langage des formes qui fera référence pour leur époque.

Leur clientèle souhaite des maisons modernes et cependant « typiques de Fès ». Les jardins ne sont plus inspirés du style andalou, mais de préférence de modèles sud-africains ou provençaux, quand ils ne suivent pas la mode de l'exotisme, qui les fait ressembler à une jungle d'Amérique du Sud. L'avant-garde se concentre sur une unique famille de plantes : les jardins de cactus sont aussi rares que les maisons minimalistes.

Dar el Aman

The Ba Mohammed family's star garden is unique. It is not based on any Eastern or Western model. And yet, it is a typical Arab-Islamic garden: surrounded by arches, decorated with colourful mosaics and geometrically laid out fountains and flowerbeds.

When the house was built by Pasha Abd Al Kari in 1860, this inner courtyard must have looked quite different, probably much simpler. Laid out as a typical *wasat al-dār* (inner courtyard) it must have had a fountain in the centre and several trees offering shade. At the time of the Pasha, who was called "the generous one", a hundred people lived in this spacious building, which has two stories, several courtyards and roof terraces. Even the grandfather of the present owner, who took the estate over from the Pasha, housed a clan of 60 people here. As a farmer, he served the Sultan both faithfully and successfully and through this earned a good reputation and became prosperous. So, he could afford to be a little extravagant: sometime between the years 1920–30 he had his friend Moulay Ali Ouazzani, a fellow farmer, redesign the garden.

Moulay Ali must have been a very imaginative man, because he created a garden the likes of which had never been seen before: he divided the ca. 30 x 20 m rectangle into 21 octagonal equal-sized stars. Three of them had fountains – so far, it was all quite normal. 18 stars were filled with earth and planted like flowerbeds, as were the smaller cruciform beds in between. The artwork took up all the space except for one surrounding corridor. The family, in the meantime, had dwindled to 20 members. The once rich farmers had become impoverished: it was hard for them to stop the 1,800 m² living space from falling into decline. The

Einzigartig ist der Sterngarten der Familie Ba Mohammed. Er orientiert sich an keinem Vorbild, weder östlich oder westlich. Dennoch ist er ein typisch arabisch-islamischer Garten: von Arkaden umgeben, mit farbigen Mosaiken geschmückt, mit geometrisch angelegten Brunnen und Beeten.

Bei der Erbauung des Hauses durch Pasha Abd Al Kari im Jahre 1860 dürfte dieser Innenhof noch ganz anders ausgesehen haben. Wesentlich schlichter. Angelegt als typischer *wasat al-dār* (Innenhof) wird er mit einem Brunnen als Mittelpunkt und einigen Schatten spendenden Bäumen ausgestattet gewesen sein. Zu Zeiten des Paschas, den man „den Großzügigen" nannte, wohnten 100 Menschen in dem weitläufigen Gebäude, das über zwei Ebenen, mehrere Höfe und Dachterrassen verfügt. Auch der Großvater des jetzigen Besitzers, der das Anwesen vom Pascha übernahm, beherbergte noch eine Sippe von 60 Personen. Als Landwirt hatte er dem Sultan ebenso treu wie erfolgreich gedient und war dadurch zu Ansehen und Wohlstand gekommen. Da konnte er sich eine kleine Extravaganz leisten: Von seinem Freund Moulay Ali Ouazzani, Bauer wie er, ließ er sich zwischen 1920 und 1930 den Garten neu gestalten.

Moulay Ali muss ein phantasievoller Mann gewesen sein, denn er kreierte einen Garten, wie man ihn noch nie gesehen hatte: Er teilte das Rechteck von etwa 30 mal 20 Meter in 21 achteckige Sterne von gleicher Größe auf. Drei davon bestückte er mit Springbrunnen – so weit, so üblich. 18 Sterne jedoch wurden mit Erde gefüllt und wie Blumenbeete bepflanzt, ebenso wie die kleineren kreuzförmigen Beete dazwischen. Das Kunstwerk nimmt, bis auf einen umlaufenden Gang, den ganzen Raum ein.

Le jardin étoilé de la famille Ba Mohammed est unique en son genre. En effet, sans correspondre à aucun modèle, que ce soit occidental ou oriental, il reste un jardin arabo-islamique typique avec les arcades qui l'entourent, les mosaïques colorées dont il est orné et la disposition géométrique de ses fontaines et parterres.

Lors de la construction de la maison par le pacha Abd Al Kari en 1860, cette cour intérieure devait présenter un aspect très différent, beaucoup plus modeste. Conçue pour être un *wasat al-dār* (cour intérieure) typique, elle n'avait vraisemblablement été dotée que d'une fontaine centrale et de quelques arbres dispensateurs d'ombre. À l'époque du pacha, appelé aussi « le généreux », cent personnes occupaient les vastes bâtiments, qui comprennent deux niveaux, plusieurs cours et des toits en terrasses. Le grand-père du propriétaire actuel, qui avait repris le domaine du pacha, entretenait, quant à lui, encore une parentèle de 60 personnes. Avec son exploitation agricole, il avait servi le sultan avec autant de fidélité que de succès et y avait gagné prestige et richesse. Il pouvait donc se permettre une petite folie en faisant réaménager le jardin par son ami Moulay Ali Ouazzani, agriculteur comme lui, entre 1920 et 1930.

Moulay Ali devait être un homme plein d'imagination, car le jardin qu'il a créé ne ressemble à aucun autre. Après avoir partagé la surface rectangulaire d'environ 30 mètres sur 20 en 21 étoiles octogonales de même taille, il dota trois d'entre elles de fontaines à jet d'eau, rien de bien inhabituel jusque-là. Mais les 18 étoiles restantes ont été remplies de terre et plantées de fleurs, formant des parterres séparés par des massifs plus petits en forme de croix,

All the doors and windows open out to the *riyad*. This one is decorated with artistic wrought-iron and colourful glass mosaics.

Alle Türen und Fenster, hier mit kunstvollem Schmiedeeisen und buntem Glasmosaik, sind auf den *Riad* ausgerichtet.

Toutes les portes et les fénêtres, comme celle à grille en fer ouvragé et vitraux de couleur, donnent sur le *riad*.

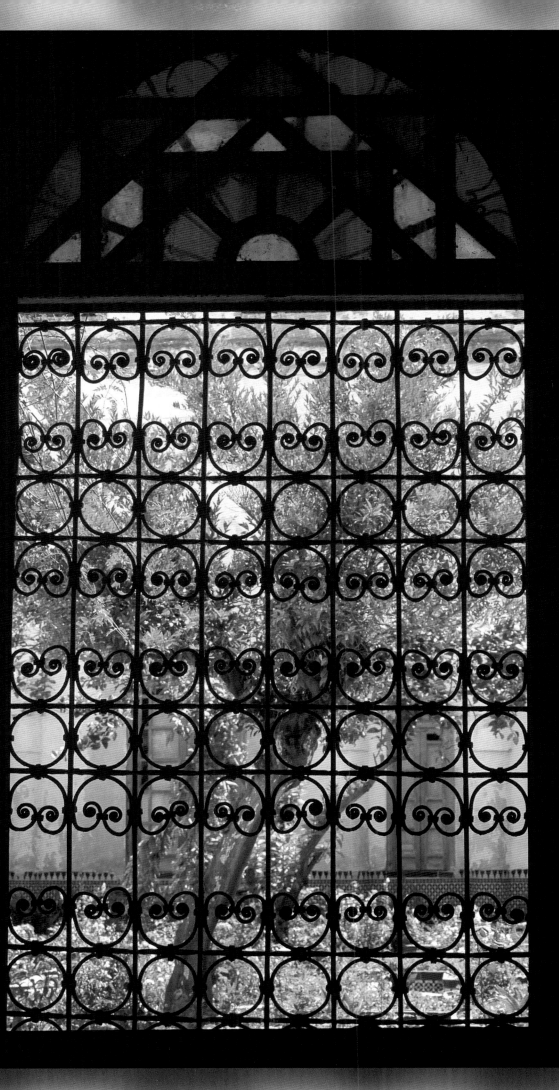

View from the huge reception salon through a beautiful double door onto a façade in decline.

Der Blick aus dem großen Empfangsraum mit der schönen Flügeltür fällt auf eine desolate Fassade gegenüber.

La vue du salon de réception avec sa belle porte à battants donne sur la façade pitoyable d'en face.

Climbing bougainvillea, rose and Indian shot dominate. Often, there is not enough money for flowers such as snapdragon and petunia.

Die kletternde Bougainvillea, Rose und Canna behaupten ihren Platz. Für andere Blumen, wie Löwenmaul und Petunie, ist oft kein Geld da.

Bougainvilliers grimpants, roses et canna défendent leur terrain. Souvent, l'argent manque, pour acheter d'autres fleurs, comme les antirrhines et les pétunias.

most expensive element to look after is the garden. Plants must be cared for, replaced and, above all, watered. Each star and each cross is surrounded by a channel, into which excess water can flow. Some fountains are broken up and scarcely provide any water now. The restoration of their marble beauty is just too expensive. However, the most costly part of all is the preservation of the precious tiled mosaics, which constantly require retouching. At one time, there were 24 *slajija* (ceramic artists) working on the design of the corridors, pillars and the raised flowerbed and fountain borders. The dominant colour is a refreshing blue; the pillars of the corridor arches are covered in sun-yellow *zellij*.

For some time now, one wing of the *Dar el Aman* (the name currently given to the former Pasha's palace) has been used to house a school for artisans. Hopefully this will help the mosaic master craftsmen of tomorrow preserve this unique garden, which is a magnificent work of art. In addition, the always-welcome visitors can contribute to the restoration with their donations.

Die Familie ist mittlerweile auf 20 Mitglieder geschrumpft. Die ehemals reichen Landwirte sind verarmt; es fällt ihnen schwer, die 1.800 Quadratmeter Wohnfläche vor dem Verfall zu retten. Am kostspieligsten ist das Bewässern des Gartens. Jeder Stern, jedes Kreuz ist umrahmt von einer Rinne, in der übertretendes Wasser abfließen kann. Einige Brunnen sind zerbrochen und spenden gar kein Wasser mehr. Das Restaurieren ihrer marmornen Schönheit ist zu teuer, insbesondere aber der Erhalt des kostbaren Kachelmosaiks, das immer wieder nachgearbeitet werden muss. 24 *slajija* (Keramikkünstler) haben einst an der Gestaltung der Gänge und Säulen, der erhöhten Beet- und Brunnenumrandungen mitgewirkt. Dominierende Farbe ist das erfrischende Blau, die Säulen des Arkadenganges dagegen tragen gelbe Sonnen aus *sillij*.

In einem Seitenflügel des *Dar el Aman* (heutiger Name des ehemaligen Palastes) ist eine Schule für Kunsthandwerker untergebracht – hoffentlich werden die Mosaik-Meister von morgen helfen, das einmalige Gartenkunstwerk zu erhalten.

de sorte que l'œuvre d'art occupe, à l'exception d'un chemin circulaire, la totalité de la surface.

La famille s'est réduite entretemps à 20 membres. En effet, les riches fermiers d'autrefois sont aujourd'hui appauvris et ont bien du mal à sauver de la ruine les 1800 mètres carrés de surface habitable. Le plus coûteux restant l'irrigation du jardin. Chaque étoile et chaque croix sont entourées d'une rigole dans laquelle l'eau peut s'écouler. Quelques fontaines sont brisées et ne donnent plus d'eau du tout, la restauration de leur beauté marmoréenne reviendrait trop cher. Le plus onéreux cependant est l'entretien des précieux carreaux de mosaïque. 24 *slajija* (artistes en céramique) ont autrefois participé à l'ornement des chemins, des colonnes et des bordures surélevées de massifs et de fontaines. La couleur dominante est un bleu frais, mais les colonnes de l'allée d'arcades présentent des soleils de *zellij* jaunes.

Une aile latérale du *Dar el Aman* (le nom actuel de l'ancien palais du pacha) abrite depuis quelque temps une école pour artisans d'art.

When the gate opens out onto the Middle Ages, you have a choice: you can go through the 800 year-old *Bab Guissa* into the oldest *médina* in Morocco, or through the *Bab Jamaï* into one of the most luxurious five-star hotels in the world.

Both are to be recommended. Those who choose to go first to the *médina*, will be able to appreciate afterwards the peace, comfort and, above all, the magnificent garden of the *Palais Jamaï* much more. On the other hand, those who decide to first enter the hotel will learn to observe the fineness of Moroccan craftwork, which they will later encounter even in the most out-of-the-way spots. For Fez is home to 30,000 *maallem* (master cratftsmen), who work in exactly the same way now as their predecessors did in days of old.

The *Palais Jamaï* was built in 1879 by the influential Jamaï brothers – grand viziers to the Sultan Moulay Hassan – in the best spot in the city, with a panoramic view of the whole of Fez. The hotel, which was established in this sumptuously furnished building in 1930, profits from this, as it offers all guests a room with a view.

That is, if the guest still has eyes for anything other than the garden, which is one of the most beautiful examples of the "Andalusian" style. The latter is the name given to all gardens which are based on the Alhambra, that often cited jewel of Moorish (Islamic) garden architecture. Most people associate this with the classical axial lines that divide up the garden, when in actual fact you can also find a linear pattern, which is also present in the Alhambra. In designing the *Palais Jamaï*, the most varied shapes were adopted, all bound to the strict geometrical order. Six quite different types of garden areas, each surrounded by its own wall, were arranged in echelons on the slope. The ones higher up have splendid *sakkaya* (wall fountains), with blue and white tiled mosaics, out of which the water flows in stages into small channels, which in turn supply a pool farther down. Each pond is equipped with an alabaster

Wo sich das Tor zum Mittelalter öffnet, hat man die Wahl: Geht man durch das 800 Jahre alte *Bab Guissa* in die älteste *médina* Marokkos – oder durch das *Bab Jamaï* in eines der luxuriösesten Fünf-Sterne-Hotels der Welt?

Empfehlenswert ist beides. Wer zuerst die *médina* wählt, weiß die Ruhe, den Komfort und vor allem den grandiosen Garten des *Palais Jamaï* hinterher umso mehr zu schätzen. Wer dagegen zuerst das Hotel betritt, trainiert das Auge für die Feinheiten des marokkanischen Kunsthandwerks, dem er später bis in die entlegensten Winkel begegnen wird. Denn Fès ist der Sitz von 30.000 *maallem* (Handwerksmeister), die heute noch genau so arbeiten wie zu vergangenen Zeiten.

Palais Jamaï wurde 1879 von den einflussreichen Brüdern Jamaï, Großwesiren des Sultan Moulay Hassan, am besten Platz der Stadt erbaut, mit Panoramablick über ganz Fès. Davon profitiert das Hotel, das 1930 in dem kostbar ausgestatteten Gebäude installiert wurde: Es bietet jedem Gast ein Zimmer mit Ausblick.

Wenn der Besucher denn noch Augen hat für etwas anderes als den Garten, der eines der schönsten Beispiele für den „andalusischen" Stil ist. So heißen alle Anlagen, die sich an der Alhambra orientieren, jenem viel zitierten Juwel maurisch-islamischer Gartenbaukunst. Dabei denken die meisten an das klassische Achsenkreuz, das zur Vierteilung des Gartens führt. Aber es gibt auch ein lineares Schema, das ebenfalls in der Alhambra zu finden ist. Bei der Anlage des *Palais Jamaï* wurden die verschiedensten Formen übernommen, alle der strengen Ordnung der Geometrie verpflichtet.

Sechs ganz unterschiedliche Gartenräume, jeweils von einer eigenen Mauer umgeben, wurden in den Hang gestaffelt. Die höher liegenden haben einen prächtigen *sakkaya* (Wandbrunnen), mit blau-weißem Kachelmosaik, aus dem das Wasser stufenweise abfließt in kleine Kanäle, die weiter unten wiederum ein

Lorsque s'ouvre la porte du Moyen-Âge, on a le choix entre parcourir le *Bab Guissa* vieux de 800 ans dans la plus ancienne *médina* du Maroc ou le *Bab Jamaï* dans l'un des hôtels cinq-étoiles les plus luxueux du monde.

Les deux valent la peine. Choisir d'abord la *médina* fait apprécier d'autant plus ensuite le calme, le confort et surtout l'imposant jardin du *Palais Jamaï*. Choisir au contraire l'hôtel en premier permet de s'exercer l'œil aux raffinements de l'artisanat d'art marocain, qu'on reverra ensuite dans le moindre recoin. Fès, en effet, loge 30 000 *maallem* (maîtres-artisans), qui travaillent encore aujourd'hui exactement comme autrefois.

Le *Palais Jamaï* a été érigé en 1879 par les influents frères Jamaï, grands-vizirs du sultan Moulay Hassan, au plus bel emplacement de la ville, d'où l'on jouit d'une vue panoramique sur tout Fès. L'hôtel, aménagé en 1930 dans les bâtiments richement meublés, a su tirer parti de cette situation et ne propose que des chambres avec vue.

Il est ensuite difficile au visiteur d'avoir des regards pour autre chose que le jardin, qui constitue l'un des plus beaux exemples du style « andalou », nom donné à tous les parcs inspirés de l'Alhambra, joyau cité entre tous de l'art des jardins maure islamique. La plupart évoqueront en premier lieu les axes classiques en croix qui divisent le jardin en quatre, mais le schéma linéaire lui aussi se retrouve à l'Alhambra. L'aménagement du *Palais Jamaï* a adopté les formes les plus diverses, mais toutes soumises à un ordre géométrique strict.

Six jardins individuels très différents les uns des autres et entourés chacun de son propre mur s'échelonnent sur la pente, les plus hauts disposent de somptueuses *sakkaya* (fontaines murales) carrelées de mosaïques bleues et blanches et d'où l'eau s'écoule par paliers dans de petits canaux, qui à leur tour alimentent un bassin situé plus bas. Chaque bassin est doté d'une vasque d'albâtre ou d'une fontaine de marbre à plusieurs degrés, le long desquels l'eau se déverse en cascades. On trouve

From a wall fountain (*sakkaya*), water flows down two steps into a tiled channel.

Aus einem Wandbrunnen (*sakkaya*) fließt das Wasser in zwei Stufen abwärts in einen gefliesten Kanal.

Une fontaine murale (*sakkaya*) fait descendre l'eau en cascade vers un canal carrelé.

Palais Jamaï

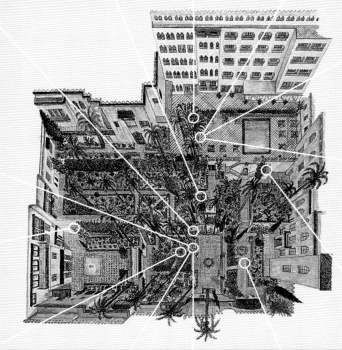

The numerous fountains are ornamented with beautiful mosaics; see detail on the left.

Mit kunstvollem Mosaik sind die zahlreichen Brunnen geschmückt, links ein Detail daraus.

Les innombrables fontaines sont artistement décorées de faïences, voir le détail à gauche.

bowl or a multi-stage marble fountain over which curtains of water cascade down. In addition, there are several large star-shaped fountains in which fine sprays of water spring out from each of their eight corners and fall into the middle of the fountain.

Those who come here from the hustle and bustle of the old city or from a noisy *souk* (market) will immediately grasp the importance of the Andalusian garden. Even when the hotel is full, visitors can find peace in any of the garden areas, in a leafy bower or under a pergola. The scents of mint, sage and rosemary, which have been used to border the flowerbeds, combine with the fragrance of countless roses that flour-

Becken speisen. Jedes Bassin ist mit einer Alabasterschale oder einem mehrstufigen Marmorbrunnen bestückt, über den sich Wasserschleier in Kaskaden ergießen. Es gibt mehrere große Brunnen in Sternform, die zusätzlich zur Mitte auch aus allen acht Ecken Fontänen sprühen.

Wer aus dem Gedränge der Altstadt oder gar von einem lärmenden *souk* (Markt) kommt, wird den Wert des andalusischen Gartens unmittelbar erfassen. Selbst wenn das Hotel voll belegt ist, findet er Ruhe in einem der Gartenräume, in einer hölzernen Laube oder unter einer Pergola. Die Düfte von Minze, Salbei und Rosmarin, die als Einfassungen der Beete dienen, mischen sich mit denen der

également plusieurs grandes fontaines en forme d'étoile, qui, non contentes de faire jaillir des jets d'eau en leur centre, le font également depuis chacun de leurs huit angles.

C'est en sortant de la cohue de la vieille ville ou d'un *souk* (marché) bruyant que le visiteur prend véritablement conscience de la valeur d'un jardin andalou. En effet, même lorsque l'hôtel est plein, il trouvera la tranquillité dans l'un des jardins, sous une tonnelle boisée ou une pergola. Les parfums de la menthe, de la sauge et du romarin plantés en bordure des parterres se mêlent alors à ceux des innombrables roses qui poussent à l'ombre de hauts palmiers. Il ne manque aucune des plan-

ish in the shade of the high palm trees. None of the plants that can be found in the Maghreb are missing; there are cypresses and jacarandas, which stretch their amazingly blue flowers high into the sky, and also pink and white tulip trees in bloom, different shades of bougainvillea, hibiscus, pomegranates, white *calla* lilies and, in front of the tennis court, a small grove of filigreed bamboo.

Here the connoisseur can complete his studies of Islamic garden art without being disturbed, since most tourists prefer to lie around the pool on the large new terrace in front of the five-storey main wing, which was added in the 1970s.

unzähligen Rosen, die im Schatten hoher Palmen gedeihen. Es fehlt keine der Pflanzen, die im Maghreb vorkommen, von Zypressen bis Jacarandas, die ihre erstaunlich blauen Blüten hoch in den Himmel recken, dazu weiß und rosa blühende Tulpenbäume, Bougainvillea in allen Farben, Hibiskus, Granatapfel, *Calla* und vor dem Tennisplatz ein kleiner Hain aus filigranem Bambus.

Ungestört kann der Kenner hier ein Studium in islamischer Gartenkunst absolvieren, denn die meisten Touristen liegen am Pool auf der großen neuen Terrasse vor dem fünfstöckigen Hauptflügel, der in den siebziger Jahren hinzu kam.

tes du Maghreb, des cyprès aux jacarandas, qui dressent leurs étonnan-
tes fleurs bleues haut dans le ciel,
sans oublier les tulipiers aux fleurs
blanches et roses, les bougainvilliers
de toutes les teintes, les hibiscus, les
grenadiers, les *callas* et, devant le
court de tennis, une petite haie de
bambous filigranés.

Le connaisseur peut ici se livrer
à une étude de l'art des jardins
islamique en toute tranquillité, car
la majorité des touristes préfèrent
pour la plupart se prélasser au bord
de la piscine ou sur la grande terrasse devant l'aile principale à cinq
étages ajoutée dans les années
soixante-dix.

Here you can find all the flowers of Morocco, from jacaranda to datura to bougainvillea.
The intensive irrigation makes a jungle-like climate.

Alle Blüten Marokkos finden sich hier, von Jacaranda über Datura bis Bougainvillea.
Durch die intensive Bewässerung entsteht fast Dschungelklima.

Toutes les fleurs du Maroc se trouvent ici, notamment les jacarandas, les daturas et les
bougainvilliers. Grâce à l'arrosage intensif, le climat ici ressemble à celui de la jungle.

Parc Bou Jloud

In the month of May the air fills with soft murmurs. Students stroll along paths holding open books and revising for their forthcoming exams. Full of pride, the inhabitants of Fez then refer to Cordoba, which was the centre of Moorish (Islamic) intellectual life 900 years ago. There too, students and scholars used to meet with each other in the gardens to study, discuss and to contemplate. In Fez, this tradition was adopted in the 14th century, when the royal city was in its heyday with 785 mosques and over 8,000 students. Since Fez lost its political and economic importance, the city has struggled to maintain at very least its reputation as Morocco's intellectual metropolis. And so, traditionally educated middle-class intellectuals watch with affection how the students in May study as they stroll: "no park is more knowledgeable than ours", they like to say.

It is certainly one of the most beautiful. It contains rare one-hundred-year-old trees, such as orange, apricot, peach and olive trees and extremely tall palm trees. Their varied shades of green provide the perfect backdrop for the brightly coloured flowerbeds with their irises, geraniums, roses, cuckoo pints and carnations. The rivers *Oued Zitoun* and *Oued Fez* both supply the different channels, which pour into countless pools and ponds. This swimmers' paradise is extremely popular with schoolboys.

Im Monat Mai ist die Luft erfüllt von leisem Murmeln. Auf allen Wegen wandeln Studenten mit aufgeschlagenen Büchern und wiederholen den Lehrstoff für die bevorstehenden Prüfungen. Voller Stolz verweisen die Bewohner von Fès dann auf Cordoba, das vor 900 Jahren Zentrum des maurisch-islamischen Geisteslebens war. Auch dort trafen sich die Studenten und Gelehrten in den Gärten, zum Lernen, Diskutieren und Kontemplieren. In Fès hat man diese Tradition im 14. Jahrhundert übernommen, als die Königsstadt mit 785 Moscheen und mehr als 8.000 Studenten ihre Blütezeit erlebte. Seit die Stadt ihre politische und wirtschaftliche Bedeutung verloren hat, kämpft Fès darum, wenigstens seinen Ruf als intellektuelle Metropole Marokkos zu erhalten. Und so betrachten die Bildungsbürger voller Wohlgefallen das gelehrige Lustwandeln der Studenten im Mai: „Kein Park ist klüger als unserer", sagen sie gern.

Einer der schönsten ist er auf jeden Fall. Hier stehen seltene hundertjährige Orangenbäume, Aprikosen, Pfirsiche, Oliven und extrem hoch gewachsene Palmen. Ihre Grünabstufungen ergeben den Hintergrund für die leuchtenden Farben der Beete mit Iris, Geranien, Rosen, Aronstab und Nelken. Die beiden Flüsse *Oued Zitoun* und *Oued Fès* speisen die verschiedenen Kanäle, die sich in zahlreiche Becken und Teiche ergießen. Ein Badeparadies, das von Knaben im Schulalter ausgiebig genutzt wird.

Au mois de mai, l'air est empli de murmures légers. Partout, on voit déambuler des étudiants aux livres ouverts, répétant leurs cours pour les examens proches. Les habitants de Fès, pleins de fierté, évoquent alors Cordoue, centre de la vie intellectuelle maure islamique il y a 900 ans, où étudiants et savants se retrouvaient aussi dans les jardins pour y apprendre, y débattre et y observer. La tradition a gagné Fès au 14e siècle, âge d'or de la cité royale aux 785 mosquées et plus de 8 000 étudiants. La ville a perdu depuis toute importance politique et économique, mais elle lutte sans répit pour conserver au moins sa renommée de métropole intellectuelle du Maroc ; et les intellectuels contemplent avec plaisir les flâneries studieuses des étudiants en mai : « notre parc est le plus cultivé de tous », aiment-ils alors à dire.

C'est en tout cas l'un des plus beaux. On y trouve des arbres aussi rares que des orangers centenaires, des abricotiers, des pêchers, des oliviers et des palmiers à la hauteur impressionnante. Ses étagements de verdure forment une toile de fond pour les couleurs lumineuses des massifs d'iris, de géraniums, de roses, d'arums et d'œillets. Les deux rivières *Oued Zitoun* et *Oued Fès* alimentent les canaux qui eux-mêmes se déversent dans de nombreux bassins et étangs, un paradis pour la baignade abondamment exploité par les écoliers.

To ensure the circulation of the air, the historic town wall was built with holes in regular distances, where birds chose to build their nests. The wall is thickly padded with pink bougainvillea.

Die historische Stadtmauer weist in regelmäßigen Abständen Löcher zur Luftzirkulation auf – hier bauen Vögel mit Vorliebe ihre Nester. Pinke Bougainvillea bildet dicke Polster.

Le mur de la cité historique présente des trous d'aération à intervalles réguliers – nids de prédilection des oiseaux. Les bougainvilliers fuchsia forment d'épais coussins.

The arched entrance as well as flower-beds are bordered by small walls. Further into the park there are cosy, overgrown spots where courting couples meet.

Der Eingang ist mit Bogengängen geschmückt, und alle Beete sind mit Mauern gefasst. Erst weiter hinten im Park gibt es verwilderte, lauschige Plätze, wo sich Paare treffen.

L'entrée est ornée d'arcades et toutes les plates-bandes sont entourées de murets. Ce n'est que plus loin dans le parc que se trouvent les coins un peu sauvages – lieux favoris des amoureux.

Each of the city's former rulers has enriched the park by adding elegant pavilions and kiosks. One of them, right next to the historic *La Noria*, houses a café. According to legend, the moaning and groaning of the water wheel are in fact the lamentations of the unfaithful wife of the Sultan, who was stabbed to death on top of the planks by a eunuch.

150 years after their creation, at the end of the 19th century Moulay al-Hassan had the gardens surrounded with high walls and kept them for the women in his palace and his harem. Today the park is open to all.

Jeder Herrscher hat den Park mit eleganten Pavillons und Kiosken angereichert. Einer davon, direkt neben der historischen *Noria,* beherbergt ein Café. Laut Legende stöhnt und ächzt das hölzerne Wasserrad von den Wehklagen der ungetreuen Frau des Sultans, die von einem Eunuchen auf den bereit liegenden Brettern erdolcht wurde.

Mulay al-Hassan ließ die Gärten Ende des 19. Jahrhunderts, 150 Jahre nach ihrer Entstehung, mit hohen Mauern umgeben und reservierte sie für die Frauen seines Palastes und seines Harems. Heute steht der Park jedem offen.

Chaque souverain a enrichi le parc d'élégants pavillons et kiosques, dont l'un, juste à côté de la *noria* historique, abrite aujourd'hui un café. Selon la légende, la roue en bois du moulin à eau gémit et fait entendre les plaintes de l'épouse infidèle du sultan, poignardée par un eunuque sur ces mêmes planches.

Moulay al-Hassan fera entourer le jardin de hauts murs à la fin du 19e siècle, soit 150 ans après sa création, et le réservera aux femmes de son palais et de son harem. Aujourd'hui, le parc est ouvert à tous.

White and cool – that's how the owner wished his villa to be and the dream was fulfilled via tiles and glassblocks.

Weiß und kühl wünschte sich der Besitzer seine Villa – mit Kacheln und Glasbausteinen wurde dieser Traum verwirklicht.

Le propriétaire souhaitait sa maison blanche et fraîche – ce rêve a été réalisé grâce aux carrelages et aux éléments de verre.

The entrance itself looks like a garden: on both sides jacaranda trees stretch their mauve flower panicles over the funnel-shaped red hibiscus blossoms and the sky-blue flowers of the climbing plumbago, whilst beneath them lies an orangey-red carpet of pelargonias. The central strip has been planted with fan palms and mulberry trees. It really is a magnificent avenue!

Five kilometres outside of Fez the Tajmouati family has laid out its own quarter, an extensive and modern version of the historic *dâr* in which a separate apartment was added for each married family member. There are 17 brothers and sisters in this family, and most have settled here. The Tajmouatis' ambition is to employ the best architects and craftsmen of the day. The siblings are locked in genteel rivalry over their houses and gardens. At the moment, most people believe that it is Khalid with his white villa the one that deserves to win.

The house is a modern-style cube. Only the white tiled façade and the inner courtyard with its rectangular frame vaguely recall the faience mosaics and stucco-decorated arches of traditional Moroccan architecture. Of course, as in all pleasure gardens, there is a pavilion too. The small building, covered in white tiles like the main house, towers over a moat.

The garden on the other hand has no traditional elements. A landscape designer from the south of France spent a year laying it out. In the end, he included a mixture of plants from Provence such as laven-

Quartier Tajmouati

Schon die Anfahrt gleicht einem Garten: Zu beiden Seiten erheben Jacarandabäume ihre malvenfarbenen Blütenrispen über die roten Trichter des Hibiscus und die himmelblauen Blüten des klimmenden Plumbago, und unter allem breitet sich der orangerote Teppich der Pelargonien aus. Der Mittelstreifen ist bepflanzt mit Fächerpalmen und Maulbeerbäumen. Wahrlich eine Prachtallee!

Fünf Kilometer außerhalb von Fès hat die Familie Tajmouati sich ihr eigenes Viertel angelegt, eine großzügige und moderne Version des historischen *dâr*, dem für jedes heiratende Familienmitglied eine eigene Wohneinheit hinzugefügt wurde. 17 Geschwister gibt es, die meisten haben sich hier niedergelassen. Der Ehrgeiz der Tajmouatis ist es, die besten Architekten und Handwerker ihrer Zeit zu beschäftigen. Die Geschwister liegen in edlem Wettstreit, wenn es um ihre Häuser und Gärten geht. Im Moment ist es Khalid mit seiner weißen Villa, dem nach Meinung der meisten die Palme gebührt.

Das Haus ist ein konsequent moderner Kubus. Nur die weiß gekachelte Fassade und der mit einem rechteckigen Rahmen angedeutete Innenhof sind ferne Reminiszenzen an die Fayence-Mosaike und Stuck verzierten Arkaden in der traditionellen marokkanischen Baukunst. Und einen Pavillon wie in jedem klassischen Lustgarten gibt es auch. Das kleine Gebäude, weiß gekachelt wie das Haupthaus, thront über einem Wassergraben.

Der Garten dagegen kommt ohne überlieferte Elemente aus. Ein Land-

La montée elle-même semble déjà un jardin : de chaque côté, des jacarandas dressent leurs grappes de fleurs mauves par-dessus les entonnoirs rouges de l'hibiscus et les corolles bleu ciel du plumbago grimpant, le tout sur le tapis déployé des pélargoniums rouge-orange. La bande centrale est plantée de palmiers éventails et de mûriers. En vérité, une allée d'apparat !

À cinq kilomètres de Fès, la famille Tajmouati a aménagé son propre quartier, version moderne et généreuse du *dâr* historique, auquel on ajoutait une unité d'habitation individuelle pour chaque membre de la famille qui se mariait. Aujourd'hui, ils sont 17 frères et sœurs, dont la plupart se sont installés ici. L'orgueil des Tajmouati est de toujours employer les meilleurs architectes et artisans de leur temps, et les frères et sœurs se livrent à une noble rivalité lorsqu'il s'agit de leurs maisons et jardins. Pour le moment, la palme revient, de l'avis de presque tous, à Khalid et à sa villa blanche.

La maison est un cube moderne et rationnel. Seules la façade carrelée de blanc et la cour intérieure marquée par un cadre rectangulaire semblent de lointaines réminiscences des arcades ornées de mosaïques en faïence et de stuc de l'architecture marocaine traditionnelle. Sans oublier le pavillon, élément indispensable de tout jardin d'agrément classique : carrelé de blanc comme la maison, le petit bâtiment trône ici au-dessus d'un fossé rempli d'eau.

Le jardin, en revanche, ne présente plus le moindre élément traditionnel. Un paysagiste du sud de la France s'est employé un an durant à son

Yucca whipplei with its pointed leaves builds the shape of a perfect ball. The curvilinear flowerbed houses many Mediterranean and exotic plants.

Eine perfekte Kugel bildet *Yucca whipplei* mit ihren spitzen Blättern. Die geschwungene Rabatte beherbergt mediterrane und exotische Pflanzen.

Le *yucca whipplei* forme une boule parfaite avec ses feuilles pointues. Le parterre ondulé exhibe ses plantes méditerranéennes et exotiques.

der, rosemary, sage and mimosas, with exotic cacti, agaves and Phymosia. Here and there he placed rare types of grass and bamboo species and enriched the whole garden with the customary bougainvilleas, oleanders and pomegranates.

Nevertheless, the garden offers something special. Several old millstones and mighty boulders introduce an unusual tone that can be found nowhere else in Morocco. The garden as a whole appears astonishingly natural and peaceful due to the prevailing greyish-green backdrop.

schaftsgestalter aus Südfrankreich hat sich ein Jahr lang Zeit genommen, um ihn anzulegen. Schließlich hat er Pflanzen der Provence, wie Lavendel, Rosmarin, Salbei und Mimosen, mit Exoten wie Kakteen, Agaven und Phymosia gemischt, hier und da seltene Gräser und Bambusarten platziert, und das Ganze mit den landesüblichen Bougainvilleen, Oleandern und Granatäpfeln angereichert. Alte Mühlsteine und mächtige Findlinge setzen ungewöhnliche Akzente, die man sonst nirgends in Marokko findet. Insgesamt wirkt der Garten erstaunlich naturnah und ruhig, da die Farbe Graugrün als Hintergrund überwiegt.

aménagement et a finalement mêlé les plantes provençales, comme la lavande, le romarin, la sauge et le mimosa, à d'autres plus exotiques, comme les cactus, l'agave et le phymosia, plaçant ça ou là des herbes ou des espèces de bambou rares et complétant l'ensemble par les indispensables bougainvilliers, lauriers-roses et grenadiers. Plusieurs meules anciennes et autres blocs massifs confèrent au tout des accents plutôt inhabituels, qu'on ne retrouve nulle part ailleurs au Maroc. L'impression générale est celle d'un jardin étonnamment proche de la nature et calme, en raison de la couleur gris-vert qui domine à l'arrière-plan.

An unusual mixture of plants: yucca (left), and from top left to bottom right: *phymosia umbellata*, agave and bougainvillea in the background, gazania, opuntia and *echinocactus grusonii*, pomegranate in flower, aloe and *echinocactus grusonii*.

Ungewöhnliche Pflanzenmischung: Yucca (links), *Phymosia umbellata*, Agave vor Bougainvillea, Gazanie, Opuntie vor Schwiegermuttersitz, gefüllte Granatapfelblüte, Aloe vor Schwiegermuttersessel (von links oben).

Inhabituel mélange de plantes: Yucca (à gauche), *phymosia umbellata*, agave devant un bougainvillier, gazanie, opuntia devant un échinocactus, fleur de grenadier double, aloès devant un échinocactus (en partant d'en haut à gauche).

Meknès –
The City of Olives
Ort der Oliven
Le Lieu des olives

Meknès has always been overshadowed by its shining neighbour, Fez, which most rulers chose to be their capital. Only Moulay Ismail (1672–1727) chose the rural Meknasat az-zeitoun (Meknès of the olives) as the seat of government. The Sultan, who had a passion for splendour and for building, grafted a monumental Ville impériale onto the simple Berber town. The grounds were protected by 40-kilometre long palace walls; up to the médina it was even separated by a triple girdle wall. The whole complex, which was built in two sections, contained incredibly large mosques, fortresses, parade grounds, granaries and mews. The huge palaces had spacious gardens and large pools.

On the outskirts of this city of palaces, rose an isolated complex of buildings comprising the fort, the watchtower and the harem. The massive pisé building was apparently covered in gardens and pavilions on the upper floor and was planned as a place of refuge for the concubines, out of the 500 that the despotic ruler possessed, who had fallen out of favour. Literary sources speak of wonderful grounds, but the present-day guards at Heri al-Mansour claim that the roof gardens were only laid out in the 1960s, whilst in the past the banned ladies of the harem had to take their open-air baths in the scorching sun on shadeless terraces. However, because of the badly dilapidated state of the granary underneath, the controversial roof gardens were closed. What is indisputable is that Meknès was once famous for its abundance of gardens. And one of its peculiarities is the mixture of kitchen and ornamental gardens. Even the grounds of the place used for official and social functions contained vegetable gardens, orangeries and groves of fruit trees. This is related to the history of the city, which lies in one of the most fertile regions of the country between the Middle Atlas and the Atlantic plains and has in many different ways remained connected to its rural surroundings.

Meknès stand immer im Schatten der strahlenden Nachbarin Fès, die von den meisten Herrschern als Hauptstadt gewählt wurde. Nur Moulay Ismail (1672–1727) erkor das bäuerliche Miknâsat al-Zaytûn (Meknès, Ort der Oliven) zum Regierungssitz. Der bau- und prunksüchtige Sultan pfropfte dem schlichten Berberort eine monumentale Ville impériale auf. Die Anlage war von 40 Kilometer langen Palastmauern geschützt, zur médina hin sogar durch einen dreifachen Mauergürtel getrennt. Zu dem Gesamtkomplex, der in zwei Abschnitten realisiert wurde, zählten Moscheen, Festungen und Paradeplätze, Getreidespeicher und Stallungen von unvorstellbarer Größe. Die riesigen Paläste verfügten über weiträumige Gärten und große Wasserbassins. An der Peripherie der Palaststadt erhebt sich ein isolierter Baukomplex, der Fort, Wachturm und Harem in einem war. Der massige Bau aus Stampflehm soll auf der oberen Etage Gärten und Pavillons getragen haben und war als Zufluchtsort für jene der über 500 Konkubinen des despotischen Herrschers gedacht, die in Ungnade gefallen waren. Literarische Quellen sprechen von wunderbaren Anlagen, aber die heutigen Wärter des Hury al-Mansûr behaupten, dass die Dachgärten erst in den 1960er Jahren angelegt wurden, während die verbannten Haremsdamen ihr Luftbad dazumal in glühender Sonne auf unbeschatteten Terrassen nehmen mussten. Wie auch immer, wegen Baufälligkeit der darunter liegenden Kornspeicher sind die umstrittenen Dachgärten geschlossen worden.

Unbestreitbar ist, dass Meknès einst berühmt war für den Reichtum an Gärten. Und eine Besonderheit ist die Vermischung von Nutz- und Ziergärten. Selbst die Repräsentationsanlagen der Paläste enthielten immer auch Gemüsegärten, Orangerien und Obsthaine. Das hängt mit der Geschichte dieser Stadt zusammen, die in einer der fruchtbarsten Regionen zwischen Mittlerem Atlas und den atlantischen Ebenen liegt und auf vielfältige Weise mit ihrer ländlichen Umgebung verbunden geblieben ist.

Meknès a toujours été éclipsée par sa rayonnante voisine Fès, choisie comme capitale par la plupart des souverains du Maroc. Seul Moulay Ismail (1672–1727) fera de la champêtre Miknâsat al-Zaytûn (Meknès, lieu des olives) le siège de son gouvernement. Le sultan amoureux de l'architecture et du faste greffera sur le modeste village berbère une monumentale Ville impériale. l'ensemble était protégé par le rempart du palais long de 40 kilomètres et séparé de la médina par une triple ceinture de murailles. Le complexe dans sa totalité, réalisé en deux étapes, comptait des mosquées, des forteresses et des places de parade, ainsi que des greniers à céréales et des écuries, fantastiques par leur seule étendue. Les immenses palais disposaient par ailleurs de vastes jardins et de grands bassins.

À la périphérie de la ville de palais se dresse un complexe isolé qui rassemblait à l'époque fort, tour de garde et harem. Le bâtiment massif d'argile foulée aurait porté des jardins et des pavillons au dernier étage et était conçu pour servir de refuge à celles des plus de 500 concubines du souverain despotique qui étaient tombées en disgrâce. La littérature parle de merveilles, mais selon les gardiens actuels du Hury al-Mansûr, les jardins en terrasse n'ont été aménagés que dans les années 1960 et les bannies du harem prenaient leur bain d'air sous le soleil brûlant de la terrasse dénuée de toute ombre. Aujourd'hui, et quoi qu'il en soit, les jardins à l'existence contestée sont fermés en raison du délabrement des greniers à grain des étages inférieurs.

Nul ne saurait en revanche contester que Meknès fut autrefois célèbre pour sa richesse en jardins, avec pour particularité le mélange des jardins de rapport et d'agrément. En effet, même les parcs de réception des palais englobaient toujours des jardins potagers, des orangeries et des vergers, tradition qui se rattache à l'histoire de cette ville, située dans l'une des régions les plus fertiles du pays, entre le Moyen-Atlas et la plaine atlantique, et restée liée de multiples manières à son environnement rural.

Hotel Transatlantique

When the day draws to a close, a magical moment begins in Meknès. Before dusk falls, the storks come flying in. Like cut-out figures, their silhouettes stand out against the soft red evening sky when they swoop down in dozens and alight on the *médina* perches which they have been using since time immemorial.

Count yourself lucky if you have a room with a balcony in the *Hôtel Transatlantique*. From this box seat one has a clear view of the impressive medieval panorama and the invasion of storks. Around 7.30 P.M., the cries of the Muezzin rising up in manifold voices conclude the evening spectacle – the guest has arrived in the eternal Maghreb. It was no different in the days of the *Marabout*, whose domed tomb is hidden away amongst oleander and orange trees in the extensive hotel garden.

Only a few guests go that far. Most stay at the large oval pool and look down on the tangle of roofs and narrow alleyways of the *médina* – good preparation for a walk through the fascinating, but exhausting labyrinth with its seductive markets.

After that, the visitor is ready for the garden. It is heralded at the entrance by the palm and orange trees and the bougainvillea. The middle section of the approach is like a brightly coloured flowerbed with *lantana*, snapdragons, sunflowers and hollyhocks.

Some guests are very lucky: a few apartments on the ground floor have their own small gardens,

Wenn der Tag zu Ende geht, beginnt ein magischer Moment in Meknès. Bevor die Dämmerung hereinbricht, kommen die Störche geflogen. Wie Scherenschnitte heben ihre Silhouetten sich ab gegen den sanftroten Abendhimmel, wenn sie sich zu Dutzenden im Sinkflug niederlassen auf ihre von altersher angestammten Plätze in der *médina*.

Wohl dem, der dann ein Zimmer mit Balkon im *Hôtel Transatlantique* hat. Von diesem Logenplatz aus hat er freien Blick auf das beeindruckende mittelalterliche Panorama und die Invasion der Störche. Um 19.30 Uhr beschließen die aus der Altstadt in vielfältigen Stimmen heraufklingenden Rufe der Muezzin das abendliche Schauspiel – der Gast ist angekommen im ewigen Maghreb. So und nicht anders war es schon zu Zeiten des *marabout*, dessen kuppelgekrönte Grabstätte versteckt zwischen Oleander und Orangen im weitläufigen Garten des Hotels liegt.

Nur wenige Gäste dringen bis dorthin vor. Die meisten bleiben am großen ovalen Pool und schauen hinab auf das Dächer- und Gassengewirr der *médina* – eine gute Vorbereitung auf den Gang in das faszinierende, aber anstrengende Labyrinth mit seinen verführerischen Märkten. Danach ist man reif für den Garten. Er kündigt sich schon vor dem Eingang mit Palmen, Orangen und Bougainvillea an. Der Mittelstreifen der Auffahrt ist wie ein buntes Bauernbeet mit Lantana, Löwenmäulchen, Sonnenblumen und Stockrosen bepflanzt.

A treat for every visitor is the sunset over the hostoric *médina* of Meknès: swarms of storks fly in and the Muezzin call from every minaret.

Ein Genuss für jeden Hotelgast ist der Sonnenuntergang über der historischen *médina* von Meknès: Schwärme von Störchen fallen jetzt ein, und von allen Minaretts ruft der Muezzin.

Le coucher de soleil au dessus de la *médina* historique de Meknès est un délice pour chaque visiteur de l'hôtel : des essaims de cigognes arrivent de toute part et de chaque minaret résonne l'appel du muezzin.

Lorsque le jour touche à sa fin, commence un moment magique à Meknès : avant l'arrivée du crépuscule, les cigognes arrivent en volant. Leurs silhouettes se détachent sur le rouge doux du ciel lorsqu'elles descendent et se posent par douzaines aux endroits qu'elles occupent depuis des générations dans la *médina*.

C'est alors une grande chance de bénéficier d'une chambre avec balcon à l'*Hôtel Transatlantique*. Depuis cette loge, on jouit d'une vue parfaitement dégagée sur l'impressionnant paysage médiéval et l'invasion des cigognes. À 19 h 30, les mille voix des muezzins faisant résonner leurs appels de la vieille ville viennent compléter le spectacle vespéral,

l'hôte se sent enfin arrivé au Maghreb éternel. Il en était déjà ainsi et non autrement au temps du *marabout*, dont la sépulture couronnée de coupoles se cache entre les lauriers-roses et les orangers du vaste jardin de l'hôtel.

Seuls peu d'hôtes s'avancent jusque là. La plupart préfèrent rester au bord de la grande piscine ovale,

d'où ils contemplent d'en haut le labyrinthe des toits et des ruelles de la *médina*, une bonne préparation avant d'aller parcourir ce dédale fascinant mais épuisant et ses marchés alléchants. C'est en revenant que l'on est mûr pour le jardin. Il s'annonce dès avant l'entrée avec des palmiers, des orangers et des bougainvilliers. La bande centrale de l'ascension,

clearly separated from the others by luxuriantly flowering bougainvillea hedges, interspersed with small rose and orange trees. Otherwise, the large garden with its olive, citrus and plum trees and neatly laid-out flowerbeds is open to all interested guests.

When they sit down on the bar terrace visitors sense how highly this garden is respected, and above all the use of aromatic plants: every breath of wind blows over new fragrances, clearly intensified by the constantly flowing water from the tiled wall fountain. It is hard to imagine a pleasanter way of passing the time until the evening invasion of storks.

Einige Apartments im Parterre haben jeweils einen eigenen kleinen Garten, von den anderen säuberlich abgetrennt durch üppig blühende Hecken aus Bougainvillea, bepflanzt mit Rosen und Orangenbäumchen. Ansonsten steht der große Garten mit seinen Oliven-, Zitrus- und Pflaumenbäumen und den säuberlich angelegten Blumenbeeten allen Gästen offen. Wie sehr darauf geachtet wurde, vor allem aromatische Pflanzen zu verwenden, spürt der Gast, wenn er sich auf der Terrasse der Bar niederlässt: Jeder Windhauch trägt neue Düfte heran, die von dem ständig fließenden Wasser des gefliesten Wandbrunnens offenbar noch verstärkt werden. Angenehmer kann man die Wartezeit bis zum Abend mit der neuerlichen Invasion der Störche kaum überbrücken.

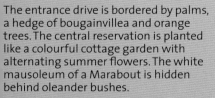

This wall fountain near the bar has seen Charles de Gaulle and Winston Churchill take their drinks, with the sun going down behind the palm trees. The Transatlantique, founded in 1925, was a dwelling place for the allied forces during World War II.

Neben diesem Wandbrunnen bei der Bar haben schon Charles de Gaulle und Winston Churchill ihre Drinks genommen, während die Sonne hinter den Palmen unterging. Das „Transatlantique", 1925 gegründet, diente den Alliierten im Zweiten Weltkrieg als Standort.

Déjà Charles de Gaulle et Winston Churchill ont pris un verre près de la fontaine murale du bar, tandis que le soleil se couchait derrière les palmiers. Le « Transatlantique », fondé en 1925, servait de base aux alliés pendant la deuxième guerre mondiale.

The entrance drive is bordered by palms, a hedge of bougainvillea and orange trees. The central reservation is planted like a colourful cottage garden with alternating summer flowers. The white mausoleum of a Marabout is hidden behind oleander bushes.

Palmen, Bougainvillea und Orangenbäume säumen die Auffahrt zum Hotel. Der Mittelstreifen ist wie ein buntes Beet mit wechselnden Sommerblumen. Versteckt hinter Oleanderbüschen liegt das weiße Mausoleum eines Marabout.

L'allée qui mène à l'hôtel est bordée d'une haie de bougainvilliers, d'orangers et de palmiers. La bande du milieu ressemble à un jardin campagnard avec ses annuelles de toutes les couleurs. Derrière les lauriers-roses, se cache le mausolée du marabout.

ensuite, semble une plate-bande colorée avec ses lantanas, ses petites gueules-de-loup, ses tournesols et ses roses trémières.

Quelques appartements du rez-de-chaussée possèdent leur propre petit jardin, soigneusement séparé des autres par des haies à la floraison exubérante de bougainvilliers et planté de rosiers et de petits orangers. Sinon, le grand jardin, avec ses oliviers, citronniers et pruniers, ainsi que ses parterres de fleurs entretenus avec soin, est ouvert à tous les hôtes. Il faut s'installer à la

terrasse du bar pour réaliser à quel point on a veillé à choisir essentiellement des plantes odorantes : chaque souffle de vent apporte de nouveaux parfums, que l'eau qui coule sans interruption de la fontaine murale carrelée semble encore fortifier. Il est difficile de passer plus agréablement le temps jusqu'au soir et la nouvelle invasion des cigognes.

Haras de Meknès

The perfect lawn and snow-white wooden fences make you believe Haras to be a well-kept English stud farm – but for the palm trees. The main building presents itself with Moorish battlements.

Mit seinen perfekten Rasenflächen und den schneeweißen Holzzäunen könnte man den Haras für ein gepflegtes englisches Gestüt halten – wären da nicht die alles überragenden Palmen. Mit maurischen Zinnen präsentiert sich das Hauptgebäude.

Avec son gazon impeccable et ses clôtures d'une blancheur immaculée, le haras pourrait passer pour une écurie anglaise – si il n'y avait les palmiers surplombant l'ensemble. Le bâtiment principal arbore des créneaux mauresques.

The Arabian stud farm in Meknès is considered to be the most important and most active in the whole of North Africa. The pedigree of their pure thoroughbreds can be traced far back; long before the existence of mare books, the inhabitants of the desert learned the bloodlines by heart and handed them down orally from generation to generation.

According to legend, God created the Arabian horse from a handful of wind. And then he made the following promise to it: "I will fill your masters' hearts with love for you". At least that is the Bedouins' story of how the thoroughbred Arabian horse was born. Indeed, they and their descendants often love the "son of the wind" above all else. Breeding these fiery horses with gentle eyes is the privilege of Kings.

Moulay Ismaïl, who turned Meknès into a royal city, is said to have created stables for 12,000 horses. Many guides claim that the ruler's precious Arabian horses were housed in the enormous *Heri es Souani* granary. But that is a myth. The arched rooms that were as high as a house with their 2 to 3 metres thick walls – which ensured constantly cool

Das Arabergestüt in Meknès gilt als das wichtigste und aktivste in ganz Nordafrika. Der Stammbaum seiner Vollblüter lässt sich weit zurückverfolgen; lange bevor es ein Stutenbuch gab, haben die Wüstenbewohner die Blutlinien auswendig gelernt und mündlich überliefert.

Die Legende will, dass Gott das Araberpferd aus einer Handvoll Wind erschuf. Und dann versprach er diesem Geschöpf: „Ich werde das Herz deines Herrn anfüllen mit Liebe zu dir." So jedenfalls erzählen die Beduinen die Geburt des Vollblut-Arabers. In der Tat lieben sie und ihre Nachkommen den „Sohn des Windes" oft mehr als alles andere. Die Zucht des feurigen Pferdes mit den sanften Augen ist das Privileg der Könige.

Moulay Ismail, der Meknès zur Königsstadt machte, soll Stallungen für 12.000 Pferde angelegt haben. Viele Fremdenführer behaupten, die kostbaren Araber des Herrschers seien in dem gewaltigen Getreidespeicher *Heri es Souani* untergebracht gewesen. Doch das ist eine Mär. Die haushohen überwölbten Räume mit ihren zwei bis drei Meter dicken Mauern, die für gleichmäßig

Le haras de chevaux arabes de Meknès passe pour être le plus important et le plus actif de toute l'Afrique du Nord. L'arbre généalogique de ses pur-sang peut être remonté très loin car, longtemps avant les premiers stud-books, les habitants du désert apprenaient déjà par cœur et transmettaient oralement les lignées de leurs chevaux.

La légende veut que Dieu ait créé le cheval arabe à partir d'une poignée de vent condensée et lui ait ensuite promis : « je remplirai les cœurs de tes maîtres d'amour pour toi ». Ainsi du moins les bédouins racontent-ils la naissance du pur-sang arabe. Et il est vrai que souvent, ils aiment plus que tout le « fils du vent » : l'élevage du cheval fougueux au doux regard est d'ailleurs un privilège de roi.

Moulay Ismail, qui avait fait de Meknès une ville royale, y aurait fait construire des écuries pour 12 000 chevaux. Nombreux sont les guides qui affirment aux étrangers que les précieux arabes du souverain étaient en fait logés dans l'immense grenier à céréales *Heri es Souani*. Rien n'est plus faux, d'autant plus que les pièces voûtées de la hauteur d'une maison, avec leurs murs épais de deux à trois mètres garantissant une

In this royal stud farm, the wild *lantana camara* is made to grow in long hedges. The cypresses, too, are kept in form as small columns.

Das zum Verwildern neigende Wandelröschen *(Lantana camara)* wird im königlichen Gestüt zu meterlangen Hecken erzogen, und auch bei den Zypressen wird darauf geachtet, dass sie kompakte Säulen bleiben.

Les *lantanas*, qui tendent volontiers à retourner à l'état sauvage, forment au haras de longues haies impeccables. De même pour les cyprès, qui sont soignés de près pour former des colonnes compactes.

temperatures – were only used for storing supplies. The Sultan's famous stud was situated farther south in the *Heri al-Mansour,* an 8,000 square metres building, which also had granaries in the basement.

Since 1912, the royal stud farm, *Haras de Meknès,* has been located on the edge of the city, where the French Protectorate masters' cavalry settled. As in the days of the Sultan, care and attention are lavished on these noble creatures and they are kept in surroundings worthy of a palace, with radiant white arches and well-kept lawns framed by extensive flowerbeds. For some inhabitants of Meknès the *Haras* are the most beautiful gardens in the city – and the Arabian horses nature's most beautiful blossoms.

kühle Temperaturen sorgen, waren nur für die Vorratshaltung geeignet. Die berühmte Zucht des Sultans stand dagegen weiter südlich im *Hury al-Mansûr,* einem 8.000 Quadratmeter großen Gebäude, das im Untergeschoss ebenfalls Getreidespeicher beherbergte.

Seit 1912 ist das königliche Gestüt, *Haras de Meknès,* am Rande der Stadt untergebracht, wo die Kavallerie der französischen Protektoratsherren sich niedergelassen hatte. Wie zu des Sultans Zeiten werden die edlen Geschöpfe gehegt und gepflegt und in einer Umgebung gehalten, die einem Palast würdig wäre, mit strahlend weißen Arkaden und gepflegten Rasenflächen, die von reichhaltigen Blumenbeeten gerahmt werden. Es gibt Bewohner von Meknès, die den *Haras* für den schönsten Garten der Stadt halten – und das Araberpferd für die schönste Blüte der Natur.

température fraîche et régulière, n'auraient pu convenir à autre chose qu'aux réserves alimentaires. Le célèbre élevage du sultan était installé plus au sud, dans le *Hury al-Mansûr,* un bâtiment de 8 000 mètres carrés abritant également des greniers à céréales dans ses sous-sols.

Depuis 1912, le haras royal *Haras de Meknès* est situé en bordure de la ville, là où la cavalerie française avait pris ses quartiers pendant le protectorat. Comme au temps du sultan, les nobles créatures sont choyées, soignées et logées dans un environnement digne d'un palais, avec ses arcades d'un blanc lumineux et ses pelouses soigneusement entretenues encadrées de massifs de fleurs variées. Certains habitants de Meknès tiennent le *Haras* pour le plus beau jardin de la ville et le cheval arabe pour la plus belle fleur de la nature.

The Arabs bred in Haras de Meknès are of most noble blood, as can be read on the red labels on their stables which lie in the shade of the arches. This stud farm is considered to be the best in North Africa.

Von edelstem Blut sind die Araber, die im Haras de Meknès gezüchtet werden, das signalisieren rote Schilder an ihren Stallboxen, die im Schatten hinter Bogengängen liegen. Das Gestüt gilt als bestes in Nordafrika.

Le chevaux arabes élevés au haras de Meknès sont du plus pur sang, comme le signalent les petits panneaux rouges sur les portes de leurs boxes, qui se trouvent à l'ombre sous les arcades. Le haras est considéré comme le meilleur d'Afrique du Nord.

The Olive Tree, the sacred tree

Olivenbaum, heiliger Baum

L'Olivier, arbre sacré

I will marry him, even if he is old, because he has olive trees, says the Arab proverb. The olive tree is the most important fruit tree in Morocco, which is one of the three biggest exporters of olives in the world. The tree was long believed to have originated in Asia. Only recently have people begun to believe that the olive tree appeared in Africa after the last Ice Age. In archaeological excavations on the edge of the Sahara, traces of charcoal and pollen were found from an olive tree dating back to 12,000 BC.

In the Bible, the Koran and the old scriptures, the olive tree was the most celebrated, praised and revered tree. Consequently the branch the dove carried back to Noah's Ark in its bill could only have been from an olive tree. It symbolised the pledge of peace, the reawakening of the earth and the first gift of renewed fertility.

In old cultures and religious faiths, the olive tree was associated with the myth of redemption. The olive tree is also a symbol of triumph, although only if the victory has been won without shedding any blood – the winners of the first Olympic Games received crowns made out of olive branches.

Year in, year out, the olive tree remains green. It only changes its leaves once every three years. If properly acclimatised, it can grow to heights of 12–15 metres. The young tree has a smooth, straight trunk, which only becomes knobbly, gnarled, cracked and hollow as it gets older. Its wood is very hard and the branches are a greyish green colour. The leaves can be identified by their long, pointed shape and their colour: dark green on top and a silvery colour on the underside. The top of the leaf is protected from the blazing summer heat by a type of shining

Heirate ihn, auch wenn er alt ist, denn er hat Olivenbäume, lautet ein arabisches Sprichwort. Der Olivenbaum ist der wichtigste Obstbaum Marokkos, das weltweit eines der drei größten Exportländer für Oliven ist. Seinen Ursprung sah man lange in Asien. Erst seit kurzem neigt man zu der Annahme, dass der Olivenbaum nach der letzten Eiszeit in Afrika aufgetaucht ist. Bei archäologischen Ausgrabungen am Rande der Sahara fand man Spuren von Holzkohle und Pollen eines Olivenbaums, die auf 12.000 Jahre vor Christus datiert wurden.

In der Bibel, im Koran und in den alten Schriften war der Olivenbaum der meist besungene, gelobte und verehrte Baum. So konnte der Zweig, den die Taube in ihrem Schnabel nach der Sintflut auf die Arche Noah brachte, nur der eines Olivenbaums sein. Er symbolisierte das Friedenspfand, das Wiedererwachen der Erde und das erste Geschenk neuer Fruchtbarkeit. In allen Kulturen und Glaubensrichtungen wird der Olivenbaum mit dem Mythos der Erlösung in Verbindung gebracht. Der Olivenbaum ist auch Symbol des Triumphs, allerdings nur, wenn der Sieg unblutig errungen wurde – die Sieger der ersten Olympischen Spiele bekamen eine Olivenkrone.

Jahraus, jahrein bleibt der Olivenbaum grün. Er wechselt seine Blätter nur alle drei Jahre. Wenn er sich gut akklimatisiert, erreicht er eine Höhe von zwölf bis fünfzehn Metern. Der junge Baum hat einen glatten, geraden Stamm, der erst mit dem Alter knotig, knorrig, rissig und hohl wird. Sein Holz ist sehr hart. Die Äste haben eine graugrünliche Färbung. Die Blätter erkennt man an ihrer langen,

N'hésite pas à l'épouser, même s'il est vieux, car il possède des oliviers, dit un ancien proverbe arabe. L'olivier est l'arbre fruitier le plus important au Maroc, l'un des trois premiers pays exportateurs d'olives du monde. On a longtemps cru que l'olivier venait d'Asie et ce n'est que depuis peu qu'on penche pour l'hypothèse selon laquelle il serait apparu en Afrique après la dernière période glaciaire. Des fouilles archéologiques à la limite du Sahara ont permis de découvrir des traces de charbon de bois et du pollen d'un olivier, datés de 12 000 ans avant Jésus-Christ.

Dans la Bible, le Coran et les textes anciens, l'olivier est l'arbre le plus cité, le plus loué et le plus vénéré. Le rameau porté par la colombe dans son bec jusqu'à l'arche de Noé après le déluge ne pouvait donc être qu'un rameau d'olivier. Il représentait alors un gage de paix, le réveil de la terre et le premier présent de sa fertilité renouvelée. Toutes les cultures et religions associent l'olivier au mythe de la Rédemption. Il peut aussi symboliser le triomphe, mais uniquement lorsque la victoire a été remportée sans effusion de sang ; les vainqueurs des premiers Jeux Olympiques se voyaient remettre une couronne d'olivier.

Bon an, mal an, l'olivier reste toujours vert. Il ne renouvelle ses feuilles que tous les trois ans. Lorsqu'il est bien acclimaté, il peut atteindre une hauteur de douze à quinze mètres. Les jeunes arbres possèdent un tronc lisse et droit, qui ne devient qu'avec l'âge noueux, rugueux, fendillé et creux. Son bois est très dur. Les branches ont une teinte gris-vert. Les feuilles se reconnaissent à leur forme longue et pointue et à leur couleur, vert foncé sur le dessus et argentée sur

insulating layer through which no moisture can escape. The tree's flowering period at the start of May is extremly short – only lasting 8 days – but during this short time it attracts veritable squadrons of insects.

The olive tree only bears fruit after seven years, after which its production rises steadily until it is 35 years old. After that the tree will regularly produce olives until the grand old age of 150. It is no wonder that this tree is the symbol of a settled way of life, peace and bourgeois order – hence, only a nation that commits itself to these virtues can enjoy the harvests.

 The Valley of the River Drâa, the longest river in Morocco, was once famous as the olive valley – nowadays not one single olive tree remains. Several consecutive years of drought and the increasing need for firewood have led to the disappearance of these beautiful trees.

The olive consists of the peel, the pulp and a hard stone, which contains the oil-bearing seed. When ripe, the pulp contains 65% water, 25% fat and 1% cellulose. The stone hardens during the first two weeks of August and only after that does the pulp form. During its growth, which lasts for six months, the olive turns dark green or black. In the intermediate stages, the fruit is light green, whitish, reddish, violet or brown.

Every year, the harvest of edible olives takes place at the end of September whilst olives destined for the production of oil are picked from December to February. The bitter taste of the edible olives is removed by soaking them for six weeks in a bath of water that is changed daily.

The instruments used in the pressing process have changed over the centuries, but the production itself has not. Today, as in days gone by, the olives are thoroughly washed and any leaves removed, as they would make the oil taste bitter. Then the fruit is ground using heavy grinding-stones. Extra virgin oil, extracted from the first cold pressing, provides the best quality oil (1% acidity). In Morocco, the most important oil producers are found in the regions around Fez, Meknès and Marrakech.

spitzen Form und an ihrer Farbe, auf der Oberseite dunkelgrün, auf der Unterseite silbrig. Die Oberseite schützt eine Art glänzende Isolierschicht, durch die keine Feuchtigkeit nach außen entweichen kann, gegen die sommerliche Sonnenglut. Die Blütezeit Anfang Mai ist kurz, sie dauert nur acht Tage, zieht während dieser kurzen Zeit aber wahre Insektengeschwader an.

Früchte trägt er erst nach sieben Jahren, erhöht dann seine Produktion bis zum Alter von 35 Jahren, danach trägt er regelmäßig bis zum stolzen Alter von 150 Jahren. Kein Wunder, dass er als Symbol für Sesshaftigkeit, Frieden und bürgerliche Ordnung steht – nur ein Volk, das sich diesen Tugenden verschreibt, kommt in den Genuss der Ernten. Das Tal des Drâa, des längsten Flusses Marokkos, war einst berühmt als das Tal der Oliven – heute wächst dort keine einzige mehr. Mehrere Jahre der Trockenheit hintereinander und der zunehmende Bedarf an Brennholz haben zum Verlust der schönen Bäume geführt.

Die Olive besteht aus Fruchtschale, Fruchtfleisch und einem harten Kern, der die das Öl enthaltende Mandel umschließt. Reif enthält das Fruchtfleisch 65% Wasser, 25% Fett und 1% Zellulose. Der Kern erhärtet sich in der ersten Augusthälfte, erst danach bildet sich das Fruchtfleisch. Während des Wachstums, das sechs Monate dauert, färbt sich die Olive dunkelgrün oder schwarz. In den Zwischenstadien ist sie hellgrün, weißlich, rötlich, violett oder braun. Die Ernte der Speiseoliven findet Ende September statt, Öl-Oliven erntet man ab Dezember und bis Ende Februar. Den bitteren Geschmack der Speiseoliven entzieht ein sechs Wochen langes Bad in täglich gewechseltem Wasser.

Die Instrumente der Pressung haben sich über die Jahrhunderte geändert, nicht aber die eigentliche Herstellung. Damals wie heute wäscht man die Oliven gründlich und entfernt alle von der Ernte übrig gebliebenen Blätter, die das Öl bitter machen würden. Dann werden die Früchte ganz von schweren Mahlsteinen zermahlen. Das Olio Extra Vergine, die erste Kaltpressung, ergibt die beste Qualität (1% Säure). In Marokko befinden sich die wichtigsten Öl-Herstellungen bei Fès, Meknès und Marrakesch.

le dessous. La face supérieure est protégée de l'ardeur du soleil estival par une sorte de couche isolante luisante, qui empêche toute humidité de s'échapper vers l'extérieur. La courte floraison a lieu début mai et ne dépasse pas, en général, huit jours, mais attire alors de véritables escadrons d'insectes.

L'olivier ne donne des fruits qu'après sept ans, il augmente alors sa production jusqu'à l'âge de 35 ans, puis continue de donner régulièrement jusqu'à l'âge canonique de 150 ans. Rien d'étonnant donc à ce qu'il symbolise la sédentarité, la paix et l'ordre social. Seul un peuple qui s'adonne à ces vertus peut espérer profiter des récoltes. La vallée du Drâa, le plus long fleuve du Maroc, était autrefois connue comme étant la vallée des olives. Plus aucun olivier n'y pousse encore aujourd'hui : plusieurs années successives de sécheresse et le besoin croissant en bois de chauffage ont suscité la perte de magnifiques arbres.

L'olive se compose d'une peau, de chair et d'un noyau dur qui entoure l'amande contenant l'huile. Lorsqu'elle est mûre, la chair contient 65 % d'eau, 25 % de graisse et 1 % de cellulose. Le noyau durcit pendant la première moitié du mois d'août et la chair ne se forme qu'ensuite. Pendant sa croissance, qui dure six mois, l'olive prend une teinte vert foncé ou noire. Aux étapes intermédiaires de développement, elle peut être vert clair, blanchâtre, rougeâtre, violette ou brune. La récolte des olives de table a lieu fin septembre, celle des olives à huile à partir de décembre jusqu'à fin février. Le goût amer des olives disparaît au cours d'un bain de six semaines dans de l'eau changée quotidiennement.

Les outils pour presser ont changé au cours des siècles, mais pas la méthode de production ellemême. Aujourd'hui comme hier, on commence par laver soigneusement les olives et retirer toutes les feuilles restées de la récolte, qui rendraient sinon l'huile amère. Les fruits sont ensuite broyés entiers par de lourdes meules de pierre. L'huile extra vierge, la première pression à froid, donne la meilleure qualité (1 % d'acidité). Au Maroc, les plus grandes fabriques d'huile sont situées près de Fès, de Meknès et de Marrakech.

The youngest of the four royal cities – the others being Marrakech, Fez and Meknès – is without a doubt also the most elegant. Even the médina of Rabat is clear and clean – its narrow streets as sparkling white as the villas in the new town. Rabat is a prosperous and noble city, with administrative and diplomatic districts and the largest university in the country. Its temperate climate appears to permit no excesses; there is hardly any nightlife here.

And yet, this city was once notorious as a pirate's nest. Its strategic, prominent position on the Bou Regreg estuary leading out to the Atlantic predestined Rabat as a starting-point for all kinds of campaigns. It was first used by orthodox Islamic religious warriors. The ribat (fortified monastery) they built in the 10th century was later converted into a fortress by the Almohad rulers and extended to make a palace. The pirates first arrived at the beginning of the 17th century. Then Andalusian refugees from Rabat and the neighbouring town of Salé got together and founded an independent republic – and began the lucrative piracy. This dubious heyday lasted a good 200 years. Then the harbour shipping department, and above all the advent of the steamers, put an end to these lucrative wheelings and dealings. Rabat sank into oblivion.

This changed in 1912 when, under the French Protectorate, the city was chosen as the country's administrative seat. And, when Morocco regained its independence in 1956, Mohammed V turned it into a royal city once again. Rabat had already been a royal city during the 12th and 18th centuries, although only for short periods. In the meantime, however, it had become the "most royal" of the four royal cities.

Die jüngste der vier Königsstädte – die anderen sind Marrakesch, Fès und Meknès – ist ohne Zweifel die eleganteste. Selbst die médina von Rabat ist übersichtlich und sauber, ihre Gassen sind so strahlend weiß wie die Villen der Neustadt. Rabat ist eine wohlhabende und gediegene Stadt, mit Verwaltungs- und Diplomatenviertel und der größten Universität des Landes. Sein gemäßigtes Klima scheint keine Exzesse zuzulassen, Nachtleben findet kaum statt.

Und doch war diese Stadt einst berühmt-berüchtigt als Piratennest. Ihre strategisch hervorragende Lage an der Mündung des Bou Regreg in den Atlantik prädestinierte sie als Ausgangspunkt für Feldzüge aller Art. Das nutzten zuerst orthodoxe islamische Glaubenskrieger. Die von ihnen Ende des 10. Jahrhunderts errichtete ribat (befestigte Klosterburg) wurde später von den Almohaden-Herrschern als Festung ausgebaut und um einen Palast erweitert.

Die Piraten kamen erst Anfang des 17. Jahrhunderts. Damals taten sich andalusische Flüchtlinge aus Rabat und der Nachbarstadt Salé zusammen, gründeten eine unabhängige Republik – und begannen mit der einträglichen Piraterie. Gut 200 Jahre hielt diese zweifelhafte Blütezeit an. Dann setzte das Versanden des Hafens, vor allem aber das Aufkommen der Dampfschiffe dem lukrativen Treiben ein Ende. Rabat versank in Bedeutungslosigkeit.

Das änderte sich 1912, als die Stadt unter französischem Protektorat zum Verwaltungssitz des Landes wurde. Und bei der Unabhängigkeit Marokkos 1956 machte Mohammed V. sie wieder zur Königsstadt, was Rabat auch im 12. und 18. Jahrhundert schon war, jedesmal nur für kurze Zeit. Mittlerweile jedoch hat sie sich zur „königlichsten" der vier Königsstädte entwickelt.

La plus jeune des quatre villes royales – les autres étant Marrakech,
Fès et Meknès – est incontestablement la plus élégante. À Rabat, même
la médina est claire et propre, avec ses ruelles tout aussi blanches et
éclatantes que les villas de la ville nouvelle. Rabat est en effet une ville
aisée et distinguée possédant un quartier administratif, un quartier
diplomatique et la plus importante université du pays. Son climat
tempéré ne semble donner lieu à aucun excès et la vie nocturne y est
quasiment inexistante.

Et pourtant, cette ville a autrefois eu la réputation d'être un nid de
pirates mal famé. Sa situation stratégiquement exceptionnelle à l'embouchure du Bou Regreg dans l'Atlantique l'a de tous temps prédestinée
pour les campagnes de tous les types. Les premiers à l'exploiter seront
les guerriers islamiques orthodoxes. Le ribat (château-fort-couvent
fortifié) qu'ils érigent à la fin du 10e siècle sera plus tard transformé en
forteresse par les souverains Almohades et agrandi d'un palais.

Les pirates n'arrivent qu'au début du 17e siècle. Des réfugiés andalous
de Rabat et de la ville voisine de Salé s'étaient associés pour fonder une
république indépendante et commencer une entreprise de piraterie
des plus rentables. Cette prospérité douteuse durera près de 200 ans,
puis l'ensablement du port, mais surtout l'arrivée des bateaux à vapeur,
mettront fin à cette activité lucrative. Rabat sombrera alors dans
l'insignifiance.

Les choses changent en 1912 lorsque, sous le protectorat français, la
ville devient capitale administrative du pays. Plus tard, en 1956, lors de
l'indépendance du Maroc, Mohammed V lui rend le titre de ville royale,
qu'elle avait déjà possédé aux 12e et 18e siècles, mais à chaque fois seulement pour de courtes périodes. Aujourd'hui, la ville est devenue « la plus
royale » des quatre villes royales.

Rabat –
Royal Capital
Königliche
Hauptstadt
Capitale royale

Casbah des Oudaïa

The *Casbah des Oudaïa* was once an impregnable fortress, emerging from *er ribat* (the fort). The name Rabat is a shortened and corrupted form of *Ribat al-Fath*, literally 'fort of conquest'. The Kasbah is named after the Oudaïa, a tribe of bellicose Arab nomads who devotedly served the former Sultans. Most of the fortress' 2.5-metres thick and 8–10 metres high walls date back to the 12th century. Only the walls of the Andalusian garden were built 500 years later. Originally, they surrounded the *mechouar* (royal parade ground), where once the tyrant Moulay Ismaïl's guard exercised before he led them into bloody battles.

At the beginning of the 20th century, in the palace courtyard, which was surrounded by arches and decorated with a shallow marble fountain basin in the centre, a *riyad* was laid out in the best Moroccan tradition. A five-storey angular tower, which now houses a library, rose above this courtyard. It is integrated into the four wings of the royal complex, which, in addition to the living quarters, also contained a *hammam* and a small mosque. In the large salon that was formerly used for official receptions, there is now a museum of old Moroccan craftwork.

From here, the visitor can go across the bridges over the moats in the garden. Moreover, one immediately comes upon a curiosity: a small *noria* (water wheel) which is turned by a donkey in order to scoop up water. The great wealth of flowers in the *riyad* is simply captivating. The formally structured flowerbeds are bordered with red hibiscus hedges

Einst war die *Casbah des Oudaïa* eine uneinnehmbare Festung, hervorgegangen aus *er ribat*, der Klosterburg, der Rabat seinen Namen verdankt. Die Kasbah ist nach dem Stamm der Oudaïa benannt, kriegerischen arabischen Nomaden, die den frühen Sultanen ergeben dienten. Die 2,50 Meter dicken und acht bis zehn Meter hohen Wälle der Festung stammen zum größten Teil aus dem 12. Jahrhundert. Nur die Mauern des andalusischen Gartens entstanden erst 500 Jahre später. Ursprünglich umschlossen sie den *mechouar* (großer Ehrenhof), wo einst die Garde des Despoten Moulay Ismaïl exerzierte, bevor sie in ihre blutigen Schlachten zog.

Anfang des 20. Jahrhunderts wurde in dem von Arkaden umgebenen Palasthof, dessen Mitte ein flaches Brunnenbecken aus Marmor ziert, ein *Riad* in bester marokkanischer Tradition angelegt. Überragt wird er von einem fünfstöckigen eckigen Turm, der jetzt eine Bibliothek beherbergt. Er ist integriert in die vier Flügel der fürstlichen Anlage, die außer Wohngebäuden auch ein *hammam* und eine kleine Moschee enthält. Im großen Salon, der früher offiziellen Empfängen diente, befindet sich heute ein Museum für altes marokkanisches Kunsthandwerk.

Von hier aus kann man die Brücke über den Wassergraben in den Garten nehmen und stößt sofort auf eine Sehenswürdigkeit: eine kleine *noria*, die zum Wasser schöpfen von einem Esel bewegt wurde. Der *Riad* nimmt durch seinen Blütenreichtum gefangen. Die streng gegliederten

La *Casbah des Oudaïa* fut autrefois une forteresse imprenable sous l'autorité du *er ribat*, le château-fort-couvent auquel Rabat doit son nom. La Casbah, quant à elle, a été nommée d'après la tribu des Oudaïa, nomades arabes guerriers et serviteurs dévoués des anciens sultans. Les remparts de la forteresse, épais de 2,50 mètres et hauts de huit à dix mètres, ont été pour la plupart érigés au 12e siècle. Seuls les murs du jardin andalou sont 500 ans plus jeunes. Ils entouraient à l'origine le *mechouar* (grande cour d'honneur), où la garde du despote Moulay Ismaïl avait coutume de faire l'exercice avant de partir pour ses campagnes sanglantes.

Au début du 20e siècle, un *riad* a été aménagé dans la meilleure tradition marocaine dans la cour du palais entourée d'arcades et ornée en son centre d'un bassin plat en marbre. Il est surplombé par une tour angulaire à cinq étages, qui abrite aujourd'hui une bibliothèque et est intégrée aux quatre ailes du domaine princier, lequel, outre les bâtiments d'habitation, comprend aussi un *hammam* et une petite mosquée. Le grand salon qui servait autrefois aux réceptions officielles présente désormais un musée d'ancien artisanat d'art marocain.

De là, on peut emprunter le pont qui enjambe le fossé rempli d'eau du jardin, pour se trouver aussitôt face à une curiosité : une petite *noria* actionnée par un âne où puiser de l'eau. Le *riad*, lui, captive par la richesse de sa flore. Les parterres rigoureusement délimités sont enchâssés dans des haies d'hibiscus aux fleurs

The five-storey tower that the sultan used for his guests offers the best view over the famous garden.

Der fünfstöckige Turm, den der Sultan einst gern Gästen überließ, bietet den besten Blick über den Garten.

C'est de la tourelle à cinq étages, que le sultan cédait autrefois à ses invités, que l'on a la meilleure vue du célèbre jardin.

The great wealth of flowers and blossoming trees in the "Casbah des Oudaïa" is unusual for a parc open to the public.

Für einen öffentlichen Park befinden sich in der „Casbah des Oudaïa" ungewöhnlich viele blühende Bäume und Blumen.

La « Casbah des Oudaïa » offre une multitude de fleurs et d'arbres fleuris, fait surprenant dans un jardin public.

in bloom. Some are very elegantly planted with white carnations, white agapanthus and ferns. Many are closely packed with marguerites; those in the shade are white and those pampered by the sun an orangey-yellow colour. Yellow irises are common, but so are the simple pink and white busy lizzies. The datura with their enormous white

or yellow trumpet-shaped flowers are real showpieces, as are the magnificent morning glories with their equally large blue flowers.

Date palms, orange trees and oleanders, which grow as high as trees in this area, provide shade. The long arboured walkway is covered with grape vines and is a favourite meeting place for courting couples.

Beete sind eingefasst mit rot blühenden Hibiskus-Hecken. Manche
wurden ganz elegant nur mit weißen Nelken, blauem Agapanthus
und Farn bepflanzt. Viele sind dicht
bei dicht mit Margeriten bestückt,
wobei jene, die im Schatten stehen,
weiß sind, während die von der
Sonne verwöhnten gelb-orange
leuchten. Gelbe Schwertlilien sind

häufig zu sehen, aber auch schlichte
Fleißige Lieschen in Weiß und Rosa.
Zu echten Schaustücken entwickeln
sich die ungehindert wuchernden
Datura mit riesigen weißen oder gel-
ben Blütentrompeten und auch die
Prachtwinden mit ebenso großen
blauen Blüten.

    Schatten spenden Dattelpalmen,
Orangen und Oleander, der hier

rouges. Certains ont été fort élé-
gamment plantés exclusivement
d'œillets blancs, d'agapanthes bleus
et de fougères. Beaucoup sont
peuplés de marguerites en rangs
serrés, blanches pour celles qui sont
à l'ombre et d'un jaune-orange lumineux pour celles qui bénéficient
des rayons solaires. On trouve également de nombreux iris jaunes, mais

aussi de modestes impatientes blanches et roses. Quant aux daturas qui
prolifèrent en toute liberté, ils forment de véritables spectacles à eux
seuls, avec leurs énormes corolles
en trompettes blanches ou jaunes,
aussi gigantesques que les fleurs
bleues des somptueux volubilis.

    L'ombre est dispensée par des
palmiers dattiers, des orangers et

The dome-shaped pavilion, which rises above a spring, is only a few steps away.

After a walk through the garden, the visitor feels strong enough for a drink in the *Café Maure*, which, with its sweeping view over the Kasbah, the estuary and across to Rabat's sister town, Salé, has always been regarded as a favourite meeting place for shady characters.

Baumhöhe erreicht. Ein langer Laubengang ist mit Wein überrankt und dient Liebespaaren als bevorzugter Treffpunkt. Von dort sind es nur wenige Schritte zum kuppelförmigen Pavillon, der sich über einer Quelle erhebt.

Nach einem Gang durch den Garten fühlt sich jeder stark genug für einen Drink im *Café Maure*, das mit seinem weitreichenden Blick über die Kasbah und die Flussmündung hinweg bis hinüber zur Schwesterstadt Salé immer schon Treffpunkt für zwielichtige Gestalten gewesen sein soll ...

des lauriers-roses, qui atteignent ici la hauteur d'arbres. Une longue charmille envahie par la vigne est le lieu de rendez-vous favori des couples d'amoureux, à quelques pas seulement du pavillon à coupole qui se dresse au-dessus d'une source.

Après un tour de jardin, le visiteur se sent assez de force pour une boisson au *Café Maure* qui, avec sa large vue sur la Casbah et l'embouchure du fleuve jusqu'à la ville-jumelle de Salé, est depuis toujours le lieu de rencontre de personnages incertains ...

Euphorbia (left), poinsettia, *agapanthus*, and *ipomoea* are in spectacular bloom. Papyrus proliferates in the water basin next to the reception hall.

Euphorbie (links), Poinsettie, Agapanthus und Ipomea blühen hier ungewöhnlich prachtvoll. Papyrus wuchert im Wasserbecken vor dem Empfangsgebäude.

Euphorbe (à gauche), poinsettie, agapanthe et ipomée offrent ici une floraison d'une splendeur surprenante. Le bassin d'eau devant le bâtiment de l'entrée est envahi de papyrus.

La Tour Hassan

The unfinished Tower of Hassan is considered to be Morocco's most important monument. This sumptuously decorated building, visible from miles away, is a reminder that at the end of the 12th century Rabat is said to have been a world-class metropolis. *La Tour Hassan* is the uncompleted minaret of the Great Hassan Mosque, destined to be the second largest in the world, but was never finished.

The hotel named after *La Tour Hassan* lies in the centre of Rabat, not far from the landmark. It too claims to be a world achievement. In addition to all the facilities that are to be expected from an international hotel – from fitness centre to office service – in Morocco it is above all the garden that creates a sense of luxury.

Directly in front of the lobby there is a sunken patio, enclosed by high ochre-coloured walls decorated with arches. A marble fountain, surrounded by elaborate artistically coloured mosaics lays emphasis on the centre. From there the path leads towards the garden via a two-part flight of steps, which surrounds a filigreed tile pattern wall fountain. Fountains and water displays constitute the most important design elements in any *riyad*. There are several fountains, the most beautiful of which is an octagonal mosaic star, which lies in the middle of the water channel that cuts the grounds in

Der unvollendete Hassanturm gilt als das bedeutendste Monument Marokkos. Das weithin sichtbare, reich verzierte Bauwerk erinnert daran, dass Rabat schon Ende des 12. Jahrhunderts eine Metropole von Weltrang sein sollte. *La Tour Hassan* ist das nicht fertig gestellte Minarett einer Moschee, die als zweitgrößte der Erde geplant war, aber nie fertig gestellt wurde.

Das nach *La Tour Hassan* benannte Hotel liegt nicht weit von dem Wahrzeichen entfernt mitten im Zentrum. Auch hier besteht der Anspruch, zur Weltspitze zu gehören. Neben allen Einrichtungen, die man von einem internationalen Hotel heute erwartet – vom Fitnesscenter bis zum Büroservice –, ist es vor allem der Garten, der ein Gefühl für Luxus in Marokko vermittelt.

Direkt vor der Lobby liegt ein abgesenkter Patio, umgeben von hohen ockerfarbenen Mauern mit Arkadenverzierung. Seine Mitte betont ein Marmorbrunnen, umgeben von kunstvollem farbigem Mosaik. Von da aus führt der Weg in den Garten über eine zweigeteilte Treppe, die einen Wandbrunnen vor filigranem Fliesen-Muster umschließt. Wasserspiele sind wie in jedem *Riad* das wichtigste Gestaltungselement. Es gibt mehrere Brunnen, der schönste, ein achteckiger Stern aus Mosaik, liegt mitten im Wasserkanal, der die Anlage in zwei Hälften unterteilt, die wiederum von blau-weiß gekachel-

La tour Hassan inachevée passe pour être le monument le plus significatif du Maroc. L'édifice visible de loin et richement orné rappelle que Rabat était dès la fin du 12e siècle une métropole de rang mondial. *La Tour Hassan* est le minaret inachevé d'une mosquée prévue pour être la deuxième plus grande du monde, mais jamais terminée.

L'hôtel du même nom, *La Tour Hassan*, n'est guère éloigné de l'emblème de la ville, en plein centre. Lui aussi a l'ambition d'appartenir à l'élite mondiale. Outre tous les services qu'un hôtel international se

doit aujourd'hui de proposer – du centre de remise en forme aux services de bureau –, c'est surtout le jardin qui, au Maroc, inspire un sentiment de luxe.

Juste devant le hall, un patio surbaissé est entouré de hauts murs ocre au décor d'arcades. Son centre est occupé par une fontaine de marbre entourée de superbes mosaïques colorées. Le chemin y mène au jardin par un escalier bipartite, qui ceinture une fontaine murale recouvrant des carreaux aux motifs filigranés. Comme dans tout *riad,* les jeux d'eau constituent l'élément principal du décor et les fontaines sont nombreuses. La plus belle, une étoile à huit branches de mosaïque, est placée au milieu du canal qui coupe le domaine en deux moitiés, elles-mêmes à leur tour divisées par des chemins carrelés de bleu et de blanc en « jardinets ». Ces derniers

The garden courtyard, ornamented with precious tiles and marble fountains, is held in the traditional style.

Traditioneller Gestaltung verpflichtet ist der mit wertvollen Kacheln und Marmorbrunnen dekorierte Gartenhof.

Le jardin dans la cour, décoré avec des carrelages précieux et des vasques de marbre, doit beaucoup à l'exemple traditionnel.

Every detail, from wall fountain to amphora, adds to the over-all impression of the garden.

Jedes Detail, vom Wandbrunnen bis zur Amphore, trägt zum geschlossenen Gesamteindruck des Gartens bei.

Chaque détail, de la fontaine murale à l'amphore, participe à l'impression d'ensemble du jardin.

two halves; both sections are in turn subdivided into "small gardens" by blue and white tiled paths. In quite an unusual way they consist of lawns containing geometrically-shaped flowerbeds.

The garden is pleasantly shaded by high palm trees, which were already here when the garden was laid out by a woman in 1965. She also planted the now mighty araucarias, which draw attention to themselves by their remarkable height. The large square pool is fairly new and was added to the grounds in 1998.

ten Wegen in „Gärtchen" unterteilt werden. Diese bestehen – ganz ungewöhnlich – aus Rasen, in den Blumenbeete in geometrischen Formen eingelassen wurden.

Der Garten wird angenehm beschattet von hohen Palmen, die schon hier standen, als er 1965 von

einer Frau angelegt wurde. Sie ließ auch jene mittlerweile mächtige Araukarie pflanzen, die mit ihrem bemerkenswerten Wuchs alle Aufmerksamkeit auf sich zieht. Der große quadratische Pool dagegen wurde erst 1998 in die Anlage eingefügt.

se composent – étrangement – de pelouses où sont enchâssés des massifs floraux aux formes géométriques.

Le jardin est agréablement ombragé par de hauts palmiers, qui étaient déjà là lors de sa création en 1965 par une femme paysagiste.

Elle a également fait planter l'araucaria, devenu depuis énorme, et dont la croissance étonnante attire l'attention de tous. La grande piscine carrée, elle, n'a été ajoutée qu'en 1998.

Paris Fleurs

A colourful variety like an agricultural show is typical for the "Marché aux Fleurs" in Rabat – but the flowers are sold only wrapped in cellophane.

Bunte Vielfalt wie auf einem Bauernmarkt kennzeichnet den „Marché aux Fleurs" in Rabat – aber verkauft werden die Blumen nur in Cellophan.

Même si la multitude de fleurs colorées du « Marché aux Fleurs » de Rabat se présente comme sur un marché campagnard, elles ne sont vendues que sous cellophane.

If you buy a bunch of flowers in the large flower market on Moulay Hassan Square, do not expect it to be tied up and packaged for you while you wait. At most stalls you can find ready-made bunches, wrapped in thick cellophane, as is customary in Morocco. On rare occasions a seller at a stall might allow you to choose the type or colours of flowers you want from their merchandise; and you can then put the bouquet together by yourself. In any case, cut flowers always stand in big clay vessels, which we would be more likely to use as outer pots.

Most stalls in the market obtain their goods from the surrounding area. Or, like Lahsen Lafkik, whose stand is called *Paris Fleurs,* they cultivate their own flowers. His market garden is located in a rural outlying district of Salé, which lies on the opposite bank of the river Bou Regreg from Rabat. A farmer's son, Lafkik was taught to work with flowers by an uncle. In 1990 he was able to acquire the 10-hectare plot of land in Salé, half of which he uses for fruit and vegetables whilst the other is reserved for flowers.

The road that leads there is lined with oleander bushes. It leads to enormous fields, on which blue asters, multicoloured gladioli, delicate baby's breath and all shades of blue larkspur grow. The ground appears to be pure sand, and, without the ditches between the fields, it is unlikely that anything would ever prosper here. Hibiscus and ferns are covered with plastic tarpaulins – protection from the sun in Morocco is as important as protection from frost in our latitudes.

An avenue leads to the greenhouses, lined on the right with avocados and on the left with bamboo. Hortensias and fuchsias are grown under cover, as well as foliage plants such as aralias, palm trees and rubber plants. Visitors can buy freshly cut flowers in a bamboo hut here.

Wer auf dem großen Blumenmarkt am Platz Moulay Hassan im Zentrum von Rabat einen Strauß ersteht, muss auf das Binden und Verpacken nicht warten. An den meisten Ständen stehen fertige Blumengebinde bereit, die nach Landessitte von üppigen Cellophan-Hüllen umgeben sind. Ganz selten bietet ein Händler seine blühende Ware nach Sorten oder Farben sortiert an, sodass der Käufer sich sein Bukett selber zusammen stellen kann. Auf jeden Fall stehen die Schnittblumen immer in bauchigen Tongefäßen, die man bei uns eher als Übertöpfe verwenden würde.

Die meisten Markthändler beziehen ihre Ware aus dem nahen Umland. Oder sie bauen ihre Blumen selbst an, wie Lahsen Lafkik, der seinen Stand *Paris Fleurs* nennt. Sein Gartenbaubetrieb liegt in einem ländlichen Randgebiet von Salé, das Rabat am anderen Ufer des Bou Regreg gegenüberliegt. Bauernsohn Lafkik hat bei einem Onkel die Arbeit mit den Blumen erlernt. 1990 konnte er das zehn Hektar große Grundstück in Salé erwerben, die Hälfte davon dient dem Anbau von Obst und Gemüse, die andere Hälfte ist für Blumen reserviert.

Die Anfahrt ist gesäumt von Oleanderbüschen. Sie führt zu riesigen Feldern, auf denen blaue Sternastern, vielfarbige Gladiolen, zartes Schleierkraut und Rittersporn in allen Blau-Schattierungen wächst. Der Boden wirkt wie schierer Sand, ohne die Wassergräben zwischen den Feldern würde hier wahrscheinlich nichts gedeihen. Hibiskus und Farn sind mit Plastikplanen abgedeckt – Sonnenschutz ist in Marokko so wichtig wie in unseren Breitengraden der Frostschutz.

Zu den Gewächshäusern führt eine Allee, die rechts von Avocados und links von Bambus gesäumt wird. Hortensien, Fuchsien und Scheinblatt werden unter Dach herangezogen, ebenso Blattpflanzen wie Aralien, Palmen und Ficus. In einer Bambushütte können Besucher ganz frisch geschnittene Blumen kaufen.

Le client qui achète un bouquet sur le grand marché aux fleurs de la place Moulay Hassan, au centre de Rabat, ne doit en aucun cas s'attendre à l'emporter lié et emballé. La plupart des stands présentent des gerbes de fleurs toutes prêtes, abondamment entourées, selon l'usage ici, de feuilles de cellophane. Il est très rare de voir un vendeur proposer sa marchandise triée par espèce ou couleur afin que le client puisse composer lui-même son bouquet. Par ailleurs, les fleurs coupées sont toujours placées dans des récipients de terre ventrus, qui serviraient plutôt de cache-pot chez nous.

La plupart des marchands font venir leur marchandise des environs immédiats. Ou alors ils cultivent euxmêmes leurs fleurs, comme Lahsen Lafkik, dont le stand porte le nom de *Paris Fleurs.* Son exploitation horticole est située dans une région rurale en périphérie de Salé, la ville qui fait face à Rabat sur l'autre rive du Bou Regreg. Fils de paysan, Lafkik a appris chez un oncle le travail des fleurs jusqu'en 1990, où il a pu acquérir son terrain de dix hectares à Salé. La moitié est consacrée à la culture de fruits et de légumes, l'autre moitié est réservée aux fleurs.

L'entrée est bordée de lauriersroses. Elle mène à d'immenses champs où poussent des asters bleus, des glaïeuls multicolores, du gypsophile léger et des pieds-d'alouette de toutes les nuances de bleu. Le sol semble être essentiellement sablonneux et sans les fossés remplis d'eau entre les champs, rien ne pourrait sans doute pousser ici. Les hibiscus et les fougères sont recouverts de bâches de plastique, la protection contre le soleil revêtant au Maroc l'importance de celle contre le gel à nos latitudes.

Une allée mène aux serres, bordées à droite d'avocatiers et à gauche de bambous. Les hortensias et les fuchsias sont cultivés sous un toit, de même que des plantes vertes comme les aralies, les palmiers et les ficus. Dans une cabane de bambous, les visiteurs peuvent acheter des fleurs fraîchement coupées.

This is how the plants destined for the market are grown: ferns and hibiscus as well as foliage plants are protected from the sun; *lantana,* avocado, fan palm, and *hydrangea* (bottom row) grow in the open.

So wachsen Blumen für den Markt heran: Farne und Hibiskus ebenso wie Grünpflanzen unter schützendem Sonnendach; *Lantana,* Avocado, Fächerpalme und Hortensie (untere Reihe) unter freiem Himmel.

C'est ainsi que grandissent les fleurs destinées au marché : fougères et hibiscus tout comme les plantes vertes à l'abri du soleil ; *lantana,* avocats, palmiers éventail et hortensias (en bas) à l'air libre.

The Pomegranate

In the Garden of Eden there was fruit in abundance. But out of all the fruits it was the innocent apple that was blamed for the fall from grace. This was probably due to a misunderstanding. The Latin words *malus* (bad or sin) and *malum* (apple) sound so similar that it may well be that the first bible illustrators mistook evil for an apple. In any case, they pressed an apple into the hand that Eve stretched out to Adam. It could have been any fruit, because the Latin text said it came from "The tree of knowledge of good and evil".

Whatever happened, the most important biblical 'apple' is the pomegranate, a member of the *Punicaceae* family and botanically unrelated to our apple. It is far more likely that the pomegranate was the forbidden fruit – after all it has a reputation of being the apple of love in many countries and cultures. Besides, it was indigenous to the biblical lands, whilst the ordinary apple was found primarily in Central Europe. The pomegranate probably came from Babylon and spread throughout the warmer climatic zones. It must have been cultivated in Cyprus quite early on because, according to myth, Aphrodite personally planted the seeds of the *granatum* (Latin for "having many seeds") in the fertile earth. The Roman goddess of love, Venus, is also said to have been particularly fond of this fruit.

The red juice of the pomegranate, or many-grained apple, was regarded as the nectar of lovers and its abundance in seeds a symbol of fertility. The extent to which the decorative *punica granatum* has inspired many people's imagination can be seen in the passionate lines of the German poet, Else Lasker-Schüler: "Pomegranates are resplendent/Hot as love

Der Granatapfel

Im Garten Eden gab es Früchte im Überfluss. Doch ausgerechnet der unschuldige Apfel soll Schuld am Sündenfall sein. Wahrscheinlich steckt dahinter nichts als ein Missverständis. Da die lateinischen Wörter *malus* (schlecht) und *malum* (Apfel) so ähnlich klingen, könnte es sein, dass die ersten Bibel-Illustratoren das Böse mit dem Apfel verwechselt haben. Jedenfalls drückten sie der nackten Eva einen Apfel in die verlockend nach Adam ausgestreckte Hand. Dabei könnte es irgendeine Frucht gewesen sein, denn gemeint war im lateinischen Text „Der Baum der Erkenntnis des Guten und des Bösen".

Wie auch immer, der wichtigste biblische Apfel ist der botanisch mit unserem Apfel nicht verwandte Granatapfel, der zur Familie der *Punicaceae* zählt. Er wäre als Frucht der Verführung viel wahrscheinlicher, schließlich hat er in allen Ländern und Kulturen einen Ruf als Liebesapfel. Außerdem war er auf biblischem Boden heimisch, während der normale Essapfel in erster Linie in Mitteleuropa vorkam. Der Granatapfel stammt wahrscheinlich aus Babylonien und breitete sich in allen wärmeren Klimazonen aus. In Zypern muss er schon früh angebaut worden sein, denn der Mythos behauptet, Aphrodite habe dort eigenhändig Kerne des *Granatum* (lateinisch für „körnerreich") in den fruchtbaren Boden gelegt. Auch der römischen Liebesgöttin Venus wird eine Vorliebe für diese Frucht zugeschrieben.

Der rote Saft der „Granate", wie sie früher oft genannt wurde, galt als der Nektar der Liebenden und ihr Samenreichtum als Symbol aller Fruchtbarkeit. Wie sehr der dekorative *punica granatum* die Phantasie der Menschen beflügelte, belegen leidenschaftliche Zeilen der Dichterin Else Lasker-Schüler:

La Grenade

Dans le jardin d'Éden, on trouvait des fruits en abondance. Et pourtant, c'est justement l'innocente pomme qui serait responsable de la chute de l'homme. Sans doute ne faut-il voir là rien d'autre qu'un malentendu : comme les mots latins *malus* (le mal) et *malum* (la pomme) ont des sonorités si proches, il se pourrait que les premiers illustrateurs de la Bible aient confondu le mal et la pomme. Ils ont en tout cas placé une pomme dans la main d'Eve nue, tendue vers Adam dans un geste de séduction, alors qu'il aurait pu s'agir de n'importe quel autre fruit. Le texte latin n'évoque-t-il pas simplement « l'arbre de la connaissance du bien et du mal ».

Quoi qu'il en soit, la plus importante des pommes bibliques n'est autre que la grenade qui, sur le plan botanique, n'est en rien apparentée à notre pomme, puisqu'elle appartient à la famille des *Punicaceae*. Elle est en effet beaucoup plus vraisemblable en fruit de la séduction, car tous les pays et toutes les cultures lui ont attribué la réputation de pomme d'amour. De plus, elle est chez elle dans les régions bibliques, tandis que la pomme ordinaire pousse essentiellement en Europe centrale. La grenade est probablement originaire de Babylone et s'est répandue peu à peu dans toutes les régions à climat chaud. Elle a certainement été cultivée très tôt à Chypre, car la mythologie affirme qu'Aphrodite y aurait semé de sa main des graines de *Granatum* (latin, « riche en graines ») dans le sol fertile, et on attribue également à la déesse romaine de l'amour, Vénus, une préférence pour ce fruit.

Le jus rouge des « granates », comme on les appelait souvent autrefois, passait pour être le nectar des amoureux et leur abondance de graines était un symbole de fertilité et de fécondité. La *punica granatum* si

in the night!/Red as love in the night!/As the fire in my cheeks" (from "Die schwarze Bhowanéh").

Pomegranates with their "little crown", their hard, yellowish-red skin and the delicious, pearl-shaped seeds with their red pulp are appreciated both for their decorative appearance and their refreshing sweet and sour taste. In the Middle Ages they were used in the preparation of meals or for their juice. They were also consumed for medicinal purposes to treat gall-bladder conditions and tapeworm. Pomegranates were also highly sought-after as gifts for hosts or as burial offerings. Golden bells were cast in the shape of this fruit and pieces of jewellery created. They adorned wall paintings, were woven into patterns for fabrics and rugs and used to decorate grand buildings. King Solomon had faithful reproductions made of four hundred pomegranates in order to decorate the capitals of columns in his temple. Since then, the unmistakable honeycomb-like mosaic of the cut fruit has often been used as a pattern on temple friezes and columned halls. It also appeared on embroidery patterns on High Priests' gowns. It is no wonder that the pomegranate, along with the olive, date, fig, grape, almond and carob were regarded as the seven symbolic fruits of the Bible, which promised special blessings.

In Rome the pomegranate in the hand of Juno was a symbol of marriage. Thanks to its flaming red, fragrant flowers, the tree became the symbol of love, followed by fertility. In expectation of bearing many children, brides in ancient Rome wore headdresses made from pomegranate twigs. In India, pomegranate juice, considered a cure for infertility, was used to help women who had not been blessed with children. In ancient China too, the fruit expressed the desire for countless offspring; they liked to give pictures of cut open pomegranates at weddings. Moreover, the Chinese use the same character for "one hundred seeds" and "one hundred sons". The pomegranate, along with the peach and the fingered citron, constitute the "three fruits of happiness", the fruits of abundance.

„Granatäpfel prangen / heiß wie die Liebe der Nacht! / Rot, wie die Liebe der Nacht! / Wie der Brand meiner Wangen" (aus „Die schwarze Bhowanéh").

Die Granatäpfel mit ihren „Krönchen", ihren harten, gelbroten Schalen und ihrem köstlichen, perlenförmigen Innern werden sowohl wegen ihres dekorativen Aussehens als auch wegen ihres erfrischenden süß-säuerlichen Geschmacks geschätzt. Schon im Mittelalter verarbeitete man sie zu Speisen oder Säften. In der Medizin wurden sie gegen Gallenbeschwerden und Bandwürmer eingesetzt. Begehrt waren sie auch als Grabgaben und Gastgeschenke. Nach ihrem Abbild wurden goldene Glocken gegossen und Schmuckstücke gearbeitet, sie zierten Wandmalereien, wurden in Stoff- und Teppichmuster gewebt und dekorierten herrschaftliche Bauten. König Salomon ließ für die Säulen seines Tempels vierhundert Granatäpfel naturgetreu nachbilden, um damit die Kapitelle schmücken zu lassen. Das unverwechselbare, wabenartige Mosaik der aufgeschnittenen Frucht wurde seither als Muster an Tempelfriesen und Säulenhallen häufig wiederholt. Es tauchte auch in Stickmustern von Gewändern der Hohen Priester auf. Kein Wunder, dass Granatäpfel neben Oliven, Datteln, Feigen, Trauben, Mandeln und Johannisbrot zu den sieben symbolischen Früchten der Bibel zählten, die besonderen Segen verhießen.

In Rom war der Granatapfel in der Hand der Juno ein Symbol der Ehe. Der Baum wurde dank seiner flammend roten, duftenden Blüten zum Sinnbild der Liebe, gefolgt von Fruchtbarkeit. Römische Bräute trugen in Erwartung häufiger Mutterfreuden Kränze aus Zweigen des Granatapfelbaums. In Indien galt der Saft des Granatapfels als Heilmittel gegen ausbleibenden Kindersegen. Auch im alten China drückte die Frucht den Wunsch nach zahlreichen Nachkommen aus, man schenkte sich zur Hochzeit gern das Bild eines halb geöffneten Granatapfels, und die Chinesen verwenden für die Begriffe „hundert Kerne" und „hundert Söhne" das selbe Schriftzeichen. Zusammen mit dem Pfirsich und der Fingerzitrone bildet der Granatapfel die „drei Glücksfrüchte", Früchte des Überflusses.

décorative a donné des ailes à l'imagination des hommes, comme en témoignent ces vers passionnés de la poétesse Else Lasker-Schüler : « Grenades luisantes/ aussi ardentes que l'amour de la nuit ! / Aussi rouges que l'amour de la nuit ! / Tel le feu de mes joues » (tiré de « Die schwarze Bhowanéh / La noire Bhowanéh »).

Les grenades et leur « petite couronne », leur peau dure rouge et jaune et leur chair de perles savoureuses sont appréciées autant pour leur aspect décoratif que pour leur goût aigre-doux rafraîchissant. Au Moyen-Âge déjà, on en faisait des desserts et des jus. En médecine, elles étaient employées contre les douleurs biliaires et le ver solitaire. Elles tenaient également lieu de présent funèbre ou aux invités. Sur leur modèle ont été fondues des cloches en or et des bijoux créés, elles ont orné des peintures murales, ont été tissées dans les motifs d'étoffes ou de tapis et ont décoré les bâtiments seigneuriaux. Le roi Salomon fit reproduire fidèlement quatre cent grenades pour en orner les chapiteaux des colonnes de son temple et la mosaïque gaufrée, unique en son genre, du fruit coupé a depuis été répétée à de multiples reprises dans les frises des temples et des salles hypostyles. Elle est également apparue parmi les motifs brodés sur les vêtements des grands prêtres. Rien d'étonnant donc, si la grenade fait partie, avec l'olive, la datte, la figue, le raisin, l'amande et la caroube, des sept fruits symboliques de la Bible, sources de bénédiction exceptionnelle.

À Rome, la grenade dans la main de Junon était un symbole du mariage. L'arbre, lui, avec ses fleurs parfumées d'un rouge flamboyant, était l'emblème de l'amour suivi de la fécondité. Les mariées romaines portaient, dans l'attente des futures joies maternelles, des couronnes de branches de grenadiers. En Inde, le jus de grenade était considéré comme un remède à l'absence d'enfant au foyer. Et dans la Chine ancienne, le fruit exprimait le désir d'une descendance nombreuse ; l'image d'une grenade ouverte en deux était un cadeau de mariage apprécié et, aujourd'hui encore, les Chinois utilisent le même caractère pour dire « cent graines » et « cent fils ». Avec la pêche et le citron, la grenade est l'un des « trois fruits porte-bonheur », fruits de l'abondance.

Tanger

At the point where Europe and Africa, the Mediterranean and the Atlantic meet, Tanger opens up like a Roman amphitheatre with a view over the wide bay and the magnificent beach. No wonder people came from all over the world to this "white city": adventurers, smugglers, spies and drug dealers, the hunters and the hunted, but also romantics and eccentrics, painters and writers. Tanger is an open minded city. Tanger's golden age as an "international zone" lasted from 1912 to 1956. After that, many Europeans left but, since 1980, this provincial capital has experienced a revival as an industrial base, commercial and passenger harbour and tourist attraction.

Originally called Tingis, Tanger is the oldest continually inhabited settlement in Morocco, as shown by prehistoric finds from the Palaeolithic Age. Because of its strategic position on the Strait of Gibraltar, it was always hotly disputed and particularly favoured by the Europeans as a bridgehead to Africa. However, the city was first immortalised as a myth by artists in their paintings and books: from Delacroix to Matisse, from Pierre Loti to Paul Bowles, who considered Tanger to be the place that gave him both "wisdom and ecstasy".

Wo Europa und Afrika, das Mittelmeer und der Atlantik aufeinander treffen, da öffnet sich Tanger wie ein römisches Amphitheater mit Ausblick auf die weite Bucht und den herrlichen Strand. Kein Wunder, dass sie von überall her in die „weiße Stadt" kamen, die Abenteurer, die Schmuggler, Spione und Drogenhändler, die Gejagten und die Suchenden, aber auch die Romantiker und Exzentriker, die Maler und Schriftsteller. Tanger – offene Stadt. Als „internationale Zone" erlebte es von 1912 bis 1956 sein goldenes Zeitalter. Danach zogen sich viele Europäer zurück, aber als Industriestandort, Handels- und Passagierhafen und als Touristenattraktion ist die Provinzhauptstadt seit 1980 wieder im Aufschwung begriffen.

Tanger, ursprünglich Tingis, ist die älteste ständig bewohnte Siedlung Marokkos, das beweisen prähistorische Funde aus der Altsteinzeit. Wegen seiner strategischen Lage an der Straße von Gibraltar war es immer heiß umkämpft und als Brückenkopf zu Afrika bei Europäern besonders beliebt. Zum Mythos aber wurde es erst durch die Künstler, die Tanger in ihren Bildern und Büchern verewigten, von Delacroix bis Matisse, von Pierre Loti bis Paul Bowles, der das weiße Tanger für den Ort hielt, der ihm „gleichzeitig Weisheit und Ekstase" gab.

Au point de rencontre de l'Europe et de l'Afrique, de la Méditerranée et de l'Atlantique, Tanger s'ouvre tel un amphithéâtre romain, avec vue sur la vaste baie et ses magnifiques plages. Rien d'étonnant si de partout sont venus à la « ville blanche » aventuriers, contrebandiers, espions et trafiquants de drogue, pourchassés et chasseurs, mais aussi romantiques et excentriques, peintres et écrivains. Tanger, ville ouverte, a connu son âge d'or entre 1912 et 1956, en tant que « zone internationale ». De nombreux Européens se sont ensuite retirés, mais depuis 1980, la capitale de province est de nouveau en plein essor en tant que site industriel, port de commerce et de passagers et centre touristique.

Tanger, à l'origine Tingis, est le plus ancien site habité sans interruption du Maroc, des découvertes préhistoriques du paléolithique l'attestent. Située à un emplacement stratégique sur la route de Gibraltar, elle n'a cessé de faire l'objet de combats acharnés et a toujours été très appréciée des Européens comme tête de pont vers l'Afrique. Quant à sa dimension mythique, Tanger la doit aux artistes qui l'ont immortalisée dans leurs livres et tableaux. De Delacroix à Matisse, de Pierre Loti à Paul Bowles, qui tenait la blanche Tanger pour le lieu par excellence lui inspirant « à la fois sagesse et extase ».

Private Gardens
Private Gärten
Jardins privés

In Tanger a whole garden culture has developed which, despite its proximity to Andalusia, has no relation to Moorish-Arab culture. A type of "English garden close to nature and sprinkled with exotic plants", has gained acceptance here. This is clearly due to the influence of British immigrants, who brought the tradition of garden design and the latest gardening trends with them from England. As born plant lovers, they also seized the opportunity to add new species to their horticultural repertoire; plants they could not grow at home because it was too cold.

Tanger is the only Moroccan city where private gardens have become famous. This certainly cannot simply be ascribed to their beauty, it is also due to the fact that artists and prominent figures from all over the world have been guests in these gardens, and have then gone on to describe their visits. In other cities, in contrast, foreigners were in general only allowed to visit the public palace gardens; the private sphere is very closely protected in Arab society.

One peculiarity of the gardens in Tanger is that they have had to be laid out in terraces, since the city lies on the undulating foothills of the Rif Mountains. These different levels open up very attractive design possibilities; the English garden designer Waller was the first person to turn them into an eye-catching feature at the beginning of the last century. As on the Mediterranean coast, strong winds and the lack of water are problematic here. However, the Mediterranean style of garden does not have many followers in Tanger.

In Tanger hat sich eine ganz eigene Gartenkultur entwickelt, die mit der maurisch-arabischen – trotz der Nähe zu Andalusien! – nichts zu tun hat. Durchgesetzt hat sich eine Art „naturnaher englischer Garten, gewürzt mit exotischen Pflanzen". Das ist eindeutig dem Einfluss der britischen Immigranten zu verdanken, die sowohl die Tradition der Gartengestaltung als auch die neuesten grünen Trends aus England mitbrachten. Als geborene Pflanzenliebhaber nahmen sie außerdem die Möglichkeit wahr, ihrem Pflanzenrepertoire neue Spezies hinzuzufügen, denen es in ihrem Heimatland zu kühl gewesen wäre.

Tanger ist die einzige marokkanische Stadt, in der einige private Gärten Berühmtheit erlangt haben, was sicher nicht nur ihrer Schönheit zuzuschreiben ist, sondern der Tatsache, dass in diesen Gärten Künstler und Prominente aus aller Welt zu Gast waren, die über ihren Aufenthalt gesprochen und geschrieben haben. In anderen Städten dagegen durften Fremde fast nur die öffentlichen Gärten der Paläste besuchen, die private Sphäre wird in der arabischen Gesellschaft sehr geschützt.

Eine Besonderheit der Tanger-Gärten ist, dass sie alle terrassenförmig angelegt werden mussten, weil die Stadt an den hügeligen Ausläufern des Rif-Gebirges liegt. Durch die verschiedenen Ebenen eröffnen sich reizvolle Gestaltungsmöglichkeiten, die der englische Gartendesigner Waller Anfang des letzten Jahrhunderts als Erster augenfällig zu nutzen wusste. Problematisch sind Wassermangel und scharfe Winde, ähnlich wie an den Küsten des Mittelmeeres. Dennoch hat der mediterrane Gartenstil in Tanger kaum Anhänger gefunden.

The English introduced mixed borders: here, exotic plants like the agave are sprinkled in. Arabic gardens with their colourful tiles are less frequently found.

Engländer brachten die „mixed borders" mit – hier mischen sich Exoten wie Agaven hinein. Den arabischen Garten mit bunten Fliesen findet man seltener.

Ce sont les Anglais qui ont importé les « mixed borders » – ici, des espèces exotiques comme les agaves s'y sont glissées. Plus rare, le jardin arabe aux faïences de couleur.

Une culture du jardin très particulière s'est développée à Tanger, n'ayant rien à voir – malgré la proximité de l'Andalousie – avec le style maure-arabe. Un type de jardin, qu'on pourrait qualifier de « jardin anglais naturel épicé de plantes exotiques », s'est imposé, sans aucun doute sous l'influence des immigrants britanniques, qui ont amené avec eux, outre la tradition du paysagisme, les dernières tendances en Angleterre. Amoureux des plantes-nés, ils ont également su exploiter la possibilité d'ajouter à leur herbier de nouvelles espèces, pour lesquelles le climat de leur pays natal aurait été trop froid.

Tanger est la seule ville du Maroc où quelques jardins privés ont atteint une certaine célébrité, due sans aucun doute, bien plus qu'à leur beauté, aux artistes et personnalités du monde entier qui y ont séjourné et en ont ensuite fait le récit parlé et écrit. Dans d'autres villes en effet, les étrangers étaient tout juste autorisés à pénétrer dans les jardins publics des palais, la vie privée étant très protégée dans la société arabe.

L'une des particularités des jardins de Tanger est qu'ils sont tous aménagés en terrasses, car la ville est elle-même située sur un contrefort vallonné du Rif. La succession des différents niveaux ouvre d'intéressantes possibilités d'aménagement, que l'architecte-paysagiste anglais Waller a su le premier exploiter avantageusement au début du siècle dernier. Il reste le problème du manque d'eau et celui des vents forts, semblables à ceux de la côte méditerranéenne. Pourtant, le style de jardin méditerranéen n'a fait que peu d'adeptes à Tanger.

Dar Kharroubia

The eccentric David Herbert wanted the plants in his garden to spread freely. The only condition was a full view over his beloved Tanger from every terrace.

Nahezu ungezähmt, so wollte es der englische Exzentriker David Herbert, durften sich die Pflanzen in seinem Garten ausbreiten. Nur der Ausblick auf sein geliebtes Tanger musste auf jeder Terrasse frei gehalten werden.

Les plantes ont quasiment envahi le jardin, comme le souhaitait l'excentrique anglais, David Herbert. Il n'y a que sur les terrasses que la vue sur son Tanger adorée devait rester libre.

Everyone in the quarter knows the way to *Dar Kharroubia*. After all, for centuries this house with its terracotta-coloured façade was a place of pilgrimage for artists, writers, nobles and inquisitive people from all over the world especially from England. Indeed, that was where David Herbert, the second son of the fifteenth Earl of Pembroke and Montgomery, was born, and there he grew up amongst the higher ranks of the European nobility. The prospect of a grey, foggy country life made him leave his homeland at an early age. He longed for warmth and a more colourful landscape and, after spending some time in Berlin and New York, he settled for the rest of his long life in Tanger. In this free zone for individualists David Herbert evolved into the most colourful of all birds of paradise. And at the same time into one of the most desirable – everybody thronged to his hospitable house, where each room was painted in a different vibrant colour. In the garden many famous film stars (in his youth Sir Herbert himself had taken part in silent films), well-known socialites and above all writers such as Truman Capote, Alberto Moravia and Jean Genet sat beneath the bougainvillea and the oleander. David Herbert travelled through the Maghreb with Jane and Paul Bowles; Paul led the team of literary figures and, like a magnet, drew others to Tanger. Herbert and the Bowles even crossed the desert in style in a Jaguar, with suitcases, hatboxes and picnic hampers …

David Herbert died in 1995, but visitors continued to come to hear these stories and to see how the legendary figure had lived. His heir and partner, Jdaoudi Noureddine transformed *Dar Kharroubia* into an exclusive small guesthouse. And thus, bustling activity once again fills the house and the garden continues to be a meeting place for international

Den Weg zum *Dar Kharroubia* kennt jeder im Viertel. Schließlich war das Haus mit der terrakottafarbenen Fassade jahrzehntelang Wallfahrtsort für Künstler, Literaten, Adlige und Neugierige aus aller Welt – vor allem aber aus England. Dort nämlich wurde David Herbert, zweiter Sohn des fünfzigsten Earl of Pembroke und Montgomery, geboren und wuchs im Kreise des europäischen Hochadels auf. Die Aussicht auf ein graues, nebliges Landleben ließ ihn sein Heimatland flüchten, kaum war er flügge. Er sehnte sich nach Wärme und Farbe und ließ sich, nach Stationen in Berlin und New York, für den Rest seines langen Lebens in Tanger nieder. In diesem Freihafen für Individualisten entwickelte David Herbert sich zum buntesten aller Paradiesvögel. Und zum begehrtesten – *tout le monde* drängte in sein gastfreies Haus, in dem jedes Zimmer in einer anderen kräftigen Farbe gestrichen war. In seinem Garten saßen unter Bougainvillea und Oleander viele Leinwandgrößen (Sir Herbert hatte in seiner Jugend selbst in Stummfilmen mitgewirkt), berühmte Socialites und vor allem Schriftsteller wie Truman Capote, Alberto Moravia und Jean Genet. Mit Jane und Paul Bowles, der die Riege der Literaten anführte und wie ein Magnet andere nach Tanger zog, reiste David Herbert durch den Maghreb. Sogar die Wüste durchquerten sie stilvoll im Jaguar, mit Reisekoffern, Hutschachteln und Picknickkoffern …

David Herbert starb 1995, aber Besucher kommen immer noch, um diese Geschichten zu hören und zu sehen, wie die Legende lebte. Sein Freund und Erbe Jdaoudi Noureddine hat *Dar Kharroubia* zu einem exklusiven kleinen Gästehaus umgestaltet. So kommt es, dass nach wie vor reges Treiben herrscht und der Garten immer noch Treffpunkt internationaler Reisender ist. Es gibt meh-

Dans le quartier, tout le monde connaît le chemin du *Dar Kharroubia*. La maison à façade couleur de terre cuite n'a-t-elle pas été pendant des décennies un lieu de pèlerinage pour les artistes, gens de lettres, nobles et curieux du monde entier, essentiellement d'Angleterre. C'est là aussi que David Herbert, deuxième fils du cinquantième comte de Pembroke et Montgomery, a vu le jour et a grandi au sein de la haute noblesse de toute l'Europe. La perspective d'une vie à la campagne grise et brumeuse lui fait fuir son pays natal dès qu'il peut voler de ses propres ailes. Regrettant la chaleur et la couleur, il s'installera à Tanger pour le reste de sa longue vie, après avoir fait halte à Berlin et New York. Dans ce port ouvert à tous les individualistes, David Herbert devient le plus coloré des oiseaux de paradis, et le plus envié. Tout le monde se presse alors dans sa demeure accueillante, dont chaque pièce est peinte d'une couleur vive différente. Dans le jardin prendront place, parmi les bougainvilliers et les lauriers-roses, de nombreuses stars de l'écran, des personnalités célèbres et surtout des écrivains comme Truman Capote, Alberto Moravia et Jean Genet. Avec Jane et Paul Bowles, qui dirige la section des gens de lettres et en attire comme un aimant sans cesse d'autres à Tanger, David Herbert voyage également à travers le Maghreb, n'hésitant pas à traverser le désert en grand style dans des Jaguars pleines de malles de voyage, de cartons à chapeaux et de valises de pique-nique …

David Herbert est mort en 1995, mais les visiteurs continuent de venir pour entendre ces histoires et voir comment a vécu la légende. Son compagnon et héritier Jdaoudi Noureddine a converti le *Dar Kharroubia* en un petit hôtel raffiné. Il arrive donc encore aujourd'hui que règne une grande agitation et le jardin est tou-

visitors. There are several terraces and a veranda behind the house decorated with wall paintings. The shutters were used for botanical illustrations. Sir Herbert was – and in this he was a typical Englishman – a fanatical plant-lover. Every last nook and cranny of the property was cultivated or at least crammed with flowerpots. The overriding impression is one of a rampant green jungle, in which the tone is set by *wisteria,* oleander, roses, *agapanthus* and colourful bird of paradise flowers.

rere Terrassen und eine Veranda hinter dem Haus, die mit Wandmalereien geschmückt ist. Die Fensterläden wurden für botanische Illustrationen genutzt. Sir Herbert war – hierin ganz Engländer – ein fanatischer Pflanzenliebhaber. Keine Ecke des Grundstücks, die nicht bepflanzt oder mindestens mit Töpfen dicht an dicht bestückt wäre. Haupteindruck ist der eines wuchernden grünen Dschungels, in dem Glyzinien, Oleander, Rosen, *Agapanthus* und Strelitzien farbige Akzente setzen.

jours le lieu de rencontre des voyageurs du monde entier. Derrière la maison se trouvent plusieurs terrasses et une véranda ornée de peintures murales. Les volets des fenêtres en sont occupés par des illustrations botaniques. En effet, Sir Herbert était – en cela très Anglais – un fanatique des plantes et le moindre recoin de la propriété est planté, ou au moins garni de pots en rangs serrés. Le plus impressionnant reste la jungle verte et luxuriante où glycines, lauriers-roses, rosiers, *agapanthes* et strélitzias mettent des notes de couleur.

Each room in this terracotta-coloured house is painted in a different shade. The veranda with Moorish arches is held in blue, with a wall painting of Sir Herbert's favourite birds: parrots. He was also very fond of potted plants – they are crammed in every free corner of house and garden.

Im terrakottafarbenen Haus hat jedes Zimmer eine andere Farbe. Die Veranda mit den maurischen Bögen trägt auf blauem Grund ein Wandgemälde, das Sir Herberts geliebte Papageien zeigt. Topfpflanzen liebte er ebenso, sie zieren jede freie Ecke in Haus und Garten.

Dans la maison aux murs couleur terre-cuite, chaque pièce est peinte d'une couleur différente. Le véranda aux arcades mauresques est décorée d'une fresque sur fond bleu, représentant les perroquets, que Sir Herbert affectionait. Il aimait aussi les plantes en pot, qui occupent tous les coins libres de la maison et du jardin.

The fashioned jungle can be enjoyed from many comfortable spots – or you can go on an expedition of discovery, where you might spot a locust, sitting in perfect mimicry on a palm leaf (above left). The butterfly on the white *calla* lily (top right) will catch even the amateur's eye.

Den gestalteten Dschungel kann man von vielen Sitzplätzen aus genießen – oder man geht auf Entdeckungsreise, und erkennt dann vielleicht die Heuschrecke, die in perfekter Mimikry auf einem Palmblatt sitzt (links unten). Der Schmetterling auf der *Calla* (rechts oben) entgeht auch dem ungeübten Auge nicht.

On peut profiter de cette jungle façonnée en paressant sur l'un des nombreux sièges. Ou partir à l'aventure, à la recherche du grillon, parfait de mimétisme sur sa feuille de palmier (en bas à gauche), ou du papillon assis sur la *calla*, qui n'échappe pas même à l'œil non exercé.

Le Jardin Magique

The gravel path lined with rubbish on either side appears to lead straight to nowhere. The nearby sea can only be imagined – you certainly don't expect to find one of Tanger's famously beautiful gardens around here. However, the announced pink wall with the *jardin magique* (magical garden) hidden behind finally appears.

Ahmed, the owner of this lovely piece of land, thought up this name for his green oasis, which really does do its name justice – even if it is not obvious at first glance. Straight after entering, you find yourself in front of a pond, which was actually planned as a swimming pool but, due to technical problems, could not be finished and ducks now bathe there.

However, the "mysterious jungle" that fascinates all visitors begins right behind the pool. Narrow paths run up and downhill through the lush vegetation, because this plot of land is hilly, despite lying so close to the sea. As a result, several terraces have been created, offering a different view around each bend.

The closer you get to this small house, the clearer the view of the garden. On each of the terraces there is a seat, each one so lovingly decorated you feel tempted to linger for a while. That is exactly what Ahmed and his wife, Anna, intended. Indeed, they only use the garden as a weekend refuge, and as a stage for their spectacular parties.

When there is a party at the *jardin magique*, the whole of Tanger scrambles to get an invitation. This is not only because of the garden's unique atmosphere, but also thanks to Anna's highly developed flair for decoration. Her talent is not just used for arranging the tables; it is also expressed in the unusual positioning of some of the plants. That is why the innocent spider plants spread out in dense clumps on either side of a flight of steps, make a

Der rechts und links von Unrat gesäumte Schotterweg scheint geradewegs ins Nichts zu führen. Das nahe gelegene Meer kann man nur erahnen – nein, hier erwartet man nicht einen in ganz Tanger für seine Schönheit berühmten Garten. Doch schließlich findet man die angekündigte rosa Mauer und den dahinter versteckten *jardin magique* – den magischen Garten.

Diesen Namen hat Ahmed, der Besitzer, sich für seine grüne Oase ausgedacht, und sie wird diesem vielversprechenden Namen in der Tat gerecht. Auch wenn das nicht gleich auf den ersten Blick zu erkennen ist. Sofort nach dem Eintreten steht man vor einem Teich, der eigentlich als Swimmingpool geplant war, aber aufgrund eines technischen Problems nicht fertig gestellt werden konnte und nun erst einmal von den Enten zum Baden genutzt wird. Doch gleich dahinter beginnt der „geheimnisvolle Dschungel", der jeden Besucher fasziniert. Schmale Wege führen durch üppige Vegetation hinauf und hinunter, denn auch dieses Grundstück ist hügelig, obwohl es so nahe am Meer liegt. Dadurch entstehen verschiedene Terrassen, und nach jeder Biegung bietet sich ein anderer Anblick. Je mehr man sich dem kleinen Haus nähert, umso deutlicher wird die wahre Bestimmung des Gartens. Auf jeder der Terrasse befindet sich ein Sitzplatz, jeder einzelne davon so liebevoll dekoriert, dass man sich zum Verweilen verführt fühlt. So ist es von Ahmed und seiner Frau Anna auch geplant, der Garten dient ihnen nämlich nur als Wochenendrefugium. Und als Bühne für ihre spektakulären Feste.

Wenn im *jardin magique* gefeiert wird, reißt sich ganz Tanger um eine Einladung. Das liegt nicht nur an der einmaligen Atmosphäre des Gartens, sondern auch an Annas ausgeprägtem Gespür für Dekoration. Dieses Talent setzt sie nicht nur für die

Le sentier caillouteux bordé à droite et à gauche d'immondices semble mener directement à nulle part. On devine à peine la mer toute proche ; non, on ne s'attend pas à trouver par-là un jardin célèbre dans tout Tanger pour sa beauté. Et pourtant, on finit par tomber sur le mur rose annoncé et le *jardin magique* qu'il dissimule.

Le nom a été imaginé par Ahmed, le propriétaire, pour son oasis de verdure, et elle rend véritablement justice à cette annonce si prometteuse. Même si on ne s'en rend pas compte au premier abord. Dès après l'entrée, on fait face à un étang, prévu à l'origine pour être une piscine, mais qui n'a pu être achevé en raison de problèmes techniques et sert aujourd'hui tout au plus de baignoire aux canards. Juste derrière commence la « mystérieuse jungle » qui fascine tous les visiteurs.

D'étroits sentiers montent et descendent à travers la végétation luxuriante, car le terrain est vallonné, malgré sa proximité avec la mer, et donc divisé en terrasses toutes différentes, de sorte que chaque tournant offre une autre vue. Plus on s'approche de la petite maison, plus on comprend la véritable fonction du jardin. Sur chaque terrasse se trouve un endroit où s'asseoir, et chacun est si amoureusement décoré que le visiteur ne peut qu'être séduit et se sentir invité à rester. C'est là l'objectif d'Ahmed et de sa femme Anna, le jardin ne leur sert que de refuge pendant les weekends et de tribune pour leurs fêtes somptueuses.

Tout Tanger s'arrache les invitations aux fêtes du *jardin magique*. La raison en est, certes, l'atmosphère unique du jardin, mais aussi le sens très développé d'Anna pour la décoration. Un talent qui s'exprime, outre dans les arrangements de tables, dans la disposition inédite de certains végétaux. Elle a ainsi massé

Dense green welcomes the visitor at the entrance. Paths and passageways are kept narrow so the garden doesn't lose its mysterious flair at first sight.

Dichtes Grün umfängt den Besucher schon im Eingangsbereich. Wege und Durchgänge sind schmal gehalten, damit der Garten sein Geheimnis nicht auf den ersten Blick preisgibt.

Dès l'entrée, le visiteur est entouré d'une épaisse végétation. Chemins et passages sont volontairement étroits, pour ne pas dévoiler trop tôt le secret du jardin.

This garden has bizarre plants placed at unusual spots, like the green lily on the steps and the *sedum morganianum* on the post.

Bizarre Pflanzen an ungewöhnlichen Orten sind Kennzeichen dieses Gartens, wie die Grünlilien auf der Treppe und das *Sedum morganum* auf dem Pfosten.

Une caractéristique du jardin : les plantes bizarres en des lieux inhabituels, comme le *Chlorophytum* sur l'escalier ou le *Sedum morganum* sur le poteau.

Garden owners are known to be excellent hosts – they are experts in the art of decoration.

Die Gartenbesitzer werden als Gastgeber gerühmt – auch weil sie die Kunst des Dekorierens perfekt beherrschen.

Les propriétaires du jardin sont également des hôtes célébrés – entre autres, parce qu'ils maîtrisent parfaitement l'art de la décoration.

really grand entrance. Amazing is the bizarre *sedum morganum* which coils up like the snake in paradise in the most unexpected places, and falls out of high hanging flowerpots onto visitors.

The garden's water supply is as mysterious as the name suggests: without the three springs hidden behind iron railings, the *jardin magique* would be precisely what it appears to be: a fata morgana …

Arrangements der Tische ein, es kommt auch in der ungewöhnlichen Platzierung mancher Pflanzen zum Ausdruck. So hat die harmlose Grünlilie, in Massen zu beiden Seiten einer Treppe eingesetzt, einen geradezu herrschaftlichen Auftritt. Und das bizarre *Sedum morganum* windet sich wie die Schlange im Paradies an den überraschendsten Stellen aus hoch hängenden Ampeln dem Besucher entgegen.

Geheimnisvoll wie der Name es verspricht, ist übrigens die Wasserversorgung des Gartens: Ohne die drei hinter Eisengittern verborgenen Quellen wäre der *jardin magique* das, was er zu sein scheint – eine Fata Morgana …

d'inoffensives Fleurs-araignées des deux côtés d'un escalier pour une montée véritablement princière, et l'étrange *Sedum morganum* tombe de vases suspendus en l'air face au visiteur avant de s'enrouler ensuite, tel le serpent du Paradis, aux endroits les plus inattendus.

Quant à l'alimentation en eau du jardin, elle est aussi mystérieuse que son nom le promet : sans les trois sources cachées par des grilles de fer forgé, le *jardin magique* ne serait que ce qu'il semble être : un mirage …

Villa Palma

Annie Lambton has achieved something that many people dream of, which is the stoke of good luck that changes your life completely in an instant. For this writer it was her bestseller about "Jackie and her sister" what made her dreams come true. For more than twenty years now Annie has lived in the *Villa Palma* situated on one of the hills that surround Tanger.

Going through the typical Arab ivy-covered gate with its cast-iron grille, you reach a raised bed in which a single palm tree acts as a solitary guard. Its trunk is sumptuously decorated in the Moroccan style: there are bromelias here too, climbing up the host tree. Busy lizzies have been planted around the palm tree and the flowerbed wall is decorated with shallow dishes containing *echeveria*. A small flight of steps leads down to the garden itself, which is actually quite small and so profusely overgrown that it is not really feasable to enter, you can only go around it. A narrow, paved path leads past the high trees that were planted as a screen and around the central flowerbed. A variety of datura, hibiscus, white *calla* lilies, Indian shot and hortensias grow close together here. Particularly dramatic is the clump of bird of paradise flowers, which stand out against a lemon tree.

With such riotous vegetation, it is no wonder that Annie prefers to enjoy her garden from above: the large roof terrace not only provides a superb view over the property, but also allows hospitable Annie to receive many guests. This is not only important for private reasons – she organises Moroccan dinners for small groups. If you are lucky, you might be allowed to enter the most romantic part of the *Villa Palma*: the magnificent, terracotta-coloured garden room.

Annie Lambton ist etwas gelungen, von dem viele Menschen träumen: Der eine, ganz große Wurf, mit dem sich das Leben schlagartig verändert. Für die Schriftstellerin war es der Bestseller über „Jackie und ihre Schwester", der ihren Traum Wirklichkeit werden ließ. Seit mehr als zwanzig Jahren lebt Annie nun in der *Villa Palma* auf einer Anhöhe Tangers.

Durch das typisch arabische, efeuberankte Portal mit seinem gusseisernen Gitter gelangt man zunächst zu einem Hochbeet, in dem eine einzelne Palme den einsamen Wächter spielt. Nach marokkanischer Manier ist ihr Stamm reich verziert: hier sind es Bromelien, die an dem gastlichen Baum empor klettern. Rund um die Palme wachsen Fleißige Lieschen, die Mauer des Beets schmücken flache Schalen mit *Echeveria*. Ein paar Treppenstufen führen hinunter in den eigentlichen Garten, der zwar klein, aber dafür so üppig bewachsen ist, dass man ihn nicht wirklich betreten, sondern nur umkreisen kann. Ein schmaler, mit Steinen gepflasterter Weg führt an den als Sichtschutz gepflanzten hohen Bäumen entlang rund um das zentrale Beet. Datura, Hibiskus, *Calla* und Canna, aber auch Hortensien wachsen hier dicht an dicht. Besonders dramatisch hebt sich ein Strelitzien-Massiv vor einem Zitronenbaum ab.

Bei einer so überhand nehmenden Vegetation ist es kein Wunder, dass Annie ihren Garten am liebsten von oben genießt: Die große Dachterrasse ermöglicht nicht nur einen einmaligen Blick auf das Grundstück, sondern erlaubt Annie auch, viele Gäste zu empfangen. Das ist ihr nicht nur aus privaten Gründen wichtig – sie organisiert marokkanische Dinner für kleine Gruppen. Wer Glück hat, bekommt so Zutritt zur romantischsten Ecke der *Villa Palma*: das wunderschöne, terrakottafarbene Gartenzimmer.

Author Annie likes her favourite plants to grow in clumps: aloe, paradise flower and a variety of different ferns.

Schriftstellerin Annie lässt ihre Lieblingspflanzen in Massen auftreten: Aloen, Strelitzien und eine Sammlung verschiedener Farne.

Annie fait apparaître ses plantes préférées en masses : aloès, strélitzies ainsi qu'une collection de fougères différentes.

Annie Lambton a réussi quelque chose dont beaucoup rêvent : le grand coup unique qui change radicalement toute une vie. Pour l'écrivain, c'est le best-seller « Jackie et ses sœurs » qui a transformé son rêve en réalité : depuis plus de vingt ans, Annie habite la *Villa Palma*, sur une hauteur de Tanger.

Le portail typiquement arabe, entouré de lierre et pourvu d'une grille en fer forgé, donne d'abord accès à un haut massif, où un palmier joue les gardiens solitaires. Comme toujours au Maroc, son tronc est richement décoré, ici de bromélies qui grimpent à l'assaut de leur arbre-hôte. Tout autour poussent des impatientes, tandis que les murs du massif sont ornés de coupes plates garnies d'*Echeveria*. Quelques marches descendent au jardin proprement dit, petit mais si densément peuplé qu'on ne peut pas vraiment y pénétrer, mais seulement en faire le tour. Un sentier étroit pavé de pierres mène le long des hauts arbres plantés pour se protéger des regards et fait le tour du massif central. Daturas, hibiscus, arums et *cannas*, mais aussi hortensias, y poussent en rangs serrés. Un groupe de strélitzias ressort spectaculairement contre un citronnier.

Face à une végétation aussi luxuriante, on comprend sans peine qu'Annie apprécie le plus son jardin d'en haut : le vaste toit en terrasse offre non seulement une vue unique sur l'ensemble du terrain, mais permet à l'hospitalière Annie de recevoir de nombreux invités. Elle ne le fait d'ailleurs pas uniquement à titre privé, mais organise aussi des dîners marocains pour de petits groupes. Les plus chanceux peuvent alors accéder au recoin le plus romantique de la *Villa Palma* : la magnifique pièce couleur de terre cuite avec jardin.

Le Consulat

In order to be able to buy the property of their dreams, Patricia and Abdelkader Erzini had to commit themselves to taking over the Swedish honorary consulate, which has been housed in this spacious two-storey house since 1964. This is how in 1976 Patricia ended up looking after the affairs of Swedish citizens, and also how she ended up taking care of the huge plot surrounding *Le Consulat*.

The garden was laid out by their predecessor, who she describes as an "expert and an enthusiast": a Scandinavian man, who was very fond of all kinds of Mediterranean plants and trees and cultivated as many as possible in the garden.

Patricia resembles him. One of the first things she did was to plant a bed with *aeonium arboreum* on the long side of the large lawn. The vigorous green leaf rosettes are indigenous to the Atlantic coast of Morocco and consequently prosper here without any problems. On the other hand, Patricia experimented with other plants in order to see if they would do well on this plot of land: "We have strong winds summer and winter alike". She is particularly proud of a coral tree *(erythrina crista-galli)*, which has flourished in this garden for 22 years and is now three metres high. This plant, with its strikingly attractive coral to scarlet red racemes, is mostly grown as a potted shrub, which is kept in an unheated greenhouse during the winter.

Many things in the garden have remained exactly as they were when

Um das Anwesen ihrer Träume erwerben zu können, mussten Patricia und Abdelkader Erzini sich verpflichten, das schwedische Honorarkonsulat zu übernehmen, das nämlich war seit 1964 in dem geräumigen zweistöckigen Haus untergebracht. So kommt es, dass Patricia sich seit 1976 um die Angelegenheiten schwedischer Bürger kümmert – und um das riesige Grundstück, das *Le Consulat* umgibt.

Der Garten wurde angelegt von ihrem Vorgänger, den sie als „Kenner und Enthusiast" beschreibt: „Ein Skandinavier, der sich für alle verfügbaren mediterranen Pflanzen und Bäume begeisterte und so viele wie möglich davon in den Garten setzte."

Ihr geht es ähnlich. Eine ihrer ersten Taten war es, an der Längsseite des großen Rasenstücks ein Beet mit *Aeonium arboreum* anzulegen. Die kräftig grünen Blattrosetten sind an der Atlantikküste Marokkos heimisch, entsprechend problemlos breiten sie sich hier aus. Mit anderen Pflanzen dagegen experimentierte Patricia, um zu sehen, ob sie sich auf diesem Stück Land wohl fühlen würden: „Wir haben heftige Winde, im Sommer wie im Winter." Besonders stolz ist sie auf einen Korallenbaum *(Erythrina crista-galli)*, der jetzt schon seit 22 Jahren bei ihr gedeiht und drei Meter hoch geworden ist. Meistens wird die Pflanze mit ihren auffallend attraktiven korallen- bis scharlachroten Blütentrauben als Strauch im Kübel gezogen, der im Winter ins Kalthaus kommt.

Pour pouvoir acquérir la propriété de leurs rêves, Patricia et Abdelkader Erzini ont dû s'engager à reprendre la charge du consulat honoraire de Suède, qui occupait depuis 1964 la grande maison de deux étages. Depuis 1976, Patricia gère donc les affaires des citoyens suédois, et s'occupe de l'immense terrain qui entoure *Le Consulat*. Le jardin a été aménagé par leur prédécesseur, qu'elle décrit comme « connaisseur et enthousiaste » par ces mots : « Un Scandinave qui se passionnait pour toutes les plantes et arbres méditerranéens qu'il pouvait trouver et dont il a planté le plus possible dans le jardin ».

Elle ne se comporte elle-même pas autrement. L'un de ses premiers gestes a été d'aménager un massif d'*Aeonium arboreum* sur le long côté de la grande pelouse. Les rosettes de feuilles d'un vert vif sont chez elles sur la côte atlantique du Maroc et s'étendent donc sans problème. Avec d'autres plantes en revanche, Patricia a dû expérimenter, pour voir si elles se sentiraient bien sur ce terrain où « les vents sont violents, en été autant qu'en hiver ». Elle est très fière notamment d'un arbre-corail *(Erythrina crista-galli)* qui prospère ici depuis 22 ans et atteint aujourd'hui une hauteur de trois mètres : cette plante aux remarquables grappes de fleurs d'une magnifique couleur corail à écarlate est généralement cultivée sous forme d'arbuste dans un baquet qu'on rentre pour l'hiver.

Le jardin est resté en grande partie tel qu'il était lors de sa reprise.

The view back towards the house shows how well the mixture between profuse growth and calming lawn has turned out.

Der Blick zurück aufs Haus zeigt, dass die Mischung aus üppiger Bepflanzung und ruhigen Rasenflächen gelungen ist.

La vue que l'on a du jardin vers la maison confirme à quel point le mélange de calmes pelouses et de végétation luxuriante est réussi.

it was taken over. Patricia is particularly happy with the tall old trees, the palm trees, cedars and cypresses. She herself created the rose pergola behind the house, to the right of the swimming pool. Going down a few steps one reaches the garden itself, which lies on a slightly downward-sloping terrain. Several parallel paths lead up and down the hill. All of the larger paths are covered in natural stone slabs.

The borders, uniformly planted with sage, have proven to be simple and effective. Choosing from the many different species of *salvia*, Patricia has added a blue-flowering one here and a pink one there. Decisions of this kind have enabled her to look after the extensive grounds with the help of only one gardener. All the same, there is plenty of work to do, because Patricia, who formerly lived in a town house with an inner courtyard, was so used to potted plants that she decorated the grounds of the consulate with countless light-coloured clay pots. They contain above all amaryllises, cacti and pansies. The most original thing is Patricia's particular fondness for hanging semicircular pots of deep blue lobelias from the trunks of the palm trees as far as her arms can stretch.

Vieles blieb im Garten so, wie es bei der Übernahme war. Vor allem über die hohen alten Bäume, die Palmen, Zedern, Zypressen, ist Patricia froh. Sie selbst legte eine Rosenpergola hinter dem Haus an, rechter Hand vom Swimmingpool. Von da geht es einige Stufen hinunter in den eigentlichen Garten, der an einem leicht abschüssigen Gelände liegt. Mehrere parallel verlaufende Pfade führen mal hügelan, mal abwärts. Alle größeren Wege sind mit Natursteinplatten belegt.

Als einfach und wirkungsvoll haben sich Rabatten mit einer einheitlichen Bepflanzung von Salbei erwiesen. Von den vielen verschiedenen *Salvia*-Arten hat Patricia mal nur eine blau blühende, mal eine pinke gewählt. Entscheidungen dieser Art machen es ihr möglich, die ausgedehnte Anlage nur mit Unterstützung eines Gärtners zu pflegen. Es bleibt auch so noch genügend Arbeit, denn Patricia, die vorher in einem Stadthaus mit Innenhof lebte, hatte sich so an Topfpflanzen gewöhnt, dass sie auch das Gelände des Konsulats mit unzähligen hellen Tontöpfen dekoriert. Vor allem Amaryllis, Kakteen und Stiefmütterchen wachsen darin. Am originellsten aber ist Patricias Vorliebe dafür, tiefblaue Lobelien in halbrunden Töpfen an die Stämme der Palmen zu hängen, so weit ihr Arm reicht.

Potted plants show to advantage here, too: lobelias hanging from the trunks of palm trees and cacti in bloom on a wall.

Hier kommen auch Topfpflanzen zur Geltung: mit Lobelien an den Stämmen der Palmen und mit blühenden Kakteen auf einer Mauer.

Ici, même les plantes en pot sont mises en valeur : des lobélies sur le tronc des palmiers et des cactus en fleurs sur un muret.

Les vieux et hauts arbres, palmiers, cèdres, cyprès, notamment, réjouissent Patricia. Elle-même a planté une pergola de roses derrière la maison, à droite de la piscine. De là, quelques marches descendent au jardin proprement dit, qui occupe un terrain légèrement escarpé. Plusieurs sentiers parallèles y montent et descendent la colline, et les chemins plus importants sont tous pavés de dalles de pierre. Les plates-bandes plantées exclusivement de sauge se sont avérées faciles à entretenir et pleines d'effet. Parmi les multiples variétés différentes de *Salvia,* Patricia a choisi, ici seulement une aux fleurs bleues, ici une de couleur rose, et ce type de décision lui a permis de n'entretenir la vaste propriété qu'avec l'aide d'un seul jardinier. Même ainsi, il reste cependant encore suffisamment de travail, d'autant plus que Patricia, qui a vécu auparavant dans une maison de ville avec cour intérieure, s'était tellement habituée aux plantes en pot qu'elle a aussi décoré le jardin du Consulat avec une multitude de pots de terre claire. Ce sont essentiellement des amaryllis, des cactus et des pensées qui y poussent, mais Patricia cultive aussi une préférence des plus originales, des lobélies d'un bleu intense dans des pots semi-circulaires accrochés aux troncs des palmiers, aussi loin que ses bras peuvent porter.

The low dry wall carries pots with spectacular *hippeastrum*. The decorative *aeonium* is indigenous to Morocco.

Die niedrige Trockenmauer trägt Töpfe mit prächtigen Rittersternen *(Hippeastrum)*. Das dekorative *Aeonium* ist in Marokko heimisch.

Le mur bas est agrémenté d'amaryllis magnifiques en pot. L'*Aeonium* si décoratif est une plante indigène du Maroc.

Villa Calpe

If you go up the hill from the harbour through the noisy, narrow alley in the direction of the *souk*, you will go past an inconspicuous gateway, behind which lies a peculiar enclave of private hospitality. Going through a tunnel-like passageway, at the end of which a vibrant pink bougainvillea adds one of the few coloured notes to this garden, you will reach the *Villa Calpe*. Its overgrown flight of steps makes the dainty villa appear larger than it actually is. The garden too is basically tiny: just a generous terrace to the left of the house and two narrow flowerbeds on two levels. However, the lack of space has not prevented Simon Cohen from making something quite special out of the inheritance from his aunt.

Simon, who was once the manager of a large hotel in Tanger, loves guests above all. That is why the garden must be flexible too, in order to fit in with his changing moods regarding the decor. One day for example he will create an impressive display with a whole row of potted ferns, the next day it might be with agaves. Sometimes he even lays out a kilim and brightly coloured cushions on the shady terrace, thereby radically changing its appearance. He is full of imaginative ideas regarding ways to reuse the remains from his many parties: he stands empty champagne bottles on their head and uses them to border the flowerbeds behind the house.

The walls all around are totally overgrown: *wisteria*, ivy, jasmine, bougainvillea and cup of gold vine (*solandra maxima*) protect Simon's

Geht man vom Hafen die schmale laute Gasse hügelaufwärts in Richtung *souk*, kommt man an einem unauffälligen Tor vorbei, hinter dem eine skurrile Enklave privater Gastlichkeit liegt. Durch einen tunnelartigen Gang, an dessen Ende eine Bougainvillea von kräftigem Rosa einen der wenige farbigen Akzente in diesem Garten setzt, gelangt man zur *Villa Calpe*. Wegen ihrer reich bewachsenen Freitreppe wirkt die zierliche Villa größer, als sie tatsächlich ist. Auch der Garten ist im Grunde winzig: eine großzügige Terrasse links vom Haus und dahinter zwei schmale Rabatten auf zwei Ebenen. Doch der Mangel an Platz hat Simon Cohen nicht daran gehindert, aus dem Erbe seiner Tante etwas ganz Besonderes zu machen.

Simon, der einst Direktor eines großen Hotels in Tanger war, liebt Gäste über alles. Daher muss auch der Garten flexibel sein, um sich seinen jeweiligen Dekorationslaunen anzupassen. Mal platziert er zum Beispiel eine ganze Reihe Farne in Töpfen zu einem eindrucksvollen Ensemble, mal sind es Agaven. Manchmal legt er auch einen Kelim und bunte Kissen auf die schattige Terrasse, womit er ihr Aussehen radikal verändert. Selbst mit den Überbleibseln seiner vielen Feste geht Simon äußerst einfallsreich um: Leere Champagnerflaschen werden auf den Kopf gestellt und dienen den Rabatten hinter dem Haus als Beeteinfassung.

Die Mauern ringsum sind über und über bewachsen: Glyzinien, Efeu, Jasmin, Bougainvillea und Goldkelch

Lorsqu'on prend depuis le port la ruelle étroite et bruyante qui monte la colline en direction du *souk*, on passe devant une porte discrète, qui cache une étrange enclave d'hospitalité privée. Un passage rappelant un tunnel, à l'extrémité duquel un bougainvillier aux fleurs d'un rose soutenu procure l'une des rares notes de couleur au jardin, mène à la *Villa Calpe*. Son escalier extérieur richement planté fait paraître la villa gracile plus grande qu'elle ne l'est en réalité. Le jardin lui aussi est en fait minuscule : une terrasse généreuse à gauche de la maison et, par derrière, deux étroits parterres sur deux niveaux. Le manque de place n'a cependant pas empêché Simon Cohen de transformer en un endroit très particulier l'héritage de sa tante.

Simon, autrefois directeur d'un grand hôtel de Tanger, aime par-dessus tout recevoir. Il lui fallait donc un système de jardin souple, qu'il pourrait adapter à ses idées de décoration du moment. Il peut ainsi lui arriver de créer un ensemble frappant en disposant une multitude de fougères en pots, ou parfois aussi des agaves. Ou alors il place un kilim et des coussins de couleurs sur la terrasse ombragée, changeant totalement son apparence. Et même les reliquats de ses nombreuses fêtes sont utilisés par Simon avec une imagination débordante : les bouteilles de champagne vides sont placées sur la tête pour tenir lieu de rebords aux plates-bandes de derrière la maison.

Les murs tout autour sont littéralement envahis : glycines, lierre, jasmin, bougainvilliers et solandra

The high doors and two-winged flight of steps make the house appear much larger than it actually is. Creeping plants grow in numerous pots.

Die hohen Türen und die zweigeteilte Freitreppe lassen das schmale weiße Haus größer wirken, als es ist. Aus zahlreichen Töpfen ranken Pflanzen, die sich wie ein Schleier über die Brüstung ergießen.

Les portes hautes et l'escalier extérieur en deux parties font paraître l'étroite maison blanche plus grande qu'elle n'est en réalité. Une multitude de fleurs en pot déverse des flots de végétation luxuriante.

little paradise form inquisitive eyes. A narrow pebble-covered path runs along behind the house. Here, on the upper level, there is a special feature, which has since been frequently copied in Tanger: the pet cemetery. Simon values his four-legged companions so much that he has dedicated a proper grave with a commemorative stone to each of his deceased dogs and cats: "After all, they accompany us for many years – we can't just 'dispose' of them…"

Potted plants are set on every step of each wing of the curved flight of steps.

Beide Flügel der geschwungenen Freitreppe tragen Topfpflanzen auf jeder Stufe.

Chacune des ailes de l'escalier extérieur incurvé est décorée de plantes en pot sur chaque marche.

(Solandra maxima) schützen Simons kleines Paradies vor neugierigen Blicken. Ein schmaler, mit Kieselsteinen befestigter Weg führt hinter dem Haus entlang. Hier, auf der höher gelegenen Ebene, befindet sich eine Besonderheit, die inzwischen in Tanger viel kopiert wird: der Haustierfriedhof. Simon schätzt seine vierbeinigen Lebensgefährten so sehr, dass er jedem seiner verstorbenen Hunde und auch den Katzen ein richtiges Grab mit Gedenkstein gewidmet hat: „Schließlich begleiten sie uns viele Jahre lang – da kann man sie doch nicht einfach ‚entsorgen' …"

Potted ferns are standing in line, waiting to be watered. The many potted plants in this garden are a proof that a passionate garden lover lives here.

In Reih und Glied warten Töpfe mit Farn darauf, gegossen zu werden. Auch die zahlreichen Topfpflanzen im Garten zeugen davon, dass hier ein leidenschaftlicher Pflanzenliebhaber lebt.

Sagement alignées, les fougères attendent d'être arrosées. Les innombrables plantes en pot du jardin attestent de la passion que leur porte le maître des lieux.

(Solandra maxima) protègent le petit paradis de Simon des regards curieux. Un chemin étroit recouvert de graviers longe l'arrière de la maison. Là, une légère éminence présente une particularité, entre-temps très copiée à Tanger : le cimetière des animaux domestiques. Simon aime tant ses compagnons à quatre pattes qu'il a dédié à chacun de ses chiens et chats morts une véritable tombe avec plaque commémorative : « après tout, ils nous accompagnent de longues années, on ne peut quand même pas simplement les ‹ éliminer › quand ils sont morts … ».

Every animal that spent its life with Simon Cohen, be it cat or dog, is given its own grave.

Ob Hund oder Katze, jedes Tier, das sein Leben mit Simon Cohen teilte, bekommt sein eigenes Grab.

Que ce soit chien ou chat, chaque animal ayant jamais partagé la vie de Simon Cohen a droit à sa tombe personnelle.

Dar Golzean

The American painter, Elena Prentice, has a wonderful view over Tanger – "the white city by the sea" – from the study in the first floor of her house. This is a view she has known since she was a young child; her grandfather was the first American ambassador in Morocco and is buried in Tanger. But *Dar Golzean*, the two-storey white house with the dark green shutters is no family inheritance. Elena only acquired it at the end of the 1990s. Then she had the house – which, like so many others of its kind in Tanger, flaunted its resplendent Moroccan colours – painted inside and out in austere white. Her dark wood furniture contrasts effectively against this backdrop. The atmosphere is reminiscent of a Spanish manor house or a South American *hacienda*.

The garden, on the other hand, displays its British influence. The influential English landscape designer, Waller, after whom a square was named in Tanger, laid it out at the beginning of the 20th century. It is said that it was Waller who brought the silk worm to northern Morocco. In order to help the animals settle in, he planted at least one mulberry tree in each of the gardens he designed. He also left his "signature" on this plot of land – a wonderful mulberry tree grows down below on the terraced slopes. There is a good view of the tree from the roof terrace of the guesthouse situated near the pool.

Many of the tall old trees that add character to the garden date back to Waller's days: different species of palm trees, fig trees and cypresses. Rambling roses climb up

Die amerikanische Malerin Elena Prentice hat von ihrem Studio im ersten Stock ihres Hauses einen grandiosen Blick über Tanger, die „weiße Stadt am Meer". Es ist eine Aussicht, die ihr seit Kindestagen vertraut ist: Ihr Großvater war der erste amerikanische Botschafter in Marokko und liegt in Tanger begraben. Aber *Dar Golzean,* das zweistöckige weiße Haus mit den dunkelgrünen Fensterläden, ist kein Familienerbe, Elena hat es erst Ende der 1990er Jahre erworben. Und sie ließ das Haus, das wie so viele in Tanger in marokkanischer Farbenfreude prunkte, innen und außen in strengem Weiß streichen. Vor diesem Hintergrund heben sich ihre Möbel aus dunklem Holz wirkungsvoll ab. Die Atmosphäre erinnert an ein spanisches Herrenhaus oder eine südamerikanische Hazienda.

Der Garten dagegen steht unter britischem Einfluss. Er wurde Anfang des 20. Jahrhunderts von dem einflussreichen englischen Landschaftsarchitekten Waller angelegt, nach dem sogar ein Platz in Tanger benannt ist. Es heißt, Waller habe die Seidenraupe nach Nordmarokko gebracht. Damit sie heimisch werden konnte, pflanzte er in jeden von ihm gestalteten Garten mindestens einen Maulbeerbaum. Seine „Signatur" hat er auch auf diesem Grundstück hinterlassen – ein wunderbarer Maulbeerbaum wächst tief unten an den terrassierten Hängen. Von der Dachterrasse des Gästehauses, das nahe beim Pool steht, hat man einen guten Blick darauf.

Aus Wallers Zeiten stammen noch viele der hohen alten Bäume, die dem Garten Charakter geben:

Depuis son studio au premier étage de sa maison, l'artiste peintre américaine Elena Prentice a une vue grandiose sur Tanger, la « ville blanche au bord de la mer ». Ce paysage lui est familier depuis son enfance, car son grand-père a été le premier ambassadeur américain au Maroc et est enterré à Tanger. Mais *Dar Golzean*, la maison blanche à deux étages aux volets vert foncé, n'est pas un héritage familial, Elena ne l'ayant acquise qu'à la fin des années 1990. Elle a fait peindre l'intérieur et l'extérieur de la maison, qui, comme tant d'autres à Tanger, faisait étalage des couleurs vives si appréciées des Marocains, d'un blanc strict, un fond sur lequel ses meubles de bois sombre se détachent avec force. L'atmosphère en rappelle aujourd'hui celle d'une demeure seigneuriale espagnole ou d'une hacienda sud-américaine.

Le jardin, en revanche, est marqué par l'influence britannique. Il a été aménagé au début du 20ᵉ siècle par l'architecte-paysagiste anglais Waller, alors très influent et dont une place porte le nom à Tanger. On dit que Waller aurait introduit le ver à soie dans le nord du Maroc et, pour que ce dernier puisse s'y acclimater, aurait planté au moins un mûrier dans chacun des jardins composés par lui. Une « signature » qu'il a également laissée ici : un superbe mûrier pousse tout en bas de la pente en terrasses, on le voit très bien depuis le toit en terrasse de la maison d'hôtes, à côté de la piscine.

Bon nombre des vieux et hauts arbres qui donnent son caractère au jardin datent aussi de l'époque Waller : diverses espèces de palmiers,

The flowers of the *tecomaria capensis* stretch into the sky; in the background, the white balustrades of the roof terrace.

Vor der weißen Balustrade der Dachterrasse recken sich die Blüten der *Tecomaria capensis* in den Himmel.

Devant la balustrade blanche de la terrasse, les fleurs de *Tecomaria capensis* s'élancent vers le ciel.

249

some of the trunks. In this garden climbing plants are allowed to grow freely. Morning glory, plumbago, crossvine, sweet peas, *nasturtiums* – they all proliferate giving a wild touch to this flourishing, well-established garden.

Elena Prentice, who spends several months each year here, has a preference for abundantly blooming summer flowers such as Mexican asters, love-in-a-mist *(nigella damascena)*, *lavatera* and, above all, farewell-to-spring. With its two-coloured 10 cm long funnel-shaped flowers, the *clarkia amoena* steals the show from the countless roses.

verschiedene Palmenarten, Feigen, Zypressen. An manchen von ihnen ranken Kletterrosen empor. In diesem Garten dürfen sich Kletterpflanzen ungehindert ausbreiten, Prunkwinden, Plumbago, Bignonia, Wicken, Kapuzinerkresse – alles wuchert und gibt dem eingewachsenen alten Garten etwas Wildes.

Elena Prentice, die mehrere Monate im Jahr hier verbringt, hat eine Vorliebe für reich blühende Sommerblumen wie Cosmeen, Jungfer im Grünen *(Nigella damascena)*, Lavatera und vor allem Godetien – die *Clarkia amoena* stiehlt mit ihren zweifarbigen, bis zu zehn Zentimeter großen Trichterblüten sogar den unzähligen Rosen die Schau.

figuiers, cyprès. Certains d'entre eux sont assaillis par des rosiers grimpants. Toutes les plantes grimpantes peuvent par ailleurs s'étaler librement dans ce jardin : volubilis, plumbagos, bignonias, pois de senteur, ou capucines, tout pousse à foison et donne au vieux jardin une apparence presque sauvage.

Elena Prentice, qui passe ici plusieurs mois de l'année, avoue une préférence pour les fleurs d'été à riche floraison, comme les cosmos, Nigelles de Damas *(Nigella damascena)*, mauves, et surtout godétias, la *Clarkia amoena* et ses fleurs en entonnoir bicolores pouvant atteindre dix centimètres vole même la vedette aux innombrables roses.

A rose arbour spans a path that leads to the lower part of the garden. The pool is set next to the house.

Ein Rosenbogen überspannt den Weg in den unteren Teil des Gartens. Der Pool liegt direkt beim Haus.

Dans la partie basse du jardin, une arche couverte de roses. La piscine se trouve tout près de la maison.

Plants that grow in the painter's garden are the aloe, *datura* lily, fare-well-to-spring, vine, love-in-a-mist and the rose.

Pflanzen aus dem Garten der Malerin: Aloe, Datura, Schwertlilien, Godetie, Duftwicken, Jungfer im Grünen, Rosen.

Les plantes du jardin de l'artiste : aloès, datura, iris, godétie, pois de senteur, nigelle, roses.

253

Bab Essalam

Many people have praised this garden. Whilst it was still owned by the French poetess Louise de Vilmorin, a woman whose great elegance was equalled by her intelligence, the house was used for large parties which are still fondly remembered today, and the beauty of the grounds is still highly praised. Even Lady Baird was so impressed that, after her first walk around the place, she exclaimed jubilantly, "It's mine, it's mine!". Thus, she set the seal on the negotiations to buy the house, even before she had set foot in it: "I have fallen in love with the garden" she said.

For a woman well into her eighties the journey there alone is a major undertaking: usually Lady Baird drives her own car – with her lap-dog as sole companion – from Norfolk in England to Tanger, stopping in Marseille to take the ferry. According to Lady Baird, every time she goes there the mere sight of the garden refreshes her so much that she forgets all the stress and strain of the journey. She only requires the help of her gardener Ahmed in order to keep everything in tidy.

Measuring at least 10,000 square metres, the plot is situated on a steep escarpment and is divided into a large number of terraces. An inconspicuous gate serves as the entrance. Only after walking through a wisteria covered pergola and up a steep flight of steps you catch a glimpse of the house: a three-storey pale pink and white villa. From the paved square in front of the house

Diesen Garten haben viele schon gerühmt. Als er sich noch im Besitz der französischen Dichterin Louise de Vilmorin, einer ebenso eleganten wie intelligenten Frau, befand, wurden hier große Feste gefeiert, die man heute noch lobt – ebenso wie die Schönheit der Anlage. Auch Lady Baird war davon so beeindruckt, dass sie nach einem ersten Rundgang jubilierte: „It's mine, it's mine!" Damit besiegelte sie die Kaufverhandlungen, noch bevor sie einen Fuß ins Haus gesetzt hatte: „Ich habe mich in den Garten verliebt."

Allein die Anreise ist für eine Frau, die gut in ihren Achtzigern ist, keine Kleinigkeit: Lady Baird fährt grundsätzlich mit ihrem eigenen Auto, nur ihren Schoßhund als Begleiter, vom englischen Norfolk nach Tanger, mit Zwischenstation in Marseille, wo sie die Fähre nimmt. Allein der Anblick des Gartens, sagt sie, erfrischt sie jedesmal so sehr, dass sie alle Strapazen vergisst. Ihr genügt die Hilfe ihres Gärtners Ahmed, um alles in bester Ordnung zu halten.

Das Grundstück von mindestens 10.000 Quadratmetern liegt an einem Steilhang und ist in viele Terrassen gegliedert. Ein unscheinbares Tor dient als Eingang, erst wenn man eine mit Glyzinien bewachsene Pergola durchschritten und eine steile Treppe abwärts genommen hat, bekommt man das Haus zu sehen: eine dreistöckige Villa in Zartrosa und Weiß. Der gepflasterte Platz davor gibt den Blick frei auf andere Hügel und Häuser von Tanger. Von

Ce jardin a déjà reçu les éloges de beaucoup. Lorsqu'il était encore en possession de la poétesse française Louise de Vilmorin, une femme aussi élégante qu'intelligente, de grandes fêtes y étaient célébrées, qui aujourd'hui encore suscitent l'émerveillement, tout comme la beauté de l'endroit. Lady Baird, elle aussi, en sera tellement impressionnée qu'après une première visite, elle jubilait déjà « It's mine, it's mine ! » C'est d'ailleurs ainsi qu'elle conclura les négociations de vente, avant même d'avoir mis un pied dans la maison : « Je suis tombée amoureuse du jardin ».

Le voyage seul, pour cette femme ayant largement dépassé les quatre-vingt ans, n'est pas une mince affaire : Lady Baird ne se déplace en principe qu'avec sa propre voiture et accompagnée de son seul bichon, entre la ville anglaise de Norfolk et Tanger, faisant une halte à Marseille où elle prend le ferry. La seule vue du jardin, déclare-t-elle, la rafraîchit à chaque fois à un point tel qu'elle en oublie toutes ses fatigues. Et pour tout conserver dans le meilleur des ordres, l'aide de son jardinier Ahmed lui suffit.

Le terrain, d'au moins 10 000 mètres carrés, est situé sur une pente escarpée et divisé en nombreuses terrasses. Un portail discret tient lieu d'entrée et ce n'est qu'après avoir traversé une pergola plantée de glycines et descendu un escalier raide que la maison s'offre aux regards : une villa à trois étages rose tendre et blanche. L'emplacement pavé qui la précède

Orange-red aloe flowers and white climbing rose increase the charm of the façade of the main house, held in a delicate pink.

Orangerot blühende Aloe und weiße Kletterrose erhöhen den Charme der zartrosa Fassade des Haupthauses.

Aloès orangé en fleurs et rosier grimpant blanc rehaussent le charme de la façade rose tendre de la maison principale.

The entrance gate is small and modest, but just a few steps down into the garden a stupendous panoramic view over Tanger opens up, framed by wisteria and crowned by a palm tree.

Das Eingangstor ist klein und bescheiden, aber dahinter öffnet sich nach wenigen Stufen abwärts ein überwältigender Blick auf das Panorama von Tanger, gerahmt von Wisteria und gekrönt von einer Palme.

La porte d'entrée est plutôt petite et modeste. En revanche, la vue sur Tanger, qui s'offre au bout de quelques marches, encadrée de glycines et couronnée d'un palmier, est époustouflante.

Behind the house, a pergola overgrown with wisteria leads up to the garden proper. The steps are made of natural stone slabs and are bordered by thick, light-green ferns.

Hinter dem Haus geht es rechter Hand durch eine mit Wisteria berankte Pergola aufwärts in den eigentlichen Garten. Die Treppe aus Natursteinen wird gesäumt von kräftigen hellgrünen Farnwedeln.

À droite derrière la maison, on passe par une pergola couverte de glycines pour descendre dans le jardin proprement dit. L'escalier en pierres naturelles est bordé d'épaisses fougères vert tendre.

there is a sweeping view over other hills and houses in Tanger. From there, the path winds its way around corners and up and down steps before finally reaching the garden itself. In spite of its well-kept appearance, the garden looks wildly romantic due to the large number of plants that have been here since the 1930s and cover every square meter of the grounds. Large terraced areas are covered in grass and bordered by flowerbeds and all the banks are laid out as beds. A jungle-like wall of trees, shrubs and flowers runs downhill to the left and right of the main garden.

You never get the impression that you are walking on some kind of showpiece; thanks to the accomplished terraces and divisions, it feels like an intimate, small garden. This applies in particular to the part with the large walled and tiled terrace that was intended for receptions. Palm and banana trees act as a screen, roses, *agapanthus*, pelargoniums and above all aloes add colour. The round pool, next to which papyrus and ferns grow, is the peacocks' favourite spot. These beautiful birds dominate the garden fanning their tail feathers out in their impressive courtship displays.

The lower third of the grounds, with its flat dry-stone walls and sparsely planted agaves and other similar "architectural" plants, was only laid out a few years ago and differs from the old part.

Some people dislike this barrenness, others find it elegant and modern. This section was designed under the aegis of Sheika Fatima, a lady who apparently left Tanger because she was lovesick, thus leaving the door open for Lady Baird who keeps the garden precisely as she came to know and love it.

da führt der Weg mit Treppen und Kurven in den eigentlichen Garten. Der wirkt bei aller Gepflegtheit wild romantisch, wegen der Vielzahl der Pflanzen, die hier schon seit den 1930er Jahren zu Hause sind und jeden Quadratmeter bedecken. Große terrassierte Flächen sind mit Rasen bedeckt und mit Blumenrabatten eingefasst, Böschungen sind durchgehend als Beete gestaltet. Links und rechts der Hauptanlage zieht sich ein dschungelartiger Wall aus Bäumen, Sträuchern und Blumen den Hang abwärts.

Nie hat man den Eindruck, sich auf einem „Präsentierteller" zu bewegen, dank der gekonnten Abstufungen und Unterteilungen fühlt man sich überall wie in einem intimen kleinen Garten. Das trifft besonders auf jenen Teil zu, der mit seiner großen ummauerten und gekachelten Terrasse für Empfänge geplant wurde. Palmen und Bananenstauden sorgen für Sichtschutz, Rosen, *Agapanthus*, Pelargonien und blühende Aloen geben Farbe. Das runde Wasserbecken, an dem Papyrus und Farne wachsen, ist der Lieblingsplatz der Pfauen, die radschlagend den Garten beherrschen.

Das untere Drittel des Geländes mit seinen flachen Trockenmauern und sparsamen Anpflanzungen von Agaven und ähnlichen „architektonischen" Pflanzen wurde erst vor wenigen Jahren angelegt und unterscheidet sich sehr vom alten Teil. Manche mögen diese Kargheit nicht, andere finden sie elegant und modern. Gestaltet wurde dieser Teil unter der Ägide von Sheika Fatima, die Tanger angeblich aus Liebeskummer verließ und so den Weg frei machte für Lady Baird, die den Garten so erhält, wie sie ihn kennen und lieben lernte.

dégage la vue sur les autres collines et maisons de Tanger. Un chemin y mène, par plusieurs escaliers et méandres, au jardin proprement dit. Bien que parfaitement entretenu, ce dernier fait l'effet d'un romantisme échevelé, en raison de l'abondance des plantes, installées ici depuis les années 1930 et qui ne laissent pas un mètre carré libre. De vastes surfaces en terrasse sont plantées de gazon et entourées de parterres fleuris, tandis que les talus sont tous aménagés en massifs. À gauche et à droite de l'espace principal, un rempart d'arbres, de buissons et de fleurs forme une véritable jungle qui descend la pente.

Jamais le visiteur n'a l'impression d'évoluer sur une scène de théâtre, car les étagements et divisions, impeccablement réalisés, le font se sentir partout comme dans un petit jardin intime. Notamment dans la partie qui, avec sa grande terrasse pavée entourée de murs, était prévue pour les réceptions. Palmiers et bananiers y protègent des regards, tandis que rosiers, agapanthes, pélargoniums, et surtout aloés, y apportent des touches de couleurs. Le bassin rond où poussent papyrus et fougères est l'endroit préféré des paons, qui règnent sur le jardin en faisant la roue.

Le tiers inférieur du terrain, avec ses murs secs et plats et ses plantations clairsemées d'agaves et d'autres plantes « architecturales », n'a été aménagé qu'il y a quelques années et se distingue fortement de la partie plus ancienne. Cette austérité ne plaît pas à tout le monde, mais certains la trouvent élégante et moderne. Cette partie du jardin a été arrangée sous l'égide de Sheika Fatima, qui aurait quitté Tanger à la suite d'un chagrin d'amour, ouvrant ainsi la voie à Lady Baird, qui ellemême a choisi de conserver le jardin dans l'état où elle a appris à le connaître et à l'aimer.

The garden extends down a steep hill. The picturesque pavilion stands on the upper half.

Der Garten zieht sich den steilen Hügel weit hinunter. Der hübsche Pavillon liegt in der oberen Hälfte.

Le jardin descend loin en suivant la pente raide. Le joli pavillon se trouve dans la moitié du haut.

The huge trumpet-like blossoms of the datura span over the path like an arch.

Die großen Trompetenblüten der Datura spannen einen Bogen über den Weg.

Les grandes fleurs des daturas s'étendent en arche par dessus le chemin.

Peacocks love trees with a view. A densely grown flowerbed does not attract them.

Einen Baum mit Aussicht suchen sich die Pfauen gern. Die dicht bepflanzten Beete dagegen meiden sie.

Les paons affectionnent « un arbre avec vue ». En revanche, ils évitent les plates-bandes trop touffues.

263

Dar Serfaty

Dar Serfaty is perched high on a hill above Tanger, where the most coveted plots of land are to be found. At first glance the front garden looks European with its well-kept lawns and beds and its modern, white spherical lamps and decorative plant containers. Only the pond, generously stocked with gold fish and large-leafed plants such as banana trees and Swiss cheese plants, creates an exotic atmosphere; bizarre rocks add to this impression.

The path runs along the right of the house to the small but splendid swimming pool from where the visitor has a sensational view of Tanger. You scarcely want to move from this spot. But this would be a pity because the garden has much more to offer. In front of the house on the left there is a passageway to the "Arab" side, which leads out into an enclosed inner courtyard with a blue and white tiled floor. Glass roofing turns the patio into a veritable winter garden where elephant ear, Swiss cheese plants, banana and palm trees flourish in large decorative pots and amphoras, while bougainvilleas cover the walls. Doors and windows with round arches, and especially the oversized old Moroccan lanterns, turn the room into something magical, straight out of the Thousand and One Nights.

Next you enter a classical riyad, a walled inner courtyard with pools and channels, which divide the garden into four equal-sized beds. Here the tiles have been kept green and white; the house wall in the background is a terracotta colour. Red pelargoniums grow in abundance.

After crossing a terrace you come to the large reception room, a fea-

Hoch oben auf einem Hügel über Tanger, wo die begehrtesten Grundstücke liegen, befindet sich Dar Serfaty. Der Vorgarten wirkt zunächst europäisch: gepflegter Rasen und Rabatten, moderne weiße Kugellampen, dekorative Pflanzgefäße. Nur der Teich, großzügig mit Goldfischen und großblättrigen Pflanzen wie Bananenstauden und Monstera bestückt, hat exotisches Flair. Bizarre Felsbrocken tragen zu dem Eindruck noch bei.

Rechts am Haus entlang führt der Weg zum kleinen, aber feinen Pool – und zu einem sensationellen Blick über Tanger. Da möchte man sich kaum mehr fortbewegen. Was aber schade wäre, weil der Garten noch einiges zu bieten hat. Schon vor dem Haus gibt es links einen Durchgang zur „arabischen" Seite, von wo man zunächst in einen geschlossenen Innenhof mit blau-weiß gekacheltem Boden kommt. Eine gläserne Überdachung macht den Patio zum veritablen Wintergarten, in dem Elefantenohr, Fensterblatt, Banane und Palme in dekorativen großen Töpfen und Amphoren gedeihen und Bougainvillea die Wände bedeckt. Türen und Fenster mit Rundbögen, vor allem aber die überdimensionalen antiken marokkanischen Laternen geben dem Raum etwas Märchenhaftes à la Tausendundeine Nacht.

Danach kommt man in einen klassischen Riad, einen ummauerten Innenhof mit Wasserbecken und Kanälen, die den Garten in vier gleich große Beete aufteilen. Hier sind die Kacheln weiß-grün gehalten, die Hauswand im Hintergrund ist terrakottafarben. Es wachsen rote Pelargonien im Überfluss.

Über eine Terrasse gelangt man in den großen Empfangsraum, über

Who wants to dive into the water if he can enjoy this view over the bay of Tanger? Traditional Moroccan tiles ornament this pool that rather invites to look than to swim.

Wer will bei diesem Ausblick auf die Bucht von Tanger noch untertauchen? Traditionelle marokkanischen Fliesen schmücken den Pool, der mehr zum Schauen denn zum Schwimmen einlädt.

Qui peut avoir envie de plonger devant une telle vue sur la baie de Tanger ? Des faïences marocaines traditionnelles embellissent la piscine, qui invite plus à la contemplation qu'à la natation.

D*ar Serfaty* est situé haut sur
une colline qui domine Tanger, parmi les terrains les
plus recherchés. Le jardin de devant
semble au premier abord plutôt européen : pelouses soignées et parterres, lampadaires sphériques blancs et
modernes, jardinières d'ornement.
Seul l'étang, généreusement pourvu
de poissons rouges et de plantes à
grandes feuilles telles que bananiers
et monsteras, donne une impression

d'exotisme, encore renforcée par les
étranges blocs rocheux.

Le long de la maison à droite, le
chemin mène à une petite, mais jolie,
piscine, et à une vue sensationnelle
sur Tanger. On voudrait ne pas avoir à
s'en détacher, ce qui serait pourtant
dommage, car le jardin a encore des
merveilles à offrir. Devant la maison,
un passage à gauche mène au côté
« arabe » et débouche d'abord dans
une cour intérieure fermée au sol

pavé de bleu et de blanc. Une toiture
vitrée fait de ce patio un véritable
jardin d'hiver où prospèrent Oreilles
d'éléphants, Monsteras délicieux, bananiers et palmiers dans de grands
pots et des amphores des plus déco-
ratifs, tandis que des bougainvilliers
recouvrent les murs. Les portes et
fenêtres aux arcs en plein cintre,
mais surtout les anciennes lanternes
marocaines surdimensionnées, confèrent à la pièce un caractère féerique

digne des Mille et une nuits. On arrive ensuite dans un *riad* classique,
une cour intérieure entourée de
murs avec bassins et canaux, qui
séparent le jardin en quatre parterres
de même taille. Les carreaux sont ici
blancs et verts, le mur de la maison
à l'arrière-plan est couleur de terre
cuite et des pélargoniums rouges
croissent à profusion.

Il faut passer par une terrasse
pour gagner la grande salle de récep-

The covered patio and the garden courtyard, designed in the style of a classical *riyad*, are very traditional. The goldfish pond in front of the house adds a little exotic flair.

Ganz der Tradition verpflichtet zeigen sich der überdachte Patio und der als klassischer *Riad* angelegte Gartenhof. Der Goldfischteich vor dem Haus hat eher exotisches Flair.

Dans le plus pur respect de la tradition, se présentent le patio couvert et la cour, arrangée à la manière d'un *riad* classique. L'étang aux poissons rouges devant la maison paraît plutôt exotique.

ture which used to be found in all Moroccan houses. From there, a few steps lead into the wildest part of the garden, which only gradually opens up and is far more extensive than it appears at first glance. Because of the problem irrigation poses here, as is the case in all large gardens in Tanger, the rest of the garden has been allowed to develop "almost naturally". Thus, the indigenous *Aeonium* spreads out, covering everything in a decorative carefree manner ...

den früher jedes marokkanische Haus verfügte. Von da aus tritt man über einige Treppenstufen in den wildesten Teil des Gartens, der sich nur nach und nach erschließt und viel weitreichender ist, als er am Anfang erscheint. Da die Bewässerung wie in allen großen Gärten Tangers Probleme bereitet, darf sich der Rest des Gartens „naturnah" entwickeln – was bedeutet, dass sich das heimische *Aeonium* in dekorativer Unbekümmertheit flächendeckend ausbreitet ...

tion dont disposait autrefois chaque maison marocaine. De là, quelques marches mènent à la partie la plus sauvage du jardin, qui ne se dévoile alors plus que peu à peu et s'avère beaucoup plus vaste qu'il ne le paraissait au début. En raison de l'irrigation qui, comme dans tous les grands jardins de Tanger, pose problème, on laisse le reste du jardin se développer « naturellement », ce qui signifie que l'*Aeonium* local prospère et occupe le terrain dans une insouciance des plus décoratives ...

Those who believe that behind the white, bougainvillea covered walls they will immediately come upon garden of the *Santa Barbara* villa are wide off the mark. Of course, a lawn with palm trees and an araucaria lead to the villa which, with its sparkling white battlements, is reminiscent of a Moorish fortress; however, on the other side of the house it becomes interesting from a botanical point of view. From the roof there is a breathtaking view over the garden itself, one of the largest and most beautiful privately owned gardens. The vegetation is so luxuriant that it creates the impression that a light mist is constantly rising from the ground. Deep green lawns are broken up by almost black Italian cypresses, opulent flowerbeds and metre-high palm trees. Like almost all plots of land in Tanger, *Santa Barbara* lies on a slope; so many different types of atmosphere can be created here on the different levels. Because of this, the stone paved terrace with the adjoining lawn and cypresses planted to the left and right of the path appear somewhat Italian. Meanwhile, the centre of the garden with its pebbled path, which runs through colourful flowerbeds, looks rather English. The deeper into the garden one goes, the more exotic it appears. There is, for example, a long, passionflower-covered pergola running along a dry-stone wall, which is in turn completely overgrown with geraniums. In the *Santa Barbara* garden the geraniums have more surprises in store for the visitor: they climb straight up the trunks of a group of palm trees, way over two metres high!

Santa Barbara

The different silhouettes of araucaria, agave and palm tree show off beautifully in front of the façade of the house, held in the typical Moorish style, complete with battlements and arched windows.

Mit ihren unterschiedlichen Silhouetten heben sich Araukarie, Agave und Palme eindrucksvoll von der typisch maurischen Fassade des Hauses ab, die von Zinnen und Fensterbögen bestimmt ist.

Les silhouettes variées de l'araucaria, de l'agave et du palmiers se détachent de façon impressionnante de la façade typiquement mauresque de la maison. Celle-ci est dominée par les créneaux et les arches des fenêtres.

Wer glaubt, hinter der weißen, mit Bougainvillea bewachsenen Mauer sofort im Garten der Villa *Santa Barbara* zu stehen, hat weit gefehlt. Sicher, eine Rasenfläche mit Palmen und einer Araukarie führen zu der Villa, die mit ihren blütenweißen Zinnen an eine maurische Festung erinnert, doch botanisch interessant wird es erst auf der anderen Seite des Hauses. Besonders vom Dach aus bietet sich ein atemberaubender Blick auf den eigentlichen Garten, einen der größten und schönsten in Privatbesitz. So üppig ist die Vegetation, dass man den Eindruck hat, es steigt permanent ein leichter Nebel vom Boden auf. Satt grüner Rasen wird unterbrochen durch fast schwarze Säulenzypressen, opulente Blumenbeete und meterhohe Palmen. Wie fast alle Grundstücke in Tanger liegt auch *Santa Barbara* an einem Hang, so dass hier durch die unterschiedlichen Ebenen viele verschiedene Atmosphären entstehen konnten. So wirkt die steingepflasterte Terrasse mit dem anschließenden Rasenstück und den links und rechts vom Weg gepflanzten Zypressen eher italienisch. Die Gartenmitte mit ihrem Kieselsteinweg, der durch bunte Blumenrabatten führt, mutet indes eher englisch an. Je tiefer man in den Garten gelangt, desto exotischer wirkt er. Da gibt es zum Beispiel eine lange, mit Passiflora überrankte Pergola, die an einer Trockenmauer entlang verläuft, die wiederum komplett mit Pelargonien zugewachsen ist. Im Garten von *Santa Barbara* hält die Pelargonie noch mehr Überraschungen bereit: Hier erklimmt sie nämlich gleich bei einer Gruppe von Palmen den Stamm – und das weit über zwei Meter hoch!

Ceux qui croient qu'il suffit de passer le mur blanc envahi de bougainvillées pour se trouver dans le jardin de la villa *Santa Barbara* sont loin du compte. Certes, une pelouse plantée de palmiers et d'un araucaria précède la villa, qui rappelle une forteresse maure avec ses créneaux ivoire, mais les choses ne deviennent intéressantes sur le plan botanique que de l'autre côté de la maison. Depuis le toit notamment, la vue sur le véritable jardin est à couper le souffle. C'est l'un des plus grands et des plus beaux jardins privés, la végétation y est si abondante qu'on a l'impression de voir en permanence un léger nuage monter du sol. Le gazon vert foncé est couvert de cyprès presque noirs, d'opulents massifs de fleurs et de palmiers hauts de plusieurs mètres. Comme presque tous les jardins de Tanger, *Santa Barbara* est situé en pente et les différents niveaux permettent de créer autant d'atmosphères différentes. Ainsi, la terrasse pavée de pierre, la pelouse contiguë et les cyprès plantés à gauche et à droite du chemin sont plutôt italiens, tandis que le milieu du jardin et son allée de graviers entre des plates-bandes colorées rappelle le style anglais. Plus on descend dans le jardin, plus il devient exotique avec, par exemple, la longue pergola couverte de passiflores courant le long d'un mur sec, lui-même totalement envahi de pélargoniums. Pélargoniums qui, dans le jardin de *Santa Barbara*, réservent encore d'autres surprises au visiteur, puisqu'ils y grimpent sur le tronc d'un groupe de palmiers, et à plus de deux mètres de haut !

The tiles of the star-shaped fountain on the main terrace are painted in Majorelle-blue. Three gardeners tend the 6,000 square metres of garden that has its own spring.

Majorelleblau leuchten die Fliesen des Sternbrunnens auf der großen Terrasse. Drei Gärtner pflegen den 6.000 Quadratmeter großen Garten, der über eine eigene Quelle verfügt.

Le carrelage de la fontaine en forme d'étoile sur la grande terrasse est d'un bleu majorelle lumineux. Trois jardiniers prennent soin du jardin, qui fait 6 000 mètres carrés et dispose d'une source.

Aromatic and Medicinal Plants

In the Thousand and One Nights it is written that "If an ill person enters Nur ad-Din's Garden, he will leave as a raging lion". The combination of a wide variety of different plants brought about a miraculous change on him, for in that garden... "You could find all types of fruit and aromatic plants, green herbs and flowers; there were henna flowers, jasmine, black pepper, amber-scented spikenard, all kinds of roses, plantain, myrtle, in brief, all sorts of fragrant herbs". This garden quite clearly fits the description of the earthly model of the Koran's Garden of Paradise. Indeed, in Paradise useful things are combined with beautiful things. Whatever pleases our senses is also good for our body and soul. However, it is true that first priority has clearly been given to the sense of smell. The aromatic plants are those most frequently praised.

If there could only be one flower in the Garden of Paradise, it would have to be the rose. According to legend, in the 10th century Berbers on their pilgrimage to Mecca were so impressed by the beauty and sweet scent of the *rosa damascena*, the Damask rose, that they took a few cuttings back with them to Morocco. Since then, thousands of wild, intensively fragrant roses have grown at the foot of the ochre-coloured High Atlas mountains at an altitude of 1,500 metres, despite the cold, the wind and the lack of water.

The only thing quite as captivating as the rose is the white jasmine. Moreover, these small, star-shaped jasmine flowers, which children in North Africa like to make into aromatic necklaces, are a credit to any garden.

The classical repertoire of the Garden of Paradise originally consisted of seven flowers: apart from the rose and jasmine there was the violet, the daffodil,

Duft- und Medizinal-pflanzen

Über den Garten des Nur al-Din heißt es in Tausendundeine Nacht: „Wenn ein Kranker ihn betrat, verließ er ihn als reißender Löwe." Die wundersame Verwandlung wurde bewirkt durch das Zusammenspiel verschiedenster Pflanzen, denn in jenem Garten „... befanden sich alle Früchte und duftenden Pflanzen, grüne Kräuter und Blumen; da waren Jasmin, Hennablüten, Pfefferpflanzen, Ambranarden, Rosen jeglicher Art, Wegerich, Myrten, kurz, duftende Kräuter von allen Arten". Ganz offensichtlich ist hier das irdische Abbild des koranischen Paradiesgartens beschrieben. Im Paradies nämlich verbindet sich das Nützliche mit dem Schönen. Was unsere Sinne erfreut, das ist auch heilsam für unsere Seele und unseren Körper. Allerdings wird dem Geruchssinn eindeutig Vorrang eingeräumt. Es sind die Duftpflanzen, die am häufigsten gepriesen werden.

Wenn es nur eine einzige Blume im Paradiesgarten gäbe, dann wäre es wohl die Rose. Die Legende erzählt, dass im 10. Jahrhundert Berber auf der Pilgerreise nach Mekka so von der Schönheit und dem Duft der *Rosa damascena,* der Rose von Damaskus, beeindruckt waren, dass sie einige Stecklinge zurück nach Marokko brachten. Seither wachsen am Fuß der ockerfarbenen Berge des Hohen Atlas in 1500 Metern Höhe, der Kälte, dem Wind und der Trockenheit zum Trotz, Tausende wilder, intensiv duftender Rosen.

So betörend wie die Rose duftet nur noch der weiße Jasmin. Außerdem sind die sternförmigen kleinen Jasmin-Blüten, die Kinder in Nordafrika gerne auffädeln und zu aromatischen Colliers verarbeiten, eine Zierde für jeden Garten.

Zum klassischen Repertoire des Paradiesgartens zählten ursprünglich sieben Blumen: Außer Rose

Plantes aromatiques et médicinales

Les Mille et une nuits rapportent du jardin de Nur al-Din que : « lorsqu'un malade y pénétrait, il en ressortait comme un lion féroce ». Cette extraordinaire transformation aurait été opérée par l'action combinée des plantes les plus diverses, car dans ce jardin « ... se trouvaient toutes les espèces de fruits et de plantes aromatiques, d'herbes vertes et de fleurs ; y poussaient le jasmin, le henné, les poivriers, le nard ambré, les roses de toutes les variétés, le plantain, le myrte, bref, toutes les sortes d'herbes aromatiques ». De toute évidence, c'est ici une représentation terrestre du paradis coranique qui nous est décrite. Car au Paradis, en effet, l'utile se mêle au beau et ce qui ravit nos sens est aussi salutaire à notre âme et à notre corps. La priorité n'en est pas moins incontestablement accordée, parmi les sens, à l'odorat et ce sont les plantes aromatiques qui se voient le plus souvent vantées.

S'il n'y avait qu'une seule fleur dans le jardin du Paradis, ce serait sans aucun doute la rose. La légende raconte qu'au 10e siècle, des Berbères en pèlerinage vers La Mecque auraient été tellement impressionnés par la beauté et le parfum de *rosa damascena,* la Rose de Damas, qu'ils en auraient rapporté quelques plants au Maroc. Depuis ce temps, des milliers de roses sauvages au parfum intense poussent au pied des montagnes ocre du Haut-Atlas à une altitude de près de 1500 mètres, défiant le froid, le vent et la sécheresse.

Seul le jasmin blanc répand un parfum aussi enchanteur que celui de la rose. De plus, ses petites fleurs en forme d'étoile, que les enfants d'Afrique du Nord aiment à enfiler en colliers odorants, sont un ornement pour chaque jardin.

Le jardin du Paradis classique comportait à l'origine sept fleurs : outre la rose et le jasmin, la violette,

Allium   *Chrysanthemum*   *Nerium oleander*   *Datura*   *Salvia*   *Natur morte*   *Acanthus*   *Salvia*

the iris, the lily and the bear's breeches. The latter, also know as *acanthus hungaricus,* is not scented but is indispensable, because it radiates such dignity. Its broadly lobed leaves have inspired architects building the curved tops of Corinthian columns. All seven "flowers of paradise" first reached Europe with the crusades.

Medicinal plants are still grown in the *bustân,* next to flowers and herbs. They too arrived in Europe with the crusades and became established in monastery gardens. In the Middle Ages, monasteries were used as infirmaries and the monks devoted themselves to both prayer and medicine. Alexander Neckham, the Abbot of Cirencester who died in 1217, left behind instructions for how a monastery garden should be laid out in his book *De naturis rerum:* "roses and lilies, sunflowers, violets and mandrakes decorate the garden. Parsley, fennel and mugwort, coriander, sage, savory, hyssop and spearmint should be planted there. Along the garden paths there should be wild celery, lettuce, cress and peonies. There need to be beds for onions, leeks, garlic, pumpkins and shallots. Cucumbers, poppies, daffodils and bear's breeches ennoble the garden. Pot herbs such as sorrel, mallow, anise, mustard, white pepper and wormwood also have a part to play in the garden".

One can thus assume that this concept corresponds pretty well to the gardens the crusaders found in the Islamic monasteries and palatial cities to which the infirmaries also belonged. In his Canon of Medicine, *Al-Qanun fi al-Tibb,* written in 1021, the most famous Arab doctor, Abu Ali Ibn Sina (980–1037) described over 800 plants and their effect on the human organism. He already knew that mallow soothed burns and camomile healed wounds and inflammations. Today, all the plants that were named in the old scriptures can be found in any large Moroccan Garden of Paradise. But nowadays hardly anyone is concerned about their therapeutic effect; it is the beauty and scent of the flowers and herbs that delight all visitors to the gardens – and keep them healthy.

und Jasmin auch Veilchen, Narzisse, Iris, Lilie und Bärenklau. Der letztere, auch *Acanthus* genannt, duftet nicht, ist aber dennoch unverzichtbar, weil er soviel Würde ausstrahlt. Seine tief gelappten Blätter inspirierten Architekten zu den geschwungenen Spitzen der korintihischen Säulen. Alle sieben „Paradiesblumen" kamen erst mit den Kreuzzügen nach Europa.

Medizinalpflanzen wuchsen im *bustân* immer schon neben Blumen und Kräutern. Auch sie kamen mit den Kreuzzügen nach Europa und fanden Eingang in die Klostergärten. Klöster dienten im Mittelalter als Krankenstation, und die Mönche widmeten sich dem Gebet ebenso wie der Medizin. Alexander Neckham, der 1217 als Abt von Cirencester starb, hinterließ genaue Instruktionen zur Anlage eines Klostergartens in seiner *De naturis rerum:* „Rosen und Lilien, Sonnenblumen, Veilchen und Alraunen schmücken den Garten. Dort sollte man Petersilie, Fenchel und Beifuss, Koriander, Salbei, Bohnenkraut, Ysop, grüne Minze pflanzen. Entlang der Gartenwege wilder Sellerie, Salat, Kresse und Pfingstrosen. Es müssen Beete für Zwiebeln, Lauch, Knoblauch, Kürbis und Schalotten angelegt werden. Gurke, Mohn, Osterglocke und Bärenklau veredeln den Garten. Auch Suppenkräuter, wie Sauerampfer, Malven, sowie Anis, Senf, weißer Pfeffer und Wermut leisten ihre Dienste in einem Garten."

Man kann davon ausgehen, dass dieses Konzept ziemlich genau den Gärten entspricht, wie Kreuzritter sie in islamischen Klöstern und Palaststädten, zu denen auch Krankenhäuser gehörten, vorfanden. Der berühmteste unter den arabischen Ärzten, Abu Ali Ibn Sina (980–1037), beschrieb in seinem Medizin-Kanon (1021) über 800 Pflanzen und ihre Wirkung auf den menschlichen Organismus. Er wusste schon, dass die Malve Verbrennungen beruhigt und Kamille bei Wunden und Entzündungen die Heilung fördert. Heute noch findet man alle Pflanzen, die in den alten Schriften genannt werden, in jedem größeren marokkanischen Paradiesgarten. Aber um ihre Heilwirkung kümmert sich kaum jemand; es sind die Schönheit und der Duft der Blumen und Kräuter, die jeden Gartenbesitzer erfreuen – und gesund halten.

le narcisse, l'iris, le lis et l'acanthe. Cette dernière, Acanthus, ne sent rien mais n'en reste pas moins indispensable pour l'incomparable noblesse qu'elle exhale. Ses feuilles profondément lobées ont inspiré les architectes pour les sommets élancés des colonnes corinthiennes. Les sept « fleurs de paradis » ne sont toutes arrivées en Europe qu'avec les Croisades.

Les plantes médicinales, quant à elles, ont toujours été cultivées dans les *bustân* avec les fleurs et les herbes. Elles aussi ont été importées en Europe à la suite des Croisades et introduites dans les jardins des cloîtres. Au Moyen-Âge, les couvents tenaient lieu d'hôpitaux et les moines se consacraient autant à la prière qu'à la médecine. Alexander Neckham, abbé de Cirencester mort en 1217, laissera dans son De naturis rerum des instructions précises pour l'aménagement d'un jardin de cloître : « Roses et lis, ainsi que tournesols, violettes et mandragores ornent le jardin. Y planter persil, fenouil et armoise, coriandre, sauge, sarriette, hysope et menthe verte. Le long des allées, du céleri sauvage, de la salade, du cresson et des pivoines. Des parterres doivent être aménagés pour les oignons, poireaux, ail, citrouilles et échalotes. Concombres, pavot, narcisses et acanthe rehaussent le jardin. Sans oublier les herbes potagères comme l'oseille, la mauve, l'anis, la moutarde, le poivre blanc et l'absinthe, qui peuvent rendre des services ».

On peut s'imaginer sans peine que ce concept de jardin correspond assez exactement à ceux que les croisés ont trouvés dans les cloîtres islamiques et les villes de palais, qui comprenaient également des hôpitaux. Le plus célèbre des médecins arabes, Abu Ali Ibn Sina (980–1037), décrit dans son canon de médecine (1021) plus de 800 plantes et leur action sur l'organisme humain. Il savait déjà que la mauve apaise les brûlures et que la camomille favorise la cicatrisation des plaies et inflammations. Mais si aujourd'hui encore, on trouve dans chacun des grands jardins de paradis marocains les plantes citées par les textes anciens, bien peu sont ceux qui s'intéressent encore à leurs vertus curatives, seuls la beauté et le parfum des fleurs et des herbes réjouissent encore les propriétaires de jardins, et les conservent en bonne santé.

Datura   *Rosa*   *Rosa*   *Hemerocallis*   *Papaver*   *Alcea rosea*   *Rosa*

Public Gardens
Öffentliche Gärten
Jardins publics

Public parks and gardens in Tanger are clearly different from those in the four royal cities. In the latter case they are places of peaceful contemplation, whilst in Tanger at first glance they look like war memorials: cannons are the most striking and frequently found "decoration". This can be explained by the city's exposed location, as the gateway to Africa and the entrance to two seas. This makes Tanger a bone of contention coveted by many different nations and tribes. The city's owners have thus changed frequently throughout its history. In these circumstances it is important to look as if you are capable of defending yourself...

A collection of 30 historic cannons from different countries – above all Spain and Portugal, but also Morocco – are to be found in the *Parc de la Mendoubia*. This warfare equipment which dates back to the 17th century is made of cast bronze. Next to the cannons the famous dragon trees *(dracaena)* have a hard time making themselves visible, despite the fact that they are over 800 years old and certainly worthy of admiration. Some fig trees here have also reached this legendary age. With their widely spreading crowns they provide shade for entire squares in the Mendoubia Park, which adjoins the *Grand Socco* (large market), the heart of the city.

The Sultan's Garden, which follows the classical Andalusian pattern, seems better kept and brighter. Apart from that, there are few typical Islamic gardens in Tanger. Also missing are the large royal gardens with olive trees, orange groves and enormous fountains, like the ones in the royal cities, which beckons you to have picnics in them. It is noticeable that Tanger opens onto the sea and is exposed to influences of many different kinds.

Die Parks und öffentlichen Anlagen in Tanger unterscheiden sich wesentlich von jenen in den vier Königsstädten. Sind sie dort Orte friedlicher Kontemplation, so sehen sie in Tanger auf den ersten Blick wie kriegerische Mahnmale aus: Kanonen sind der augenfälligste und häufigste „Schmuck". Das erklärt sich aus der exponierten Lage der Stadt, die als Tor zu Afrika gilt und Zugang zu zwei Meeren hat. Das machte sie zum begehrten Zankapfel der verschiedensten Nationen und Stämme, und so wechselten im Laufe der Geschichte immer wieder ihre Besitzer. Da wird es wichtig, wehrhaft zu wirken ...

Eine Sammlung von 30 historischen Kanonen aus den verschiedensten Ländern – vor allem aus Spanien und Portugal, aber auch aus Marokko – befindet sich im *Parc de la Mendoubia*. Die Kriegsgeräte stammen aus dem 17. Jahrhundert und sind aus Bronze gegossen. Neben ihnen haben es die berühmten Drachenbäume *(Dracaena)* schwer, Aufmerksamkeit auf sich zu ziehen, obwohl sie über 800 Jahre alt und jede Bewunderung wert sind. Auch einige Feigen haben hier dieses sagenhafte Alter erreicht. Mit ihren weit ausladenden Kronen beschatten sie ganze Plätze im Mendoubia-Park, der sich direkt an den *Grand Socco* (großer Markt), das Herzstück der Stadt, anschließt.

Gepflegter und heiterer wirkt der Garten des Sultans, der dem klassischen andalusischen Muster folgt. Ansonsten findet man in Tanger wenige typisch islamische Anlagen. Auch fehlen hier große königliche Gärten mit Oliven- und Orangenhainen und riesigen Wasserbecken, wie sie in den Königsstädten zum Picknick einladen. Man merkt, dass die Stadt zum Meer hin geöffnet und vielen Einflüssen ausgesetzt ist.

The site above the open bay made it necessary to have fortified buildings. The old canons are still on display in the Sultan's garden.

Die Lage an der offenen Bucht zum Atlantik machte wehrhafte Bauten nötig – die Kanonen von damals sind heute noch im Garten des Sultans zu sehen.

La situation auprès de la baie donnant sur l'Atlantique nécessitait des bâtiments en état de se défendre – les canons de jadis peuvent toujours être admirés dans le jardin du sultan de nos jours.

Les parcs et jardins publics de Tanger se distinguent beaucoup de ceux des quatre cités royales. S'ils sont dans ces dernières des lieux de contemplation pacifique, ils semblent à Tanger dès le premier regard des mémoriaux guerriers, dont les canons sont « l'ornement » le plus manifeste et le plus fréquent. Cela s'explique par la situation exposée de la ville, porte de l'Afrique et accès à deux mers : véritable pomme de discorde entre les différentes nations et tribus, ses possédants n'ont cessé de changer au cours de l'histoire. On comprend donc l'importance que revêt l'apparence de la puissance ...

Le *Parc de la Mendoubia* présente une collection de 30 canons historiques de tous les pays, essentiellement d'Espagne et du Portugal, mais aussi du Maroc. Les engins de guerre remontent au 17e siècle et ont été coulés dans le bronze. À côté d'eux, les célèbres dragonniers *(Dracaena)* ont bien du mal à attirer l'attention, malgré leur âge de plus de 800 ans, qui les rend digne de toute admiration. Quelques figuiers ont aussi atteint cet âge fabuleux et ombragent des places entières de leurs larges cimes dans le parc de la Mendoubia, directement contigu au *Grand Socco* (grand marché), le cœur de la ville.

Le jardin du sultan, de style andalou classique, semble en comparaison mieux entretenu et plus gai. On ne trouve sinon que peu de parcs typiquement islamiques à Tanger. Les vastes jardins royaux, leurs oliveraies, orangeraies et immenses bassins, qui invitent au pique-nique dans les villes royales, manquent également. On remarque fortement que la ville est ouverte sur la mer et exposée à de multiples influences.

Jardin du Sultan

A gate built in 1888 – *Bab Riad Soltane* – leads to the Sultan's Garden. First one crosses a unique arched courtyard which, with its central fountain and the marble columns, befits the peaceful mood of the garden. Large pieces of pottery from Tétouan decorate this courtyard, which belongs to the Moroccan craftwork museum. The museum is housed in the former Sultan's palace.

The archaeological museum is now located in another wing of the *Dar el Makhzen*, in the part of the building where the kitchens used to be. Here too, there is a pretty little inner courtyard with a fountain.

The highlight of a walk around the Pasha's palace, built at the end of the 17th century and added to several times since then, is, without a doubt, the well-tended Andalusian style garden. It is the only one of its kind in Tanger.

As a proper *riyad* it is enclosed by high walls, its centre marked out by a marble fountain surrounded by precious mosaics. Axial lines subdivide the ground plan into four parts, each containing small orange trees and flowers. A long, wooden arboured walk – overgrown with thick foliage from grape vines – gives this garden, which was also usually used for social functions, a somewhat unusual private and intimate atmosphere. Today it is also used as an

---

Ein Portal aus dem Jahr 1888 – *Bab Riad Soltane* – führt zu den Gärten des Sultans. Zunächst durchquert man den einzigartigen Arkadenhof, der mit seinem zentralen Wasserbecken und den marmornen Säulen bereits einstimmt auf die Ruhe des Gartens. Große Keramiken aus Tétouan schmücken diesen Hof, der zum Museum für marokkanisches Kunsthandwerk gehört, das im ehemaligen Sultanspalast untergebracht ist.

In einem anderen Flügel des *Dar el Makhzen*, wo einst die Küchen waren, befindet sich heute das archäologische Museum. Auch hierzu gehört ein schöner kleiner Innenhof mit Brunnen.

Höhepunkt des Rundgangs im Palast des Paschas, der Ende des 17. Jahrhunderts errichtet und seither mehrfach umgebaut wurde, ist zweifellos der gepflegte Garten im andalusischen Stil. Es gibt keinen zweiten dieser Art in Tanger. Als echter *Riad* ist er von hohen Mauern eingeschlossen, seine Mitte markiert ein marmorner Brunnen, umgeben von kostbaren Mosaiken. Ein Achsenkreuz unterteilt den Grundriss in vier Teile, die mit Orangenbäumchen und Blumen bepflanzt sind. Ein langer hölzerner Laubengang, überrankt vom dichten Blätterwerk des Weins, gibt diesem Garten, der immer auch der Repräsentation diente, etwas ungewöhnlich Privates

---

Un portail de 1888 – *Bab Riad Soltane* – mène aux jardins du sultan. On commence par traverser l'extraordinaire cour aux arcades qui, avec son bassin central et ses colonnes de marbre, prépare déjà à l'atmosphère calme du jardin. De grandes céramiques de Tétouan décorent la cour, qui fait aujourd'hui partie du musée d'artisanat d'art marocain, installé dans l'ancien palais du sultan.

Une autre aile du *Dar el Makhzen*, où se trouvaient autrefois les cuisines, abrite aujourd'hui le musée archéologique et comprend également une jolie petite cour intérieure avec fontaine.

Le clou de la visite du palais, érigé à la fin du 17ᵉ siècle et transformé à de multiples reprises depuis, est sans conteste le jardin soigné de style andalou. Il n'en existe aucun autre de ce type à Tanger. Véritable *riad*, il est enclos de hauts murs et son centre est marqué par une fontaine de marbre entourée de précieuses mosaïques. Deux axes en croix divisent le plan en quatre parties plantées de petits orangers et de fleurs. Une longue charmille de bois, sur laquelle grimpe l'épais feuillage d'une vigne, confère à ce jardin, dont le rôle a également toujours été représentatif, quelque chose d'inhabituel, de privé et d'intime. Aujourd'hui, il sert également de lieu d'exposition à des chapi-

---

The marble fountain lies in the shade of a pergola overgrown with vine, just as it is recommended in early gardening treatises. In the background, the minaret of the Kasbah mosque.

Der marmorne Brunnen wird beschattet von einer mit Wein bewachsenen Pergola, wie frühe Gartentraktate es vorschreiben. Im Hintergrund das Minarett der Kasbah-Moschee.

La vasque de marbre est protégée par une pergola couverte de vigne, comme le préconisaient d'anciens traités de paysagisme. À l'arrière-plan, on aperçoit le minaret de la mosquée de la casbah.

The Sultan's garden was designed not only for representation, there is also an orchard with banana and orange trees. To the right, a beautiful example of Islamic portals.

Der Garten des Sultans wurde nicht nur zur Repräsentation angelegt, er hat auch einen Obstgarten mit Bananen und Orangen. Rechts ein besonders schönes arabisches Tor.

Le jardin du sultan n'était pas seulement un jardin d'agrément, il contient également un verger avec des bananiers et des orangers. À droite, une porte arabe particulièrement belle.

exhibition area for Punic and Roman capitals, columns, remains of statues and inscribed tombstones.

At the end of a visit one should cross the *mechouar* (royal parade ground) in front of the palace and go through the *Bab er Raha* to the small terrace from which there is a stunning view of the Bay of Tanger – with Cap Malabata on the opposite side – over the harbour and out to the Spanish coast only 14 kilometres away.

und Intimes. Heute dient er auch als Ausstellungsfläche für punische und römische Kapitelle, Säulen, Reste von Statuen und Grabsteine mit Inschriften.

Zum Abschluss eines Besuchs sollte man den *Mechouar* (Versammlungsplatz) vor dem Palast überqueren und durch das *Bab er Raha* auf die kleine Terrasse treten – hier hat man einen überwältigenden Ausblick auf die Bucht von Tanger mit dem gegenüber liegenden Cap Malabata, auf den Hafen und die nur 14 Kilometer entfernte spanische Küste.

teaux, colonnes, restes de statues et pierres tombales inscrites puniques et romains.

Pour terminer la visite, traverser le *Mechouar* (place de rassemblement) devant le palais et pénétrer par le *Bab er Raha* sur la petite terrasse : la vue y est grandiose sur la baie de Tanger et le Cap Malabata qui lui fait face, ainsi que le port et la côte espagnole, distante de seulement 14 kilomètres.

Musée Forbes

Eccentric characters have always been attracted to Tanger like moths to the light. The multifaceted radiance of the *Ville Blanche* in which Arab, African and European influences converge fascinates those in search of a stage for their own performance. One of the most spectacular backdrops was built by the American magazine mogul and billionaire Malcolm Forbes. His snow-white property on Rue Shakespeare in the western part of the *médina* could be a fata morgana come true to a Hollywood star. Actually one of the James Bond adventures has already been filmed here. Other films may follow, as the house is now free since the 115,000 tin soldiers held in the *Musée des Miniatures Militaires* were moved to the Louvre in 1998. The inhabitants of Tanger were very sorry to lose these tin soldiers because the show of light and sound in which the little soldiers portrayed the great battles of history attracted many visitors. What is worse, however, is that when the museum closed all the statues in the garden were also removed, something many people regarded as downright vandalism.

At the same time, however, the garden is still one of the most beautiful in Tanger. At first glance it seems very formal with its paths laid out in a cross shape and covered in cool blue and white tiles. The flowerbed borders, made of the same tiles, are particularly high and kept scrupulously free of all overgrowing plants. The way the beds are planted contrasts with this: the most popular summer flowers

Exzentriker strebten stets nach Tanger wie Motten zum Licht. Das facettenreiche Strahlen der *Ville blanche*, in der sich arabische, afrikanische und europäische Einflüsse mischen, fasziniert jeden, der eine Bühne für seine Selbstdarstellung sucht. Eine der spektakulärsten Kulissen baute sich der amerikanische Zeitschriftenmogul und Milliardär Malcolm Forbes. Sein schneeweißes Anwesen im Westen der *médina* an der Rue Shakespeare könnte die Wirklichkeit gewordene Fata Morgana eines Hollywoodstars sein. In der Tat wurde hier bereits ein James-Bond-Abenteuer gedreht. Weitere Filme könnten folgen, denn das Haus ist frei, seit die 115.000 Zinnsoldaten, die das *Musée des Miniatures Militaires* fest in ihrer Hand hatten, 1998 abgezogen und in den Louvre gewandert sind.

Die Bewohner von Tanger haben den Abzug sehr bedauert, denn die Ton- und Lichtshow, in der die kleinen Soldaten die großen Schlachten dieser Welt nachstellten, zog viele Besucher an. Schlimmer aber ist, dass bei der Schließung des Museums auch alle Statuen aus dem Garten entfernt wurden, was viele geradezu als Vandalismus empfinden.

Dabei ist der Garten immer noch einer der schönsten, die man in ganz Tanger finden kann. Auf den ersten Blick wirkt er sehr streng mit seinen kreuzförmig angelegten Wegen, die mit kühlen Kacheln in Blau-Weiß belegt sind. Die Beeteinfassungen aus denselben Kacheln sind besonders hoch und peinlich von allen überwachsenden Pflanzen frei ge-

De tous temps, les personnages les plus excentriques ont été attirés par Tanger comme les papillons de nuit par la lumière. Le rayonnement aux mille facettes de la *Ville blanche* où se mêlent les influences arabes, africaines et européennes fascine tous ceux qui cherchent une tribune pour se mettre en scène eux-mêmes. Dans ce contexte, l'une des coulisses les plus spectaculaires a été construite par le magnat de la presse et milliardaire américain Malcolm Forbes. Sa propriété d'un blanc de neige, située à l'ouest de la *médina*, dans la rue Shakespeare, pourrait être la vision devenue réalité d'une star d'Hollywood. D'ailleurs, une aventure de James Bond y a déjà été tournée. D'autres films pourraient suivre, car la maison est vide depuis la retraite en 1998 pour le Louvre des 115 000 soldats de plomb qui constituaient l'essentiel des collections du *Musée des Miniatures Militaires*.

Les habitants de Tanger ont beaucoup regretté ce départ, car le spectacle son et lumière où les petits soldats rejouaient les grandes batailles de ce monde attiraient de nombreux spectateurs. Mais il y a plus grave encore, avec la fermeture du musée, toutes les statues ont également été retirées du jardin, ce que beaucoup considèrent comme un véritable acte de vandalisme.

Le jardin n'en reste pas moins l'un des plus beaux de Tanger. Il semble à première vue plutôt sévère, avec ses chemins en forme de croix pavés de froids carreaux bleus et blancs. Les rebords des massifs ornés du même pavage sont particulièrement

This fantastic palace was once the seat of the Mendoub, representative of the Sultan. The American billionaire Malcolm Forbes turned it into a museum.

Ehemals war der phantastische Palast Sitz des Mendoub, des Sultansvertreters. Der amerikanische Milliardär Malcolm Forbes machte ein Museum daraus.

Ce palais fantastique servait autrefois de résidence au mendoub, le représentant du sultan. Le milliardaire américain Malcolm Forbes l'a transformé en musée.

such as larkspur, poppies, snap-dragons, daylilies and yarrow flourish here, planted close together. Geraniums create a lush pink clump; the only thing to rival their dominance is a cluster of red and pink roses. The use of sweet peas is quite unusual. These flowers cover everything in sight in a carefree manner with their dark red or lilac-pink flowers. In the thick green foliage of an old fig tree, on the other hand, a "window" has been cut out to provide a view over Tanger.

Palm trees often come in pairs, emphasising the symmetry of the paths just like the two fountains, whose basins stand on high columns. And a small pavilion surrounded by scented plants invites you to linger, as if it were a pasha's pleasure garden...

The Forbes Museum is placed high on the cliffs, with a panoramic view over the bay. The garden is laid out symmetrically, enclosed by white balustrades. A decorative urn is set in the middle of the flight of steps, padded by ivy and hydrangeas.

Das Forbes-Museum sitzt hoch über der Steilküste mit Panoramablick über die Bucht. Der Garten ist streng symmetrisch angelegt und mit weißen Balustraden eingefriedet. Eine Pflanzurne mitten auf der Freitreppe sitzt auf einem „Polstersessel" aus Efeu und Hortensien.

Le musée Forbes est situé au dessus de la falaise et offre une vue panoramique de la baie. Le jardin est agencé de manière strictement symétrique et entouré de balustrades blanches. Une urne forme le centre de l'escalier extérieur, assise sur « un fauteuil » composé de lierre et d'hortensias.

hauts et tristement débarrassés de toute plante tentée de dépasser. Le contraste avec la plantation des massifs n'en est que plus fort : les fleurs d'été les plus en vogue y poussent en rangs serrés, où se mêlent pieds-d'alouette et pavots, gueules-de-loup, hémérocalles et achillées, les pélargoniums formant à eux seuls un large massif rose. Seule l'accumulation de roses rouges et roses produit un effet semblable. En revanche, l'emploi de pois de senteur, qui recouvrent tranquillement tout ce qu'ils peuvent escalader de leurs fleurs rouge sombre ou lilas, est tout à fait inhabituel. De même que la « fenêtre » découpée dans la cime verte et épaisse d'un vieux figuier pour libérer la vue sur Tanger.

Les palmiers se présentent souvent deux par deux, soulignant la symétrie des chemins, comme les deux fontaines aux vasques posées sur de hautes colonnes. Enfin, un petit pavillon, entouré de plantes odorantes invite à rester, comme s'il s'agissait du jardin d'agrément d'un pacha ...

halten. Im Kontrast dazu steht die Bepflanzung der Beete: Dicht bei dicht gedeihen hier die beliebtesten Sommerblumen wie Rittersporn und Mohn, Löwenmaul, Taglilie und Schafgarbe. Pelargonien bilden ein üppiges rosa Massiv. Ähnlich dominant wirkt nur noch die Anhäufung roter und pinker Rosen.

Ganz ungewöhnlich ist der Einsatz von Duftwicken, die mit ihren dunkelroten oder lilapinken Blüten unbekümmert alles bedecken, was sie überranken können. In das dichte grüne Dach einer alten Feige wurde dagegen ein „Fenster" geschnitten, damit der herrliche Blick auf Tanger freigegeben ist.

In diesem Garten kommt eine Palme selten allein. Meistens treten sie zu zweit auf, was die Symmetrie der Wege betont, genau wie die beiden Brunnen, deren Wasserschalen auf hohen Säulen stehen. Und ein von Duftpflanzen umringter kleiner Pavillon lädt zum Verweilen, als wär's der Lustgarten eines Paschas ...

Few gardens are as well-kept as that of the Forbes Museum. No dry leaf obstructs the majestic silhouette of the palm tree, the white marble fountains are flawless. No wonder all the plants are so healthy, be they roses, sweet peas, larkspur, daylily, or aloe.

Wenige Anlagen sind so gepflegt wie der Garten des Forbes-Museums. Kein abgestorbenes Blatt stört die majestätische Silhouette der Palmen, kein Schmutz hat die Chance, sich auf dem weißen Marmor der Brunnen festzusetzen. Kein Wunder, dass auch alle Pflanzen gesund sind, von Rosen über Wicken, Rittersporn und Taglilie bis zur Aloe.

Peu de jardins sont aussi soignés que celui du musée Forbes. Pas une feuille morte ne gâche la silhouette majestueuse des palmiers, pas un brin de saleté n'a la chance de se déposer sur le marbre blanc des vasques. Ainsi, la santé des plantes n'étonne pas non plus, que ce soit celle des roses, des pois de senteur, des delphinums, des hémérocalles ou de l'aloès.

Hotel Gardens
Hotelgärten
Jardins d'hôtels

The best thing about the large hotel gardens in Tanger is their view: stretching far over the bay into the endless blue it is impossible to make out where the ocean ends and where the horizon begins. The gardens are mainly made up of well-kept lawns, which is good for the eyes – the calming green is refreshing after the blinding brightness of blue and white. The fact that the city lies on the slopes of a foothill of the Rif Mountains puts a limit to the creative possibilities. All tracts of land have to be terraced in order to be cultivated. That is why there are very few flowerbeds here. On the other hand, architectural elements such as arches,

flights of steps and parapets are often chosen in order to highlight the unique views.

In absolute contrast to the gardens that you find inland, which offer protection from noise, dust and the scorching sun, and are thus mostly surrounded by walls, gardens in Tanger enjoy extensive views and light breeze. They are not enclosed, but open – and have consequently also received international influences. This sometimes leads to combinations of English lawns with Islamic inner courtyards and fountains, which is unusual, but typical for Tanger, Morocco's melting pot.

Das Beste an den großen Hotelgärten in Tanger ist ihr Blick: Über weiße Häuser hinweg geht er weit über die Bucht ins endlose Blau – unmöglich zu unterscheiden, wo der Ozean aufhört und der Horizont anfängt. Da tut es dem Auge gut, dass die Gärten zum Großteil aus gepflegtem Rasen bestehen, das Grün wirkt erholsam nach dem blendenden Blau-Weiß-Kontrast. Die Tatsache, dass die Stadt an den Hängen eines Ausläufers des Rifgebirges liegt, beschränkt die Gestaltungsmöglichkeiten. Jedes Gelände muss terassenförmig gestuft werden, um es bearbeiten zu können. Deswegen findet man nur wenige Blumenrabatten. Dagegen werden oft architektonische Elemente wie Arkaden, Freitreppen und Brüstungen gewählt, um die einmalige Aussicht hervorzuheben.

Ganz im Gegensatz zu den Gärten im Inneren des Landes, die Schutz vor Lärm, Staub und sengender Sonne bieten und deswegen meist von Mauern umgeben sind, leben Gärten in Tanger vom weiten Blick und der leichten Brise. Sie sind nicht geschlossen, sondern geöffnet – und haben entsprechend auch internationale Einflüsse aufgenommen. Das führt manchmal zu Mischungen aus englischem Rasen und islamischem Innenhof mit Springbrunnen, ungewöhnlich, aber typisch für den Schmelztiegel Tanger.

Best of all is always the view. All high-class hotels have terraces and view-points which offer a view over the Strait of Gibraltar and the Atlantic.

Das Beste ist immer der Blick. Alle Luxushotels verfügen über Terrassen und Plattformen mit Aussicht auf die Straße von Gibraltar und den Atlantik.

La vue est toujours ce qu'il y a de mieux. Tous les hôtels de luxe disposent de terrasses et de plate-formes avec une vue sur le détroit de Gibraltar et l'Atlantique.

Le plus beau dans les grands jardins des hôtels de Tanger est leur vue : au-delà des maisons blanches, elle porte jusque loin dans la baie, avant de se perdre dans le bleu infini : impossible de savoir où cesse l'océan et où commence l'horizon. On apprécie alors que les jardins soient composés pour l'essentiel de pelouses bien entretenues, le vert repose l'œil après le contraste aveuglant de bleu et de blanc. La situation de la ville sur les pentes d'un contrefort du Rif limite les possibilités d'aménagement et les terrains doivent être étagés en terrasses pour pouvoir être exploités. C'est pour cette raison qu'on trouve si peu de plates-bandes fleuries mais que, en revanche, les éléments architecturaux comme les arcades, les escaliers extérieurs et les balustrades abondent, mettant en valeur la vue unique.

Contrairement aux jardins de l'intérieur des terres, qui offrent une protection contre le bruit, la poussière et le soleil brûlant, et sont généralement entourés de murs à cet effet, les jardins de Tanger vivent du vaste panorama et de la légère brise, et ne sont pas fermés, mais bien ouverts, ouverts également aux influences du monde entier. Le résultat en est parfois un mélange entre gazon anglais et cour intérieure islamique avec jet d'eau, inhabituel, certes, mais typique du creuset culturel qu'est Tanger.

Those who have never had mint tea in the *El Minzah* garden have not experienced the *joie de vivre* that Tanger conveys. The view over the sea promises infinite freedom – and the fact that it is framed by white arches gives you a sense of security. The well-kept green lawns and most of the people strolling around them display effortless elegance. It is hardly surprising that you can meet many international stars here. In the *El Minzah* the exceptional is commonplace. Everything seems possible – which explains why so many people become attached to this white city by the sea.

This five-star hotel is a second home to most of the well-known immigrants. David Herbert, who defined the social life of foreigners in Tanger for five decades, drove past each day in order to pick up post, news and the latest gossip. Even today the *El Minzah* still remains the place to go for all those looking for the right contacts. In the hotel where Rita Hayworth and Errol Flynn were immortalised in the guest book famous names continue to appear just like in days gone by. Those who cannot afford to stay the night in *the* traditional hotel in Tanger should at least have a drink there and stroll through the different garden areas.

The residence was built in 1930 and decorated in the traditional Moorish style by the – naturally eccentric – English Lord Bute. Subtropical gardens surround the bright-arcaded patio with its breathtaking view of the Strait of Gibraltar. The pool is framed by bougainvillea, palm trees and roses. A modern fitness centre was added to this legendary hotel in 1996.

El Minzah

Framed by a plain arch, the view resembles a picture. The guests are invited to walk on the lawn – and to pick oranges, too.

Gerahmt von schlichten Arkaden präsentiert sich die Aussicht wie ein Bild. Rasen betreten ist hier erwünscht – und auch die Orangen dürfen gepflückt werden.

Encadrée d'une simple arcade, la vue s'offre comme un tableau. On est prié de marcher sur le gazon – même les oranges peuvent être cueillies.

Wer nie seinen Minztee im Garten des *El Minzah* zu sich nahm, weiß nicht, welches Lebensgefühl Tanger vermittelt. Der Blick aufs Meer verheißt unendliche Freiheit – dass er von weißen Arkaden gerahmt ist, vermittelt Geborgenheit. Der gepflegte grüne Rasen und die meisten Menschen, die auf ihm wandeln, zeugen von müheloser Eleganz. Dass man hier internationalen Stars begegnet, ist keine Überraschung. Im *El Minzah* ist das Ungewöhnliche alltäglich. Alles scheint möglich – und deswegen bleiben so viele hängen in der weißen Stadt am Meer.

Das Fünf-Sterne-Hotel ist für die meisten illustren Immigranten ein zweites Zuhause. David Herbert, der für fünf Jahrzehnte das gesellschaftliche Leben der Ausländer in Tanger bestimmte, fuhr jeden Tag vorbei, um Post, Nachrichten und neuesten Klatsch einzusammeln. Auch heute noch ist das *El Minzah* Anlaufadresse für alle, die auf der Suche nach den richtigen Kontakten sind. Wo schon Rita Hayworth und Errol Flynn sich im Gästebuch verewigten, tragen sich nach wie vor große Namen ein. Wer es sich nicht leisten kann, in *dem* Traditionshotel Tangers zu nächtigen, sollte hier wenigstens einen Drink nehmen und einen Gang durch die verschiedenen Gartenbereiche machen.

Erbaut wurde die Residenz im maurischen Stil 1930 vom – natürlich exzentrischen – englischen Lord Bute. Um den heiteren Arkaden-Patio mit der atemberaubenden Aussicht auf die Straße von Gibraltar gruppieren sich subtropische Gärten. Bougainvilleen, Palmen und Rosen umrahmen den Pool. Seit 1996 hat das legendäre Hotel auch ein modernes Fitnesscenter.

Ceux qui n'ont jamais pris leur thé à la menthe dans le jardin du *El Minzah* ne savent rien du sentiment de vie qu'inspire Tanger. La vue sur la mer est la promesse d'une liberté infinie, tandis que son cadre d'arcades blanches donne un sentiment de sûreté et d'abri. La pelouse verte et bien entretenue, ainsi que la plupart des gens qui y déambulent, témoignent d'une élégance instinctive. Rien d'étonnant donc si on y rencontre des stars internationales. Au *El Minzah*, l'inhabituel est le quotidien et tout semble possible. C'est pour cette raison qu'il semble à tant de gens impossible de se détacher de la ville blanche au bord de la mer.

L'hôtel cinq étoiles est pour la plupart de ces illustres immigrants un deuxième foyer. David Herbert, qui a présidé la vie sociale des étrangers de Tanger pendant cinq décennies, passait chaque jour y prendre le courrier et y apprendre les nouvelles et les dernières rumeurs. Aujourd'hui encore, le *El Minzah* est la première adresse pour tous ceux qui sont à la recherche de contacts utiles. Le livre d'or où se sont immortalisés Rita Hayworth et Errol Flynn voit encore s'inscrire de grands noms. Et si vous ne pouvez vous permettre de passer la nuit à l'hôtel de référence de Tanger, il faut au moins y prendre quelque chose et y faire un tour dans les différents jardins.

La résidence de style mauresque a été construite en 1930 par le lord anglais – et donc forcément excentrique – Lord Bute. Autour du clair patio à arcades et de sa vue à couper le souffle sur le détroit de Gibraltar se groupent des jardins subtropicaux. La piscine, elle, est entourée de bougainvilliers, palmiers et rosiers et, depuis 1996, l'hôtel légendaire possède également un centre de remise en forme des plus modernes.

Le Mirage

Like an illusion and true to its name, *Le Mirage*, the famous hotel on the most north-westerly point of the African continent, emerges like a white crest on the dark red cliffs. But it is a dream come true for the brothers Abdeslam and Ahmed Chekkour, who have built one of the most beautiful hotels in Morocco here, 14 kilometres west of Tanger. This three-level hotel has been skilfully set into the steep escarpment and contains 30 suites, each with its own terrace or veranda – an exclusive view of the Atlantic is guaranteed.

Dazzling white balustrades run like a wall around the whole grounds, which thus resemble an enclosed village, especially since each bungalow has its own flat red roof. This, combined with the extensive green lawns, makes the whole ensemble reminiscent of a manor house with paddocks in New England.

On the other hand, the countless large and small flowerbeds, which accompany all the terraces and paths and turn the slopes into seas of flowers, are as colourful as farmhouse gardens. Here, red and pink geraniums, only known as balcony decorations in the cooler climes of Europe, prove to be frequently flowering bedding plants, which can stay outside all winter. The *tagetes* and busy lizzies bloom equally tirelessly at the foot of the high fan palms. Pale pink double roses can be found at the pool, next to the pink flowering oleander. In contrast, a single bed along the window frontage of the restaurant is reserved for the red roses. Opposite there is a clump of mallows, hibiscus and lantana. "We wanted to create a Mediterranean atmosphere", say the owners.

Wie ein Trugbild – und nichts anderes bedeutet *Le Mirage* – taucht das berühmte Hotel an der äußersten Nordwestspitze des afrikanischen Kontinents auf: als wäre es eine weiße Schaumkrone auf den dunkelroten Klippen. Aber es ist der Wirklichkeit gewordene Traum der Brüder Abdeslam und Ahmed Chekkour, die 14 Kilometer westlich von Tanger eines der schönsten Hotels Marokkos errichtet haben. Auf drei Ebenen geschickt in den Steilhang eingebettet liegen 30 Suiten, jede mit eigener Terrasse oder Veranda – exklusiver Blick auf den atlantischen Ozean garantiert.

Blendend weiße Balustraden ziehen sich wie eine Mauer um die gesamte Anlage, die dadurch wie ein eingefriedetes Dorf wirkt, zumal jede Wohneinheit ihr eigenes flaches rotes Dach hat. Zusammen mit den weiten grünen Rasenflächen erinnert das Ganze an einen Herrensitz mit Pferdekoppeln in Neu-England.

Bunt wie Bauerngärten sind dagegen die unzähligen großen und kleinen Beete, die jede Terrasse und jeden Weg begleiten und jeden Hang in ein Blumenmeer verwandeln. Pelargonien in Rot und Rosa, im kühleren Europa nur als Balkonschmuck bekannt, bewähren sich hier als fleißig blühende Beetpflanzen, die auch im Winter draußen bleiben. Ebenso unermüdlich blühen Tagetes und Fleißige Lieschen zu Füßen der hohen Fächerpalmen.

Am Pool finden sich gefüllte zartrosa Rosen, neben dem rosa blühenden Oleander. Den roten Rosen dagegen ist eine eigene Rabatte entlang der Fensterfront vor dem Restaurant reserviert. Gegenüber erhebt sich ein Massiv mit Malven, Hibiskus und

Telle une illusion – c'est bien le sens du nom *Le Mirage* – le célèbre hôtel surgit à la pointe nord-ouest la plus extrême du continent africain : une couronne d'écume blanche posée sur les brisants rouge sombre. Tel est le rêve devenu réalité des frères Abdeslam et Ahmed Chekkour, qui ont construit à 14 kilomètres à l'ouest de Tanger l'un des plus beaux hôtels du Maroc. Habilement enchâssées sur trois niveaux dans la pente escarpée, 30 suites, chacune dotée de sa propre terrasse ou véranda, offrent une vue unique sur l'océan Atlantique.

Des balustrades d'un blanc aveuglant s'étirent comme un mur tout autour de la propriété, à laquelle elles font prendre l'aspect d'un village clos, une impression encore renforcée par le fait que chaque unité d'habitation possède son propre toit plat et rouge. Avec les vastes pelouses vertes, l'ensemble rappelle une demeure seigneuriale de Nouvelle-Angleterre et son paddock.

Les innombrables massifs de toutes tailles qui flanquent terrasses et chemins et transforment chaque versant en une mer de fleurs, en revanche, sont aussi colorés que des jardins potagers. Les pélargoniums rouges et roses, qui dans la froide Europe ne sont connus que comme ornement pour balcons, s'avèrent ici des plantes à massifs à floraison énergique qui restent dehors toute l'année. Tout aussi infatigables, les œillets d'Inde et les impatiences fleurissent le pied des hauts palmiers-éventails. Les roses doubles rose tendre occupent les abords de la piscine, à côté du laurier-rose à fleurs roses, tandis que les roses rouges ont un massif qui leur est réservé devant le restaurant, le long des fenêtres. En face se dresse un massif de mauves,

The successful brothers began with the restaurant, which they called the *Grottes d'Hercule*. The luxury hotel, whose kitchens have the same good reputation the restaurant had, developed from there. After the meal, guests like to walk the four kilometres from Cap Spartel, where the hotel is located, to the famous limestone Caves of Hercules, which in prehistoric times were probably inhabited. Some of these rock chambers are currently open to visitors.

Lantana. „Wir haben uns eine mediterrane Stimmung gewünscht", erklären die Besitzer.

Angefangen haben die erfolgreichen Brüder mit einem Restaurant, das sie *Grottes d'Hercule* nannten. Daraus entwickelte sich das Luxushotel, dessen Küche denselben guten Ruf hat wie vordem das Restaurant. Gäste gehen nach dem Essen gern die vier Kilometer vom Cap Spartel, auf dem das Hotel steht, zu den berühmten Herkulesgrotten, Kalksteinhöhlen, die in prähistorischer Zeit wahrscheinlich bewohnt waren und zum Teil besichtigt werden können.

d'hibiscus et de lantana. « Nous voulions une atmosphère méditerranéenne », expliquent les propriétaires.

Les frères ont d'abord connu le succès avec un restaurant appelé *Grottes d'Hercule*, à partir duquel s'est développé l'hôtel de luxe, dont la cuisine jouit de la même réputation que le restaurant auparavant. Après le repas, les hôtes aiment à parcourir les quatre kilomètres qui séparent le cap Spartel, sur lequel est construit l'hôtel, des célèbres grottes d'Hercule, cavités calcaires qui ont probablement été habitées aux temps préhistoriques et peuvent être visitées en partie.

On the one side, the flight of steps ornamented with beautiful tiled mosaics leads down to the garden while on the other side it leads further down right onto the beach.

Die Treppe mit dem schönen Fliesen-Mosaik führt auf einer Seite in den Garten und auf der anderen noch weiter hinunter bis direkt an den Strand.

L'escalier avec sa belle mosaïque de faïence conduit d'un côté au jardin, de l'autre, il descend bien plus bas jusqu'à la plage.

You had better not suffer from vertigo, if you want to enjoy the view from up on the cliffs. Many a guest prefers to stay on the calming green lawn.

Schwindelfrei sollte man sein, wenn man die Aussicht so hoch oben von den Klippen genießen will. So manchem Gast ist das beruhigende Grün des gepflegten Rasens lieber ...

Mieux vaut ne pas avoir le vertige, si l'on veut profiter de la vue du haut des falaises. Bien des clients lui préfèrent l'effet tranquillisant des vertes pelouses ...

Tea in Morocco

All greetings in Morocco are warm – in fact, very warm and beautifully sweet. And that is exactly how the mint tea that is drunk here on all occasions should be. With tea business deals are made, friendships are born, reunions are celebrated, families united, speeches opened and meals ended – or it is simply used to kill time.

Tea is omnipresent. And it is a relatively new acquisition. It only arrived in Morocco in 1854 brought by English traders who, because of the Crimean War, could not deliver it to Russia and therefore unloaded their cargoes in Tanger and Mogador (Essaouira). They also brought the samovar for preparing the tea and gold-plated cups to drink out of. But the Moroccans did not keep them.

From the very start they used small straight glasses, sometimes with a gold edge (a reminiscence of the rejected cups?), but most sumptuously decorated with filigreed coloured patterns. Perhaps it was the use of glasses that lead the English to mockingly refer to the tea as "Moroccan whisky".

The fact is that the Moroccans immediately made it their national drink and developed their own recipe, and a whole ritual for its preparation. It is based on the green, unfermented tea that was developed in China. The Moroccan touch is acquired through the addition of fresh mint – out of which refreshing infusions had always been made. Now

Tee in Marokko

Heiß ist jede Begrüßung in Marokko – siedendheiß und zuckersüß. So nämlich muss er sein, der Minztee, der zu jedem Anlass getrunken wird. Mit Tee werden Geschäfte besiegelt, Freundschaften geschlossen, Wiedersehen gefeiert, Familien vereint, Gespräche eröffnet und Mahlzeiten beendet – oder es wird damit ganz einfach die Zeit totgeschlagen.

Tee ist allgegenwärtig. Dabei ist er eine relativ neue Errungenschaft. Erst 1854 wurde er in Marokko eingeführt, und zwar durch englische Händler, die wegen des Krim-Krieges nicht nach Russland liefern konnten und ihre Schiffsladungen deswegen in Tanger und Mogador löschten. Sie brachten auch den Samowar für die Zubereitung mit und vergoldete Tassen zum Trinken. Doch davon hielten die Marokkaner nichts. Sie nahmen von Anfang an kleine gerade Gläser, manchmal mit Goldrand – Reminiszenz an die verweigerten Tassen? –, meist jedoch reich mit filigranem farbigem Muster dekoriert.

Vielleicht ist es der Gebrauch von Gläsern, der die Engländer spöttisch vom „marokkanischen Whisky" reden ließ. Tatsache ist, dass die Marokkaner ihn sofort zu ihrem Nationalgetränk machten und ihr eigenes Rezept, ja ein ganzes Ritual um die Zubereitung herum entwickelten. Grundlage ist grüner, unfermentierter Tee, wie er in China entwickelt wurde. Die marokkanische Note bekommt er durch das

Le Thé au Maroc

Au Maroc, la réception est toujours brûlante : bouillante et très sucrée. C'est ainsi que doit se boire le thé à la menthe, servi à toute occasion. Des affaires sont conclues, des amitiés confirmées, des retrouvailles célébrées, des familles réunies, des discussions ouvertes et des repas terminés autour d'un verre de thé, quant on n'y tue pas simplement le temps.

Le thé est omniprésent au Maroc. Il s'agit pourtant d'une acquisition relativement récente, puisqu'il n'a été introduit dans le pays qu'en 1854, par des négociants anglais que la Guerre de Crimée empêchait de livrer en Russie et qui déchargeaient donc leurs navires à Tanger et Mogador. Ils apporteront également le samovar pour la préparation du thé et des tasses à dorure pour sa dégustation, mais les Marocains ne tiendront aucun compte de ces dernières et utiliseront dès le début de petits verres droits, parfois ornés d'une bordure dorée – réminiscence des tasses refusées ? – mais le plus souvent richement décorés de motifs filigranés colorés.

Peut-être est-ce l'emploi de verres qui fera parler les Anglais en se moquant de « whisky marocain ». En tout cas, les Marocains feront aussitôt du thé leur boisson nationale et développeront même leur propre recette et tout un rituel autour de sa préparation. La base en est du thé vert, non fermenté, tel qu'on en produit en Chine. La spécificité marocaine vient de

this herb was to lend its special fresh aroma to green tea. There are different species of mint and the best one comes from Marrakech and Meknès. It is also sold as "nana-tea": *nâa-naa* being the Arabic word for mint tea.

Two trays are needed for the tea ceremony. On one there is a copper samovar and three containers: the first for sugar, the second for the green tea leaves and the third for the fresh mint. They are washed beforehand and carefully dried with a clean cloth. On the second tray there are small glasses – usually more glasses than the number of guests present – and the typical bulbous teapot with its long spout and pointed lid.

To do things properly, boiling water should first be poured quickly over the tea leaves, in order to get rid of any dust and bitterness. After a rapid rinse, this liquid is poured away. Only then is the carefully folded bundle of mint put into the teapot and a large piece of cone-shaped sugar loaf placed on top, which, with its weight, keeps the leaves on the bottom of the pot. This time the infusion has to be left to brew for a few minutes before the host pours out the first glass – just to see if the tea is the right colour. The boiling liquid then goes back into the pot before being poured back into the glass shortly afterwards, this time to be tasted. This action can continue for some time before the host is satisfied with the result.

Only then does he serve the tea to his guests. It is poured out in a high arch, because only after the jet of tea has had the longest possible contact with the air can the complete aroma develop. Usually glasses are only filled halfway. Thus, it is generally topped up three times in succession. But let the guest who refuses say his prayers! To refuse tea in Morocco is considered the ultimate insult.

Hinzufügen frischer Minze – aus der übrigens immer schon Aufgüsse zum Trinken gemacht wurden. Jetzt verleiht sie dem grünen Tee das ganz spezielle, frische Aroma. Es gibt verschiedene Sorten von Minze, die beste kommt aus Marrakesch und Meknès. Sie wird auch unter der Bezeichnung „Nana-Tee" verkauft: *nâa-naa* ist das arabische Wort für Minztee.

Für das Teezeremoniell braucht man zwei Tabletts. Auf dem einen stehen der kupferne Samowar und drei Gefäße: das erste für Zucker, das zweite für die grünen Teeblätter und das dritte für die frische Minze. Die wurde vorher abgespült und vorsichtig mit einem sauberen Tuch getrocknet. Auf dem zweiten Tablett stehen die kleinen Gläser – grundsätzlich mehr als Gäste zugegen sind – und die typische bauchige Teekanne mit ihrer langen Tülle und dem spitzen Deckel.

Wenn es ganz korrekt zugeht, wird das kochende Wasser zunächst nur kurz über die Teeblätter gegossen, um sie von Staub und Bitterkeit zu befreien. Nach raschem Schwenken wird es weggegossen. Dann erst kommt das sorgfältig gefaltete Bündel Minze in die Kanne und obenauf ein großes Stück vom kegelförmigen Zuckerhut, das mit seinem Gewicht die Blätter am Boden hält. Diesmal muss der Aufguss einige Minuten ziehen, bevor der Gastgeber das erste Glas eingießt – nur zum Schauen, ob die Farbe stimmt. Der Tee kommt zurück in die Kanne, um kurz darauf wieder ins Glas gegossen zu werden, diesmal zum Kosten. Das kann einige Male so hin und her gehen, bis der Gastgeber das Ergebnis befriedigend findet. Dann erst gießt er seinen Gästen ein – in hohem Bogen, denn nur wenn der Strahl möglichst lange Berührung mit der Luft hat, entfaltet sich das volle Aroma. Jedes Glas wird grundsätzlich nur bis zur Hälfte gefüllt. Dafür wird meistens dreimal hintereinander eingeschenkt. Und wehe, der Gast verweigert sich! Einen Tee in Marokko abzulehnen, gilt als die größte Beleidigung.

l'ajout de menthe fraîche – par ailleurs bue depuis toujours en infusion – qui confère au thé vert un arôme spécifique, très frais. Il existe différentes espèces de menthe, la meilleure provient de Marrakech et de Meknès et est vendue sous l'appellation « menthe nana » : *nâa-naa* signifie en arabe thé à la menthe.

Pour le cérémonial du thé, il faut deux plateaux. Sur l'un sont posés le samovar de cuivre et trois récipients : le premier pour le sucre, le deuxième pour les feuilles de thé vert et le troisième pour la menthe fraîche. Ce dernier a été préalablement rincé et soigneusement essuyé avec un torchon propre. Sur le deuxième plateau se trouvent les petits verres – en principe en plus grand nombre que les invités présents – et la théière typique et ventrue, avec un long bec et un couvercle pointu.

Lorsque tout se déroule correctement, l'eau bouillante est d'abord versée un court instant sur les feuilles de thé, afin de les débarrasser de toute poussière et de leur amertume. Après avoir agité rapidement le tout, l'eau est jetée. Alors seulement, le bouquet de menthe soigneusement plié est posé dans la théière, avec par-dessus un gros morceau de pain de sucre conique, dont le poids maintiendra les feuilles au fond. Cette fois, on laisse infuser quelques minutes avant que l'hôte ne remplisse le premier verre, seulement pour vérifier que la couleur est correcte. Le thé est alors reversé dans la théière et peu après de nouveau dans le verre, cette fois pour goûter. Ces opérations peuvent être répétées plusieurs fois, jusqu'à ce que l'hôte soit satisfait du résultat. Alors seulement, il sert ses invités en versant de haut, car le jet doit être le plus longtemps possible en contact avec l'air pour que l'arôme se déploie pleinement. Chaque verre n'est en principe rempli qu'à moitié, mais on sert le plus souvent trois fois de suite. Et malheur à l'invité qui s'y refuserait ! Ne pas accepter un thé est au Maroc un affront parmi les plus graves qui soient.

Acknowledgments
Danksagungen
Remerciements

This book could not have been written without the support of the following people:

We would like to pay a very special thank you to HRH Mohammed VI, who was so kind to allow us to take pictures of his royal palace in Marrakech. We have to thank His Excellency, Mr. El Mrini, for obtaining this permission. Another thank you to Mr. Germain, who was our guide through the garden.

The Moroccan Tourism Centre in Germany, especially Mr. Jorio and Mrs. Ludwig, offered a lot of help regarding our travel preparations, as well as the *Offices du Tourisme* in all the Moroccan cities we have visited. Many thanks to the Moroccan Embassy in Berlin for all their information.

We are grateful for the support of Royal Air Maroc, mainly Mr. Saquihi El Mustafa. We also owe Mrs. Ahmadi of Avis a big thank you.

One part of our journey was perfectly organised by Plan Tours in Tanger. We would like to pay a special thank you to Mrs. Irene Gause and Mr. Saïd El Fassi, who openend to us a lot of doors into Moroccan gardens.

Thank you for the hospitality of the following hotels: Palais Salam/Taroudant, Tikida Garden/Marrakech, Sol Azur/Tanger, Hôtel Transatlantique/Meknès, Hotel Menzeh Zalagh/Fez, Méridien La Tour Hassan/Rabat.

We are also grateful to all landlords, who let us visit their gardens. Very useful tips were submitted by Mr Bennis (La Gazelle d'Or), Olivier Français (former director of Tikida Garden), Monsieur and Madame Lafont, Nabil Tajmouati, Dr. Berrada and Simon Cohen. A warm thank you also to Mr. and Mrs. Serfaty and their daughter, Fabienne Henzler-Serfaty, who shared a lot of their Tanger contacts with us.

While working on this book, we received an incredible amount of useful tips and information, but we could not follow all of them up. Many thanks to:

Mohamed Taroush, Jacqueline Foissac, Nouhad and Madame Azelmad, Habib Sahla, Rachid Andaloussi, Elie Moujal, Rachel Muyal, Peter Arnold, Helmut Rainalter, Zakharia Mahlali, Charly Bitton.

Another thank you to Marie-Claude Treglia, who was a great help during the translation.

In case we forgot to thank somebody, we herewith would like to excuse this.

The photographer would like to thank the following people, who proved to be a wonderful support throughout the journey with their good sense of humour, their moral spirit and their help: Florian Bohlmann, Michel Blanchard und Carina Landau. This book is dedicated to my son Alexandre, our tour guide who sometimes lacked a little bit of good humour.

Finally, thanks to all Moroccan people and their indefinite patience and friendliness towards all children. This makes their country a perfect travel place for families with children.

The author would like to thank Bea Gottschlich from Paris, who documented six text insets with care and detail.

Dieses Buch hätte ohne die freundliche Unterstützung der nachfolgend genannten Menschen nie entstehen können.

Unser besonderer Dank gilt seiner Majestät Mohammed VI., der uns freundlicherweise die Erlaubnis, den königlichen Palast von Marrakesch zu fotografieren, zukommen ließ. Für das Erwirken dieser Genehmigung bedanken wir uns herzlichst bei Seiner Exzellenz, Herrn El Mrini. Dank auch an Herrn Germain, der uns durch den Garten führte.

Für die Hilfe bei den Vorbereitungen unserer Reise möchten wir uns zuallererst bei dem Marokkanischen Fremdenverkehrsamt in Deutschland, namentlich bei Herrn Jorio und Frau Ludwig, bedanken. Herzlichen Dank auch an die Offices du Tourisme der von uns besuchten Städte. Der marokkanischen Botschaft in Berlin sei für ihre Informationen gedankt.

Für die freundliche Unterstützung gilt unser Dank auch Royal Air Maroc und ganz besonders Herrn Saquihi El Mustafa. Auch dem Autoverleih Avis (besonders Frau Ahmadi) sei auf diesem Wege gedankt.

Ein Teil unserer Reise wurde von Plan Tours in Tanger angenehm reibungslos organisiert. Hierfür gilt unser besonderer Dank Frau Irene Gause und Herrn Saïd El Fassi, dem wir dafür danken möchten, dass er uns die Türen zu vielen Gärten in Tanger geöffnet hat.

Für die Gastfreundschaft, die man uns in den folgenden Hotels bezeugt hat, herzlichen Dank: Palais Salam/Taroudant, Tikida Garden/Marrakesch, Sol Azur/Tanger, Hôtel Transatlantique/Meknès, Hotel Menzeh Zalagh/Fès, Méridien La Tour Hassan/Rabat.

Natürlich gilt unser Dank all den Gartenbesitzern, die uns freundlicherweise ihre Türen geöffnet haben. Für nützliche Hinweise möchten wir uns außerdem bei Frau Bennis (La Gazelle d'Or), Olivier François (ehemaliger Direktor des Tikida Garden), Monsieur und Madame Lafont, Nabil Tajmouati, Dr. Berrada und Simon Cohen bedanken. Unser besonderer Dank gilt Herrn und Frau Serfaty und deren Tochter, Fabienne Henzler-Serfaty, denen wir in Tanger viele Kontakte zu verdanken haben.

Während der Arbeit an diesem Buch haben wir unzählige interessante Tipps und Informationen bekommen, denen wir nicht immer folgen konnten. Herzlichen Dank an:

Mohamed Taroush, Jacqueline Foissac, Nouhad und Madame Azelmad, Habib Sahla, Rachid Andaloussi, Elie Mouyal, Rachel Muyal, Peter Arnold, Helmut Rainalter, Zakharia Mahlali, Charly Bitton.

Und ein Dankeschön an Marie-Claude Treglia für Übersetzungs-Hilfe.

All diejenigen, die wir möglicherweise vergessen haben, möchten wir an dieser Stelle um Entschuldigung bitten.

Der besondere Dank der Fotografin gilt folgenden Personen, die sie auf ihren Reisen durch gute Laune, moralische Unterstützung und Tatkraft besonders unterstützt haben: Florian Bohlmann, Michel Blanchard und Carina Landau. Dem nicht immer so gut gelaunten Reisebegleiter möchte ich das Buch widmen: meinem Sohn Alexandre. An dieser Stelle übrigens noch ein letztes Dankeschön für die wunderbare Geduld und Freundlichkeit der Marokkaner allen Kindern gegenüber, sie machen damit ihr Land zum idealen Reiseziel für Eltern ...

Der besondere Dank der Autorin gilt Bea Gottschlich, Paris, für die ausführliche Dokumentation zu sechs Inset-Texten.

Ce livre n'aurait pû voir le jour sans l'aide des personnes suivantes :

Nos respectueux remerciements à Sa Majesté Mohammed VI, qui nous a très aimablement fait transmettre l'autorisation de photographier le jardin du Palais Royal de Marrakech. Nous sommes particulièrement redevables de cette autorisation à Son Excellence, Monsieur El Mrini. Merci également à Monsieur Germain, qui a guidé la visite.

Nos plus vifs remerciements s'adressent à l'Office du Tourisme Marocain en Allemagne, et spécialement à Monsieur Jorio et Madame Ludwig. Merci également à tous les offices du tourisme des villes que nous avons visitées. Merci à l'ambassade du Maroc en Allemagne pour les informations qu'elle nous a fournies.

Pour son généreux soutien, merci à Royal Air Maroc et tout spécialement à Monsieur Saquihi El Mustafa. Nous souhaitons également remercier la société Avis, et particulièrement Madame Ahmadi.

Une partie de notre voyage a été organisée avec beaucoup d'efficacité par la société Plant Tours de Tanger. Pour cela, grand merci à Madame Irene Gause et à Monsieur Saïd El Fassi, qui nous a ouvert de nombreuses portes à Tanger.

Merci pour leur hospitalité aux hôtels suivants :

Palais Salam/Taroudant, Tikida Garden/Marrakech, Sol Azur/Tanger, Hôtel Transatlantique/Meknès, Hôtel Menzeh Zalagh/Fès, Méridien La Tour Hassan/Rabat.

Il va de soi que nous sommes reconnaissantes à toutes celles et tous ceux qui nous ont ouvert les portes de leur jardin – qu'ils en soient tous remerciés. Pour leur conseils avisés, nous remercions particulièrement Madame Bennis (La Gazelle d'Or), Olivier François (ancien directeur de l'hôtel Tikida Garden), Monsieur et Madame Lafon, Nabil Tajmouati, Dr. Berrada et Simon Cohen. Grand merci à Monsieur et Madame Serfaty, ainsi qu'à leur fille, Fabienne Henzler-Serfaty, pour les nombreuses introductions qu'ils nous ont généreusement fournies à Tanger.

Pendant la préparation de ce livre, nous avons reçu une foule de conseils intéressants, même s'il ne nous a pas toujours été possible de suivre toutes les pistes. Merci à :

Mohammed Taroush, Jacqueline Foissac, Nouhad et Madame Azelmad, Habib Sahla, Elie Mouyal, Rachel Muyal, Rachid Andaloussi, Peter Arnold, Helmut Rainalter, Zakharia Mahlali, Charly Bitton.

Merci à Marie-Claude Treglia pour avoir répondu à notre appel de dernière minute.

D'avance, toutes nos excuses à ceux que nous aurions oubliés de citer ici.

La photographe souhaite particulièrement remercier ici les personnes suivantes, qui, grâce à leur bonne humeur, leur soutien moral et leur dynamisme, ont été d'une aide précieuse: Florian Bohlmann, Michel Blanchard et Carina Landau.

Je souhaite dédier ce livre à celui de mes compagnons de route qui n'a pas toujours été d' humeur égale: mon fils, Alexandre.

Enfin, je souhaite remercier tous les Marocains pour leur extraordinaire gentillesse et patience avec les enfants, faisant de leur pays une destination de rêve pour les parents ...

L'auteur souhaite remercier tout particulièrement Béa Gottschlich, Paris, pour la documentation nécessaire aux chapîtres intermédiaires.

Hotels with Gardens
Hotels mit Gärten
Hôtels avec des jardins

Some hotels are open to the public, you can have tea time or visit the gardens. Other hotels, however, are exclusively for hotel guests, public visitors are not welcome. It is advisable to phone the hotel before visiting it to obtain the required information.
The phone prefix for calls from Europe is ☎ **OO 212**
From the United States: ☎ **O11 212**
More information:
Moroccan Tourist Office, London, UK
☎ 020-743 700 73
Moroccan Tourist Board (ONMT), New York, NY ☎ 212-557 25 20

TAROUDANT
Melià Palais Salam
Kasbah, entrance at the historical city wall
☎ (08) 85 21 30 ✆ (08) 85 26 54
La Gazelle d'Or
Drive from Bab Tangrount along the Western Wall of the Médina 1.5 km on the Route de Marrakech, then turn left.
☎ (08) 85 20 39 ✆ (08) 85 27 37

OULED BERHIL
Hotel Palais Riad Hida
Situated in the village Ouled Berhil, 45 km out of Taroudant, on the way to Marrakech. Directly behind the mosque and kasbah
☎ (08) 53 10 44 ✆ (08) 53 12 26

MARRAKECH
Palmeraie Golf Palace
Les Jardins de la Palmeraie
☎ (04) 30 10 10 ✆ (04) 30 50 50
Tikida Garden
Circuit de la Palmeraie
approx. 8 km out of the city centre
☎ (04) 30 90 99 ✆ (04) 30 93 43
Riad Enija
Ursula Haldimann, Rahba Laktima, Derb Mesfioui 9
☎ (04) 44 09 26 ✆ (04) 44 27 00
La Mamounia
Avenue Bab Jdid, *near the Koutoubia*
☎ (04) 44 89 81 ✆ (04) 44 46 60

FEZ
Palais Jamaï
Bab Guissa, Fès el Bali
☎ (05) 63 50 90 ✆ (05) 63 50 96
Menzeh Zalagh
10, rue Mohammed Diouri
☎ (05) 93 22 34 ☎ (05) 62 55 31
✆ (05) 65 19 95

MEKNÈS
Hotel Transatlantique
Zankat el Meriniyine
☎ (05) 52 50 50 ✆ (05) 52 00 57

RABAT
La Tour Hassan
26, rue Chellah
☎ (07) 70 42 01 (07) 72 14 02 (07) 73 25 31
✆ (07) 72 54 08 (07) 73 18 66

TANGER
Dar Kharroubia
Jamâa el Mokrâa, Place du Cadi
☎ (09) 33 58 46 ✆ (09) 93 47 57
El Minzah
85, rue de la Liberté, Ville Nouvelle
☎ (09) 93 87 87 ✆ (09) 93 45 46
Le Mirage
14 km west of Cape Spartel, located above the Hercules caves
☎ (09) 33 34 91 ✆ (09) 33 34 92

In manchen Hotels genügt es, einen Tee zu nehmen, um den Garten besichtigen zu dürfen, in anderen sind kurzfristige Besucher nicht erwünscht, da haben nur Hotelgäste Zutritt. Im Zweifel vorher telefonisch anfragen.
Die Telefonvorwahl von Deutschland aus ist ☎ **OO 212**
Informationen über *Staatlich Marokkanisches Fremdenverkehrsamt* Graf-Adolf-Straße 59, 40210 Düsseldorf
☎ 0211-370551/2 ✆ 0211-374048

TAROUDANT
Melià Palais Salam
Kasbah, Eingang liegt in der historischen Stadtmauer
☎ (08) 85 21 30 ✆ (08) 85 26 54
La Gazelle d'Or
Ab Bab Tangrount an der Westmauer der Médina ca. 1,5 km auf der Route de Marrakech, dann links
☎ (08) 85 20 39 ✆ (08) 85 27 37

Hotel Palais Riad Hida
45 km außerhalb von Taroudant auf der Straße nach Marrakesch im Dorf Ouled Berhil, kurz hinter Moschee und Kasbah
☎ (08) 53 10 44 ✆ (08) 53 12 26

MARRAKECH
Palmeraie Golf Palace
Les Jardins de la Palmeraie
☎ (04) 30 10 10 ✆ (04) 30 50 50
Tikida Garden
Circuit de la Palmeraie
etwa 8 km außerhalb des Zentrums
☎ (04) 30 90 99 ✆ (04) 30 93 43
Riad Enija
Ursula Haldimann, Rahba Laktima, Derb Mesfioui 9
☎ (04) 44 09 26 ✆ (04) 44 27 00
La Mamounia
Avenue Bab Jdid, *nahe der Koutoubia*
☎ (04) 44 89 81 ✆ (04) 44 46 60

FÉS
Palais Jamaï
Bab Guissa, Fès el Bali
☎ (05) 63 50 90 ✆ (05) 63 50 96
Menzeh Zalagh
10, rue Mohammed Diouri
☎ (05) 93 22 34 (05) 62 55 31
✆ (05) 65 19 95

MEKNÈS
Hotel Transatlantique
Zankat el Meriniyine
☎ (05) 52 50 50 ✆ (05) 52 00 57

RABAT
La Tour Hassan
26, rue Chellah
☎ (07) 70 42 01 (07) 72 14 02 (07) 73 25 31
✆ (07) 72 54 08 (07) 73 18 66

TANGER
Dar Kharroubia
Jamâa el Mokrâa, Place du Cadi
☎ (09) 33 58 46 ✆ (09) 93 47 57
El Minzah
85, rue de la Liberté, Ville Nouvelle
☎ (09) 93 87 87 ✆ (09) 93 45 46
Le Mirage
14 km westlich am Cap Spartel, oberhalb der Herkules-Grotten
☎ (09) 33 34 91 ✆ (09) 33 34 92

Dans certains hôtels, il suffit de prendre un thé pour pouvoir visiter le jardin, dans d'autres, celui-ci reste reservé aux clients. Dans le doute, mieux vaut se renseigner par téléphone.
Le préfixe depuis l'Europe est ☎ **OO 212**
On peut également se renseigner auprès de l'Office national marocain du tourisme :
En France : 161, rue St. Honoré, 75001 Paris, ☎ 01.42.60.47.24/63.50
En Belgique : 66, rue du Marché-aux-Herbes , 1000 Bruxelles, ☎ 02. 512.21.82
En Suisse: Schifflande 5, 8001 Zurich, ☎ 01.252.77.52

TAROUDANT
Melià Palais Salam
Dans la casbah, l'entrée se trouve dans le mur d'enceinte.
☎ (08) 85 21 30 ✆ (08) 85 26 54
La Gazelle d'Or
Depuis Bab Tangrount, mur ouest de la Médina, suivre sur environ 1,5km la route de Marrakech, puis tourner à gauche.
☎ (08) 85 20 39 ✆ (08) 85 27 37

OULED BERHIL
Hotel Palais Riad Hida
À Ouled Berhil, depuis Taroudant à 45 km en direction de Marrakech, juste derrière la mosquée et la casbah
☎ (08) 53 10 44 ✆ (08) 53 12 26

MARRAKECH
Palmeraie Golf Palace
Les Jardins de la Palmeraie
☎ (04) 30 10 10 ✆ (04) 30 50 50
Tikida Garden
Circuit de la Palmeraie
à environ 8 km du centre.
☎ (04) 30 90 99 ✆ (04) 30 93 43
Riad Enija
Ursula Haldimann, Rahba Laktima, Derb Mesfioui 9
☎ (04) 44 09 26 ✆ (04) 44 27 00
La Mamounia
Avenue Bab Jdid, *près de la Koutoubia*
☎ (04) 44 89 81 ✆ (04) 44 46 60

FÉS
Palais Jamaï
Bab Guissa, Fès el Bali
☎ (05) 63 50 90 ✆ (05) 63 50 96
Menzeh Zalagh
10, rue Mohammed Diouri
☎ (05) 93 22 34 (05) 62 55 31
✆ (05) 65 19 95

MEKNÈS
Hotel Transatlantique
Zankat el Meriniyine
☎ (05) 52 50 50 ✆ (05) 52 00 57

RABAT
La Tour Hassan
26, rue Chellah
☎ (07) 70 42 01 (07) 72 14 02 (07) 73 25 31
✆ (07) 72 54 08 (07) 73 18 66

TANGER
Dar Kharroubia
Jamâa el Mokrâa, Place du Cadi
☎ (09) 33 58 46 ✆ (09) 93 47 57
El Minzah
85, rue de la Liberté, Ville Nouvelle
☎ (09) 93 87 87 ✆ (09) 93 45 46
Le Mirage
Au Cap Spartel, à 14km à l'Ouest, au dessus de la grotte d'Hercule.
☎ (09) 33 34 91 ✆ (09) 33 34 92

Public
Gardens
Öffentliche
Gärten
Jardins
publics

In nearly every Marrocon city you can visit a public garden. Most of these gardens are closed at dusk.

MARRAKECH
Agdal
Located in suburb around the palace, south of Mechouar el Oustani (Inner Mechouar)
Menara
Avenue de la Ménara
2 km southwest of Bab el Jédid
Majorelle
Guéliz, Ville Nouvelle, Avenue Yacoub el Mansour
Open daily from 8 to 12 A.M. and from 3 to 7 P.M.; in winter open from 8 to 12 A.M. and from 2 to 5 P.M.

FÉS
Parc Bou Jloud
The park streches from Fès el Jédid and Fès el Bali. The best entrance is a small gate at the end of Grande Rue de Fès el Jédid.

MEKNÈS
Haras de Meknès
Avenue Ahmed-ben-Hmad-di-Ghoussi
Open Monday to Friday from 9 to 12 A.M. and 2 to 5 P.M. No entrance fee.

RABAT
Casbah des Oudaïa
You can enter the beautiful Andalusian garden, belonging to the museum Oudaia, through a gate in the wall west of the Café Maure.
Open daily from 8.30 to 12 A.M. and 2.30 to 6 P.M. except Tuesday and holidays.

TANGER
Jardin du Sultan
Pass the Patio of the Pillars in Dar el Makhzen. The Morrocan museum of arts and crafts is located in the former palace of the sultan.
Open daily from 9 to 11.45 A.M. and 3 to 6.15 P.M. except Tuesday.
Musée Forbes
West of Médina along the Rue Shakespeare; the former museum of tin soldiers is closed, but you can visit the garden.
📞(09) 93 36 06.

In fast jeder Stadt Marokkos gibt es öffentliche Gärten, die besichtigt werden können. Bei den meisten werden die Tore bei Einbruch der Dämmerung geschlossen.

MARRAKECH
Agdal
im Palastviertel, südlich vom Mechouar el Oustani (Innerer Mechouar)
Menara
Avenue de la Ménara
2 km südwestlich vom Bab el Jédid
Majorelle
Guéliz, Ville Nouvelle, Avenue Yacoub el Mansour
Täglich von 8–12 Uhr und von 15–19 Uhr geöffnet, in den Wintermonaten von 8–12 Uhr und von 14–17 Uhr

FÉS
Parc Bou Jloud
Der Park erstreckt sich zwischen Fès el Jédid und Fès el Bali. Am besten durch ein kleines Tor am Ende der Grande Rue de Fès el Jédid zu erreichen.

MEKNÈS
Haras de Meknès
Avenue Ahmed-ben-Hmad-di-Ghoussi
Montag–Freitag 9–12 und 14–17 Uhr. Eintritt frei

RABAT
Casbah des Oudaïa
Der schöne andalusische Garten, der zum Musée des Oudaïa gehört, ist westlich vom Café Maure durch einen kleinen Mauerdurchgang zu erreichen. Täglich von 8.30–12 Uhr und von 14.30–18.00 Uhr geöffnet, außer dienstags und an Feiertagen.

TANGER
Jardin du Sultan
Über den großen Säulenpatio im Dar el Makhzen an der Place de la Casbah zu erreichen. Im ehemaligen Sultanspalast ist das Museum für marokkanisches Kunsthandwerk untergebracht. Geöffnet täglich außer dienstags von 9.00–11.45 Uhr und von 15.00–18.15 Uhr.
Musée Forbes
Westlich der Médina an der Rue Shakespeare gelegen. Das ehemalige Zinnsoldaten-Museum ist geschlossen; der Garten kann auf Anfrage besichtigt werden
📞(09) 93 36 06.

Dans la plupart villes marocaines, il y a des jardins publics que l'on peut visiter. Leurs portes ferment en général avec le coucher du soleil.

MARRAKECH
Agdal
quartier du Palais, au Sud du Mechouar el Oustani (Mechouar intérieur)
Menara
Avenue de la Ménara
2 km au sud-ouest de Bab el Jédid
Majorelle
Ville nouvelle, quartier du Guéliz, au coin de l'avenue Yacoub el Mansour. Ouvert tous les jours de 8–12 h et de 15–19 h, pendant les mois d'hiver de 8–12 h et de 14–17 h.

FÉS
Parc Bou Jloud
Le parc s'étend entre Fès el Jédid et Fès el Bali. On y accède le plus facilement par une petite porte au bout de la Grande Rue de Fès el Jédid.

MEKNÈS
Haras de Meknès
Avenue Ahmed-ben-Hmad-di-Ghoussi
Du lundi au vendredi de 9–12 h et de 14–17 h. Entrée libre.

RABAT
Casbah des Oudaïa
On accède au joli jardin andalou qui fait partie du musée des Oudaïa par une petite porte à l'ouest du Café Maure. Ouvert tous les jours de 8.30–12 h et de 14.30–18 h, sauf le mardi et jours de fête.

TANGER
Jardin du Sultan
On y accède par les arcades de dar el Makhzen, place de la Casbah. Dans l'ancien Palais du Sultan se trouve un musée d'artisanat marocain. Ouvert tous les jours, sauf mardi, de 9–11.45 h et de 15–18.15 h.
Musée Forbes
À l'ouest de la Médina, rue Shakespeare. L'ancien musée de soldats de plomb est fermé; on peut éventuellement demander une autorisation spéciale pour visiter le jardin
📞(09) 93 36 06.

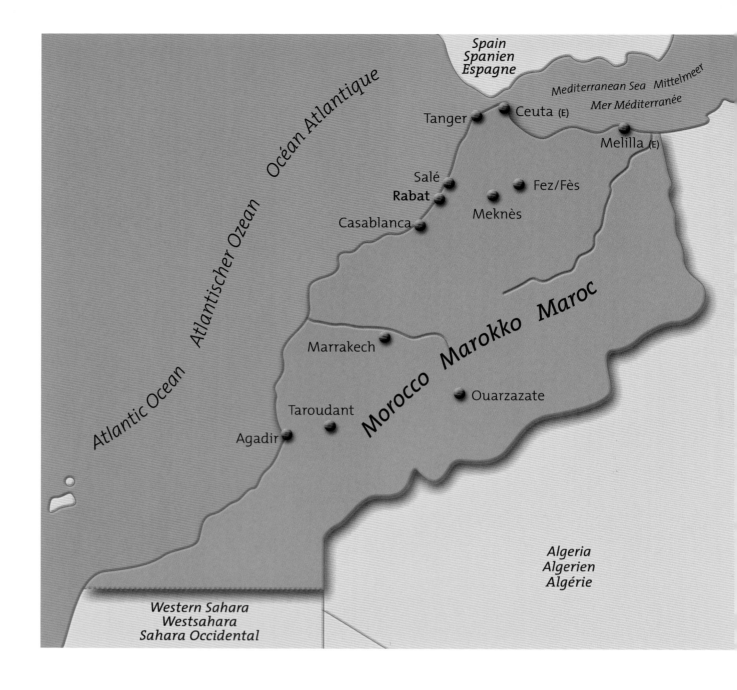

Bibliography
Bibliografie
Bibliographie

Ingeborg Lehmann: *Marokko –* Polyglott 1999

Marokko – Berlitz Reiseführer 1996

Marokko – Baedeker Allianz Reiseführer 1996

Hartmut Buchholz: *Marokko –* DuMont Richtig Reisen 1998

Marokko – Merian Februar 1999

Maroc – Guides Bleus Évasion Hachette 1999

Simon Russell/Pamela Windo: *Escape to Morocco –* Fodor's 2000

Bienvenue à Marrakech – ACR Edition 1994

Hugues Demeude: *Marokko –* Benedikt Taschen 1998

Marie-Pascale Rauzier: *Couleurs du Maroc –* Flammarion 1999

Stefano Bianca: *Hofhaus und Paradiesgarten –* C.H. Beck 1991

Arnaud Maurières/Eric Ossart: *Orientalische Gärten –* Christian Verlag 2001

Attilio Petruccioli: *Der islamische Garten* – DVA 1995

Christa von Hantelmann/Dieter Zoern: *Gärten des Orients –* DuMont 1999

Narjess Ghachem-Benkirane/ Philippe Saharoff: *Marrakech, Demeures et jardins secrets –* ACR Edition 1990

Quentin Wilbaux/Michel Lebrun: *Marrakech, Le secret des maisons-jardins –* ACR Edition 1999

Mohammed El Faïz/Rachid Bendaoud: *Jardins de Marrakech –* Actes Sud 2000

Irène Menjili-de Corny: *Jardins du Maroc –* Le Temps Apprivoisé 1991

Herbert Ypma: *Marokko modern –* Knesebeck 1997

Lisa Lovatt-Smith: *Moroccan Interieurs –* Taschen 1995

Lisl & Landt Dennis: *Living in Morocco –* Thames and Hudson 1998

Alexandra Bonfante-Warren: *Moroccan Style –* Friedman/Fairfax 2000

James F. Jereb: *Arts and Crafts of Morocco* – Thames and Hudson 1995

Edith Wharton: *In Morocco –* 1920

Pierre Loti: *Im Zeichen der Sahara –* dtv 2000
Original title: *Au Maroc –* Paris 1890

Elias Canetti: *Die Stimmen von Marrakesch –* Hanser 1994

Paul Bowles: *The Sheltering Sky –* The Ecco Press 1945
Their heads are green and their hands are blue – The Ecco Press 1957
Points in Time – The Ecco Press 1982